# Self-Consuming Artifacts

# Self-Consuming Artifacts

*The Experience of Seventeenth-Century Literature*

BY STANLEY E. FISH

University of California Press, Berkeley, Los Angeles, London

University of California Press
Berkeley and Los Angeles, California
University of California Press, Ltd.
London, England
Copyright © 1972, by
The Regents of the University of California
ISBN: 0-520-02230-0
Library of Congress Catalog Card Number: 76-187747
Printed in the United States of America

## For Susan Meredith Fish

". . . full of sweet dayes and roses,
A box where sweets compacted lie."

George Herbert, *Vertue*

In all his long discourse, I dare not claim to have said anything worthy. . . . A wise man, in that book of his we name Ecclesiasticus, spoke thus concerning thee: "We speak many things, and yet attain not: and the whole consummation of our discourses is himself." When therefore we shall have attained to thee, all those many things which we speak, and attain not, shall cease: one shalt thou abide, all things in all; one shall we name thee without end, praising thee with one single voice, we ourselves also made one in thee.

AUGUSTINE, De Trinitate

My propositions serve as elucidations in the following way: anyone who understands me eventually recognizes them as nonsensical, when he has used them—as steps—to climb up beyond them. (He must, so to speak, throw away the ladder after he has climbed up it.) He must transcend these propositions, and then he will see the world aright.

WITTGENSTEIN, Tractatus Logico-Philosophicus

Literature is like phosphorus: it shines with its maximum brilliance at the moment when it attempts to die.

ROLAND BARTHES, Writing Degree Zero

# Contents

# To the Reader

Prefaces are usually defensive and this preface will be no exception, for I must begin by explaining what I do not do. I do not in the following pages say very much about such familiar subjects as skepticism (in its various strains), Neoplatonism, allegory (I do not use the word in my chapter on *The Pilgrim's Progress*), the vestarian controversy, praisings of folly, typology, arts of preaching, Renaissance anatomies, the tradition of paradox, the techniques of meditation, the conventions of polemic, the Baroque. It is not that I am uninterested in these matters or think them unimportant, it is just that I am more interested in the experience that might lead one to invoke these labels or categories and I have left the labeling and categorizing to others. Of course, I have categories of my own—self-consuming and self-satisfying, to name just two—but as the reader will discover, they are categories of experience rather than of style or party affiliation, and therefore they are (or at least are intended to be) not taxonomic, but explanatory.

I must also explain what I *have* done, and especially why I have done it at such length. The number of pages in this book is to a large extent a function of my critical assumptions. This is not the place to state them (the reader may consult, if he wishes, the appendix, "Literature in the Reader"), but in general they rest on the belief that reading is an activity, and that meaning, insofar as it can be specified, is coextensive with that activity, and not, as some would hold, its product. For the questions "what is this work about?" and "what does it say?", I tend to substitute the question "what is happening?" and to answer it by tracing out the shape of the reading experience, that is by focusing on the mind in the act of making sense, rather than on the sense it finally (and often reductively) makes. This results in a criticism that may at times seem interminable, although it is in fact always less exhaustive than it should be, given the theory and its assumptions. The reader who feels burdened, however, should know that the following chapters are simultaneously self-contained units and components in a larger argument; this means that, with the exception of the seventh and eighth, they can be read in isolation, although it goes without saying that from the author's point of view the ideal reading would be a sequential one.

Again proceeding defensively, I would like to anticipate two questions. The first is, do I intend my analyses to be extended to other works by these same authors? The answer is yes and no, yes in the special case of Robert Burton, no (with qualifications) in the case of the others. The experience of reading Milton's *Areopagitica* is not at all like the experience of reading *The Reason of Church Government,* and each of these would have to be distinguished from the experience of reading *The Ready and Easy Way;* similarly Bacon's *Essays* make quite different demands on the reader than does *The Advancement of Learning* (a difference for which Bacon himself provides the theoretical terms). In general, then, the descriptions yielded by this kind of analysis are not generalizable (reading has to be done every time) although the procedures that yield the descriptions are. Of course, some generalizations can be hazarded with more safety than others. I would be surprised if parts of my description of *Death's Duell* were not applicable to other Donne sermons, and at some level (not necessarily the most helpful) the poems of Herbert's *The Temple* can be regarded as related manifestations of a single strategy. On the other hand (or is it the third?) I would expect that the interest of a comparison between the two parts of *The Pilgrim's Progress* would lie more in the differences revealed than in the similarities. I trust that I have been sufficiently evasive to make my point clear.

The second question is, to what extent do I mean to restrict the genre of self-consuming artifacts to either the seventeenth century or to the Platonic-Augustinian tradition? This question has already been asked by friends who have been kind enough to read portions of the manuscript and have exclaimed (variously), "why, that's just like Sterne, or Byron, or Beckett, or Borges, or concrete poetry." The answer is that I am not here making a claim beyond that made for the works I discuss, but, on the other hand, I will be pleased if others find this study helpful to their consideration of more modern (or, for that matter, more ancient) documents. As a matter of fact, I tend to find self-consuming artifacts everywhere I look, but this may be simply because I have been writing this book for more than six years. At any rate, as the reader will notice, I have epigraphs from Wittgenstein and Roland Barthes, in addition to a book jacket by courtesy of Jean Tinguely. These speak for themselves, as opposed to speaking for me. That is, they allow me to play the time-honored academic game of making a very large claim in such a way as to escape responsibility for it.

Responsibility (or culpability) should also be escaped by the following, who have helped: Jonas Barish, Channa Bloch, Gale Carrithers, Ira Clark, John Coolidge, Jackson Cope, Kimberly Davis, Walter Davis, Ruth Fox, Donald Friedman, Donald Howard, Richard Lanham, Lawrence Lapidus, Arthur Marotti, William McClung, Richard Rodriguez, Thomas Sloan, Harry Smallenburg, George Starr, John Sullivan, Helen Vendler, Samuel Westgate, Joan Webber, Susan Welling. To this long list (which I find not embarrassing but heartening), I would add the names of two who do bear responsibility: Paul Alpers, who by giving a sympathetic and rigorous reading to a particularly troublesome chapter (it will not be identified) helped me to solve a problem that had persisted through many revisions; and Stephen Booth, from whom I have been happily stealing ideas since the day we met.

The writing of this book was made possible by two grants-in-aid; one in the form of a Humanities Research Professorship awarded by the University of California at Berkeley, and the other a fellowship from the John Simon Guggenheim Memorial Foundation.

A small portion of Chapter II has appeared in the *Critical Quarterly* (Spring, 1971). An early and much shorter version of Chapter III was printed in *ELH* (December, 1970). Nearly the whole of Chapter IV was published in the Autumn, 1971, issue of *English Literary Renaissance*. Portions of Chapter V are included in an essay written for Earl Miner's *Seventeenth Century Imagery* (California, 1971).

S. E. F.

I

# The Aesthetic of the Good Physician

INTRODUCTION

This book has four theses, which are at once discrete and interdependent. The first is historical and is concerned with the opposition of two kinds of literary presentation. In the following pages these kinds will be variously distinguished, but for the purposes of this introduction we can label one "rhetorical"—in the sense defined and attacked by Plato in the *Gorgias*—and the other "dialectical." A presentation is rhetorical if it satisfies the needs of its readers. The word "satisfies" is meant literally here; for it is characteristic of a rhetorical form to mirror and present for approval the opinions its readers already hold. It follows then that the experience of such a form will be flattering, for it tells the reader that what he has always thought about the world is true and that the *ways* of his thinking are sufficient. This is not to say that in the course of a rhetorical experience one is never told anything unpleasant, but that whatever one is told can be placed and contained within the categories and assumptions of received systems of knowledge.

A dialectical presentation, on the other hand, is disturbing, for it requires of its readers a searching and rigorous scrutiny of everything they believe in and live by. It is didactic in a special sense; it does not preach the truth, but asks that its readers discover the truth for themselves, and this discovery is often made at the expense not only of a reader's opinions and values, but of his self-esteem. If the experience of a rhetorical form is flattering, the experience of a dialectical form is humiliating.

Obviously the risk, on the part of the dialectician, of so proceeding, is considerable. A reader who is asked to judge himself may very well decline, but should he accept the challenge, the reward that awaits him—a better self than the self he is asked to judge—will be more than commensurate with his efforts. For the end of a dialectical experience is (or should be) nothing less than a *conversion*, not only a changing, but an exchanging of minds. It is necessarily a painful process (like sloughing off a second skin) in the course of which both parties forfeit a great deal; on the one side the applause of a pleased audience, and on the other, the satisfaction of listening to the public affirmation of our values and prejudices. The relationship is finally less one of speaker to hearer, or author to reader than of physician to patient, and it is as the "good physician" that the dialectician is traditionally known.

The metaphor of the good physician is one of the most powerful in western literature and philosophy. In the Christian tradition it belongs preeminently to God, who, as Augustine tells us, "setting out to cure men, applied Himself to cure them, being at once the Physician and the Medicine. . . . He applied humility as a cure . . . and cleanses . . . with certain medicinal adversities." [1] These cleansing powers are also given by God to his minister, who, in the words of Milton, "beginning at the prime causes and roots of the disease sends in . . . divine ingredients of most cleansing power . . . to purge the mind . . . a rough and vehement cleansing medicin . . . a kind of saving by undoing." [2] And in Plato's dialogues, these are the powers (and intentions) of the philosopher king, who, rather than catering to the pleasure of his charges, will "combat" them, "prescribing for them like a physi-

[1] *On Christian Doctrine*, trans. D. W. Robertson (New York, 1958), pp. 15–16. All references to this tract are to Robertson's edition and translation unless otherwise noted. For a detailed and authoritative discussion of the good-physician metaphor, especially as it appears in the tradition of Christian rhetoric, see Winfreid Schleiner, *The Imagery of John Donne's Sermons* (Providence, 1970), pp. 68–85. See also Rudolf Arbesmann, "The Concept of *Christus Medicus* in St. Augustine," *Traditio*, X (1954), 1–28, and D. C. Allen, "Donne's Knowledge of Renaissance Medicine," *JEGP*, XLII (1943), 322–342.

[2] *The Reason of Church Government* in *Complete Prose Works of John Milton*, Vol. I, ed. Don Wolfe et al. (New Haven, 1953), pp. 846–847.

cian." [3] The good physician, then, may be philosopher, minister, teacher, or even deity, but whatever his status, his strategy and intentions are always the same: he tells his patients what they *don't* want to hear in the hope that by forcing them to see themselves clearly, they may be moved to change the selves they see.

What exactly is the nature of this change? The question leads directly to my second thesis and to another opposition, an opposition between two ways of looking at the world. The first is the natural way of discursive, or rational, understanding; its characteristic motion is one of distinguishing, and the world it delivers is one of separable and discrete entities where everything is in its proper place. The second way is antidiscursive and antirational; rather than distinguishing, it resolves, and in the world it delivers the lines of demarcation between places and things fade in the light of an all-embracing unity. In a dialectical experience, one moves, or is moved, from the first to the second way, which has various names, the way of the good, the way of the inner light, the way of faith; but whatever the designation, the moment of its full emergence is marked by the transformation of the visible and segmented world into an emblem of its creator's indwelling presence ("Thy word is all, if we could spell" [4]), and at that moment the motion of the rational consciousness is stilled, for it has become indistinguishable from the object of its inquiry.

It follows then (and this is my third thesis) that a dialectical presentation succeeds at its own expense; for by conveying those who experience it to a point where they are beyond the aid that discursive or rational forms can offer, it becomes the vehicle of its own abandonment. Hence, the title of this study, *Self-Consuming Artifacts,* which is intended in two senses: the reader's self (or at least his inferior self) is consumed as he responds to the medicinal purging of the dialectician's art, and that art, like other medicines, is consumed in the workings of its own best effects. The good-physician aesthetic, then, is finally an anti-aesthetic, for it disallows to its productions the claims usually made for verbal art— that they reflect, or contain or express Truth—and transfers the

[3] *Gorgias,* 521a. The translation is by W. C. Helmbold in his edition for The Library of Liberal Arts (Indianapolis, New York, 1952), p. 99.

[4] George Herbert, "The Flower," 1.21.

pressure and attention from the work to its effects, from what is happening on the page to what is happening in the reader. A self-consuming artifact signifies most successfully when it fails, when it points *away* from itself to something its forms cannot capture. If this is not anti-art, it is surely anti-art-for-art's-sake because it is concerned less with the making of better poems than with the making of better persons.

My fourth thesis is personal, and will not be argued explicitly in these pages. It is the extension of the aesthetic of the good physician into a general principle of literary criticism: the proper object of analysis is not the work, but the reader. This is, of course, the "affective fallacy" as it has been invented and defined by Wimsatt and Beardsley: "The Affective Fallacy is a confusion between the poem and its *results* (what it *is* and what it *does*) . . . It begins by trying to derive the standards of criticism from the psychological effects of the poem and ends in impressionism and relativism. The outcome . . . is that the poem itself as an object of specifically critical judgment, tends to disappear (*The Verbal Icon*, Kentucky, 1954, p. 21)." I would reply that this is precisely what happens when we read—the work as an object tends to disappear—and that any method of analysis which ignores the affective reality of the reading experience cuts itself off from the source of literary power and meaning. I do not ask my own readers to commit themselves to this position [5] or even to consider it, if they find the issues it raises uninteresting or distracting. The burden of the argument in the following chapters is carried by the historical thesis, which finds its validation in the words of the authors themselves, in Bunyan's promise that "This book will make a traveller of thee," in Herbert's declared desire to "Ryme thee to good and turn delight into a sacrifice," in Milton's repeated entreaties to an understanding he is in the process of rectifying, and in Burton's plain declaration "Thou thyself art the subject of my discourse." All of these enroll themselves in the tradition of the good physician, which begins, as everything begins, with Plato.

[5] For a fuller exposition see my "Literature in the Reader: Affective Stylistics," first published in *New Literary History, II* (1970), 123–162, and here reprinted as an appendix.

PLATO: WORDS AS SEEDS

At a crucial point in the *Gorgias,* Callicles, in response to what he thinks to be the manifest absurdities of the doctrine Socrates is expounding, cries out: "Socrates, are we to take you seriously? . . . For if you're serious and what you say is really true, won't human life have to be turned completely upside down? Everything we do, it seems, is the exact opposite of what we ought to do (49, 481)." [6] Socrates has been arguing that since the perpetrator of an injury is more to be pitied than the party he injures (because to do wrong is to do violence to one's own soul), punishment and correction are the greatest goods an individual or the state can tender; and conversely, if we wish to injure an enemy, "we must do everything in our power . . . to prevent his being brought to justice . . . but if he is, we must devise how he may escape paying the penalty (48, 481)." Callicles' objection is the obvious one of common sense, "but no one thinks of these matters as you do," and in this (implied) opposition between what men do according to their common lights and what men ought to do in the light of a truth they seem not to perceive lies nearly the whole of Plato's philosophy of mind. That philosophy is both antisensible and antirational, and its cornerstone is a profound distrust of the systems of value and modes of perception indigenous to human life. As Plato describes it in the *Phaedrus* and elsewhere, human life is a declination from a higher state in which the individual soul once gazed upon reality itself, "without shape or color, intangible." A soul that has "through some mischance" fallen from this state to earth spends its time here trying to recover the vision it once enjoyed; but the very impulse or "mischance" that occasioned its fall in the first place continues to block the desired return and the result is a divided being in the simultaneous and warring control of two opposing appetites:

> Every human soul by reason of its nature has had a view
> of Reality, otherwise it could not have entered this human

[6] The first of these numbers refers to the page in Helmbold's edition (see note 3), the second to the traditional paragraph numbering.

form of ours. But to derive a clear memory of those real truths from these earthly perceptions is not easy for every soul—not for such as have only a brief view in their former existence, or for such as suffered the misfortune, when they fell into this world, to form evil connections . . . forgetting the holy vision they once had. Few indeed remain who can still remember much (249–250).[7]

While the natural motion of the soul is (like that of Milton's fallen angels) ascent, the motion of the form it has assumed is downward toward the realm of "earthly perceptions," of sensibles, and the pressure exerted by these sensibles is a pressure in favor of forgetting and against remembering. Remembering is painful and difficult because it requires the reorientation of the soul toward a reality that is simultaneously its natural object and yet, because of the incarnation it has suffered, wholly alien. Consequently, the soul which has some measure of success in freeing itself from the fetters of sense will be moving in a direction diametrically opposed to that of its fellows, who are likely to respond with derision and abuse: "He separates himself from the busy interests of men and approaches the divine. He is rebuked by the vulgar as insane, for they cannot know that he is possessed by divinity (32, 249)." The "vulgar" on the other hand are possessed by common sense, by the visible and insistent reality that presses in on them from all sides, and from that perspective the actions of the heavenly aspirant are at best incomprehensible and at worst evidence of derangement. If this is a Platonic doctrine it is also obviously Christian. The relevant scriptural verses are I Cor. 3:17, 19: "If any man among you seemeth to be wise in this world, let him become a fool that he may be wise." "For the wisdom of this world is foolishness with God." What is perhaps the most affecting literary embodiment of the tension between an egocentric and a theocentric vision was written by someone who in all probability had never read Plato at all: "So I saw in my Dream, that the Man began to run; Now he had not run far from his own door, but his Wife and Children perceiving it, began to cry after him to return: but the Man put

---

[7] The translation is by W. C. Helmbold and W. G. Rabinowitz in their edition for The Liberal Arts Press (New York, 1956), p. 33. Subsequent references will cite first the page in this edition and then the traditional paragraph numbering.

his fingers in his Ears, and ran on crying, Life, Life, Eternal Life: so he looked not behind him, but fled towards the middle of the Plain." [8]

Whether this action is described as separating oneself from the busy interests of men, or fleeing the things of this world, or some other more abstractly philosophical formulation, its constituents and implications remain the same: the individual soul is asked to reject as partial and distorting the version of reality yielded by the senses and by a merely rational wisdom and raise itself to the point where the truly and wholly real once again comes into view. In this process, not only are the objects of sense put aside, but the values which were in large part responsible for the appeal of those objects are replaced by the values accompanying a progressively widening vision. In the end, the triumphant soul can look down at this pinprick of a world and, in the manner of Chaucer's Troilus, laugh at all of those things for which at one time he would have died. In these terms, Callicles' objection to Socrates' line of reasoning—"if you're serious . . . won't human life have to be turned upside down"—is the highest of compliments, and, incidentally, a capsule statement of what is necessary if the wandering and dispossessed soul is to come home.

Plato's name for this education of the soul, this inversion of the values human life urges on us, this remembering, is dialectic, the prodding of the individual mind to the rigorous examination of the notions it has always rested in, with a view toward refining and in some cases rejecting them. The end of dialectic is not so much the orderly disposition of things in the phenomenal world, as the transformation of the soul-mind into an instrument capable of seeing things in the phenomenal world for what they really are (turning things upside down), imperfect and inferior reflections of a higher reality whose claim on our thoughts and desires is validated as earthly claims are discredited. It follows that the course of a dialectical investigation will be unpredictable and to some degree haphazard, since the turns of the argument, its advances and backslidings, will vary according to the degree to which the minds involved are in bondage to the realm of sensibles.

[8] John Bunyan, *The Pilgrim's Progress*, ed. J. B. Wharey, rev. R. Sharrock (Oxford, 1960), p. 10.

The success a teacher-dialectician has, if he has one, will be measured not in the number of propositions he has proved, but in the number of illuminations he has provoked, in the horizons he has widened; and the locus of a dialectical experience is not the spoken or written word but the mind in which the word is working. There the action takes place and there the triumphs or failures are recorded. In fact, the value of a word or a proposition in a dialogue is determined less by its truth-content than by its effectiveness in stimulating further inquiry and thereby contributing to the progressive illumination of the aspiring mind. This is what Socrates means when he talks in the *Phaedrus* of words as "seeds," "Words which bring their possessor to the highest degree of happiness possible (71)." And it is to the *Phaedrus* that we now turn, not only for an authoritative account of dialectic but for what is perhaps the supreme example of the dialectical mode in operation.

The point of the *Phaedrus* is usually taken to be the distinguishing of good rhetoric and writing from bad, and the basis for this reading is the text itself:

> *Socrates.*   Then this will be quite obvious to anyone: there is nothing in itself disgraceful about writing speeches.
> *Phaedrus.*   Why should there be?
> *Socrates.*   But the disgrace comes in when the speaking and the writing is not good, when it is, in fact, disgracefully bad.
> *Phaedrus.*   That is perfectly obvious.
> *Socrates.*   What then is the way to distinguish good writing from bad (44, 258)?

In the discussion that follows, the Sophist position—that a good rhetorician need only know the opinions men hold on a subject rather than the truth about it—is refuted and Socrates goes on to argue that a truly scientific rhetoric requires an exact knowledge of "the truth about any given point" and of the various kinds of audiences on whom that truth may at some future time be urged: "Since it is in fact the function of speech to influence souls, a man who is going to be a speaker must know how many types of souls there are . . . men of a special sort under the influences of speeches of a particular kind are readily persuaded to take action of a definite sort because of the qualitative correlation that obtains between speech and soul (63, 271)." Only when these two abilities —to specify and distinguish things and to specify and recognize souls—are joined will the art of speech be perfected: "Unless a man reckons up the various natures of his future audience and gains the capacity to divide existent things according to their classes and to compass them by a single kind in each case in which they are severally one, he will never attain such science in speech as it is possible for a man to achieve (66, 274)." Soon after this summary statement Socrates asks, "Then shall we take it for granted that the subject of science and the lack of it in speech has been adequately treated?" and Phaedrus replies "Surely (67, 273)"; the note of finality is unmistakable and satisfying.

Unfortunately, any view of the *Phaedrus* based on the simple opposition of good to bad speech-writing runs immediately afoul of the condemnation in the last few pages of anything written or formally delivered. This embarrassment has been the cause of many articles, usually entitled "The Unity of the *Phaedrus*," in which the offending section is somehow accounted for, usually by explaining it away. I do not wish to take issue with any of these, but rather to suggest that the inconsistency is less a problem to be solved than something to be noticed, and as something noticed it seems to me to be the key to the way the dialogue works. Rather than a single sustained argument, the *Phaedrus* is a series of discrete conversations or seminars, each with its own carefully posed question, ensuing discussion, and firmly drawn conclusion; but so arranged that to enter into the spirit and assumptions of any one of these self-enclosed units is implicitly to reject the spirit and assumptions of the unit immediately preceding. This is a pattern which can be clearly illustrated by the relationship between the speech of Lysias and the first speech delivered by Socrates. Lysias' speech is criticized for not conforming to the definition of a good discourse: "every discourse, like a living creature, should be so put together that it has its own body and lacks neither head nor feet, middle nor extremities, all composed in such a way that they suit both each other and the whole (53, 264)." Socrates, in fact, is careful to rule out any other standard of judgment: it is the "arrangement" rather than the "invention" or "relevance" that concerns him as a critic. Subsequently, Socrates' own effort on the same theme is criticized for its impiety, an impiety, moreover, that is compounded by its effectiveness as a "piece of rhetoric." (So well ordered is it, that although Socrates breaks off in mid-flight, Phaedrus is able to supply the missing half.) [9] In other words, Lysias' speech is bad because it is not well put together and Socrates' speech is bad because it is well put together.

Although neither Socrates nor Phaedrus acknowledges the contradiction, the reader, who has fallen in, perhaps involuntarily, with the standards of judgment established by the philosopher himself, is certainly confronted with it, and asked implicitly to do something with it. What he does, or should do, is realize that in the condemnation of Socrates' speech a new standard (of impiety) has been introduced, one that invalidates the very basis on which the discussion, and his reading experience, had hitherto been proceeding. At that moment, this early section of the dialogue will have achieved its true purpose, which is, paradoxically, to bring the reader to the point where he is no longer interested in the issues it treats, because he has come to see that the real issues exist at a higher level of generality. Thus, in a way peculiar to dialectical form and experience, this space of prose and argument will have been the vehicle of its own abandonment.

Nor is that by any means the end of the matter. This pattern, in which the reader is first encouraged to entertain assumptions he probably already holds and then is later forced to reexamine and discredit those same assumptions, is repeated again and again. In the course of exploring the subject of good and bad writing, Socrates asks, "If a speech is to be well and fairly spoken, must not the . . . speaker know the truth about the matters he intends to discuss?" and Phaedrus objects that he has heard something quite different, that an orator "may neglect what is really good and beautiful and concentrate on what will seem so; for it is from what seems to be true that persuasion comes, not from the real truth (46, 260)." Socrates immediately rejects this position and

---

[9] Helmbold & Rabinowitz, p. 22 (241): "But I thought you were only in the middle of it. I thought you were going on to say as much about the non-lover and how he ought to be preferred, enumerating all his good points."

we naturally anticipate an argument asserting the interdependence of rhetoric and truth, much in the manner later made familiar by Aristotle and Cicero. In fact, that is exactly what Socrates promises, to "convince the fair Phaedrus that if he doesn't give enough attention to philosophy, he will never become a competent speaker on any subject (47, 261)." In one sense we are not disappointed; but in another sense we get more than we bargained for. Socrates begins as might have been expected, by explaining that the art of speaking requires one to be "able to produce every possible sort of resemblance between comparable objects as well as . . . expose the attempts of others to produce resemblances through obfuscation (49, 261)." This seems not only scientific, but moral. But then suddenly, before either Phaedrus or the reader is aware of it, the argument takes a funny little turn and knowledge of the truth is declared necessary because ignorance would impair the orator's ability to *deceive:*

> *Socrates.*   When a man sets out to deceive someone else without being taken in himself, he must accurately grasp the similarity and dissimilarity of the facts . . .
>    Will it then be possible for an expert rhetorician regularly to lead his auditors step by step through a maze of similarities from the truth to its opposite or will he be able himself to avoid such pitfalls if he does not know the truth about each point he makes?
> *Phaedrus.*   Never!
> *Socrates.*   So, my friend, any man who does not know the truth, but has only gone about chasing after opinions, will produce an art of speech which will not only seem ridiculous, but no art at all (50, 262).

It is important to note that the conclusion to this amazing sequence ("So, my friend") is delivered as if nothing at all had changed since the question (whether the orator must know the truth) was first posed. The attentive reader, however, can hardly accept Socrates' QED with the equanimity Phaedrus evidences, for the content of the key terms has been blurred in the interim. While art and truth have been joined in one context—the ruthlessly practical context of manipulative rhetoric—a wedge has been driven between them in another—the moral context assumed at the beginning of the discussion. The reader now begins to inhabit two opposing worlds of discourse, although the two are represented by the same linguistic components. There is (1) the truth about things and (2) the truth that is, or should be, the goal of all investigative inquiry and efforts at persuasion. And corresponding to these are two concepts of persuasion, one in which the auditor is brought along step-by-step to an apparently rational conclusion, which may well be the opposite of truth, and another in which the auditor is brought *up* to a vision, to a point where his understanding is so enlarged that he can see the truth immediately, without the aid of any mediating process or even of an orator. This distinction is not made in the text; it is rather a distinction between what is happening in the surface narrative, in the self-enclosed world of Socrates and Phaedrus, and what is happening in the mind of the reader. It is he, not Phaedrus, who notes the contradictions and non sequiturs and is moved by them to reach new levels of insight (or at least he is given the *opportunity* to do so). That is, for the reader, the unfolding dialogue provides a series of stimuli to intellectual growth that is in some sense progressive: to the earlier insight that a well-made speech is not necessarily a true speech (in the moral sense), the reader must now add the further (and extending) insight that "well madeness" is likely to be a weapon in the arsenal of Truth's enemies. So that what was at first a standard of judgment (good writing) to which Socrates, Phaedrus *and* the reader repaired, is now seen to be positively deleterious to the higher standard now only gradually emerging from the give-and-take of the dialogue.

The important word in my last sentence is "seen," for it suggests that what is being processed by the *Phaedrus* is not an argument or a proposition, but a vision. As an argument, in fact, the dialogue makes no sense, since Socrates is continually reaching conclusions which he subsequently, and without comment, abandons. But as an attempt to refine its reader's vision it makes a great deal of sense; for then the contradictions, the moments of blurring become invitations to examine closely premises too easily acquiesced in. The reader who accepts this invitation will find, on retracing his steps, that statements and phrases which had seemed unexceptionable are now suspect and dubious (the concept of a "competent speaker," for example, on rereading, is less unambiguously positive than it was when Socrates introduced it as the basis of the discussion), and that lines of reasoning which had seemed proper and to the point are now disastrously narrow. Of course the phrases, statements, premises, and conclusions haven't changed (as Socrates remarks later, "written words . . . go on telling you the same thing over and over"), the reader has, and with each change he is able to dispense with whatever section of the dialogue he has been reading, because he has passed beyond the level of perception it represents.

To read the *Phaedrus,* then, is to use it up; for the value of any point in it is that it gets *you* (not any sustained argument) to the next point, which is not so much a point (in logical-demonstrative terms) as a level of insight. It is thus a *self-consuming artifact,* a mimetic enactment in the reader's experience of the Platonic ladder in which each rung, as it is negotiated, is kicked away. The final rung, the level of insight that stands (or, more properly, on which the reader stands) because it is the last, is, of course, the rejection of written artifacts, a rejection that, far from contradicting what has preceded, corresponds exactly to what the reader, in his repeated abandoning of successive stages in the argument, has been doing.

If an interpretation in which the work disappears seems strange, I invite my readers to substitute this more conventionally literary account, although the end result is the same: in the *Phaedrus,* there are two plots; Socrates and Phaedrus are busily building up a picture of the ideal orator while the reader is extracting, from the same words and phrases, a radical criticism of the ideal.[10] The two merge in the final assertion—"no work . . . has ever been written or recited that is worthy of serious attention (73, 278)"—which is problematical only if it is considered apart from the experience of the reader. That is, the reader who some time ago joined with Socrates and Phaedrus in an attempt to distinguish good from bad writing is not the same reader who hears

[10] This description will hold, as we shall see, for Milton's *The Reason of Church Government,* many of Herbert's poems, Bacon's *Essays,* Bunyan's *The Pilgrim's Progress,* and Burton's *Anatomy of Melancholy.*

Socrates reject writing in favor of the "serious pursuit of the dialectician (71, 276)"; he has changed (largely as a result of having been pursued by a dialectician) and one measure of his change is the fact these last pages are neither surprising nor disconcerting; rather, they are confirming, for they state explicitly an intuition that has been growing in the reader's mind, at the same rate as that mind itself has been growing.

In short, the *Phaedrus* is what it urges: "a discourse which is inscribed with genuine knowledge in the soul of the learner (70, 276)." Although a piece of writing itself, it escapes the criticism leveled at written artifacts because it does not exhibit the characteristics of those artifacts. Specifically, its words do not "go on telling you the same thing over and over (69, 275)," for as a result of passing through them, the reader is altered to such an extent that if he were to go back they would mean quite differently. The value of such words lies not in their truth content or in their answerability to a speaker's state of mind (literally speaking, Socrates is often lying), but in their effect; they are neither statements about the world nor expressions of a point of view (one cannot infer Plato's beliefs from any assertion made in the body of the dialogue, if only because so few of them stand), but strategies directed at an audience; and as strategies, they have reference to a vision developing *within* the reader-respondent rather than to objects in the empirical field of vision. As objects themselves they do not survive the moment of speech; once they have been uttered or read and worked their effect on the reader-respondent's mind, they die, except for the life they continue to live in that effect; and that life has nothing to do with their relationship to things and concepts in the phenomenal world and everything to do with the interior motion they induce in concert with other similarly strategical words. In terms of the functions we usually assign to language—communication of facts, opinions, desires, and emotions—they are not words at all, but *seeds,* "for they can transmit their seed to other natures and cause the growth of fresh words in them, providing an eternal existence for their seed; [they] bring their possessor to the highest degree of happiness possible to attain (71, 277)."

The highest degree of happiness possible to attain is, of course, a knowledge of Reality; and if the *Phaedrus* is a model of the kind of discourse that can help the soul to this happy state, the object of its criticism is the kind of discourse that does exactly the opposite. The name Socrates gives to this inferior and dangerous mode is rhetoric and its properties, or more properly, crimes, are continually exposed in the course of the dialogue. It makes lies and impieties attractive, as Lysias and Socrates do when they blaspheme against divine love. It enables an "expert rhetorician to lead his auditors step by step through a maze of similarities from the truth to its opposite (50, 262)," initiating a movement directly contrary to the upward movement initiated by dialectic. Rather than facilitating the process of memory by which the soul ascends to its former height of vision, rhetoric and things written induce forgetfulness and complacency:

> This invention [writing] will produce forgetfulness in the souls of those who have learned it. They will not need to exercise their memories . . . calling things to mind no longer from within themselves by their own unaided powers, but under the stimulus of external marks that are alien to themselves (68, 274).
>
> No work . . . has ever been written or recited that is worthy of serious attention—and this applies to the recitations of rhapsodes also, delivered for the sake of mere persuasion, which give no opportunity for questioning or exposition—the truth is that the best of these works merely serves to remind us of what we know already (73, 277–278).

This last charge is the most damaging; for by reminding us of what we know already, artifacts constructed with a rhetorical, or persuasive, intent stabilize our knowledge at its present inadequate level. Rhetoric tends, as Robert Cushman notes, to canonize the status quo; for "to persuade is to render plausible and to render plausible is frequently to render something one believes and desires apparently conformable to what one's hearers also believe and applaud." [11] The rhetorician panders to his audience's imme-

[11] *Therapeia: Plato's Conception of Philosophy* (Chapel Hill, 1958), p. 37. Throughout this chapter I am indebted to Cushman's exposition of Plato's philosophy.

diate desires and thereby lessens the probability that it will come to see the desirability of something better. In short, he acts toward his audience much as the bad lover of Socrates' first speech acts toward his beloved, and with somewhat the same motives:

> The lover will not willingly endure to have his beloved stronger or an equal but will continually strive to make him weaker or inferior. . . . He . . . does great harm by trying to keep his favorite from many other advantageous associations which would tend to make a man of him, and especially from the one that would most increase his wisdom. . . . This is divine philosophy from which the lover must necessarily and strictly bar his beloved, for he fears that he would then be despised (18, 239).

The lover would be despised because divine philosophy would have the effect of refining the beloved's perceptions so that what once seemed attractive and valuable would now seem base and worthless. This picture of the bad lover, who jealously guards his prerogatives and in his selfishness does irreparable harm to the soul of his beloved, is later counterpointed in every detail by the account, in Socrates' second speech, of the actions and motives of true lovers:

> Each selects his love according to character; and as though the youth were the very God whom he once followed, the lover fashions and adorns him like an image to be the object of his worship and his veneration. So the followers of Zeus desire that the soul of their beloved should follow that God; they look for one who loves wisdom. . . . When they come upon such a person the memory of the God they followed is aroused; enraptured, they pattern their way and manner of life upon his—in so far as a man can partake of a God's ways. And they consider the beloved cause of all this and love him still more: the drafts of inspiration which they draw from Zeus they pour like Bacchants into the boy's soul, making him so far as they can exactly like their God. . . . They exhibit no jealousy or pettiness toward the loved one; rather, every act is aimed at bringing

the beloved to be as much as possible like themselves, that is, like the God they honour (36–37, 252–253).[12]

Such a pair become lovers of wisdom and therefore lovers of each other because singly and together they are growing into images and repositories of the wisdom they love. The true basis of their relationship is not sense but soul, and their final victory is an escape from sense and a meeting with the source of all goodness: "At the end of life they will have full-grown wings and cast off the burdens of the flesh. . . . Nor can human discipline or divine madness confer any greater blessing on man than this (41, 256)." At this point human discipline has no more specific name than "philosophic way of life"; later, however, it will be more precisely identified as dialectic, whose practitioners, not surprisingly, follow the same procedures and reap the same reward as do the good lovers: "the dialectician . . . finds a congenial soul [one that resembles the God he followed] and then proceeds with true knowledge to plant and sow in it words which are able to help themselves and help him who planted them; words which . . . bring their possessor to the highest degree of happiness possible for a human being to attain (71, 276)."

It is in this implied equation of the dialectician and the good lover, on the one hand, and the rhetorician-writer and the bad lover on the other, that the unity of the *Phaedrus*—so much sought for by modern commentators—is to be found. The correspondences are exact, although they are at no point spelled out by the text (the spelling is the reader's job, one more exercise in the course of education the dialogue offers him); and for the sake of convenience and for future reference they can be represented by the following two tables:

TABLE I

| Bad Lover-Rhetorician | Good Lover-Dialectician |
|---|---|
| For slightly different reasons they impede progress toward the perception of the good; one | They lead the lover-respondent toward the good by making him dissatisfied with the opinions his |

[12] It is not difficult to see how in Christian terms this becomes the doctrine of imitating Christ by loving our neighbors for His sake.

TABLE I

| *Bad Lover-Rhetorician* | *Good Lover-Dialectician* |
| --- | --- |
| because he doesn't want the beloved to become cognizant of higher pleasures than those he has to offer him; the other because he wishes only to gain applause or impose his will, and thus urges on an audience the opinions it is already known to hold. | mind is stocked with and thus inducing a motion upward. |
| Both are committed to the status quo and leave untouched the soul of the lover-respondent. | Both are committed to the purification of the soul, to the raising of the eye of the mind to the point where it is congruent with Reality. |
| Both are flatterers who provide a pleasant and comfortable experience, an ego-satisfying experience. | Both are physicians whose ministrations are often painful because they force their charges to face unpleasant truths about themselves and counsel abandonment of the values they have always lived with. |
| Both present their pitches in a form that corresponds to the sense of order built into the consciousness to which they address themselves. | Both follow no set form, but act in response to what they consider to be the best interests of their charges, and that means *breaking out* of the perceptual set they were born with. |
| Both encourage and speak to that part of the mind which is in bondage to the sensible world. | Both strive to free the mind from its enslavement to the material and visible so that it can fly to that of which the material and visible is but an imperfect reflection. |
| Both speak to a man's basest instincts. | Both speak to a man's best self and to instincts of which he may not even have been aware, i.e. may have forgotten. |

TABLE II

| *Rhetoric and Writing* | *Dialectic* |
|---|---|
| Discourse controlled by the predetermined goal of the rhetorician which is likely to be suited to the known inclinations of the audience. | Discourse controlled by the unknown but real goal (the Good, Reality) toward which dialectician and respondent make uneven, nonpatterned progress, according to the state of the soul. |
| Persuades by taking the mind from point to point, according to the laws of logic or aesthetics (beginning-middle-end) which are actually reflections of the perceptual machinery in the mind itself. Assenting to a well-made speech or a well-made syllogism is assenting to oneself. | Persuades by *changing* the mind into an instrument congruent with the reality it would perceive; this involves breaking out of built-in frames of reference and evidentiary processes. |
| Claims to contain or corral truth, or to process it; and thus discourages active and self-critical participation in the search for truth. | Claims to initiate a movement of the soul (which is the vehicle, not it) toward an experience of truth; makes no claims for itself as *truth expressive*, either at any stage or as a whole; it is strategical not expressive. |
| Knowledge as the organization of items outside the mind of the respondent. | Knowledge as the transformation of the mind *into* the object of knowledge. |
| Success independent of the moral probity of either party. | Success depends on the moral probity of both; the perception (possession) of knowledge and the attainment of moral purity are one. Knowing the good and being the good are one. |
| Satisfies present expectations and so confirms the mind in its ignorance and corruption. Canonizes community values. | Disappoints present expectations and even challenges them, and thus induces dissatisfaction with the mind's state of knowledge. |

TABLE II

| *Rhetoric and Writing* | *Dialectic* |
| --- | --- |
| Dulls, encourages pride and complacency. | Awakens, encourages humility and aspiration. |
| Secures assent to a form, and when the form is taken away, so is the force of the assent. | Secures assent to an experience; thus the assent is inner and does not depend on any form external to the mind (soul). |

These tables offer two perspectives on the same opposition, one from the vantage point of the speaker or writer, the other from that of the forms he employs. In both, the emphasis falls finally on the very different effects produced by the two kinds of forms, effects which are contrasted explicitly in the methodological alternatives Socrates poses for himself in the closing pages of the *Gorgias:* "To which treatment of the city do you urge me? . . . Is it to combat the Athenians until they become as virtuous as possible, prescribing for them like a physician; or is it to be their servant and cater to their pleasure (99, 521)?" One is tempted to pause here to consider the implications of Socrates' phrasing, the suggestion that in order truly to serve the people, one must first somehow pain them; the use of the physician metaphor, which becomes a commonplace in Christian homiletics. But for the present I would call attention to the assumption underlying this passage, to what Cushman in *Therapeia* labels "the central theme of Platonism regarding knowledge . . . that TRUTH IS NOT BROUGHT TO MAN, BUT MAN TO THE TRUTH (213)." In other words, to educate is to change, and in a sense, to convert; the end of education is not so much the orderly disposition of things, but the illumination and regeneration of minds; the end of education, to borrow from a seventeenth-century Platonist, is "to repair the ruins of our first parents by regaining to know God aright, and out of that knowledge to love him, to imitate him, to be like him, as we may the neerest by possessing our souls of true virtue which . . . makes up the highest perfection." [13] It can be truly

[13] John Milton, *Of Education* in *Complete Prose Works of John Milton,* Vol. II, ed. Ernest Sirluck et al., pp. 366–367.

said that every would-be educator, speaker, statesman, poet, preacher, faces the choice Socrates articulates in the *Gorgias*, a choice of *motives*—whether to strive selfishly for a local and immediate satisfaction or to risk hostility and misunderstanding by pursuing always the best interests of his auditors (readers, citizens, parishioners); a choice of *modes*, whether to use language and discursive modes of thought in order to construct internally coherent artifacts whose strength lies in their conformability to the limitations of the human mind, or to use language and discursive modes of thought in order to push his auditors beyond their confining horizons (the ambiguity is intentional); and, above all, a choice of *results*, whether to immure the mind even more firmly in its earthly prison or to free it by raising it to the point where it becomes congruent with the Reality it would perceive. The seventeenth-century authors who are treated in this study, with the possible exception of one, consistently choose the second of these pairs of alternatives and produce works that exhibit many of the self-consuming characteristics of Platonic dialectic; but before examining those works, I would like first to look closely at one of the documents by which the philosophical and aesthetic concerns of the *Phaedrus* and *Gorgias* were transmitted to the Christian world.

### AUGUSTINE: WORDS AS SIGNS

To the modern literary sensibility, the least acceptable tenet in Augustine's teachings on the interpretation of the Bible is likely to be his theory of figurative reading. What are we to do, he asks in the *On Christian Doctrine*, when the literal sense of a scriptural verse "seems to commend either vice or crime or to condemn either utility or beneficence (93)?" The answer he gives is at once dazzlingly simple and, from the point of view of our normal assumptions about the world and our perceptions of it, wholly subversive:

> Whatever appears in the divine Word that does not literally pertain to virtuous behavior or to the truth of faith you must take to be figurative (88).

Therefore in the consideration of figurative expressions a rule such as this will serve, that what is read should be subjected to diligent scrutiny until an interpretation contributing to the reign of charity is produced (93).

A hostile reader might rephrase these two statements in the following way: "Whenever you find something that doesn't say what it is supposed to say, decide that it doesn't mean what it says; and then *make* it say what it's supposed to say." In other words, this rule would seem to urge us to disregard context, to bypass the conventional meanings of words, and, in general, to violate the integrity of language and discursive forms of thought. To such an accusation, Augustine would no doubt reply, "That is exactly the point," for his assumption is that if a word or a sentence does not seem to contribute to the reign of charity, the fault lies in the eye that so misinterprets it; and therefore what he enjoins is a way of reading that exercises eyes prone to misinterpretation (as ours, darkly clouded, surely are) until they are sufficiently "corrected" to see what is really there. "What is really there" will always be another instance of the only lesson the Bible ever teaches: love of God and love of one's neighbor for the sake of God. Anything else is an illusion, created by the distorted glass of a limiting and darkened perspective.

Clearly this exercise, insofar as it serves to push the mind's eye beyond the confining limits of literalism, is analogous to dialectic. The difference is that the dialectician in this case is God, who has not only informed Scripture with his true meaning, but so arranged matters that the discovery of that meaning becomes a program of self-improvement:

The obscurity itself of the divine and wholesome writings was a part of a kind of eloquence through which our understandings should be benefited not only by the discovery of what lies hidden, but also by exercise (123).

Scripture teaches nothing but charity, nor condemns anything except cupidity, and *in this way shapes the minds of men* (88, my emphasis).

Earlier in *On Christian Doctrine,* Augustine outlines the course of this shaping: first, "the student . . . will discover that he has been enmeshed in the love of this world, or of temporal things (39)." This discovery arouses fear and leads him "to lament his own situation" (exactly the sequence found in the opening pages of *The Pilgrim's Progress*). As a result "he will extract himself from all mortal joy in transitory things and as he turns aside from this joy, he will turn toward the love of eternal things." When he begins to see these eternal things "glowing in the distance," he finds that "because of his weakness he cannot sustain the sight of that light" and he "purges his mind, which is rising up and protesting in the appetite for inferior things, of its contaminations (39)." Finally, he "cleanses that eye through which God may be seen by those who die to the world as much as they are able (40)" so that he "neither prefers his neighbor to the Truth nor compares him with it"; and thereafter "this holy one will be of such simple and clean heart that he will not turn away from the Truth either in a desire to please men or for the sake of avoiding any kind of adversities to himself which arise in this life (40)." What Augustine describes, of course, is a total reorientation (conversion) of being, which involves an inversion of earthly values and a rejection of conventional ways of knowing, a turning of the world, as our natural faculties receive it, upside down.

It is important to note that while this passage looks forward to Augustine's theory of hermeneutics, what it urges is not only a way of reading the Bible, but a way of reading the World, which, no less than the Bible, is God's book.[14] If the "cleansed eye" interprets the words and events of the sacred writings according to the reign of charity, that same eye will perform an identical action on the words and events of life; for, "to the healthy and pure internal eye He is everywhere (13)." And if the obscurities and difficulties of Scripture were intended medicinally to "benefit our understandings," the obscurities and difficulties of our everyday existence are to be used to the same end. In fact everything is to be used to that

14 On this and related points see J. A. Mazzeo, "St. Augustine's Rhetoric of Silence: Truth vs. Eloquence and Things vs. Signs," in *Renaissance and Seventeenth Century Studies* (New York, 1964), pp. 1–28. See especially pp. 11, 24.

end and the danger of doing otherwise is the subject of Augustine's first book:

> Some things are to be enjoyed, others to be used, . . .
> Those things which are to be enjoyed make us blessed.
> Those things which are to be used help, and, as it were, sus-
> tain us as we move toward blessedness in order that we may
> gain and cling to those things which make us blessed. If we
> . . . enjoy those things which should be used, our course
> will be impeded and sometimes deflected, so that we are re-
> tarded in obtaining those things which are to be enjoyed,
> or even prevented altogether, shackled by an inferior
> love (9).

To enjoy the things of the world is to have a *rhetorical* encounter with them; to use them is to have a *dialectical* encounter. The temptation, then, is to confuse means with ends, and the journey metaphor, somewhat submerged here, is made explicit in the next paragraph: "Suppose we were wanderers . . . miserable in our wandering and desiring to end it and to return to our native country. We would need vehicles . . . which could be used to help us to reach our homeland, which is to be enjoyed. But if the amenities of the journey and the motion of the vehicles itself delighted us, and we were led to enjoy those things which we should use, we should not wish to end our journey quickly, and, entangled in a perverse sweetness, we should be alienated from our country, whose sweetness would make us blessed (9–10)." The allegory is, of course, commonplace and transparent: our native country is the "better country" of Hebrews XI where we shall enjoy the ever-lasting bliss of those who move and sing before the Lamb; the vehicle is this temporal life and its "amenities," all those things usually referred to as the "pleasures of this world." Thus, Augustine continues, "in this mortal life, wandering from God, if we wish to return to our native country . . . we should use this world and not enjoy it, so that the 'invisible things' of God 'being understood by the things that are made' may be seen, that is, so that by means of corporal and temporal things we may compre-hend the eternal and spiritual (10)." Translated into a rule for living, this means that as we proceed through our allotted three-score-and-ten, everything we encounter is to be interpreted (and valued) not with reference to the appearance it makes in any earthly configuration, but with reference to its function in the larger design of God's providential dispensation; and every commitment into which we enter is to be regarded either as temporary or as a shadow of our greater and overriding commitment to Him. In short, we are to live in time, but for (the sake of) eternity, seeking always to discern and respond to God's meaning rather than to the meaning that leaps immediately to our carnal eyes: [15]

> We should not causelessly and vainly consider the beauty of the sky, the order of the stars, the radiance of the light, the alternations of day and night, the monthly course of the moon, the fourfold organization of the year, the fourfold harmony of the elements, the minute force of seeds. . . . In considering these things, no empty and transient curiosity is to be exercised, but a step is to be made toward those things which are immortal and which remain always.[16]

Living in these terms is a continual exercise in translation, a seeing through the literal contexts of things (objects, events, persons) to the significance they acquire in the light of a larger perspective, and thus a means of enlarging our understanding. And the dangers life holds out, the many opportunities to cling to its "perverse sweetness" and thus forget the sweetness which would make us blessed, is exactly the danger Augustine warns against when he comes to discuss the writing and hearing of sermons:

> And we should beware lest what should be said escape us while we are thinking of the artistry of the discourse (120).
> He who speaks eloquently is heard with pleasure; he who speaks wisely is heard with profit. . . . Just as things which are both bitter and healthy are frequently to be taken, so also a pernicious sweetness is always to be avoided (122–123).

[15] This, as we shall see, is the obligation that generates the dynamics of *The Pilgrim's Progress*.

[16] Quoted by D. W. Robertson in *A Preface to Chaucer* (Princeton, 1960), p. 66.

The artistry of the discourse and the artistry of the beautifully ordered natural world are regarded with an exactly equivalent ambivalence. Whether you are listening to a sermon or simply living your life, the point is to keep your eye on the object; and the object, in either context, is not the vehicle within which you are moving, but the end to which the vehicle may bring you. The forms of this mortal life and the forms of a sermon, both proceeding in time and space, are to be used much as the forms of Platonic dialogue are used, that is, *used up;* and to do otherwise, to value them for their own sake rather than for the promise they shadow, is to court the death of the soul:

> Nor can anything more appropriately be called the death of the soul than that condition in which the . . . understanding is subject to the flesh in the pursuit of the letter. He who follows the letter takes figurative expressions as though they were literal and does not refer the thing signified to anything else. For example if he hears of the Sabbath, he thinks only of one day out of the seven that are repeated in a continuous cycle; and if he hears of Sacrifice, his thoughts do not go beyond the customary victims of the flocks and fruits of the earth. There is a miserable servitude of the spirit in this habit of taking signs for things, so that one is not able to raise the eye of the mind above things that are corporal and created to drink in eternal light (84).
>
> But we are taught to love and worship one God, who made all those things whose images they venerate either as Gods or as signs and images of Gods. If it is a carnal slavery to adhere to a usefully instituted sign instead of the thing it was designed to signify, how much is it a worse slavery to embrace signs instituted for spiritually useless things instead of the things themselves? Even if you transfer your affections from these signs to what they signify, you still, nevertheless, do not lack a servile and carnal burden and veil (86).

It becomes difficult in these passages to tell whether one is being counseled against a misinterpretation of words or of things, and in fact the usual distinction between the two tends to disappear in *On Christian Doctrine* into the larger category of signs. The first paragraph in which the nature of signs is discussed is itself a tour de force of distinctions that are finally without a difference: Augustine begins by apparently denying "real objects" the status of signs: "All doctrine concerns either things or signs. . . . Strictly speaking, I have here called a 'thing' that which is not used to signify something else, like wood, stone, cattle, and so on (8)." But his "strict speaking" (*proprie*) doesn't last long and immediately he begins to qualify his two categories into one "but not that wood concerning which we read that Moses cast it into bitter waters that their bitterness might be dispelled, nor that stone which Jacob placed at his head, nor that beast which Abraham sacrificed in place of his son. For these are things in such a way that they are also signs of other things." Of course these things of which other things are signs are themselves signs: Moses' "wood" is a sign of the Cross which is a sign of the crucifixion, which as an action is a sign (and a seal) of Christ's love for man; and the ram offered by Abraham as a sacrifice is a sign of Christ's sacrifice of Himself, for the love of man; and the stone Jacob places at his head is a sign of the firmness of Christ (that pure rock) on whose love we may all rest. Not only are these things signs of other signs which are also signs, but the chain of *signify*-ing all points in the same direction.

As the paragraph continues, a new distinction between verbal signs and thing signs is introduced. "There are other signs whose whole use is in signifying, like words. For no one uses words except for the purpose of signifying something (8)." But words that are signs are also things, "for that which is not a thing is nothing at all," and therefore "every sign [every word] is also a thing (9)." Augustine forestalls the complete collapse of his categories by stipulating that "not every thing is a sign (9)"; that is, some things do not signify beyond themselves; but it becomes clear as he proceeds that one should be interested in such self-referring things only because a knowledge of them as objects will help us when they are used as signs:

> An ignorance of things makes figurative expressions obscure when we are ignorant of the nature of animals or stones or plants. . . . Thus the well known fact that a ser-

pent exposes its whole body in order to protect its head from those attacking it illustrates the sense of the Lord's admonition that we be wise like serpents. That is, for the sake of our head, which is Christ, we should offer our bodies to persecutors lest the Christian faith be in a manner killed in us, and in an effort to save our bodies, we deny God (50–51).

It is instructive to follow the line of interpretation in this example: One begins presumably with a real-life situation or problem, the persecution with which professing Christians are threatened, and looks for direction to the Scriptures. There a verse is found which counsels, somewhat obscurely, a kind of wisdom, the wisdom of the serpent. The known characteristics of actual serpents are then recalled, but only so that they can be allegorized into a reading of the verse that instructs us how properly to read the situation. A proper reading of the situation is, of course, one that issues in a response consonant with the truths of Christian faith. Such a reading, while it appears to be the result of the sequence of inter-pretation, is actually the cause of it. One does not derive from the text and the situation (and the physical properties of serpents) a general truth; rather one scrutinizes the text and the situation until a relationship between them and a general truth that is assumed is discerned, until "an interpretation contributing to the reign of charity is produced." Thus persecution is finally seen providing an opportunity to *sign*ify our love of Christ above all else, including our bodies, and the fact of persecution becomes a sign just as the "well known fact that a serpent exposes its whole body in order to protect its head" becomes useful (true) knowl-edge when it becomes a sign. "Becomes" is perhaps the wrong word. It has always been a sign; what has been transformed is not it, but the eye looking at it.

In the course of *On Christian Doctrine*, the number of areas in which figurative reading of this kind is to be the rule grows and grows until the list of things that are signs is finally all-inclusive. "Every good and true Christian," Augustine declares, "should understand that wherever he may find truth, it is his Lord's (54)." If anything in the arts (music, painting, literature) is found useful for purposes of instruction, that usefulness is to be attributed to Him, and not to any merely human artificer. And while history may be the narration of "the human institutions of the past," "history itself is not to be classed as a human institution"; rather its "creator and administrator is God (64)" whose sometimes hidden purposes give it meaning and direction. History is God's sign. Even logic is God's sign: "the truth of valid inference was not instituted by men . . . [but] by God (68)," not invented "but discovered (69)." In fact everything is instituted by God—the "order of events in time," the "location of places," the "natures of animals, plants, or minerals," the rise and fall of nations, the rise and fall of a sparrow—and man's task is always one of discovery, the discovery of His (instituted) meaning amidst the distracting camouflage of local contexts. In short, *"to the pure and healthy internal eye He is everywhere* (13)," which means that for the pure and healthy internal eye, to see correctly is to be forever producing interpretations contributing to the reign of charity.

The implications of this way of looking at the world are enormous. If all things are signs of God's loving presence and if the usefulness of all things inheres in their signifying function, the distinctions we are accustomed to make, between persons, times, places, nations, callings, etc., must be abandoned, along with the systems of value that support them. "We say amisse/This or that is:/Thy word is all, if we could spell," writes George Herbert,[17] testifying to the survival into the seventeenth century of this radically unified vision along with its attribution of all perceived differences to the carnal eyes of "uneducated" readers. In another poem Herbert extends his "levelling" insight to the hierarchy of human actions: "Nothing can be so mean/Which . . . for thy sake/Will not grow bright and clean." [18] The value of our various callings is not to be determined by the service they render to society, but by the service they *would* render to God; and in these terms all callings are equally meritorious or base, depending on whether or not they are entered into "for thy sake."

---

[17] "The Flower," ll. 19–21.          [18] "The Elixir," ll. 14–16.

Obviously such a view makes nonsense of the system of rewards and honors by which we live and, less obviously, it also makes nonsense of the traditional rationale for the deployment of the classical "three styles." In the fourth book of *On Christian Doctrine*, Augustine recalls Cicero's authoritative formulation of the relationship between style and subject matter—"he therefore will be eloquent who can speak of small things in the subdued manner, of moderate things in a temperate manner, and of grand things in a grand manner (1–13)"—and he goes on to explain why this correlation does not obtain for Christian rhetors:

> Among our orators, however, everything we say, especially when we speak to the people from the pulpit, must be referred, not to the temporal welfare of man, but to his eternal welfare and to the avoidance of eternal punishment, so that everything we say is of great importance . . . for as the Lord says, "He that is faithful in that which is least, is faithful also in that which is greater." Therefore what is least is least, but to be faithful in what is least is great (143–144).

By the end of this paragraph "least" (*minimum*) and "great" (*magnum*) have reference to a standard of judgment that is no longer operative (in the Latin the alliteration and assonance accelerate the confusing and merging of the two words), either in terms of the real world or the rhetorical world of a sermon; and the novice who has gone to Augustine's book for instruction is left with the three styles but with no directions for employing them. This is hardly what one would expect from a manual for would-be preachers, although it is true that Augustine warns us in his preliminary remarks not to expect "the rules of rhetoric which I learned and taught in the secular schools (118)." But this (negative) statement of intention only complicates the confusion, for if the rules of rhetoric do not apply to Christian teaching, why is so much of this fourth book devoted to discussing them? The answer lies not so much in the presence of the rules in the tract, as in what happens to them and to the entire world view from which they issue; and the answer lies, too, in a method of instruction very much like the method Plato employs in the *Phaedrus*.

We may begin where Augustine does, with one of the classical conundrums of rhetorical theory. Is eloquence learned from the rules, or from the example of eloquent men? Augustine first poses the question and then answers it almost immediately: "Those with acute and eager minds more readily learn eloquence by reading and hearing the eloquent than by following the rules of eloquence . . . if capacity of this kind to learn eloquence is lacking, the rules of rhetoric will not be understood (119)." Augustine then declares that the speeches of truly eloquent men are the basis of the rules, not their product: "they were eloquent whether they had learned the rules or never come in contact with them. They fulfilled them because they were eloquent; they did not apply them that they might be eloquent (120)." The rules, he concludes, are merely an ex post facto codification of what true eloquence naturally effects.

This is perfectly straightforward and not at all surprising, especially to someone familiar with Cicero's writings on the subject. What is surprising, however, is the first sentence of the next section: "But since some do these things dully, unevenly, and coldly, while others do them acutely, ornately, and vehemently, he should approach this work about which we are speaking who can dispute or speak wisely even though he can not do so eloquently (121)." If rhetoric is the art of persuasion, then the criterion for judging the products of that art has suddenly changed, as eloquence, up to this point the assumed standard of judgment, is now declared superfluous, indeed even dangerous: "But he who is foolish and abounds in eloquence is the more to be avoided the more he delights his auditor with those things to which it is useless to listen so that he thinks because he hears a thing said eloquently, it is true (121)." The new standard is wisdom (one recalls the progression in the *Phaedrus*) but its ascendancy lasts only a few moments until Augustine literally defines it out of existence: "A man speaks more or less wisely to the extent that he has become more or less proficient in the Holy Scriptures (122)." "For one who wishes to speak wisely, therefore, even though he cannot speak eloquently, it is above all necessary to remember the words of Scripture (122)." Wisdom thus defined is not wisdom as we usually understand it because it is something external to the individual, who merely attaches himself to the wisdom of someone else. In the next paragraph, both wisdom and eloquence reappear in a sentence that would seem to resolve the question as originally posed—"he who wishes to speak not only wisely but also eloquently . . . should more eagerly engage in reading or hearing the works of the eloquent and in imitating them . . . than in setting himself to learn . . . the art of rhetoric"—but the usefulness of this conclusion to Christian rhetors is somewhat impaired by the change its terms have undergone since the discussion began. Eloquence and wisdom have been taken away from the orator-preacher and given to Holy Scripture which consequently constitutes the whole of the category "works of the eloquent." Implicit in all of this, of course, is the true conclusion to which the reader is being directed: Eloquence, wisdom, and, finally, persuasion belong solely to God and, in the end, eloquence is redefined as the act of praying for its effects (142).

Two interdependent actions have been set in motion by this sequence: (1) the reader's understanding of certain concepts has been refined to the point where the concepts more or less disappear; (2) as a direct result of (1) the book begins to work against the stated intention of its author, to "say a few things concerning teaching (118)." That is, each chapter or section of what purports to be an art of preaching succeeds only in further narrowing the area in which that art and its would-be practitioners are allowed to operate. It is not a distortion to call this method dialectical; for, as in the *Phaedrus* and other works that carry this designation, the reader is first invited to consider a problem in terms with which he is likely to be familiar (and therefore comfortable) and then forced by some unexpected turn in the argument to *re*consider not the problem, but the terms. As the book unfolds, the same question is always being asked—how does one become a good preacher? (how does one tell good writing from bad?)—but to the reader whose experience has led him to redefine "good" and "preacher" and perhaps to reject "become," that question means differently every time.

In fact, after a while it becomes meaningless, because the abilities that would go to make a good preacher turn out to be either beside the point or illusory. Eloquence is, as we have seen, the first prerequisite to go by the boards, and later in the book it is dismissed peremptorily ("The speaker should not consider . . . eloquence") and replaced with a new criterion, the effectiveness of teaching: "I am not here treating the method of pleasing; I speak of the method of teaching those who wish to learn (135)." But what of those who do not wish to learn or who wish to learn pleasurably? Here Augustine seems to make the concession first yielded by Aristotle (and subsequently by every apologist for rhetoric) to the "defects of our hearers," and thus to reintroduce the possibility of an *art* of preaching:

> Therefore a certain eloquent man said, and said truly, that he who is eloquent should speak in such a way that he teaches, delights, and moves. Then he added, "To teach is a necessity, to please is a sweetness, to persuade is a victory." Of the three, that which is given first place, that is, the necessity of teaching, resides in the things we have to say, the other two in the manner in which we say it (136).

In the paragraph that follows, Augustine expands on these Ciceronian distinctions and begins to translate them into rules for effective preaching. The speaker must not only say what he wished to say, but if he desires to retain the attention of his listener, he must delight by speaking "sweetly"; and if he wishes his listener to act on what has been said, to doctrine and delight must be added exhortation, so that "he loves what you promise, fears what you threaten, hates what you condemn . . . and is moved by whatever else may be done through grand eloquence (136–137)."

But no sooner has this superstructure of a rhetorical art been reerected than it is immediately dismantled, piece by piece, simply by collapsing its parts into one another: "But . . . instruction should come before persuasion. And perhaps when the necessary things are learned, they may be so moved by a knowledge of them that it is not necessary to move them further by greater powers of eloquence (137)." This moves quickly from a statement of priorities (instruction before persuasion) to the suggestion that the first action, if successfully undertaken, makes the second unnecessary, and it proves to be only a short step from the qualifying "perhaps" to a firmly conclusive "therefore": "And therefore persuasion is not a necessity because it need not always be applied if the listener consents through teaching and even through delight also (137)." Of the three constituents of eloquence—to teach, to delight, and to move—only two remain, to teach and to delight. But this new refinement of the original definition is itself short-lived as Augustine immediately declares "But delight is not a necessity either," for "when the truth is demonstrated in speaking, an action which pertains to the function of teaching, eloquence is neither brought into play nor is any attention paid to whether the matter of the discourse is pleasing, yet the matter itself is pleasing simply because it is true (137)." With this last phrase, "simply because it is true," the cat is let out of the bag. The teaching of the truth need not be accompanied by pleasing words or forceful exhortations, because the truth itself, if it is understood, both delights and moves. Cicero's anatomization of eloquence is therefore redundant, and in place of the instruction he had been led to expect, the novice preacher is left with little more than a sense of his own superfluousness. Not only have eloquence and the verbal arts usually associated with eloquence been declared unnecessary, but teaching, which has replaced eloquence as the sine qua non of Christian rhetorical art, has been defined in such a way as to make the preacher unnecessary, except as a passive transmitter of truths whose force is independent of anything he might do. And the force of truth, of course, is to be identified finally with God, who is Truth, and therefore the sole agent of persuasion. At this point this conclusion is only implied (rather strongly), but it is not long before it surfaces along with all its implications:

> And who shall bring it about that we say what should be said through us and in the manner in which it should be said except Him, in "whose hand are both we, and our words"? . . . "Take no thought how or what to speak: for it shall be given you in that hour what to speak. For it is not you that speak, but the spirit of your Father that speaketh in you (140)."

One would think that after this assertion, with all its authority, nothing more could be said on the subject, since the subject—the art of preaching—has been shown not to exist; but Augustine continues to consider the rules of rhetoric, although, not surprisingly, as he explains them, he explains them away. From the three ends of persuasion—to move, to please, and to teach—he proceeds to the three styles traditionally associated with those ends—the grand, moderate, and subdued, or high, middle, and plain. In classical theory, the deployment of these styles is determined either by subject matter—is it grandly important, moderately important, or relatively unimportant?—or by the occasion—are we speaking in the senate, delivering an after-dinner speech, or instructing our servants in their duties? In the context of Christian rhetoric, however, these considerations do not obtain; for the single subject matter of Christian rhetors, salvation, admits to no distinction of degree and therefore to no differentiation of occasion:

> When we are speaking of the eloquence of those men whom we wish to be teachers of things which will liberate us from eternal evil or lead us to eternal good, *wherever* these things are discussed, either before the people or in private, either with one or with several, either with friends or with enemies, either in extended speech or in conversation, either in treatises or in books, either in long letters or in short, they are great things (145, emphasis mine).

With both the imitative and the occasional rationales for the three styles undermined, there would seem to be no reason to retain them; but Augustine is strangely reluctant to give them up and he advises that they be varied according to the condition of one's hearers: "when . . . speaking to those who ought to do [something] but do not wish to do it, then those great things should be spoken in the grand manner in a way appropriate to the persuasion of their minds (145)." The force of such advice, however, is likely to be blunted if the reader remembers what he has been told before and will be told again, that the "persuasion of their minds," if it occurs, is to be attributed not to him, but to God. And even the reader who has forgotten will find this section of the treatise less than helpful, simply because it becomes increasingly difficult to tell one style from another. The grand style differs from the moderate "in that it is forceful with emotions of the spirit (150)," but "even in the grand style the beginning of the discourse should always be, or almost always be, moderate (159)." Again, the grand style is used for persuading, the moderate for delighting (160), but "when praises and vituperations are eloquently spoken, although they belong to the moderate style, they so affect some that they are not only delighted . . . but also desire to live in a praiseworthy way (161)," that is, they are also persuaded. The only positive rules that emerge from these pages are firmly negative: "no one should think that it is contrary to mix these three manners (158)"; one should not employ the subdued style for "understanding," the moderate style for "willingness," and the grand style for "obedience," rather the orator should attend always "to all three ends even when he is using a single style (162)," for "who does not know that, if he is not heard with understanding, neither is he heard willingly or obediently (163)?" The climax of what is certainly to be regarded as a "rhetorical" tour de force is a long sentence describing the subdued style in the course of which the subdued style disappears:

> Plerumque autem dictio ipsa submissa, dum soluit difficilli-
> mas quaestiones et inopinata manifestatione demonstrat;
> dum sententias acutissimas de nescio quibus quasi cauernis,
> unde non sperabatur, eruit et ostendit; dum aduersarii
> conuincit errorem et docet falsum esse quod ab illo dici
> uidebatur inuictum; maxime quando adest ei quoddam
> decus non appetitum sed quodammodo naturale, et non-
> nulla, non iactanticula, sed quasi necessaria, atque, ut ita
> dicam, ipsis rebus extorta numerositas clausularum, tantas
> acclamationes excitat, ut uix intellegatur esse submissa
> (*De Doctrina Christiana Liber Quartus,* ed. and trans.
> Sister Therese Sullivan, Washington, D.C., 1930, pp. 176,
> 178).
>
> Frequently the subdued style, when it solves difficult ques-
> tions and demonstrates in unexpected ways, when it brings
> to light and sets forth most acute principles from I know
> not what caverns, as it were, in an unexpected way, when it
> shows an adversary's error and reveals that what he seemed
> to say uncontrovertibly is false, and especially if a certain

beauty is added to it, not deliberately sought but in some way natural, and a few rhythmic closings are used, not ostentatiously but, as I say, as if necessary, arising from the things discussed themselves, then it excites such acclamations that it is hardly recognized as being subdued (Robertson, p. 163).

*Submissa* frames the body of this long sentence but its appearance at the end is something of a surprise, since it is we who have lost sight of it, scarcely know it, hardly recognize it.

It is true, of course, that an insistence on flexibility, and an unwillingness to narrowly circumscribe the use of the three styles is characteristic of the best of the classical theorists, and especially of Demetrius; and, were this an isolated feature of Augustine's treatment, the interpretation I put on it would be unwarranted. But as one instance of a pervasive pattern, this discussion falls into place as a further limiting of the orator-preacher's effectiveness. It is finally not too much to say that the implications of this fourth book of *On Christian Doctrine* are wholly negative. The only positive action is the relentless expansion of the category of those things that are irrelevant (and the corresponding narrowing of the area in which the preacher is allowed to operate):

– Eloquence is irrelevant, because it is an adjunct of wisdom.

– Wisdom is irrelevant, insofar as the speaker has any responsibility for it, since to be wise he need only remember the words of Scripture.

– Persuasion and all the arts of persuasion, including the three styles, are irrelevant, since the truth alone persuades and its persuasiveness is independent of the speaker's skills and even of his intentions.[19]

[19] On this point see *On Christian Doctrine*, pp. 164–165: "But since the good faithful do not obey any man, but obediently hear that Lord who said 'All things therefore whatsoever they shall say to you, observe and do: but according to their works do ye not; for they say, and do not,' thus they may hear usefully those who do not dare to teach their own doctrines, at least not from the high place of ecclesiastical authority which sound doctrine has constituted. On this account Our Lord, before He spoke of those I have mentioned, said by way of introduction, '[They] have sitten on the chair of Moses.' Thus that chair, not their own but

– Considerations of time, place, and audience are irrelevant, for the same reasons.

All that remains, it would seem, is to declare the speaker himself irrelevant, and this is precisely the import of Augustine's final piece of advice:

> Whether one is just now making ready to speak before the people or before any other group or is composing something to be spoken later before the people or to be read by those who wish to do so . . . *he should pray that God may place a good speech in his mouth* (168, emphasis mine).

This remarkable statement stands to everything that precedes it exactly as Socrates' rejection of labored artifacts stands to the earlier sections of the *Phaedrus*. Both works conclude by discrediting the very arts in whose use they had promised instruction, and both leave their nominal addressees—the writer of speeches and the writer of sermons—strangely silent, stripped of everything usually assumed to be theirs, and wholly dependent on the one genuinely effecting force in the universe.

The fact that the fourth book of *On Christian Doctrine* is, like the *Phaedrus,* a self-consuming artifact should not be surprising to anyone who has understood books I–III, for in the universe they describe, the assumptions that make possible an art of rhetoric are invalid. Traditional oratory assumes that some things are more important than others; consequently, the persuasion it effects always involves the making of distinctions (let us do A rather than B because A will bring about X which, as an objective, is preferable to Y). Distinctions, however, are what the Christian rhetorician finally denies, for he believes in a world everywhere informed and sustained by God's presence ("to the pure and healthy internal eye He is everywhere"), a world that, because it is without parts, is without hierarchies, either of persons or actions. Techniques for dividing and distinguishing, including the

---

that of Moses, forced those to speak well who did not also act well. They did what they would in their lives, but the chair of another did not permit them to teach their own doctrines. . . . And thus they benefit many by preaching what they do not practice."

rules of rhetoric, are therefore antithetical to his purpose, which is not to persuade to a point, but to a vision in which all points are one (he works to turn the world, as we naturally know it, upside down); and his successes are marked neither by applause nor by votes, but by conversions. A further difference between the two rhetorics, because it is a difference between the world views they reflect, involves the responsibility for persuasion which in traditional theory is attributed to men and to the forms they employ. In the context of Christian assumptions, only God persuades, and He persuades independently of the vessel He chooses as a means, whether it be a man or a sermon (or, as in the case of Herbert, a poem). The practical result of this, as we have seen, is to make nonsense of the lessons rhetorical manuals usually teach; and the result of that result is the raising of a question: why write sermons at all?

It is a question Augustine himself raises in the form of an imagined objection to his citing from Matthew "Take no thought how or what to speak: for it shall be given you." What are we to say, he asks, to those who argue "that if teachers are made learned by the Holy Spirit they do not need to be taught by men what they should say or how they should say it (141)?" For his answer, Augustine goes first to the Scriptures and then to an analogy in the practice of physicians:

> Does the Apostle contradict himself when he says that men are made teachers by the operation of the Holy Spirit and at the same time tells them what and how they should teach? Or is it to be understood that the office of men in teaching even these teachers should not cease even with the generosity of the Holy Spirit assisting? For "neither he that planteth is anything, nor he that watereth; but God that giveth the increase." Whence it happens that even with the assistance of holy men, or even if holy angels themselves take part, no one rightly learns those things which pertain to life with God unless he is made by God docile to God, to whom it is said in the Psalm, "teach me to do thy will, for thou art my God." Whence also the Apostle says to that same Timothy, speaking as a teacher

to his disciple, "But continue thou in those things which thou hast learned, and which have been committed to thee, knowing of whom thou hast learned them." Medicines for the body which are administered to men by men do not help them unless health is conferred by God, who can cure without them; yet they are nevertheless applied even though they are useless without His aid. And if they are applied courteously, they are considered to be among the works of mercy or kindness. In the same way, the benefits of teaching profit the mind when they are applied by men, when assistance is granted by God, who could have given the gospel to man even though it came not from men nor through a man (142).

In these terms, teachers and ministers (whether to the body or the soul) do their work under a double obligation. They must act as if the health of their charges depended solely on the proper application of human skills, while at the same time believing that the cures these skills effect have really been effected by God, who could have done very well without them. They are, then, to continue in their professions not because their labors are either efficacious or necessary, but because Scripture commands it; and indeed the value of what they do inheres in their willingness to do it under these humiliating conditions, sacrificing the satisfaction that attends a personal success for the greater satisfaction of being an instrument of the Lord, if He so chooses. Obviously such an obligation imposes a great many difficulties, not the least of which is the avoiding of the Scylla and Charybdis of pride and despair. On the one hand there is the danger of becoming so involved in the mechanics of an art that the claims of the Lord are implicitly denied; and on the other, the equal danger of affirming those claims to the extent of doing nothing at all. What is required is a mode of action that is simultaneously assertive and self-effacing, a difficult balance which Augustine achieves here by continually calling attention to the ultimate insufficiency of the very procedures he is discussing (and therefore to the insufficiency of his present effort). This is a self-protective device which also protects the reader. It allows Augustine to teach without running the (personal) risk of claiming more for his teaching than it alone could perform (Augustine thus follows the counsel of the Apostle to Timothy), and it prevents the reader from placing too much trust in the lessons he is all the while learning. In other words, the reader gets more than he bargained for and more, perhaps, than he would have wished. He is given the tools with which to fashion good (well-made) sermons, but he is not given a proportional faith in those tools or in the sermons they will fashion. He has his cake, but has been made to eat it too.

The obvious question remains. What would a sermon faithful to the spirit of *On Christian Doctrine* be like? Augustine never tells us in so many words, but we may infer its characteristics from what he does tell us, as well as from his own practice.

1. It would be a sermon whose strategy was to open eyes rather than to validate propositions, persuading, if it did persuade, not to a point, but to a vision.

2. Since the vision it would persuade to is of a universe in which all things ("and words also are things") are signs of God and therefore are finally not (separate things), its language could not function conventionally. The simplest syntactical string—subject-object-verb—assumes distinctions a sacramental view of the world denies, and one cannot write a sentence without placing the objects to which its words refer in relationships of subordination and dependence. In the face of this, the writer of sermons must either remain silent (hardly a feasible alternative) or contrive somehow to frustrate these dividing and distinguishing tendencies of language, perhaps by writing sentences like this one of Augustine's:

Illuc ergo venit ubi erat.
He came to a place where he was already (I, 12.12).

The first part of the sentence—"He came to a place"—establishes a world of fixed and discrete objects, and then the second half—"where he was already"—takes it away. (The effect is even swifter in Latin.) As a result, the words "He" and "place" lose their specificity, becoming finally as indistinguishable as their referents, and the forward (linear) movement of the syntax is countered by the feeling a reader has at the end of the sentence that he has returned to its beginning. Augustine, in effect, has made language defeat itself by making it point away from the temporal-spatial vision it naturally reflects.[20] Of language such as this one cannot ask the question, "what does it mean?" for in everyday terms it doesn't mean anything (as a statement it is self-consuming); in fact, in its refusal to "mean" in those terms lies its value. A more fruitful question would be "what does it do?"; and what it does is alert the reader to its inability (which is also his inability) to contain, deal with, capture, say anything about, its putative subject, Christ. The sentence is thus a ploy in the strategy of conversion, impressing upon the reader, or hearer, the insufficiency of one way of seeing in the hope that he will come to replace it with something better.

3. A sermon filled with such sentences will reproduce the same characteristics on a larger scale. There will be movement, from word to word, paragraph to paragraph, page to page, but it will be illusory. The reader-hearer will pass through doors only to find himself in the room he has just left. Sequence will not be the generator of meaning, but the marking off of discrete areas within which the audience will or will not make contact with the one true meaning, as its great author permits. (Thy will be done.)

4. Such a sermon, then, will be continually pointing away from itself, calling attention to what it is not doing (and indeed could not do), proclaiming not only its own insufficiency, but the insufficiency of the frame of reference from which it issues, the human frame of reference its hearers inhabit.

5. And therefore, a sermon that is true to Augustine's *ars praedicandi* will in the end give itself over to God, just as it will give over to God the selves of its charges. It will thus be self-

---

[20] For illuminating discussions of Augustine's attitude toward language see Mazzeo, "St. Augustine's Rhetoric of Silence," and Marcia L. Colish, *The Mirror of Language: A Study in the Medieval Theory of Knowledge* (New Haven, 1968), pp. 47–58. See especially p. 49. "Earthly ways of knowing are necessary, but they have a term. . . . In heaven the things which serve on earth as cognitive channels between God and man fall silent, for their work is done. All languages, whether literally or figuratively verbal, will cease, for the heavenly communion is beyond language."

consuming in two directions, as an object, which is to be used rather than enjoyed, and as a strategy.

These five characteristics may be taken (at least provisionally) as a paradigm description of a self-consuming artifact.

DONNE: THE WORD AS ALL

Whatever the influence of Augustine's writing on the preaching of his own time, his influence on the preaching of the seventeenth century was enormous. And in that century his chief disciple was John Donne.[21] Here is a sentence from Donne's last sermon, *Death's Duell:*

> And therefore as the *Mysteries* of our *Religion,* are *not* the *objects* of *our reason,* but *by faith we rest* on *God's decree* and purpose, (It is so, O God, because it is *thy will,* it should be so) so *Gods decrees* are ever to be considered in the *manifestation* thereof.[22]

The opening of the sentence bears two interrelated promises: its point will be made discursively, and the making of the point will take the form of a demonstrative argument, thesis and proposition, followed by a conclusion. For a time these promises are kept, and because they are kept the reader is involved in the very activity the sentence is warning against. The mysteries of our religion are *not* the objects of our reason, we are told, and yet the simple act of taking in the words "And therefore" involves us unavoidably in reasoning about the mysteries of our religion. In the logic of the experience, as opposed to the logic of the syntax, the weakest word in the first three clauses is "not," for as we nego-

---

[21] See on this point the appendix in Vol. X of the Potter-Simpson edition of the *Sermons*. See also Robert L. Hickey, "Donne's Art of Preaching," *Tennessee Studies in Literature,* I (1956); Robert L. Hickey, "Donne's Art of Memory," *Tennessee Studies in Literature,* III (1958); Dennis Quinn, "Donne's Christian Eloquence," *ELH* XXVII (1960); Dennis Quinn, "John Donne's Principles of Biblical Exegesis," *JEGP,* LXI (1962); Joan Webber, *Contrary Music: The Prose Style of John Donne* (Madison, 1963); Janel Mueller (ed.) *Donne's Prebend Sermons* (Chicago, 1971).

[22] *The Sermons of John Donne,* ed. George R. Potter and Evelyn Simpson (Berkeley, 1953–1961), Vol. X, p. 237. Citations from Donne's sermons are to this edition unless otherwise noted.

tiate the sentence, its message is less pressing (literally) than the machinery that is supposedly processing it; and although we read and understand the words, the thrust of our attention is forward, in the direction of the waiting "so" which will complete the sequence begun by "And therefore as."

But when that "so" is reached (twice, in a parenthesis), it does not complete, but disrupts the sequence, for it is the wrong "so." "It is so, O *God,* because it is *thy will,* it should be so." This is the "so" of divine fiat, of a causality more final than any that could be observed in nature or expressed in a natural language, and its appearance makes an a priori mockery of the fulfillment of the reader's expectations. Nevertheless, they are fulfilled. The second half of the demonstrative argument does arrive ("so *Gods decrees* are"), but a second too late and without the force of its earlier promise. The true force of the sentence now resides in the clash of the two "so's," one of which usurps the right of concluding from the other, leaving the reader to complete a sequence that has been emptied of its powers. Usually, a parenthesis is a momentary detour in the progress of a larger syntactical unit, but this parenthesis subverts the progress (and the claims) of the larger unit in which it occurs. Although the sentence continues, ending with a verbal and parodic echo ("therefore . . . thereof") of its beginning, it is finally an exercise in futility, which declares its own insufficiency and the insufficient faith of those who believed, even for a time, in its promise.

Obviously this sentence fulfills all the conditions of my paradigm (it is spectacularly self-consuming), and the pattern of its unfolding is a model of the entire sermon. Doctor Donne's "Own Funeral Sermon" opens by offering its auditor a striking image and inviting him to use it as a mnemonic device:

> Buildings stand by the benefit of their *foundations* that susteine and *support* them, and of their *butteresses* that comprehend and *embrace* them, and of their *contignations* that knit and *unite* them: The *foundations* suffer them not to *sinke,* the *butteresses* suffer them not to *swerve,* and the *contignation* and knitting suffers them not to *cleave.* The body of our building is in the former part of this verse: It is this, hee that *is our God* is the *God of salvation; ad*

*salutes,* of salvations in the plurall, so it is in the originall; the *God* that gives us spirituall and temporall salvation too. But of this *building,* the *foundation,* the *butteresses,* the *contignations* are in this part of the *verse,* which constitutes *our text,* and in the three divers *acceptations* of the words amongst our expositors, *Unto God the Lord belong the issues of death* (230).

What is provided here is, literally, a building or floor plan whose rooms are to be filled and furnished as we listen. Nearly every device available to the preacher's art is employed to make certain that we have the plan firmly in mind as Donne proceeds. The alliterative patterns of the first sentence do double duty: they support the assertion of the sense by combining with antistrophe and isocolon to perform a knitting and uniting action of their own; and in doing so they strengthen the probability that the image and its components will be recalled at a later point. This work continues in the following sentences: the functions of the foundation, buttresses, and contignations are restated (albeit negatively); the relationship between the image, the day's text, and the unfolding of the sermon is made explicit; and a third set of memory hooks or places is provided in "the three divers acceptations of the words amongst our expositors" and the three pronoun phrases with which Donne distinguishes them, *a morte, in morte,* and *per mortem:* "And these three considerations, our deliverance *a morte, in morte, per mortem, from death, in death,* and *by death,* will abundantly doe all the offices of the *foundations,* of the *butteresses,* of the *contignation* of this our building (231)."

This is, of course, wholly conventional and there are any number of traditions that would account for Donne's practice:

1. The tradition of artificial or place memory recently explored by Frances Yates; this would seem especially likely since as Miss Yates observes, "the commonest . . . type of mnemonic place system used was the architectural type," [23] or

2. the tradition of the *artes praedicandi,* with its many ways of opening or dividing a text, including the way of "textual precognition, an advance survey of text and content," [24] or

[23] *The Art of Memory* (Chicago, 1966), p. 3.
[24] Joan Webber, *Contrary Music* (Madison, 1963), p. 144.

3. the venerable tradition of legal rhetoric to which Bacon has recourse when he promises "I will give you at the first entrance a form or abstract of them all four, that, forthinking what you shall hear, the proof may strike upon your minds as prepared." [25]

It is not necessary to tie Donne exclusively to any one of these, since in each of them (and they were all available to him) he could have found a rationale and a set of directions for the clarity of presentation he achieves here. The directions would have varied slightly, but the rationale would have been the same: to afford the reader-auditor the comfort and satisfaction of a manageable experience, one whose contours he will be able to predict, and by predicting, control. In other words, these opening sentences constitute a promissory note, and what they promise is that the shape of what follows will correspond exactly to the shape that has been introduced into the auditor's mind. (We shall later see how Herbert makes use of this same principle and promise in his shaped poems.)

The advantages of such a procedure are obvious. What is not so obvious, perhaps, is the subtle flattery it implies. By providing us with a foreplan of his sermon, Donne pays us the compliment of assuming that we will be able to make use of it. The compliment is simultaneously to our memories and to our understandings. Our memories are presumed to be up to the task of keeping things in their appointed places (*a morte, in morte, per mortem*) and since these places are interior places in the mind, our understandings are presumed to be answerable to the dimensions of the sermon's subject. The order of the sermon will be a reflection of the ordering capability of the receiving mind, and together they (mind and sermon) will proceed to process and contain the mysteries of divinity.

Unfortunately, however, things turn out differently. The memory of the reader-auditor is taxed beyond its capacity; the distinctions represented by the components of the architectural image and by the three prepositional phrases are blurred and cease to be helpful; and the categories by means of which the mysteries of divinity were to have been anatomized become themselves the

[25] *Works,* ed. James Spedding, R. L. Ellis, and D. D. Heak (London, 14 vols., 1857–1874), VII, 689.

subject of question and debate. The result is precisely the opposite of what we are here encouraged to expect: an uncomfortable and unsettling experience in the course of which the understanding is denied the satisfaction of its own operations.

The explanation for this reversal of expectations is to be found in another memory tradition, one to which Donne explicitly refers when he declares in a sermon preached at "Lincolns Inne," "The art of *salvation*, is but the art of *memory*." In this tradition, which has its twin sources in the dialogues of Plato and the writings of Augustine, the memory functions to obliterate the very distinctions the "places," or *loci*, help us to maintain. These are distinctions of persons, places, things, actions, etc., the distinctions, in short, between the multiple forms of the natural world. In the philosophy and theology of Plato and Augustine the discreteness of these forms is an illusion, the product, in one case, of too long a sojourn in the inferior realm of sense impressions, and in the other, of too exclusive a reliance on the evidence of things seen. The dispelling of this illusion is the business of the faculty of memory. Thus, in the *Phaedrus* we read that the process of "passing from a plurality of perceptions to a unity" involves the "remembering of what our soul once saw . . . looking down upon what we now assert to be real, and gazing upwards at what is Reality itself." The aspiring philosopher "remains, always so far as he can, through memory, in the field of precisely those entities in whose presence . . . he is himself divine." And if a man makes "right use" of memory, he becomes "truly perfected," for he "separates himself," through memory, "from the busy interests of men (32, 249)." The function of memory, then, is admonitory; [26] it turns us away from the variegated beauties of the visible world to the spirit which created and still informs them. For Augustine this spirit is God, who is to be remembered even in the midst of those enticing things that lead men to "become devotees

[26] See Augustine *De Beata Vita,* where the indwelling presence of the Holy Spirit is characterized as a "certain admonition, flowing from the very fountain of truth [which] urges us to remember God, to seek him tirelessly." Quoted by Robert O'Connell, *St. Augustine's Early Theory of Man* (Cambridge, Mass., 1968), p. 197. On this and related matters see E. Gilson, *The Christian Philosophy of St. Augustine* (New York, 1960), pp. 101–105, and Robert O'Connell, *St. Augustine's Confessions: The Odyssey of the Soul* (Cambridge, Mass., 1969), pp. 118–130.

of their external products, while abandoning internally [forgetting] their own Maker (*Confessions* X, 53)." [27] "The eyes," laments Augustine, "love beautiful and diverse shapes, brilliant and pleasing colors (X, 51)." [28] These threaten to occupy the soul, but they can be crowded out if the internal eye will but fix on God's mercies: "I . . . do get my steps involved in these beautiful things, but Thou dost free me, O, Lord, Thou dost free me, 'for thy mercy is before my eyes' (X, 53)."

It is in this tradition, then, that Donne enrolls himself when he advises (following St. Bernard) that "wee . . . place *all Religion* in the memory":

> The art of *salvation,* is but the art of *memory.* When God gave his people the *Law,* he proposes nothing to them, but by that way, to their memory; *I am the Lord your God, which brought you out of the land of Egypt;* Remember but that. And when we expresse Gods mercy to us, we attribute but that faculty to God, that he *remembers* us; *Lord, what is man, that thou art mindfull of him?* And when God works so upon us, as that *He makes his wonderfull works to be had in remembrance,* it is as great a mercy, as the very doing of those wonderfull works was before. It was a *seal* upon a *seal,* a seal of *confirmation,* it was a *sacrament* upon a *sacrament,* when in instituting the *sacrament* of his *body and his bloud,* Christ presented it so, *Doe this in remembrance of me. Memorare novissima,* remember the *last* things, and *fear* will keep thee from sinning; *Memorare praeterita,* remember the *first* things, what God hath done for thee, and *love,* (love, which, mis-placed, hath transported thee upon many sins) love will keep thee from sinning. *Plato* plac'd *all learning* in the memory; wee may place *all Religion* in the memory too: All knowledge, that seems new today, says *Plato,* is but a remembring of *that,* which your soul knew before. All instruction, which we can give you today, is but the remembring you of the mercies of God, which

---

[27] *Confessions,* trans. Vernon J. Bourke (New York, 1953), p. 310.
[28] *Ibid.,* p. 308.

have been *new every morning* . . . let them but remember thoroughly, and then as it follows there, *They shall turn unto the Lord, and all the kindreds of the Nations shall worship him.* Therefore *David* makes *that* the key into this Psalme; *Psalmus ad Recordationem, a Psalm for Remembrance.* Being lock'd up in a close prison, of multiplied calamities, this turns the key, this opens the door, this restores him to liberty, if he can *remember (Sermons,* Vol. II, 73–74).

These are large claims (one could almost believe that Bunyan was reading this sermon as he wrote the Doubting-Castle episode of *The Pilgrim's Progress*), and it is obvious from this passage that memory, while it is only one of the faculties of the soul, is more than a third among equals. The will is perverse unless it be informed aright; and the understanding that ought to inform the will intrudes itself into the very areas from which, by fiat, it is excluded ("Thy judgements are unsearchable and thy ways past finding out") so that "truly the Memory is oftner the Holy Ghost's Pulpit that he preaches in, than the Understanding": [29] *"Let God make his wonderful works to be had in remembrance. . . .* This is the faculty that God desires to work upon; and therefore if thine understanding cannot reconcile differences . . . if thy will cannot submit itself to the ordinances of thine own church, go to thine own memory." [30] To the extent that this recourse to memory bypasses or obviates the operation of the understanding, it is the opposite of the memory which forms the basis of the classical mnemonic systems. Whereas, in one tradition things are fixed in their respective places, in the other, a growing awareness of God's immanence makes all places and things one. In one tradition the categories by means of which the visible world is divided and made manageable are validated, while in the other those categories are collapsed when they are discovered to contain the same essence. One tradition calls upon and exalts the powers of the rational understanding, while the other asks the

[29] *The Sermons of John Donne,* VIII, 261. Donne's conception of memory is discussed in those places cited in note 21. Pp. 30–35 of Janel Mueller's introduction (Donne's *Prebend Sermons*) are particularly succinct and helpful.

[30] *Ibid.,* II, 237.

rational understanding to abdicate in favor of the revealed word.
In brief, to remember God is to forget everything else, because, as
Thomas Browne declares, "he onely is, all others . . . are something but by a distinction (*Religio Medici,* I. 35)"; it is that distinction, between God and everything else, which one tradition
preserves and the other denies.

I would like to suggest that *Death's Duell* is built in part on
the tension between these venerable traditions. At first it appears
that the apparatus of the rhetorical or artificial memory will be
employed in the service of the Christian-Platonic memory and
that we will be able to anatomize and contain the Word within
the structures of rational thought; but as the sermon unfolds, the
two kinds of memory work against each other: the memory of
"what God hath done" occupies all the supposedly discrete categories established in the artificial memory and thereby undermines
the distinctions those categories support.

This process begins almost at once, even as the components of
the mnemonic image are supposedly being established. As Donne
proceeds to "open" his text, the prose continues to move in the
direction of clarity and order: "For *first* the *foundation* of this
*building* . . . is laid in this; That *unto* this *God the Lord belong
the issues of death,* that is, it is in his power to give us an *issue*
and deliverance, even then when wee are brought to the jawes and
teeth of death, and to the lippes of that whirlepoole, the grave
(230)." This is perfectly straightforward, even conventional,
("the jawes and teeth of death," "that whirlepoole, the grave")
and it exactly fulfills the promise of the introductory "that is."
The second "acceptation" begins by following the same pattern,
but unexpectedly it is complicated by a thrust out toward the
audience:

And then *secondly,* the buttresses that comprehend and
settle this building . . . *unto God the Lord belong the
issues of death,* that is, the disposition and *manner of our
death:* what kind of *issue,* and *transmigration* wee shall
have out of this world, whether prepared or sudden,
whether violent or naturall, whether in our perfect senses
or shaken or disordered by sicknes, there is no condemna-

tion to bee argued out of that, no Judgement to bee made upon that, for howsoever they dye, *precious in his sight is the death of his saints,* and with him are *the issues of death,* the *wayes* of our *departing* out of this *life* are in his *hands* (230–231).

The warning "there is no condemnation to bee argued . . . no Judgement to bee made" comes a split second too late, after we have been invited, indeed compelled, to judge and condemn. Only the first pairing of alternative ways of dying can be received indifferently; there are things to be said both for a death that has been anticipated and for a death that takes one unawares. The choice between "violent" and "naturall," however, is less neutral, and in the third pairing, the balance, both rhetorically and in terms of the sheer quantity of words, is heavily weighted against disorder and sickness. In short, the reader-auditor cannot help but react judgmentally to the sequence, to argue a condemnation or a commendation from the physical circumstances of a death. And in the act of judging, he is himself judged. The sentence ends by referring the matter to the true judge or, more precisely, to his word—"with him are *the issues of death.*" With him, not us, in his hands, not our minds. The rebuke is local, but its implications extend to the business in which the prose has involved us, the anatomizing and understanding of God's word.

Even at this early stage, then, there are two forces operating in the sermon, one embodied in the point-by-point unfolding of the *divisio,* and another that is subversive of that unfolding and of the presumption which underlies it. And curiously enough, the vehicle of subversion is "the *verse* which constitutes *our text*"— "*Unto this God the Lord belong the issues of death*"—which is brought in whenever the machinery of rational discourse breaks down. The pattern is established in this opening section when the expectations created by the thrust of the syntax ("Is laid in this," "consists in this") are met not by a reason or a piece of evidence, but by the bald repetition of the verse, which is put forward as if it were wholly explanatory. We look for a statement that will ask for our rational assent and find instead the self-sufficiency of the revealed Word. What we have, then, are two logics, the everyday logic of definition and inference, and the logic (or anti-logic) of divine decree. At first, these coexist uneasily in a relationship of mutual threatening, but as the sermon continues, theirs becomes an adversary relationship in which the terms exacted by the victor are no less that total surrender. The first overt clash occurs in the climactic sentence of the proem:

> And these three considerations, our deliverance *a morte, in morte, per mortem, from death, in death,* and *by death,* will abundantly doe all the offices of the *foundations,* of the *butteresses,* of the *contignations* of this our building; That he that is our *God,* is the *God of all salvation,* because *unto* this *God the Lord belong the issues of death* (231).

This sweeping period recapitulates the entire section and brings to bear all the machinery that is to attend the opening of the text, the image of a building with its architectural supports, the three "acceptations" of the verse, the three pronoun phrases to which they are attached. The weight of this machinery falls squarely on "because" which in turn invites us to transfer its burden to the reason that will presumably follow. But, once again, the anticipated reason fails to appear (despite the promise of "because") and we are deposited, as we have been before, on "the verse which constitutes our text."

When the forms of logical discourse abdicate their responsibility in this way, the audience is left in an uncomfortable position, committed both by training and instinct to rational procedures and yet increasingly aware of the irrelevance of those procedures to the business at hand. This is an intellectual, almost abstract, discomfort, but it becomes more visceral when the sermon fails us at precisely those points where the issues it raises are personally oppressive and threatening, for then we are trapped by the very mechanisms which were to have served us. This is particularly true of the long first movement which is supposedly to take us through "all our *periods* and *transitions* in this life, . . . so many passages *from death* to *death* (231)." "Periods," "transitions," and "passages" are familiar literary terms and, although their primary reference is to the progression of our lives, they refer also to the anticipated progression of this sermon; and in both contexts they promise development and change. That promise is immediately qualified, however, by the phrase *"from death to death."* The prepositions divide the phrase into discrete areas or (in temporal terms) periods, but as we go from one to the other, they are discovered to be indistinguishable. There is a passage and a transition, but the reader who negotiates them exits from one room (the architectural metaphor is, of course, Donne's) only to find himself in the room he has just left.

This is exactly the pattern on a larger scale of the entire section. We move (supposedly) from one period to another, from one section of the sermon to the next, but discover in each new period and section the same horrors we thought to escape. As a result, the experience of the sermon becomes a cycle of frustrations, at each stage of which the pressure for release is greater. Thus we are at first assaulted by an imaginative recreation of our life in the womb: "for in our mothers *wombe* wee are *dead so,* as that wee do *not know* wee *live,* not so much as wee doe in our sleepe, neither is there any *grave* so close, or so *putrid a prison,* as the *wombe* would be unto us, if we stayed in it *beyond* our time (232)." Staying in the womb makes us murderers. "In the wombe the dead *child* kills the *Mother."* Staying in the womb may deprive us of salvation. "And there in the *wombe* wee are taught *cruelty,* by being *fed with blood,* and may be *damned,* though we be *never borne* (232)." As this catalogue of terrors lengthens, the claustrophobia of the actual situation is transferred to the experience of reading (or hearing) about it; the prose envelops us in its own womb and asks a question (with the help of St. Paul) that is self-referring: *"wretched man that he is, who shall deliver* him *from this body of death* (232–233)?" The answer is given quite properly by Eve, our general mother, whose unopened womb would have been the grave of the entire race: ". . . shee might well say, *possedi virum a Domino, I have gotten a man from the Lord . . .* the *Lord* that *brought into the world* that which himselfe *had quickened;* without all this might *Eve* say, My *body had been* but *the house of death,* and *Domini Domini sunt exitus mortis,* to *God the Lord belong the issues of death* (233)."

The unburdening of Eve's womb and our exit from the womblike enclosure of the prose are effected simultaneously, but the

effecting agent is not time, but God, who intervenes to reverse
the direction events seemed to be taking. Once again the linear
movement of the sermon defaults to the verse (or half verse) it
was to have explained. The machinery of rational discourse, with
its temporal structures and spatial images, has served only to
generate perplexities ("who shall deliver?") and dilemmas
(*"damned,* though we be *never borne"*); for their resolution we
are returned to the word of God, which does not so much untie
as cut through a Gordian knot of our own (and Donne's) making.

The result is a feeling of release and relief which carries with
it a strong suggestion of closure, and for a moment we forget that
this is but the first (indeed prior to the first) of the ages of man.
This is a sweet forgetting, but its duration is less than a word:

> But then this *exitus a morte,* is but *introitus in mortem,* this
> *issue,* this deliverance *from* that *death,* the death of the
> *wombe,* is an *entrance,* a delivering over to *another death,*
> the manifold deathes of this *world.* Wee have a winding
> sheete in our Mothers wombe, which grows with us from
> our conception, and we come into the world, wound up in
> that *winding sheet,* for wee come to *seek a grave* (233).

"It is," declares Donne, "the *exaltation* of *misery* to *fall* from a
*neare hope* of *happines* (232)"; and it is just such a fall that we
experience here, not once, but twice, as the prose plunges us back
into the cycle of death and at the same time nurtures in us the
hope of escape. The miseries of the "manifold deathes of this
*world"* are at least as great as the miseries of the "death of the
wombe" and of longer duration; their description, like their living,
threatens to be interminable:

> That which we call life, is but *Hebdomada mortium, a*
> *week of deaths,* seaven dayes, seaven periods of our life
> spent in dying, a *dying seaven times over;* and there is an
> end. *Our birth dyes* in *infancy,* and our *infancy* dyes in
> *youth,* and *youth* and the rest dye in *age,* and *age* also
> dyes, and *determines all.* Nor doe all these, youth out of
> infancy, or age out of youth arise so, as a *Phoenix* out of
> the ashes of another *Phoenix* formerly *dead,* but as a *waspe*

or a *serpent* out of a *caryon*, or as a *Snake* out of *dung*. Our *youth* is *worse* then our *infancy*, and our *age worse* then our *youth*. Our *youth* is *hungry and thirsty*, after those *sinnes*, which our *infancy knew not;* And our *age* is *sory* and *angry*, that it *cannot pursue* those *sinnes* which our *youth* did. And besides, al the way, so many deaths, that is, so many deadly calamities accompany every condition, and every period of this life, as that death it selfe would bee an ease to them that suffer them. Upon this sense doth *Iob* wish that *God had not given him* an *issue* from the *first death*, from the *wombe*, *Wherefore hast thou brought me forth out of the wombe? O that I havd given up the Ghost, and no eye had seen me; I should have been, as though I had not been* (234–235).

The topos of the seven ages of man has a long and varied history before Donne employs it here; but in all its versions two characteristics remain constant: it is a device for the making of distinctions, and it is a figure of progression. Often the distinctions are qualitative and the progression is from weakness to strength, before returning in a circle to weakness: "The strength of manhood . . . is released from the tutelage of boyhood . . . the number seven multiplied by itself produces the age which is properly considered and called perfect, so that a man of this age . . . is considered ripe in wisdom." [31] Even Christianity, with its emphasis on the debilitating effects of original sin, does not abandon the more positive implications of the sequence: "the first age . . . infancy . . . submits without any resistance to the flesh, and the second age . . . boyhood . . . has not yet understanding enough. . . . But when we reach that age which can now comprehend the commandment . . . we must declare war upon vices, and wage this war keenly, lest we be landed in damnable sins." [32] The se-

[31] Macrobius, *Commentary on the Dream of Scipio,* trans. W. H. Stahl (New York, 1952), pp. 114–115.

[32] Augustine, *City of God,* XXI, 16, trans. Marcus Dods in *The Works of Aurelius Augustinus* (Edinburgh, 1871–1876), 15 vols. Most readers know the topos from Jacques's speech in *As You Like It* (Act II, scene vii, ll. 147–174) which begins with the famous line "All the world's a stage." Jacques's version is of course supremely cynical, but still his ages are distinguishable, if not exactly progressive.

quence in *Death's Duell* is quite different, as Donne empties the
topos of its conventional associations in two swift and decisive
maneuvers: first its distinguishing force is taken away, when the
last age is made the essence of every age; and then, not content
merely to arrest movement, he reverses it. Maturity brings the
maturing of sin [33] and more deadly calamities follow upon the
calamities we have already known. The effect is all the more powerful (and distressing) because the framework of the topos is not
abandoned; it remains as an area to be negotiated, but without
the sense of progression that makes its negotiation a source of
satisfaction. In short, the topos becomes a prison. This is, of
course, precisely what has happened to the sermon; its mechanisms, too, have been deprived of power and efficacy, yet they
remain, stretching before us, not, however, as a chain of inferences
leading to a triumphant conclusion, but as a succession of graves.
The forward movement (like the forward movement of the topos)
has become *de*progressive, or retrogressive, from worse to worse,
and the discomfort we are now beginning to feel is compounded
when we are forced to assign the responsibility for this declination
to ourselves. Twice in this passage we are tempted (literally) to
shift it elsewhere. For a moment, "our *youth* is *hungry and
thirsty*" is read as a complaint against the time, but the addition
of "after those *sinnes,* which our *infancy knew not*" alters the
force of the construction and leaves us with no choice but to
return the blame to ourselves. In the same way, the assertion that
"our *age* is *sory*" seems at first an invitation, readily accepted, to
self-pity ("*sory*" is read as sorrowful), until the delayed syntax
reveals that it is we who are sorry (regretful) that we are no
longer capable of the sins we enjoyed in youth. From every
direction, the sermon assaults us, with carrion, with dung, and

---

There were in the Renaissance numerous pictorial representations of the ages,
often in the form of a circle, with "mature Manhood" at the apogee and infancy
and age meeting at the bottom. There is also the tradition, descending from Hor-
ace's remarks in the *Ars Poetica,* of suiting speech and action to each of the ages,
and again the distinctions implied were qualitative and progressive. See in this
connection S. E. Fish, *John Skelton's Poetry* (New Haven, 1965), Ch. III. For a
general discussion see Franz Boll, *Die Lebensalter* (Leipzig and Berlin, 1913).

[33] For the relationship between the seven ages and the deadly sins see Morton W. Bloomfield, *The Seven Deadly Sins* (East Lansing, 1952).

with accusations, and the prospect, given the divisions and "acceptations" yet to be negotiated, is for more of the same. The distinctions and divisions that were to have marked the progress of our understanding mark, instead, the extent of our entrapment. We begin by holding on to the discursive framework of the opening sentences only to find that it now has a stranglehold on us. The architectural metaphor returns, but with a new and distressing force: "in heaven there *are many mansions;* but here upon earth *The Son of man hath not where to lay his head . . .* wee are but in *a pilgrimage,* and wee *are absent from the Lord;* hee might have said *dead,* for this whole *world* is but an *universall church-yard,* but our *common grave;* and the life and motion that the greatest persons have in it, is but as the shaking of buried bodies in their graves (234)." Again these statements apply equally to life and to this sermon. Movement is illusory; all places, real and rhetorical, are the same, all graves; all distinctions of time are but the artificial measures of an endless dying.

In the whole of the passage, and in the sermon to date, only one hope is held out:

There is an end (234).

If the unfolding of time, through the agency of her discursive structures, will not deliver us, we can at least be delivered from time; and if death itself would be an ease to those who suffer life's calamities, the linguistic equivalent of death—silence—will be an ease to us who suffer their chronicling. The sermon cannot go backward, despite the reference to Job's wish "that *God had not given him* an *issue* from the *first death,* from the *wombe*" (a wish that we might echo were it not for the earlier description of the womb as a *"grave* so close," "so *putrid a prison"*), but it can conclude; and it is the promise of concluding that Donne holds out when he allows us to anticipate the final period (again the double reference) of the ages of man: *"age* also dyes and *determines all."* In short, we are once again looking to the temporal-spatial framework of the sermon for the resolution of our difficulties, even though it has failed us so many times before. Of course, there is a difference. Earlier we were confident that discursive forms, in the service of our rational intelligences, would be

answerable to the task of identifying and processing truth; now
we hope that by exiting from those same forms we will be able to
escape a truth whose application has become distressingly personal. In both cases, however, we make the mistake of putting our
trust in what Milton calls the "rare devices of man's brain" and of
forgetting that *Domini Domini sunt exitus,* to God the Lord—and
not to sermons, or sermonists, or parishioners—belong the issues
of death.

It is a mistake and a forgetting that Donne continues to encourage, as he recalls the laments of all of those who, like us, have
wished for death and for an end: "*Eliah* himselfe, when he *fled
. . .* requested that *hee might dye,* and sayd, *It is enough, now
O Lord, take away my life.* So *Jonah . . . O Lord take, I be-
seech thee, my life from mee, for it is better for me to dye then to
live* (235)." The conclusion is obligingly drawn by Donne, who
leads us forward in the manner of Spenser's Despair: "How much
worse a death then death, is this life, which so good men would
ever change for death (235)?" In this case the "so good men" are
ourselves, who have been changing death for death, and are
ready to do so again, in the foolish hope that the passing of time
will bring us rest. The climactic sentence of this section follows
immediately, and it seems to offer the rest we have been seeking.

> But if my case bee as Saint *Paules* case, *quotidie morior,*
> that *I dye dayly,* that something heavier then death fall
> upon me every day; If my case be *Davids* case *tota die
> morificamur, all the day long wee are killed,* that not onely
> every day, but every houre of the day some thing heavier
> then death fall upon me, though that bee true of me, *Con-
> ceptus in peccatis, I was shapen in iniquity, and in sinne did
> my mother conceive me,* (there I dyed one death,) though
> that be true of me (*Natus filius irae*) I *was borne* not
> onely the child of sinne, but *the child of wrath,* of the wrath
> of *God* for sinne, which is a heavier death; Yet *Domini
> Domini sunt exitus mortis,* with *God the Lord are the issues
> of death,* and after a *Job,* and a *Joseph,* and a *Jeremie,* and
> a *Daniel,* I cannot doubt of a deliverance. And if no other
> deliverance more to his glory and my good, yet he hath the
> *keys of death,* and hee can let me out at that dore that is,

deliver me from the manifold deaths of this world, the *omni die* and the *tota die,* the *every dayes death,* and *every houres death,* by that *one death* the *final dissolution* of body and soule, the end of all (235).

This is not a real conditional; there is no doubt that everything predicated hypothetically of the first person voice is true, especially since the hypotheses correspond exactly to the facts as they have been relentlessly detailed in the preceding paragraphs. As a result, the pressure of the construction is anticipatory, pointing forward to whatever it is that will counterbalance the depressing reality of the sinner's situation. The weight of that pressure falls directly on the conjunction "yet," just as earlier it had fallen on "because" in the concluding sentence of the proem. The parallel is continued when the cascading clauses of the extended period are met not by a statement of equal length, but by the simple reinvocation of the verse that constitutes our text, *"Domini, domini. . . ."* The satisfaction we experience at this moment is a double one: we are released at last from the cycle of daily and hourly dyings, and our release coincides with the completion of one of the sermon's rhetorical divisions. For a moment it seems that what had been denied to the formal structure—a place in the expounding of God's word—is to be restored, as its cadences merge with revelation to provide the ofttime promised "end of all."

The breaking of that promise is particularly brutal:

But then is that the end of all? Is that dissolution of body and soule, the last death that the body shall suffer? (for of spirituall death wee speake not now) It is not. Though this be *exitus a morte* it is *introitus in mortem;* though it bee an *issue from* the manifold *deaths* of this *world,* yet it is an *entrance* into the *death of corruption* and *putrefaction* and *vermiculation* and *incineration,* and dispersion in and from the *grave,* in which every dead man dyes over againe (235–236).

This last reversal should disabuse us of any remaining confidence we may have had in temporal and discursive forms; they have helped us neither to escape nor to understand. Once more we are remanded back to prison just when release seemed imminent, and this second remanding, more peremptory and (apparently) final than the first, brings into sharp and pressuring focus the three prominent patterns of the sermon: the periodic defaulting of the argument to the verse it was to have explained; the persistent short-circuiting of our normal modes of discursive response (by ends that are beginnings, progressions that go backward, etc.); and the refusal of the sermon to move toward a conclusion.

Although these three patterns are to some extent discrete, they finally function as one; for together they constitute a radical subversion not only of the sermon's pretensions, but of the pretensions of those who are prepared (or so they think) to understand it and to exit from it with a portable truth. If the expository mechanisms of rational discourse will not serve, what are we to do? How are we to proceed without the support and direction (and self-satisfying comfort) they usually provide? These questions are not asked directly; they arise gradually (and unavoidably) when the habits of thought we have always found reliable fail us, and they arise more immediately when Donne follows this most recent disappointment of our expectations with a question of his own: "It was a *prerogative* peculiar to *Christ,* not to dy this death, *not to see corruption.* What gave him this priviledge (236)?"

At first this question, because it signals a change of subject, is welcomed for the relief it seems to offer from the cycle of frustrations that precedes it; but, like everything else in the sermon, that relief is temporary and illusory and in the sequence that follows the frustrations return with a new and newly personal intensity. A question, after all, implies the availability of an answer; it is one half of a maneuver in the strategy of rational inquiry; and to ask it is always to create a psychological need for its completing half. Thus, even though Donne's question is to some extent rhetorical—he doesn't expect us to answer it—the force of the interrogative draws us into its rhythm and creates in us the expectation of an answer. But rather than a single answer, Donne puts forward a series of answers, holding out each one just long enough to make it attractive, before withdrawing it. It was "Not *Josephs* great proportion of *gummes* and *spices,* that might have preserved his body . . . longer then *three dayes,* but it would not have done it for ever (236)." Was it then "his *exemption and freedome from originall sinne?"* This possibility is considered at greater length, in part because it is more theologically respectable than the natural explanation of gums and spices; after all, " 'tis true that the original sinne hath induced this corruption and *incineration* upon us." But not upon him, it seems, for "since *Christ* tooke *sinne* upon him, so farre as made him *mortall,* he had it so farre too, as might have made him see this corruption and *incineration,* though he had no *originall sinne* in himself." As the passage continues, the speculation becomes more rarified: "Did the *hypostaticall union* of both natures, *God* and *Man,* preserve him?" for this was indeed "a most powerfull *embalming,* to be embalmed with the *divine nature* it selfe, to bee embalmed with *eternity."* But even this will not satisfy the case, since "for al this powerful *embalming* . . . we see *Christ* did *dye;* and for all this *union* . . . hee became no man (for the *union* of the *body* and *soule* makes the man, and hee whose soule and body are separated by death, (as long as that state lasts) is properly no man) (236)."

With each repeating of the question—"What preserved him then?"—the pressure for an answer is more and more felt. At the same time, the explanation of the inadequacy of the answers proffered grows longer and more complicated, demanding from us increasingly precise, even scholastic, distinctions, until finally, we are met with a sentence that is literally impossible to follow:

> And therefore as in him the dissolution of *body* and *soule* was no *dissolution* of the *hypostaticall union;* so is there nothing that constraines us to say, that though the *flesh* of *Christ* had *seene corruption* and *incineration* in the grave, this had bene any *dissolution* of the *hypostaticall union,* for the *divine nature,* the Godhead might have remained with all the *Elements* and *principles* of Christs body, as well as it did with the two constitutive parts of his *person,* his *body* and his *soul* (236).

The difficulty of this sentence is to be located in the number of operations it asks us to perform consecutively and simultaneously.

From the beginning we are waiting for the conclusion introduced by "And therefore"; and within the arc of that suspension we are waiting, too, for the completion of the concessive argument introduced by "as." This second expectation is satisfied by the clause beginning "so is there"; but here two difficulties arise; this clause has imbedded within it another, and it is ruled by the nicely ambiguous "nothing that constraines us to say." In other words, the status of whatever will be asserted (or perhaps not asserted) is profoundly uncertain. To make matters even worse, the "that" clause itself contains a second concessive construction which requires a third suspension, again within the arcs of the first and second. It becomes impossible to keep the various "nos" and "thoughs" and "sos" in their respective places; the sentence collapses under the weight of its own apparatus and our efforts to understand it collapse also. By this point our stake in the answering of the original question—"What preserved him then?"—is at least as great as the difficulty and perplexity this paragraph has generated, and when Donne begins a sentence that promises to end with a flatly definitive assertion—"But this *incorruptiblenes* of his *flesh* is most conveniently plac'd in that . . ."—we strain forward in anticipation. For our troubles, we are slapped on the wrist; the long-awaited answer is spectacularly inadequate to the question, especially in the light of the distance we have traveled and the obstacles we have negotiated: *"Non dabis, thou wilt not suffer thy holy one to see corruption* (237)." This is not "the verse which constitutes our text," but it performs in the same deflating way, as an implicit criticism of the creaking machinery that has preceded its appearance (or should I say its revelation). This criticism extends to us and to our involvement with that machinery, and it is made explicit (and unavoidable) in the next sentence. "We looke no further for *causes* or *reasons* in the *mysteries of religion,* but to the *will* and pleasure of *God* (237)."

Of course, looking for causes and reasons is exactly what we have been doing, what we have been encouraged to do, and what the forms of expository prose were invented to do. The rebuke in this declaration is self-reflexive, for it includes not only the audience, but the sermon and also the sermonist who has set its now discredited processes in motion. (The editorial "we" has real, not rhetorical, force.) Those processes continue to function, but as a parody of the promise they once held out. *"Christs* body did *not see corruption,* therefore because *God* had *decreed* it should not (237)." The words "therefore" and "because" are here surrogates for every claim that has been made for the discursive movement of the sermon, and they suffer the common fate when the phrase "God had decreed" countermands them and robs them of their explanatory force.

Almost immediately, this sequence is repeated, with an even greater flourish, in the sentence with which this analysis began: "And therefore as the *Mysteries* of our *Religion,* are *not* the *objects* of *our reason,* but *by faith we rest* on *Gods decree* and purpose, (It is so, O *God,* because it is *thy will* it should be so) so *Gods decrees* are ever to be considered in the *manifestation* thereof (237)." That is to say, the mysteries of religion are not to be rationally considered at all. It is here that the true object of Donne's concern and the true object of the sermon's assault are openly identified. The undermining of the original plan, and the disallowing of its implicit claims (to explain the mysteries of our religion) is a strategy that is directed not at "Reasons," "therefores," and "becauses"—although they are the most obvious casualties—but at the presumption inherent in the act of reasoning itself. It is, therefore, a strategy directed at the audience, which is first invited to a consideration of the day's text and is then systematically frustrated in its attempt to take up that invitation. The result, as we have seen, is a progressive loss of confidence in the capacity of the sermon's structures to organize and manage its materials; and this in turn (and in time) leads to a loss of confidence in the capacities of our own understandings. Indeed it would not be an exaggeration to say that understanding, or the possibility of understanding, is what the sermon is finally "about"; for as the expectation of an orderly and manageable experience is repeatedly (and variously) disappointed, the focus of attention changes from the supposed subject of the sermon to ourselves, who become (as we always have been) the true subject; and this change is here confirmed and acknowledged by Donne when he implicitly enjoins us from further "considering."

In what follows, that injunction becomes more explicit and

more obviously subversive of our intellectual pretensions. The next large topic to be considered (or not considered) is the manner of the death we must all finally suffer; but even before the alternative forms of death are enumerated, Donne steps in (and out toward us) with a warning: "Wee may bee deceived both wayes (240)." What will deceive us is the natural tendency of the human mind to make distinctions and pass judgments on the basis of appearances, to identify our powers of discrimination with God's: ". . . wee use to comfort our selves in the death of *a friend,* if it be testified that he went away like a *Lambe,* that is, without any *reluctation.* But, *God* knowes, that may bee accompanied with a *dangerous damp* and *stupefaction,* and *insensibility* of his *present state* (240)." Here the colloquial expression "God knows" regains its original force. God *only* knows and it is an act of the greatest presumption to confuse our knowledge with His. This example of Christ Himself who "suffered *colluctations* with *death* . . . and an *agony* even to a *bloody sweate*" should be enough to prevent us from judging those who die painfully or violently. Nor is a man's unwillingness to die necessarily an indication of an unhealthy attachment to the pleasures of this world. Of course, this is not to say that in some cases such inferences may not be correct ("Wee may bee deceived *both* wayes"); the moral of this passage is unequivocal, and it becomes a virtual litany as Donne proceeds: "Make no *ill conclusions* upon any mans *loathnes* to *dye* (240)." "*Christ* himselfe hath forbidden us by his owne death to make any *ill conclusion* (241)." "*God* governes not by *examples* . . . and therefore make no *ill conclusion* upon *sudden death* nor upon distempers neyther (241)." [34] As the list of situations in the context of which conclusions are not to be drawn grows, the adjective "ill" becomes superfluous. What is being asked of us is a refraining from conclusions altogether, and a yielding of the responsibility for concluding (and everything else) to God, who is here represented, as he has been so many times before, by the verse that constitutes our text: ". . . never make *ill conclusions* upon persons overtaken

[34] It is possible that Donne may here be working *against* that part of the *Ars Moriendi* tradition which concerns itself with the opposing of good deaths to bad and with the distinguishing by signs of one from the other. See Nancy Lee Beaty, *The Craft of Dying: The Literary Tradition of the Ars Moriendi in England* (New Haven, 1970), pp. 21, 23, 64, 142, 154, 166, 173, 174, 175, and passim.

with such deaths; *Domini Domini sunt exitus mortis, to God the Lord belong the issues of death* (241)."

If there is any progress at all in this sermon, it is the progressive widening of the influence of this verse which arrogates to itself the functions of both preacher and parishioner. It is ruthlessly self-sufficient, requiring no supports, and at the same time requiring that we rely for support only on it. It begins, as we have seen, by supplanting the structures that were to have explained it, and now it supplants the faculty (of understanding) of which those structures are an extension. This, however, is but one half of the story, for the subversion of the one faculty results in the strengthening of another; the disabling of the forms of rational thought has as its corollary the triumph of the memory ("truly the Memory is oftner the Holy Ghost's Pulpit . . . than the Understanding"), not of the memory of places and distinctions, of buttresses, contignations, and foundations—these have receded from view and mind as the influence of the day's verse has grown—but the memory of God's mercy, the Christian memory whose emergence into full and exclusive prominence is the shape of our experience.

Indeed that experience is finally the sermon's true structure, although the outline of the formal structure, the structure of the artificial memory, remains visible in the articulations of its original plan; but when Donne recalls us to that plan at the end of this paragraph, the effect is to make us realize how far from it and its assumptions we have moved. "And further wee cary not this *second acceptation* . . . and passe to our *third part* (242)." The vocabulary of "parts" and "acceptations," "seconds" and "thirds" is wholly irrelevant to our present situation, for it refers to a procedure in which we no longer have any confidence and to expectations we no longer entertain. Our expectations are now of a different order and our confidence is centered elsewhere, on the verse itself and, in the final section (this "third part and last part"), on the reality of the flesh the Word became:

Now *see the end of the Lord,* sayth that *Apostle,* . . . *see the end of the Lord.* . . . The end, *that the Lord* himselfe came to, *death,* and a painefull and a shamefull death (242).

This exhortation is different from any we have met before; it asks for a more immediate and personal seeing than would be possible in the light of a merely carnal understanding. The protection of discursive reasoning, the screen it places between us and the full weight of the truth, has been removed along with its presumptions, and we are now to be brought face-to-face with the presence to whom our triune faculties have been turned. Here there will be no intellectualizing, but a merging, insofar as possible, with the object of our contemplation, for "Our *meditation* of his *death* should be more *viscerall* and affect us more because it is of a thing already done (245)": "*Christ* bled not a droppe the lesse at the last, for having bled at his *Circumcision* before, nor wil you shed a teare the lesse then if you shed some now. And therefore bee now content to consider with mee how to *This God the Lord belong'd the issues of death* (243)." The possibility of a rational ("therefore") considering is reintroduced one last time so that it can finally be laid to rest in the felt experience of the next sentence:

> That *God,* this *Lord,* the *Lord* of *Life could dye,* is a strange contemplation; That the *red Sea* could bee *drie,* That the *Sun* could *stand still,* That an *Oven* could be *seaven times heat* and *not burne,* That *Lions* could be *hungry* and *not bite,* is strange, *miraculously strange,* but *supermiraculous* that *God could dye;* but that *God would dye* is an *exaltation* of that. But even of that also it is a *superexaltation,* that *God shold dye, must dye* (243).

It is a strange contemplation indeed when the smaller part of a proportional analogy is a series of miracles. Each of the units in this sequence gives us a frame of reference in terms of which God's death could be comprehended; but the next unit always destroys it as a possible norm, and this continues until we are in the position Thomas Browne so loved to affect: "I love to lose myself in a mystery, to pursue my reason to an *O altitudo.*" With proportion and measure gone the way of reason and disquisition, we have no choice but to obey Donne's injunction to "follow this [Christ's death] home," that is, to take it to ourselves, "to consider it seriously," not as an occasion for logic-chopping or moralizing, but as the central fact of our existence to which we can give no response but acceptance: "answere you with *David, accipiam Calicem, I will take the cup of salvation;* take it, that *Cup of salvation,* his *passion,* if not into your *present imitation,* yet into your *present contemplation* (244)." Imitation of Christ, then, is to be the end of our efforts, and as a first step, Donne proposes a meditative exercise: "Take in the *whole day* from the *houre* that *Christ received* the *passeover* upon *Thursday, unto* the *houre* in which *hee dyed* the *next day.* Make *this* present *day* that *day* in thy *devotion,* and consider what *hee did,* and remember what *you have done* (245)." Even at this late stage, however, there is more to be given up, more to be taken away, a further humiliation to be suffered; for, rather than bringing us closer to Christ, the performing of this exercise serves only to widen the gulf that separates us from Him by making painfully clear the impossibility of truly conforming our lives to His. At first, the measure of conformity is comfortably abstract: "Hast thou considered that a *worthy receaving of the Sacrament* consists in a *continuation* of *holinesse after,* as well as in a *preparation* before? If so, thou hast therin also *conformed* thy selfe to him (246)." But as the questions grow shorter and more insistent, the probable answers (Donne plays both parts) become increasingly embarrassing and painful:

> About midnight he was *taken* and *bound with a kisse,* art thou not *too conformable* to him in that? Is not that *too literally,* too exactly *thy case?* . . . then hee was *examined* and *buffeted* and *delievered over* to the custody of those *officers,* from whome he received all those *irrisions,* and *violences* . . . *the spitting upon his face,* . . . and the *smartnes of blowes.* . . . How thou passedst all that time last night, thou knowest (246).

Once again the promise that this sermon has continually held out, the promise that in some way we will be able to come to terms with the death of Christ, is proffered and cruelly withdrawn. Forced to admit the irrelevance and presumption of rational inquiry, the motion of the mind, we have turned instead, at Donne's urging, to acceptance and conformity, the motion of the heart. But the will is no less corrupt than the reason ("For the good that I would I do not; but the evil which I would not, that I do"), and with each step along the way, the blows that strike at Christ strike with even more force at our self-esteem. Our affective response, which should issue in righteous action, is no less inadequate than our intellectual response, which should end in understanding, and the self-consciousness we are now feeling is the consciousness of shame (*"Thou* knowest").

There is, after all this, still another turn to Donne's screw. Having at first encouraged to conform and then made us aware of how impossible the act of conforming would be, he now tells us that conformity (even if it could be achieved) would not be enough, "that will not serve, that's not the right way, *wee presse* an utter *Crucifying* of the *sinne* that governes thee; and that *conformes* thee to Christ (247)." An "utter" conformity indeed, when the conforming agent is asked to die. The enormity of what is required of us here is reflected in the phrase "governes thee," which receives no qualifications. Sin governs us not in one, but in all respects, and therefore an utter crucifying of that sin involves nothing less than the crucifying of the self. No way of ours can be the right way and all our ways are to be given up. (This, of course, is what has been "pressed" on us all along.) And yet this death and silencing of the self and its pretensions is paradoxically an entrance into a new and better life. For while we may be unable to conform ourselves to Christ, He has already (and literally) conformed Himself to us. The way of satisfaction has been paid by Him to whom it was due (*"I* am the way"); our sins are utterly crucified in His crucifixion. So that, at this lowest point in our careers, when, in Herbert's words, all our abilities have been confounded, we receive, as a gift, what those abilities could never have won; not merely an understanding of Christ's death, but an equal portion of the fruits it has purchased:

> There wee leave you in that *blessed dependancy,* to *hang* upon *him* that *hangs* upon the *Crosse,* there *bath* in his teares, there *suck* at his *woundes,* and *lye downe in peace* in his *grave,* till hee vouchsafe you a *resurrection,* and an *ascension* into the *Kingdome,* which hee *hath purchas'd for you,* with the *inestimable price* of his *incorruptible blood.* AMEN (248).

This is more than a striking image; it is a precise statement of what has been happening to us in the course of the sermon. We begin in self-dependency, but as the motions of the self are one by one stilled, we grow gradually less self-sufficient, until we are finally left here, hanging, "in dependency." And yet this dependency is blessed, for although by means of it we are rendered powerless (*dis*abled), our powers are increased in the person of Him on whom we depend. By taking away our initiative (of both reason and will) and directing us to the figure on the cross, the sermon brings us to a felt knowledge of the state in which we always were—"In Him we live, and move, and have our being"— and it does this not despite, but because its promises have not been kept. Like the *Phaedrus* and the fourth book of *On Christian Doctrine, Death's Duell* succeeds (if it succeeds) by calling attention to what it is not doing, by transferring the burden it first assumes (the burden of containing and communicating the truth) from the words on the page (which are contradictory and circular) to the Word that is inscribed on the fleshly tables of the reader's or auditor's heart. The sermon does not inscribe that Word (it has always been there, "written not with ink, but with the Spirit of the living God") but merely reveals it; and it reveals it by removing from our line of vision the structures that obscure it and cause us to forget it. These are, of course, its own structures which, in turn, reflect the structures of our understandings; like the other self-consuming artifacts to be considered in these pages, *Death's Duell* serves us by refusing to serve us, by failing.

The preacher is, no less than we, the beneficiary of this failure; for by fashioning words and sentences that point only to their insufficiency, he displaces attention from his own efforts to the Spirit which informs them; and by emptying his art of its (claims to) power, he acknowledges his own powerlessness, becoming like us and like the shell of his sermon a vessel filled by and wholly dependent on the Lord. Of course the audience to whom Donne preached in 1630 would have had no need of this clumsy exposition, for the sublimation of his personality would have been visible to them in the figure he presented in the pulpit, gaunt, enfeebled, dying. For once, Donne's theatricalism served him well, not for the dramatization of the self, but for its consuming in the consuming of his artifact. "Not I," says the Apostle, "but the grace of God which was with me (I Cor. 15:10)." Not I, says Donne, but "thy *Master* (in the unworthiest of his servants) *lookes back upon thee* (246–247)." In answer to the prayer recommended by Augustine, God has placed a "good speech" in his mouth, and in the end Donne becomes indistinguishable from the Word he preaches, which is also the Word to which our understandings have defaulted. He loses his identity exactly at the point where we are blessed with the loss of ours, and at the point where the broken forms of his art are gathered into the verse they were to have explained. So that sermon, preacher, and parishioner dissolve together into a self-effacing and saving union with the source of their several motions.

Those who are accustomed to regard Donne as the type of the metaphysical preacher, given to ingenious puns and fanciful analogies, may find it difficult to think of his as a self-deprecating art. And yet it is by calling attention to itself that his prose becomes a vehicle of humility, for its most spectacular effects are subversive of its largest claims, which are also, by extension, the claims of the preacher. The prose of the Puritan sermon, by way of contrast, is self-effacing in style, but self-glorying (in two directions) in effect, for by making no claim to be art, it makes the largest claim of all, that it simply tells the truth. The Anglicans may *display* language, but it is the Puritans who take *pride* in language, because it is the Puritans who take language seriously.

The Puritan objections to Anglican preaching are well known and they receive their classic exposition in Perry Miller's *The New England Mind: The Seventeenth Century*. To the Puritans, Miller explains, the Anglican way of "topical preaching," preaching " 'according to the series of the words . . . especially when each one carryeth some kind of emphasis with it,' " is a "logical absurdity." [35] In place of an orderly disposition of axioms, the Anglican "weavers" offer discrete and unconnected verbal fireworks which do little to advance the argument, but merely serve the preacher "as occasions for sensual eloquence (345)." Worse still, in his

[35] Perry Miller, *The New England Mind: The Seventeenth Century* (Boston, Beacon Press, 1961), p. 345.

concern for language, the "witty" preacher defaults on his obligation to edify. His auditors are not led step-by-step according to "the order of nature," to a clear understanding of Christian doctrine, but dazzled and discomfited by all manner of "wit and conceit" and "by absurd . . . and prodigious cogitations (358)." Too many things are happening at once in an Anglican sermon and too few of them are related to one another in logical sequence. There is no opportunity for the hearer to either get or maintain his bearings, and as a result he carries little of value away with him: "When the speech is carried on like a swift stream, although it catch many things of all sorts, yet you can hold fast but a little, you can catch but a little, you cannot find where you may constantly rest; but when certaine rules are delivered, the Reader hath, alwayes, as it were at every pace, the place marked where he may set his foot." [36] In the Puritan sermon, the places are marked by the numbered sequence of axioms, and you are helped to "hold fast" to those axioms by examples and analogies which are brought in specifically to support them. This is the "right opening and expounding of the Scripture (344)" whereby preaching is made "the meanes better to convince our judgements (344)," and lest we be turned away from the meat of doctrine to the wind of words, the expounding comes to us in a plain and unaffected style.

The most significant of the objections to the Anglican way is that it "prevented understanding (359)"; for this implies that understanding, in the sense of a rational clarification, is possible. The sermon controversy is finally not about styles and their decorums but about minds and their capabilities. Both parties subscribe to the doctrine of innate depravity and testify to the inability of the fallen consciousness to comprehend the mysteries of divinity but, in practice, the Puritan sermon is designed to process that comprehension, and to the degree that it succeeds, the abilities of the hearer are magnified. Here, for example, is a passage from a sermon by John Cotton:

> We are now to speake of living by faith in our outward and temporall life: now our outward and temporall life is twofold, which wee live in the flesh. It is either a civill, or

---

[36] *Ibid.*, p. 359. The author is William Ames.

a naturall life, for both these lives we live, and they are different the one from the other: Civill life is that whereby we live, as members of this or that City, or Town, or Commonwealth, in this or that particular vocation and calling. Naturall life I call that, by which we doe live this bodily life, I meane, by which we live a life of sense, by which we eate and drinke, by which we goe through all conditions, from our birth to our grave, by which we live, and move, and have our being. And now both these a justified person lives by faith; To begin with the former.[37]

The subject is faith, but the exposition is logical, or at least methodical. The point is opened in the Ramist manner, the proposal of the subject—"living by faith"—its delimiting specification—"in our outward and temporal life"—and its division into two branches—"either a civill, or a naturall life"—which are then, themselves, further specified—"Civil life is," "Naturall life I call." The movement is always from the more general to the particular, and the reader is led by the hand (or nose) from place to place until there is nothing left to be said and no possibility of his not understanding. In the process, meanings are narrowed and flattened out; abstractions are not allowed to stand, but are at once tied down to palpable specifics; and even Scripture is emptied of its mystery and domesticated so that it refers not to Christ (in whom we live and move and have our being) but to "a life of the sense."

I do not mean to suggest that the reading or hearing of a Puritan sermon requires no effort, only that the effort is always followed by understanding. One is never asked to do more than one can and, more important, one is never asked to undo what has already been done. References backward are not, as in an Anglican sermon, complicating and unsettling, but clarifying and confirming, and repetitions, rather than expanding the area of reference, pin it down and make it manageable:

First, it hath a care that it be a *warrantable* calling, wherein we may not onely aime at our own, but at the

[37] John Cotton, *The Way of Life or Gods Way And Course in Bringing The Soule Into, Keeping it in, and carrying it on, in the wayes of life and peace* (London, 1641), p. 436.

publike good, that is a warrantable calling, *Seek not every man his owne things, but every man the good of his brother,* I *Cor.* 10:24. *Phil.* 2:4. Seek one anothers welfare; faith works all by love, *Gal.* 5:6. And therefore it will not think it hath a comfortable calling, unlesse it will not onely serve his owne turne, but the turn of other men. Bees will not suffer drones among them, but if they lay up any thing, it shall be for them that cannot work; he would see that his calling should tend to publique good (439).

The pattern of this paragraph is established in its first sentence where the phrase "publique good" (which is to be opened) is preceded and followed by "warrantable calling." The connection between them is thus made inescapable; in whatever direction the reader looks (or the hearer listens) he will find himself relating one to another. Since "publique good" also concludes the paragraph, the same forward and backward pressure is exerted on everything in the middle. There scriptural and natural proofs are marshalled in mutual support (they are not hierarchically distinguished) and in support of the original proposition, which, with slight variations, is regularly repeated. Everything leads from and toward "publique good" which is relentlessly surrounded, hemmed in, pinned down, and, in a word, known.

The movement of this paragraph is typical of the sermon as a whole. A perspective is established, and then never abandoned. Rather, it is reaffirmed and reinforced. Every step along the way is confirming; nothing is distracting; there is no sense of strain and as a result we do not strain either. It would be a mistake to think of this as artless; it is simply a different kind of art, one that involves the illusion of a simple and natural unfolding; and this is an illusion that is transferred to the operations of our understanding. Confidence in the building of the argument builds confidence in our ability to follow it.

This is, of course, a reflection of the formal strategy of a Puritan sermon which is designed to restore (or to be a means in God's restoring of) the right working of man's disordered faculties. When Adam disobeyed God's command for the sake (or so he believed) of Eve, he reversed the priorities by which the affections are properly subordinate to the reason, and as the inheritors of his error we are naturally inclined to repeat it. The urgings of our carnal appetites prevail over the urgings of the revealed word, and emotional appeals persuade us more readily than rational arguments. If this unhappy situation is to be remedied, the understanding must be regenerated and reason returned to its rightful preeminence. Regeneration is, of course, the work of the spirit, but the spirit prefers to work through natural means and especially through the means of sermons. Sermons by themselves cannot bring about conversion, but they can, in their unfolding, follow the order of conversion the spirit prefers. To this end the Puritan preacher is careful to speak to the minds of his hearers before proceeding to move the will by stimulating the affections. Edification must precede exhortation, and the form of the Puritan sermon is directly answerable to these priorities—first doctrine, then reasons, and then uses:

> The Puritan sermon quotes the text and "opens" it as briefly as possible, expounding circumstances and context, explaining its grammatical meanings, reducing its tropes and schemata to prose, and setting forth its logical implications; the sermon then proclaims in a flat, indicative sentence the "doctrine" contained in the text or logically deduced from it, and proceeds to the first reason or proof. Reason follows reason, with no other transition than a period and a number; after the last proof is stated there follow the uses or applications, also in numbered sequence, and the sermon ends when there is nothing more to be said.[38]

What this means for the auditor or reader is an absence of surprise. One is never misled in the course of a Puritan sermon; topic sentences accurately forecast the shape of what follows; the vocabulary of logical arguments is neither superfluous, nor self-defeating; similes establish points of correspondence that are always relevant, and limitedly relevant; the meaning of a word is not changed in successive appearances; rather the meaning of its first occurrence is more firmly fixed. These are all negative characteristics, but they have a positive effect. They give one the ex-

[38] Miller, *The New England Mind,* p. 332.

perience of being in control, the experience of knowing where you've been and where you're going, and, most important, of getting there.

In brief, the Puritan sermon is not self-consuming, but self-sufficient, in two directions. Its forms are sufficient to its pretensions—they open and make plain the points of Scripture—and its auditors are sufficient unto the occasion—they are able to understand that which is made plain. In its unfolding the sermon promises not only that you *shall* know the truth, but that you *can* know the truth, and it keeps both promises. The Anglican sermon, on the other hand—and *Death's Duell* is a brilliant example—consistently defaults on its promises. Its divisions and transitions do not indicate the stages of a progression, either in the argument or in the hearer's understanding; they are merely "ands," marking out areas and opportunities for illumination, even if they read literally as "buts," "althoughs," "becauses," "therefores," "firsts," "seconds," and "thirds." The movement of the sermon's central action is away from its discursive machinery (although that machinery continues to creak along) and therefore away from the listener's rational powers, which are increasingly *dis*abled (as the machinery is disabled). Here, then, is the fundamental difference between the two sermon traditions; in one the faculties are put in good working order and made answerable to the task of comprehending truth; in the other the faculties are first broken and then replaced by the object of their comprehension, "a kind of saving by undoing"; one makes linguistic forms serviceable by making them unobtrusive; the other thrusts the forms of language before us so that we may better know their insufficiency, and our own; one claims only to convey the truth and therefore claims everything; the other begins by claiming everything and then presides over the gradual disallowing of all its claims; one invites us to carry the truth away, the other to be carried away by the truth.[39]

---

[39] I am aware, of course, that these are very large conclusions to draw from a comparison of two sermons which represent the extremes of their respective traditions. One can certainly find Anglican preachers who are less metaphysical than Donne, or preachers, like Andrewes, who are metaphysical in a different way. (In this connection, see my "Structures as Areas: Sequence and Meaning in Seventeenth Century Narrative," forthcoming in the *William Andrews Clark Memorial*

We have, of course, encountered these large oppositions before, in the distinction between rhetoric and dialectic, between the bad and the good lover, between persuading to a point and persuading to a vision, between the memory of places and the Christian memory of the promise, and in the one distinction that informs all of these, between a presentation that leaves the mind

---

*Library Seminar Papers*.) And there are, of course, Puritans whose style seems anything but plain, who, as Harold Fisch points out (*Jerusalem and Albion*, London, 1964), display "a maximal use of tautology, exclamation, and rhetorical question combined with an untiring use of Biblical quotation and echo, metaphor and simile (34)." If I am right, however, the difference between Puritan and Anglican has less to do with the formally observable components of their styles than with the *use* to which those components are put. That is to say, for the Puritans, metaphor, simile, and the like are justifiable so long as they operate to aid the auditor's understanding. As William Haller observes (*The Rise of Puritanism*, New York, 1957), "the style in which the spiritual brethren chose to address the new vernacular public was called plain English not because it was imaginative or in the larger sense unliterary but because it was designed to be intelligible (133)." In other words, the style is plain not because it is free of tropes and metaphors, but because the tropes and metaphors are in the service of making plain the sense the sermonist wishes to communicate. (See on this point Larzer Ziff, "The Literary Consequences of Puritanism," *ELH*, Vol. XXX, No. 3, Sept., 1963, 297–298, *passim*.) Here, for example, is a passage from Thomas Hooker:

> The second End of Meditation is, *It settles it effectually upon the heart.* It's not the pashing of the water at a sudden push, but the standing and soaking to the root, that loosens the weeds and thorns, that they may be plucked up easily. It's not the laying of Oyl upon the benummed part, but the chafing of it, the suppleth the Joynt, and easeth the pain. It is so in the soul; Application laies the Oyl of the Word that is searching and savory, Meditation chafeth it in, that it may soften and humble the hard and stony heart: Application is like the Conduit or Channel that brings the stream of the Truth upon the soul; but Meditation stops it as it were, and makes it soak into the heart, that so our corruptions may be plucked up kindly by the Roots
>
> (*The Application of Redemption By the Effectual Work of the Word, and Spirit of Christ, for the bringing home of Lost Sinners to God*, London, 1659, as reprinted in Perry Miller and T. H. Johnson, eds., *The Puritans: A Sourcebook of Their Writings, Vol. One*, New York, 1963, p. 304).

Formally this prose is very different from Cotton's, but the effect is the same because the tropes and figures are subservient to the logic of the unfolding argument; the comparisons and analogies are always tied to the axiom they illustrate (*it settles it effectually upon the heart*); the phrase "it is so in the soul" directs the ear or eye to the connections that are to be made between the first and second halves of the passage; and the patterned repetitions ("soaking to the root"–"soak into the heart," "plucked up easily"–"plucked up kindly") make it certain that those connections will be made. This is language designed to assure the comprehension of the "meanest capacity" (Haller, *The Rise of Puritanism*, p. 134) and

complacent and self-satisfied [40] and a presentation that unsettles the mind and demands, literally, that it change.

This opposition and these distinctions are to be found everywhere in the seventeenth century, but not always in their pure forms. There is a danger in a study like this that real differences will be sacrificed to a paradigm; and it is, in part, to avoid that danger that I now turn to Francis Bacon, who is committed, more overtly than the Puritans, to the rehabilitation of man's faculties, yet shares with the Anglicans a profound distrust of those faculties. As a result, his artifacts are both self-consuming and self-satisfying, although, as we shall see, the satisfaction is very much in the future.

---

therefore it is language in which the meanest capacity has an increasing confidence, a confidence that is transferred to its own operations. What this language does not do is confuse or challenge or puzzle or call attention to itself apart from its expository and clarifying function; and therefore it never calls into question the sufficiency of its own procedures or the sufficiency of the understandings it makes plain. This suggests that my analysis of the sermon controversy would hold even if examples less stylistically "pure" than those I have introduced were brought to bear; for in every case it could be shown that while the two traditions are not always distinguishable by the formal properties of their language, they remain distinguishable in terms of the relationship between that language and the understandings of their auditors. Of course, this holds only for the first half of the century. In the Restoration, for reasons we shall consider in the epilogue, everyone is in the business of making plain.

[40] Even when the sense of a Puritan sermon is unflattering, its experience is satisfying. The hearer who attains a "true sight of sin" may be tracing out the shape of his own depravity, but it is he who is doing the tracing out; and when the job is done he can take a personal satisfaction in it.

II

# Georgics of the Mind: The Experience of Bacon's Essays

And surely if the purpose be in good earnest not to write at leisure that which men may read at leisure, but really to instruct and suborn action and active life, these Georgics of the mind, concerning the husbandry and tillage thereof, are no less worthy than the heroical descriptions of Virtue, Duty, and Felicity

*—The Advancement of Learning.*

My hope is they may be as graynes of salte, that will rather give you an appetite, then offend you with satiety
—Cancelled dedication to 1612 edition of *Essays.*

YOU MUST NEVERTHELESS EXCEPT

There has been a general recognition in the twentieth century of the close relationship between Bacon's *Essays* and his scientific program. In 1871 Edward Arber could still write that the essays are "no essential part" of Bacon's real work, "the proficiency and advancement of knowledge"; [1] but in 1923 R. S. Crane pointed out that these "Counsels Civill and Morall" speak directly to a need first articulated in *The Advancement of Learning,* and five years later Jacob Zeitlin was referring to this same body of mate-

---

[1] Edward Arber, *A Harmony of Bacon's Essays* (London, 1871), p. xxvii.

rials as "a science of pure selfishness." [2] This view of the *Essays* opened the way for a consideration of their successive revisions which were seen to correspond to the successive stages of scientific method. Thus, in the 1597 version, Bacon is "content to offer us the *disjecta membra*" without the ordering superstructure of a "methodical scheme," [3] while in the 1625 *Essays* these discrete observations are related to one another and to the abstraction they collectively illuminate by "a clear and explicit organization." [4] This description of the essays and of their progress is now standard: Bacon, Douglas Bush tells us in his volume of the *Oxford History of English Literature,* "wished to fill a gap in practical psychology and ethics, to contribute to . . . knowledge of the genus *homo* (196)." Paolo Rossi takes his text from Bush and treats the essays as "another contribution to that science of man to which Bacon dedicated for many years the best part of his inexhaustible energies." [5] And for Brian Vickers, the most recent of the commentators, the connection between these "literary productions" and Bacon's scientific labors is not a point of issue; he assumes it, and goes on to draw illuminating parallels between the style of the *Essays* and the methodology of the *Novum Organum* and other works. [6]

Yet, for all this unanimity, the casual judgments these critics make on the *Essays* suggest that they do not really understand what is scientific about them. For the most part they take their cue from Bacon's praise of Machiavelli: ". . . we are much beholden to Machiavel and others, that write what men do and not what they ought to do. For it is not possible to join serpentine wisdom with the columbine innocency, except men know exactly all the conditions of the serpent (*Sp.*, III, 430–431)." [7] To know

[2] R. S. Crane, "The Relation of Bacon's *Essays* to his Programme for the Advancement of Learning," in *Schelling Anniversary Papers* (New York, 1923), pp. 87–105. Jacob Zeitlin, "The Development of Bacon's *Essays* and Montaigne," *JEGP,* XXVII (1928), p. 503.

[3] Zeitlin, p. 507.

[4] Crane, p. 97.

[5] Paolo Rossi, *Francis Bacon: From Magic to Science* (London, 1968), p. 187.

[6] *Francis Bacon and Renaissance Prose* (Cambridge, 1968), p. 53.

[7] References are to the *Works* edited by James Spedding, R. L. Ellis, and D. D. Heath (London, 14 vols., 1857–1874), hereafter referred to as *Sp.,* followed by the appropriate volume number.

exactly what men do. This seems to be a call for objectivity, for accurate and disinterested observation of particulars; and objectivity is the quality most commonly attributed to the *Essays*.

> Bacon's essays are for the most part as impersonal, as objective, as the essays of Macauley. . . . his method was that of the detached, impersonal observer, his presentation was concise, dogmatic, formal (Zeitlin, 518, 519).
> In the *Essays* his attitude is conditioned by the whole rationale of the work toward dispassionate objective observation and analysis (Vickers, 133).
> . . . Bacon's cool objectivity . . . represents also the attitude of the scientific analyst who does not gossip and ramble, whose mind is a dry light (Bush, 195).
> It [the style of the *Essays*] thus represents a clear parallel to the scientific style of report.[8]

But if the *Essays* are objective in fact, analytic in method, impersonal in tone, and practically instructive in purpose, they are not, according to these same critics, without their problems. Zeitlin is uncomfortable with the "baldly analytic or coldly intellectual consideration" of the topics Bacon treats and he sees the essays as a battle between the "two spirits" that fight for the author's soul, the spirit of the scientist and the spirit of the moralist (512, 510). Bush speaks of the "utilitarian motives" that "keep Bacon's *Essays* in the category of admired books rather than among the well-thumbed and beloved (197)"; and he notes the simultaneous presence of "some wholly admirable counsels of moral wisdom and public and private virtue" and "an atmosphere of 'business,' of cold-blooded expediency, and sometimes of unscrupulous self-interest (196)." And while Vickers seems to dismiss the notion of any such tension existing in the *Essays*, he at least acknowledges it in passing: "I think that an unbiased analysis would show a constant and non-ambivalent dependence on traditional ethics (92)."

In short, the characterization of the *Essays* as objective, dispassionate, and concisely analytic is hardly borne out by the collective response of those who so characterize them. An impersonal report does not leave its readers wondering about the inner life

---

[8] H. Fisch, *Jerusalem and Albion* (London, 1964), p. 29.

of the author; nor does it encourage speculation as to whether its own focus is "traditional," "utilitarian," "moral," or blurred. A student of Bacon criticism may be excused if he asks, only half in jest, will the real Bacon's *Essays* please stand up?

The difficulty, I think, lies in the assumed equation of scientific and objective; for this involves the further assumption that Bacon's concern as a scientist is wholly with the form of his presentation. I would suggest, however, that his primary concern is with the *experience* that form provides, and, further, that this experience, rather than the materials of which it is composed, is what is scientific about the *Essays*. I believe such a hypothesis to be consistent with the psychological emphasis of Bacon's theoretical writings and with his repeated classification of styles according to their effect on readers and hearers; but, for now, I prefer to rest my case on the primary evidence and proceed inductively, in good Baconian fashion, to the discovery of general principles.

Let us begin by examining a section of the 1625 essay, "Of Love":

> You may observe, that amongst all the great and worthy persons (whereof the memory remaineth, either ancient or recent) there is not one that hath been transported to the mad degree of love: which shews that great spirits and great business do keep out this weak passion. You must except nevertheless Marcus Antonius, the half partner of the empire of Rome, and Appius Claudius, the decemvir and lawgiver; whereof the former was indeed a voluptuous man, and inordinate; but the latter was an austere and wise man: and therefore it seems (though rarely) that love can find entrance not only into an open heart, but also into a heart well fortified, if watch be not well kept (*Sp.*, VI, 397).

Everything about the first sentence serves to inspire confidence in its contents. Before a reader reaches the main statement, he has been assured (by the parenthesis) that it is based on exhaustive research. Both the rhythmic and argumentative stresses fall on the phrase "there is not one," and nothing that follows qualifies this absoluteness. The formal conclusion of the "which" clause is hardly necessary—it is clearly implied—but it does add to the

impression of completeness and finality, especially since the opposition of "great" and "weak," "business" and "passion," is so
strongly pointed. The form of the whole is almost syllogistic, moving from the primary proposition—there are "great and worthy
persons"—to the secondary proposition—"there is not one that
hath"—to the inevitable therefore—"which shews that." In short,
the reader is encouraged in every way possible to confer the
status of truism or axiom on the assertion this sentence makes. Of
course, there are potential ambiguities. As we read it for the first
time, "You may observe" is simply a rhetorical formula which
allows us to anticipate something unexceptionable; but, strictly
speaking, that formula includes the possibility of not performing
the action: you may observe, or, on the other hand, you may not
observe. The material in the parenthesis contains a similar "logical out," since it acknowledges indirectly the possibility of there
being a whole body of great and worthy persons whereof no memory remains, persons whose existence would call into question the
validity of the generalization that follows. Still, there is no reason
for a reader to indulge in such quibbles, and every likelihood, if
my description of the sentence's effect is accurate, that he will not.

But hardly has Bacon established his axiom before he begins
to qualify it, and insofar as the reader has accepted it, he partici-
pates in the act of qualification. Indeed he has no choice, for in
contrast to the permissive "may," Bacon begins the next sentence
with a commanding "You *must* except"; and as the exceptions
are enumerated, the force of the original statement is less and less
felt, in part because the prose is making so many new demands on
the reader. The sentence proceeds in fits, and each stage of it
seems momentarily to be the final one. First Marcus Antonius and
Appius are set apart from other "great men" and this is a simple
enough (mental) action; but then these two are distinguished
from one another and the reader is obliged to construct categories
for them: both are "great" and subject to the passion of love; but
while the weakness (voluptuous and inordinate) of one suggests
an explanation for his subjugation—Marcus Antonius can be
"handled" without disturbing the validity of the axiom—the qual-
ities of the other (wise and austere) prevent us from raising this
explanation to the level of a general truth. And meanwhile, the
emphasis of the entire experience has shifted from the original

assertion to the classification of its exceptions, so that it now seems that *no* great man is immune from the infection of love.

At this point, the words "and therefore" promise relief from this rather strenuous mental activity. Presumably a new and more inclusive axiom will be forthcoming, one which takes into account the fact of Marcus Antonius and Appius Claudius. But unlike the first (and now discredited) axiom, this one is qualified even before it is offered. The firm conclusiveness of "therefore" gives way to the equivocation of "seems" and then to the near negativity of "though rarely." By the time the reader reaches the actual statement, its status is so unclear that the question of record— whether or not great men and mad lovers constitute mutually exclusive classes—is only further muddled. The last tail-like phrase, "if watch be not well kept," introduces a new variable—the vigilance factor—which would seem to make it even more difficult to formulate a generally applicable rule.

What are we to make of this confusion? Is this the Francis Bacon whose revisions, Vickers tells us, are always in the direction of "extending, clarifying and focusing (231)"? One can answer in the affirmative, I think, if the focus of inquiry is shifted from the essay's nominal subject, love, to what I believe to be its real subject, the inadequacy of the commonly received notions about love. That is, if anything is being clarified here, it is the extent to which the confidently proffered pronouncement of the first sentence does not hold up under close scrutiny; and, moreover, the reader's experience of that clarification is somewhat chastening, since it involves the debunking of something he had accepted without question. Of course Bacon has assured this acceptance by surrounding his generalization with the paraphernalia of logical discourse and enclosing it in a rhythmically satisfying syntactical structure; but this deception (if deception is the proper word) is essential to his strategy, and that strategy is adumbrated in the *Preface* to *The Great Instauration* and in the first book of the *Novum Organum*.

PRESENT SATISFACTION VS. FURTHER INQUIRY

Although the goal of Bacon's work is the orderly disposition of an objective reality, his primary concern in the early stages of that undertaking is with his tools, and chief among these is the hu-

man mind itself. In the plot of *The Great Instauration* and especially in the first book of the *Novum Organum,* the mind has the
role of villain. Its principal crimes are

1. *A tendency to fly up too quickly to generalizations:*
The mind longs to spring up to positions of higher generality, that it may find rest there; and so after a little
while wearies of experiment . . . this evil is increased by
logic, because of the order and solemnity of its disputa-
tions (xx).[9]

2. *A tendency, not unrelated to (1), to identify its own
sense of order with the cosmic order:*
It is a false assertion that the sense of man is the measure of things. On the contrary, all perceptions, as well of
the sense as of the mind, are according to the measure of
the individual and not according to the measure of the universe (xli).

The human understanding is of its own nature prone to
suppose the existence of more order and regularity in the
world than it finds (xlv).

3. *A tendency to ignore or suppress whatever does not
accord with its own notions:*
The axioms now in use, having been suggested by a
scanty and manipular experience and a few particulars of
most general occurrence, are made for the most part just
large enough to fit and take these in. . . . And if some opposite instance, not observed or not known before, chance
to come in the way, the axiom is rescued and preserved by
some frivolous distinction; whereas the truer course would
be to correct the axiom itself (xxv).
The human understanding when it has once adopted an
opinion (either as being the received opinion or as being
agreeable to itself) draws all things else to support and
agree with it. And though there be a greater number and
weight of instances to be found on the other side, yet these

[9] References to the *Novum Organum* and the *Preface to The Great Instauration*
are from *The English Philosophers from Bacon to Mill,* ed. E. A. Burtt (New
York, 1939).

it either neglects and despises; or else by some distinction
sets aside and rejects; in order that by this great and per-
nicious predetermination the authority of its former conclusions may remain inviolate (xlvi).

4. *A tendency to assent to forms—logical, rhythmical,
syntactical—rather than to empirical evidence:*

If you look at the method of them [presently received
systems] and the divisions, they seem to embrace and comprise everything which can belong to the subject. And although these divisions are ill filled out and are, but as
empty cases, still to the common mind they present the
form and plan of a perfect science (lxxxvi).

It [the syllogism] is a thing most agreeable to the mind
of man. For the mind of man is strangely eager to have
something fixed and immovable, upon which in its wanderings and disquisitions it may securely rest (*De Aug.,
Sp.*, IV, 428).

According to Bacon, these defects of the understanding are responsible for the confused state of knowledge at the present time,
and unless they are remedied, no progress is possible. Of course in
one sense, the problem is insoluble, since these are "errors common to human nature (xlii)"; but the least (and the most) we can
do is provide "true helps of the understanding" so that "as far as
the condition of mortality and humanity allows, the intellect may
be . . . made capable of overcoming the difficulties and obscurities of nature (p. 15)." By "helps" Bacon means the method of
induction, a manner of "collecting and concluding" whose principal force is to protect the mind against itself. The general rule
is given in aphorism lviii—"let every student of nature take this
as a rule, that whatever his mind seizes and dwells upon with particular satisfaction is to be held in suspicion"—and in practice
this is translated into a determined delaying action:

The understanding must not . . . be allowed to jump
and fly from particulars to remote axioms and of almost
the highest generality (civ).

The induction which is to be available for the discovery
and demonstration of sciences and arts, must analyze na-

ture by proper rejections and exclusions: and then after a sufficient number of negatives, come to a conclusion on the affirmative instances (cv).

One must take care not to accept an axiom until it has been tried in the fire of "rejection and exclusion," and even then the acceptance should be provisional, leaving open the possibility that the discovery of new particulars will challenge its adequacy. This is a question not only of method but of communication. That is, the "cautions" Bacon would institute look in two directions, to the compilers of systems and to those who will come after them. If the mind of man is wont to assume completeness in a science merely because the form of its presentation has the appearance of completeness, that form must be altered accordingly. In place of an "artificial method" with full and articulated divisions, Bacon recommends "short and scattered sentences not linked together," aphorisms which will not give the impression that they "pretend or profess to embrace the entire art (lxxxvi)." For his part, he promises to "so present . . . things naked and open, that my errors can be marked and set aside before the mass of knowledge be further infected by them (12)." To each experiment, he will "subjoin a clear account of the manner in which I made it; that men knowing exactly how each point was made out, may see whether there be any error connected with it and may arouse themselves to devise proofs more trustworthy (21)." It will be the business of his presentation to "arouse" men rather than to "force or ensnare" their judgments (12).

This concern with a method of communication that will neutralize the "natural" errors of the understanding is on display everywhere in Bacon's writings. There is now, he complains in *The Advancement of Learning,* "a kind of contract of error between the deliverer and the receiver: he that delivereth knowledge desireth to deliver it in such form as may be best believed; and he that receiveth knowledge desireth rather present satisfaction than expectant inquiry." Such a form of delivery—Bacon terms it "Magistral"—is proper for the transmission of settled truths, but tends to discourage further inquiry. Far more fruitful is the way of "Probation" whereby knowledge is "delivered and intimated

. . . in the same method wherein it was invented (404)." [10] The opposition of "Magistral" and "Probative" is transferred in the same work to another pair of terms, "Methods" and "Aphorisms," and the advantages claimed for Aphorisms are exactly those claimed for the new induction:

> . . . the writing in Aphorisms hath many excellent virtues, whereto the writing in Method doth not approach.
>
> For first, it trieth the writer, whether he be superficial or solid: for Aphorisms, except that they should be ridiculous, cannot be made but of the pith and heart of sciences; for discourse of illustration is cut off; recitals of examples are cut off; discourse of connexion and order is cut off; descriptions of practice are cut off; so there remaineth nothing to fill the Aphorisms but some good quantity of observation: and therefore no man can suffice, nor in reason will attempt, to write Aphorisms, but he that is sound and grounded. But in Methods . . . a man shall make a great shew of art, which if it were disjointed would come to little. Secondly, Methods are more fit to win consent or belief, but less fit to point to action; for they carry a kind of demonstration in orb or circle, one part illuminating another, and therefore satisfy; but particulars, being dispersed, do not agree with dispersed directions. And lastly, Aphorisms, representing a knowledge broken, do invite men to enquire farther; whereas Methods, carrying the shew of a total, do secure men, as if they were at furthest (405).

Again, the distinction and the evaluation are made on the basis of psychological effect rather than literal accuracy. The content of aphorisms is not necessarily more true than the content of methodical writing; but one form has a more salutary effect than the other because it minimizes the possibility that the mind, in its susceptibility, will take the internal coherence of an artful discourse for the larger coherence of objective truth. Like induction and the way of probation, writing in aphorisms sacrifices present satisfaction to the hope of a fuller knowledge in the future. For Bacon, then, aphorisms are what "words as seeds" are to Plato:

[10] *Sp.,* Vol. III.

their function is heuristic rather than expressive or mimetic and they are part of an effort to bring men "to the highest degree of happiness possible" by putting them in direct touch with reality.[11]

[11] Bacon often refers to himself as a sower of seeds, the planter of a harvest that will be reaped not by him, but by those whose minds have been quickened and made fertile by his labors: "I bear myself soberly and profitably, sowing in the meantime for future ages the seeds of a purer truth (*Sp.,* IV, 104)." Men's wits, Bacon declares, live on in books "because they generate still and cast their seeds in the minds of others." "It is in knowledges as it is in plants: if you mean to remove it to grow, then it is more assured to rest upon roots than slips (*Sp.* III, 404)." (See the discussion of these and other seed images in Vickers, *Francis Bacon and Renaissance Prose,* pp. 193–198.) Bacon also uses the word "seeds" to characterize his collection of "concise sentences (*Sp.,* IV, 492)." These sentences (some of which are aphoristic) are "to be as skeins or bottoms of thread which may be unwinded at large when they are wanted (472)." The point is that "unwinding" is what they call for; in their unsystematic and provocative brevity, they "invite men both ponder that which was invented and to add and supply further (*Sp.,* III, 498)." (On this and related points see Vickers, pp. 60–96, and J. P. Stern, *Lichtenberg: A Doctrine of Scattered Occasions,* Bloomington, 1963, *passim.*) A different view is put forward by Robert Adolph in *The Rise of Modern Prose Style* (Cambridge, 1968): "For Bacon, the aphoristic style was . . . the *clearest.* In the *Novum Organum* it is Bacon's 'design' to set everything forth, as far as may be, plainly and perspicuously (56)." This is just one of the many places where Adolph betrays his misunderstanding of Bacon's rhetorical theory and practice. That misunderstanding is rooted in the assumption that Bacon's "aim" is "one of persuasively making things easier for the reader (176)." "Good Style is Public Style, a style easy to read because accessible and appropriate to the group for which it is intended. Hence Bacon's rhetorical theory and practice are strictly functional (172)." But it is precisely *because* they are satisfyingly easy to read that Bacon turns away from "methods" to aphorisms and the way of "broken knowledge." Bacon's rhetorical theory and practice are functional, but they function (at least in their early stages) to accentuate rather than remove difficulties. In general, Adolph ignores Bacon's strictures on the defects of the human understanding and he therefore attributes to Bacon notions of clarity and "utility" which might more accurately be attributed to his Restoration followers. For while clarity may be the ultimate goal of Bacon's procedures, protecting the mind against itself is their first business; and in that context the most "useful" style will be the style which rejects "easy accessibility" in favor of the slow and laborious scrutiny of everything it presents. In short, Bacon's idea of "utility" is more sophisticated than Adolph's (or Sprat's with whom Adolph tends to link him) because it is answerable to the mind as it is rather than to the mind as one might wish it to be. Of course, if the "cautions" Bacon institutes are successful, the mind may once again be a "clear glass," unclouded by errors and misconceptions; and then (but only then), when the understanding no longer distorts what is presented to it, will the transparent effortless style of the Royal Society ideal be proper for the transmission of truth. There are, then, two stages in Bacon's linguistic reform and only the second issues in a neutral mathematical style; the first is designed to make that style viable, and it completely escapes Adolph who has only two categories—

Later in *The Advancement of Learning,* Bacon turns to a consideration of the "wisdom touching Negotiation or Business," and here, too, the emphasis is on the dangers of a procedure that facilitates the mind's tendency to rest in the notions it already possesses:

> The form of writing which of all others is fittest for this variable argument of negotiation and occasions is that which Machiavel chose wisely and aptly for government: namely, *discourse upon histories or examples.* For knowledge drawn freshly and in our view out of particulars, knoweth the way best to particulars again. And it hath much greater life for practice when the discourse's attendeth upon the example than when the example attendeth upon the discourse. For this is no point of order, as it seemeth at first, but of substance. For when the example is the ground . . . it is set down with all circumstances, which may sometimes control the discourse thereupon made and sometimes supply it, as a very pattern for action; whereas the examples alleged for the discourse sake are cited succinctly and without particularity, and carry a servile aspect toward the discourse which they are brought in to make good (453).

If you are committed to a proposition, you will find evidence to support it; but if a proposition is drawn from the evidence you disinterestedly find, your commitment is to truth. In this formulation, "examples" stand to "discourse" as "particulars" stand to artificially filled out systems (including syllogisms) and Aphorisms to Methods. When a discourse is controlled by examples, its form is discovered rather than imposed and its general conclusions are independent of the author's preconceptions which, indeed, may be altered in the process of discovery; but when the

"utility" and "self revelation"—neither of which recognizes the epistemological problems that generate the method of induction. Adolph seems really to believe that when one apprehends easily and immediately, what one apprehends is therefore true; that the internal coherence of discourse is equivalent to the larger coherence of reality; that rhetorical and perceptual clarity are one and the same. Bacon was not so naive. (See Rossi, *Francis Bacon: From Magic to Science,* pp. 171, 193.)

examples carry a "servile" aspect to the discourse—that is when they are brought in to make it good, or left out because they do not make it good, or distorted so that the "axiom now in use" can be "rescued and preserved"—those preconceptions are allowed to limit what can be discovered. As A. N. Whitehead has put it, in an aphorism Bacon would have admired, "Our problem is . . . to fit the world to our perceptions, and not our perceptions to the world." [12]

### POOR AND HIGH SAYINGS

We are now in a position to define more precisely the relationship between Bacon's *Essays* and his method of scientific inquiry. The point of contact, of course, is the experience the *Essays* give. If we return to my analysis of the passage from "Of Love," and keep in mind the vocabulary of the *Novum Organum* and *The Advancement of Learning,* the correspondence between what happens in that essay and what should happen in a responsible scientific investigation is immediately apparent. First, the reader is presented with an axiomlike statement enclosed in "such form as may be best believed, and not as may be best examined." The sentence is "rounded"; the progression of its thought is apparently logical; its parts "carry a kind of demonstration in orb or circle, one . . . illuminating another, and therefore satisfy." In short, the mind's desire "to have something fixed and immovable, upon which in its wanderings and disquisitions it may securely rest" has been gratified. (One should note, in this connection, that the sentence flatters the reader, since it allows him to include himself among "all the great and worthy persons" and exclude himself from the class "mad degree of love.")

But, unexpectedly, the examples that follow do not "attend upon the discourse" but begin instead to "control and supply" it. The reader is "aroused" from his complacency and becomes involved in a refining operation in which the commonly received notion is subjected to the test of "proper rejections and exclusions." Qualification follows upon qualification with the double result that the original axiom is discredited—it is not sufficiently

[12] *The Limits of Language,* ed. *Walker Gibson* (New York, 1962), p. 14.

"wide (*N.O.*, I, cvi)" to include "new particulars"—and the possibility of formulating another is called into question.[13]

What then is the value of this experience? Obviously, it has not yielded the promised clarification of the nature of love, but in Bacon's scale of values it has yielded much more: (1) a felt knowledge of the attraction generalities have for the mind and therefore a "caution" against a too easy acceptance of them in the future; (2) an awareness of the unresolved complexity of the matter under discussion; (3) an open and inquiring mind, one that is dissatisfied with the state of knowledge at the present time. In short, the demands of the prose have left the reader in a state of "healthy perplexity," neither content with the notion he had been inclined to accept at the beginning of the experience, nor quite ready to put forward a more accurate notion of his own. This is, of course, the mental set of the scientist, observant, methodical, cautious, skeptical, and yet, in long-range terms, optimistic. (The question of just how Bacon's style contains and communicates this optimism will be taken up later.)

My description of the essay, or, more precisely, of its effects, is noteworthy for an omission; it says nothing at all about the nominal subject, love; but as I have suggested earlier, the real subject of the essay is what men think about love, or, perhaps, *how* men think about love; and I would suggest further that the same formula should be applied to the other essays, which are about how men think about friendship, fortune, dissimulation, studies, and so on. This, of course, would tend to make all of the essays one large essay in the root sense of the word—one continu-

13 In the *Colours of Good and Evil,* published with the 1597 edition of the *Essays,* Bacon is concerned to expose the fallacies of certain sophisms which "sway" the ordinary judgment simply by virtue of their imaginative and rhetorical force. "Nothing," he declares "can be of greater use and defence to the minde, then the discovering and reprehension of these coulours, shewing in what cases they hold, and in what cases they deceive." This is the task assigned to the reader in the *Essays.* In this connection one should also note Bacon's lifelong habit of collecting *antitheta,* statements for and against a certain point of view, many of which find their way into the *Essays* where they operate to jostle the mind into an awareness of the complexity and manysidedness of the subject under discussion. As Margaret L. Wiley observes ("Francis Bacon: Induction and/or Rhetoric," in *Studies in the Literary Imagination,* Vol. IV, No. 1), Bacon was throughout his career preoccupied with "dualisms on the move (72)." I would add only that what is moved by these dualisms is often the mind of his reader.

ing attempt to make sense of things, with the emphasis on the "making sense of" rather than on the "things." The alternative (and more usual) view is well represented by Anne Righter: ". . . the 1625 edition is not a tidy knitting together of various ideas which interested Bacon; it is an accumulation of disparate pieces as difficult to generalize about, or to connect internally, as Donne's *Songs and Sonets,* and it is to be read in a not dissimilar fashion." [14] This statement has been endorsed recently by Vickers who adds that the *Essays* were "not . . . composed from a consistent impelling attitude or plan (132)." Miss Righter and Vickers are no doubt correct if one looks for a consistency of content or attitude (remember the "two" Bacons who trouble Zeitlin and Bush); but there is, I think, another kind of consistency to the essays, a consistency of experience, which in turn is a reflection of what might be called an "impelling plan." The *Essays* are to be read not as a series of encapsulations or expressions, but as a refining process that is being enacted by the reader; and to some extent, the question, in any one essay, of exactly what abstraction is being refined, is secondary.

Thus, in the 1625 essay "Of Love," for example, the title merely specifies the particular area of inquiry within which and in terms of which the reader becomes involved in a characteristic kind of activity, the questioning and testing of a commonly received notion. The excerpt analyzed above is followed in the 1625 text by a sentence which begins: "It is a poor saying. . . ." The "poor saying" in question turns out to have been said by Epicurus, but the phrase might well apply (as it seems to for a moment) to the generalization that has dominated the essay to this point, "amongst all the great and worthy persons . . . there is not one. . . ." Indeed the true focus of the essay is the many "poor sayings" that have accumulated about this one abstraction; and the purpose of the essay is to initiate a search for "better sayings," sayings more in accordance with the observable facts.

This same pattern—the casual proffering of one or more familiar and "reverenced" witticisms followed by the introduction of data that calls their validity into question—is found everywhere

[14] "Francis Bacon," in *The English Mind,* ed. H. S. Davies and G. Watson (Cambridge, 1964), p. 26.

in Bacon's *Essays*. A particularly good example is the late essay "Of Usury" which moves immediately to the point other essays make only indirectly:

> Many have made witty invectives against Usury. They say that it is a pity the devil should have God's part, which is the tithe. That the usurer is the greatest sabbath-breaker, because his plough goeth every Sunday. That the usurer is the drone that Virgil speaketh of;
>
> *Ignavum fucos pecus a praesepibus arcent.* That the usurer breaketh the first law that was made for mankind after the fall, which was, *in sudore vultus tui comedes panem tuum;* not, *in sudore vultus alieni* [in the sweat of thy face shalt thou eat bread—not in the sweat of another's face]. That usurers should have orange-tawny bonnets, because they do judaize. That it is against nature for money to beget money; and the like (*Sp.,* VI, 473–474).

No practiced reader of Bacon's *Essays* will be likely to miss the sneer in "and the like"; and its effect is retroactive, extending back to the governing verb phrase, "They say." In other essays, "They say" will appear in slightly changed form as "men say" or "as has been thought," while "and the like" will be shortened to "and such"; but the implication is always the same: what men say and think about things may be far from the truth about them. In this case, the current sayings are "poor" because they have not been formulated with a view to the facts of the human condition:

> I say this only, that usury is a *concessum propter duritiem cordis* [a thing allowed by reason of the hardness of men's hearts]; for since there must be borrowing and lending, and men are so hard of heart as they will not lend freely, usury must be permitted. Some others have made suspicions and cunning propositions of banks, discovery of men's estates, and other inventions. But few have spoken of usury usefully. It is good to set before us the incommodities and commodities of usury, that the good may be either weighed out or culled out; and warily to provide, that while we make forth to that which is better, we meet not with that which is worse.

In the *Novum Organum,* Bacon uses the phrase "sciences as one would" to refer to internally coherent, but objectively inaccurate, systematizations of knowledge: "For what a man had rather were true he more readily believes (xlix)." Here, in "Of Usury," the object of the philosopher's contempt is "morality as one would," a morality of wishful thinking based on "what men ought to do" rather than on "what men do." Such a morality, he implies, may well be immoral (useless), for it leaves a man ignorant of and defenseless against the real complexity of the situations that will confront him. It is a mistake to term the essays a "science of pure selfishness" (as Zeitlin does), if by that one means that they advocate selfishness: the essays advocate nothing (except perhaps a certain openness and alertness of mind); they are descriptive, and a description is ethically neutral, although, if it is accurate, it may contribute to the development of a true, that is, responsible, ethics. The distinction is made beautifully by the last sentence in this first paragraph. The "good" of "it is good to set before us" is a purely procedural good; the "good" of "that the good may be," on the other hand, seems to have some ethical content, but more in the direction of "beneficial" than "right"; and, finally, the "better" of "make forth to that which is better" is unambiguously moral. Significantly, this "better" is placed in the future, while the emphasis is on the "making forth." Indeed, the temporal movement of the entire sentence prefigures the successive stages of a truly scientific inquiry: first the collecting of observations, then the tentative drawing out ("culling") of axioms, and finally, but only after a wary and rigorous process of "exclusions and rejections," the specification of what is "better" and what is not. At this point, what emerges as unequivocally "good" is the methodical disposition of the facts about usury, or any other "thing" and it is this task that Bacon sets his readers in the essays. The making of "witty invectives" or of unrealistic rules is, as Bacon says in the second paragraph, "idle." Talk of the "abolishing of usury," for instance, "must be sent to Utopia (475)." Bacon is even more vehement in "Of Suspicion," another late essay: "What would men have? Do they think those they employ and deal with are saints (454)?" In "Of Riches," the reader is warned, "have no abstract nor friarly contempt of them (460)" (Bacon's attitude

toward religious "sayings" will be discussed later). And the tone
of the essays in this connection is established at the very beginning, in "Of Truth": "Doth any man doubt, that if there were
taken out of men's minds vain opinions, flattering hopes, false
valuations, imaginations as one would, and the like, but it would
leave the minds of a number of men poor shrunken things, full of
melancholy and indisposition, and unpleasing to themselves (377–
378)?" Taking out of the reader's mind all vain opinions, flattering hopes, false valuations, imaginations as one would, and the
like is the business of these essays. There is no room in Bacon's
program for illusions, and especially not for the illusions projected
naturally by the order-loving, simplicity imposing, human understanding.

"Of Usury," however, is not typical of the essays because so
much of the work is done *for* the reader. In the more characteristic essay, the "vain opinions" and "false valuations" are exposed
gradually, and then only after the reader has been given an opportunity to accept them or to let them go by unchallenged. This
results in a more self-conscious scrutiny of one's mental furniture
and helps to foster the curious blend of investigative eagerness
and wary skepticism which, according to Bacon, distinguishes the
truly scientific cast of mind. "Of Adversity" is such an essay, and
for our purposes it has the advantage of being brief enough to be
quoted in full:

> It was a high speech of Seneca (after the manner of the
> Stoics), *that the good things which belong to prosperity
> are to be wished; but the good things that belong to ad-
> versity are to be admired. Bona rerum secundarum opta-
> bilia; adversarum mirabilia.* Certainly if miracles be the
> command over nature, they appear most in adversity. It is
> yet a higher speech of his than the other (much too high
> for a heathen), *It is true greatness to have in one the
> frailty of a man, and the security of a God. Vere magnum
> habere fragilitatem hominis, securitatem Dei.* This would
> have done better in poesy, where transcendences are more
> allowed. And the poets indeed have been busy with it; for
> it is in effect the thing which is figured in that strange fic-

tion of the ancient poets, which seemeth not to be without
mystery; nay, and to have some approach to the state of a
Christian; that *Hercules, when he went to unbind Prome-*
*theus* (by whom human nature is represented), *sailed the*
*length of the great ocean in an earthen pot or pitcher;* lively
describing Christian resolution, that saileth in the frail
bark of the flesh thorough the waves of the world. But to
speak in a mean. The virtue of Prosperity is temperance,
the virtue of Adversity is fortitude; which in morals is
the more heroical virtue. Prosperity is the blessing of the
Old Testament; Adversity is the blessing of the New;
which carrieth the greater benediction, and the clearer revelation of God's favour. Yet even in the Old Testament, if
you listen to David's harp, you shall hear as many hearse-
like airs as carols; and the pencil of the Holy Ghost hath
laboured more in describing the afflictions of Job than the
felicities of Salomon. Prosperity is not without many fears
and distastes; and Adversity is not without comforts and
hopes. We see in needle-works and embroideries, it is
more pleasing to have a lively work upon a sad and solemn
ground, than to have a dark and melancholy work upon a
lightsome ground: judge therefore of the pleasure of the
heart by the pleasure of the eye. Certainly virtue is like
precious odours, most fragrant when they are incensed or
crushed: for Prosperity doth best discover vice, but Adversity doth best discover virtue (*Sp.,* VI, 386).

In one of the more recent editions of the essays, "high" is
glossed as "presumptuous," but this is hardly the meaning that
will occur to the casual reader as he first moves into the essay.
More likely he will assume, too easily perhaps, but naturally, that
by "high" Bacon intends "elevated" or "exalted" or "lofty," even
"noble"; and in the same way, the parenthetical "after the manner
of the Stoics" will seem at first to be a point of identification rather
than a criticism. Only after the last word of the essay is read is
the meaning of "high" clarified, and even then "presumptuous,"
while it is more accurate than "noble," does less than justice to the
felt experience of the word's complexity. An understanding of that

complexity is the chief product of the essay, which is finally more about "high speeches" (for which read "poor sayings" or "abstract" or "friarly") and their relationship to what is than about "adversity."

This first "high speech" exhibits many of the characteristics Bacon associates with the delivery of knowledge "in such form as may be best believed and not as may be best examined." This is the form Bacon condemns in the *De Augmentis* because it "seemes more witty and waighty than indeed it is": "The labour here is altogether, *That words may be aculeate, sentences concise, and the whole contexture of the speech and discourse, rather rounding into it selfe, than spread and dilated* . . . Such a stile as this we finde more excessively in *Seneca* . . . it is nothing else but a hunting after words, and fine placing of them." [15] The "fine placing" of the words results in a pointed and schematic prose in which the argument is carried more by the clinking harmony of like endings than by the "matter." In short, one assents to the form (which is designed to satisfy the psychological needs of the receiving consciousness) rather than to the content; and this makes the Senecan style, at its most mannered, as debilitating as the "sweet falling . . . clauses" of an extreme Ciceronianism; for both persuade by alluring, and short-circuit the rational processes.

Williamson has noted how carefully Bacon's translation preserves the Senecan mannerisms, and even perfects them: "Bacon duplicates Senecan balance, suggests his transverse like-endings, but adds alliteration to the parallelism of the second member." And he adds, "If this form be considered accidental, it may be argued that the similarities could have been, but are not, avoided." [16] The similarities are not avoided because Bacon wishes to secure, at least momentarily, the extreme Senecan effect, the unthinking acceptance of this "high speech." The reader is allowed to anticipate a comfortable and untaxing journey through the essay, and this expectation is strengthened by the first word of the next sentence, "Certainly." But the second word of the sentence is "if" and suddenly the hitherto sharp outlines of the discussion are blurred. "Certainly, if" is a particularly concise instance of a pat-

15 *De Aug.,* trans. Gilbert Wats (Oxford, 1640), p. 29.
16 George Williamson, *The Senecan Amble* (London, 1951), p. 117.

tern that appears everywhere in the essays: words like "surely," "doubtless," "truly," and phrases like "in truth," "it is doubtless true," "certainly it is true" suggest strongly that what follows is to be accepted without qualification; but within a word or a phrase or, at most, a sentence Bacon drops in one of another group of words and phrases—"but," "except," "although," "nevertheless," "and yet," and the most devastating of all, "it is *also* true." The result is a change in the quality of the reader's attention, from complacency to a kind of uneasiness, an uneasiness which takes the (perhaps subconscious) form of a silently asked question: "What, exactly, is the truth about ——?" At that moment the reader is transformed from a passive recipient of popular truth into a searcher after objective truth, and this transformation follows upon the transformation of the essay from a vehicle whose form is designed to secure belief into an instrument of inquiry and examination.

This is, perhaps, too great a burden to place on the phrase "Certainly, if" in "Of Adversity." Its effect is less dramatic; it simply introduces doubt where there had been none before and that doubt, while it is unfocused, nevertheless extends to the word "adversity" which does appear in a prominent position. (Incidentally this is the only function of the sentence, to foster doubt and uncertainty; that is, its purpose is not communicative or expressive, but rhetorical; Bacon is not really interested in whether or not miracles can be defined as "the command over nature.") The reader's active involvement in the essay begins with the next sentence, which returns to the concept of "highness." However straightforwardly the first "high" had been accepted, there is something uncomfortable and awkward about the comparative "higher," and with the parenthesis ("much too high for a heathen") the word can no longer be taken as honorific. It is here that the meaning "presumptuous" comes into play and with it an implied hierarchy of authorities—heathen vs. Christian. This second "high speech," then, will be viewed with more suspicion than the first, and that suspicion will be confirmed and given body by its association in the following sentence with "poesy" and "transcendences." A third meaning of "high" now emerges—"unreal" or "remote from the world of facts"—a meaning reinforced by the phrase "strange fiction." Together with "heathen," "poesy," and "transcendences," "strange fiction" forms a system of related terms which begin to displace "adversity" as the subject of the essay. In this system, "mystery" occupies an ambiguous position: on one hand it shares with poetry "and the like" the taint of "fantasy"; and on the other it looks ahead to the more respectable category of "Christian." But that word too, coming as it does at the end of the series, cannot escape the pejorative associations that have been clustering around "high" and its equivalences. The opposition of "heathen" to "Christian" now seems less firm and controlling than it did a few moments ago and the reader is further away than ever from knowing the "truth" about adversity, largely because the authorities contending for his attention have been overtly or implicitly discredited.

In short, the effect of the first half of the essay is to disabuse the reader of whatever confidence he may have had in the sayings of heathen philosophers, poets, traffickers in mysteries, or even Christians. At this point Bacon introduces another of his "code phrases"—"But to speak in a mean"—which will be read by the initiated as, "Now that we've taken note of the opinions men commonly hold on the subject, let us look to the truth of the matter." In "Of Usury" the phrase is "to speak usefully" and in "Of Cunning," "To say truth," while in "Of Truth" the distinction implied by all these is made more fully: "To pass from theological and philosophical truth, to the truth of civil business (*Sp.,* VI, 378)." In terms of the methodology of scientific inquiry, "theological truth" is no more to be honored than any other body of commonly received notions. One of the most remarkable statements in the *Novum Organum* is this variation on the biblical commonplace, "Render therefore unto Caesar the things which be Caesar's (Luke, 20:25)":

> . . . some of the moderns have with extreme levity indulged so far as to attempt to found a system of natural philosophy on the first chapter of Genesis . . . from this unwholesome mixture of things human and divine there

> arises not only a fantastic philosophy but also an heretical
> religion. Very meet it is therefore that we be sober-minded,
> and give to faith that only which is faith's (lxv).

Being "sober-minded" means speaking "usefully" or "in a mean,"
descending from the aery heights where adversity is characterized by the image of the frail bark of flesh sailing through the
waves of the world (this is almost comical) to the level plain of
empirical observation and a plainer style: "The virtue of Prosperity is temperance, the virtue of Adversity is fortitude. . . .
Prosperity is the blessing of the Old Testament; Adversity is the
blessing of the New." But these speeches, while they are less
"lively" and metaphorical than the others, are still "high" in the
all-important sense of being above the facts; and moreover, the
parallel members and the pointed schemes operate to secure the
kind of facile assent Bacon is always warning against. Once
again, knowledge is being delivered "In such form as may best be
believed," and once again Bacon breaks the spell of his cadenced
rhythms with a characteristic qualification: "Yet, even. . . ." But
the qualifying statement has a rhythm of its own, in addition to
a network of patterned oppositions—"David's harp"–"pencil of
the Holy Ghost," "hearse-like airs"–"afflictions of Job," "carols"–
"felicities of Salomon"—and for the third time the reader is encouraged to relax while his powers of judgment are taken over
by the movement of the prose. The transverse patterning continues—"Prosperity"–"fears and distastes," "Adversity"–"comforts and hopes"—as the distinction between the two abstractions
becomes increasingly blurred. The argument, which is, of course,
rhetorical rather than logical, is helped along by the unheralded
reintroduction of "lively" language. Amidst talk of "embroideries"
and "lightsome grounds," the emotional and physical realities of
adversity fade, and when Bacon concludes "Judge therefore of
the pleasure of the heart by the pleasure of the eye" he is, in fact,
urging something his style has already effected. As the final sentence unfolds, the reader is once more in the position he occupied
at the beginning of the essay, the passive receiver of "high
speeches," assured by an introductory "certainly" that nothing
will be required of him but a nod of the head. The sentence itself

is the "highest" speech imaginable, complete with an elaborate and fanciful simile and ending with a perfect and pointed isocolon. But the effect is spoiled, intentionally of course, by a single superfluous phrase—"or crushed"—which not only upsets the symmetry of the parallel members, but serves, for the last time, to arouse the reader from the intellectual lethargy into which he has fallen. Supposedly offered as a synonym for "incensed," "crushed" is instead a comment on it and on "precious odours" and "fragrant," revealing what "incensed" and all incenselike "high speech" is designed to hide—the hard, and ultimately saving, truth. Without it the last pair of neat antitheses—"Prosperity doth best discover vice, but Adversity doth best discover virtue" —would have been received with the reverence we usually accord comforting *sententiae,* but with its near onomatopoetic sound ringing in our ears, the response is more likely to be, "that's all very nice, but. . . ." The essay ends, then as it began, with a "high speech," but in between the two the deficiencies of any speech that flies above the facts have again and again been exposed, along with the attraction such speeches hold for the mind of the reader. The question of what "adversity" is has no more been settled here than the question of what "love" is was settled in that essay. In fact, the experience of the essay is *un*settling, and therefore it meets Bacon's criteria for "useful" and "fruitful" discourse, discourse which, because it does not pretend to completeness, invites men "to enquire farther."

"Of Adversity" is perhaps the most finely wrought of Bacon's performances in this mode. None of the effects I have been describing are obvious or heavy-handed; the shifts in tone are not heralded; the machinery of the surface argument is maintained even when the alert reader's attention has been drawn away to other concerns; the essay is almost seamless, so much so that as discerning a critic as Macauley could praise it for its "eloquence . . . sweetness and variety of expression, and . . . richness of illustration." [17] This kind of "underreading" is less likely, however, when the movement from "morality as one would" to "morality as it is" is more deliberate and leisurely. In "Of Simulation

[17] "Lord Bacon" (1837), in *The Life and Works of Lord Macauley*, Edinburgh ed. VI, 240–242.

and Dissimulation," for example, the essay which follows "Of Adversity" in the 1625 edition, it would seem to me very difficult to read very far into the second paragraph without being aware of the uneasy juxtaposition of several frames of reference:

> Dissimulation is but a faint kind of policy or wisdom; for it asketh a strong wit and a strong heart to know when to tell truth, and to do it. Therefore it is the weaker sort of politics that are the great dissemblers.
>
> Tacitus saith, *Livia sorted well with the arts of her husband and dissimulation of her son;* attributing arts or policy to Augustus, and dissimulation to Tiberius. And again, when Mucianus encourageth Vespasian to take arms against Vitellius, he saith, *We rise not against the piercing judgment of Augustus, nor the extreme caution or closeness of Tiberius.* These properties, of arts or policy and dissimulation or closeness, are indeed habits and faculties several, and to be distinguished. For if a man have that penetration of judgment as he can discern what things are to be laid open, and what to be secreted, and what to be shewed at half lights, and to whom and when, (which indeed are arts of state and arts of life, as Tacitus well calleth them,) to him a habit of dissimulation is a hinderance and a poorness. But if a man cannot obtain to that judgment, then it is left to him generally to be close, and a dissembler. For where a man cannot choose or vary in particulars, there it is good to take the safest and wariest way in general; like the going softly, by one that cannot well see. Certainly the ablest men that ever were have had all an openness and frankness of dealing; and a name of certainty and veracity; but then they were like horses well managed; for they could tell passing well when to stop or turn; and at such times when they thought the case indeed required dissimulation, if then they used it, it came to pass that the former opinion spread abroad of their good faith and clearness of dealing made them almost invisible (*Sp.,* VI, 387).

The first paragraph is apparently an unqualified indictment of dissembling and dissemblers. The linear movement of the prose is unimpeded; the logical ligatures which direct and control the syntax are at once firm and unobtrusive; and, as is so often the case in the early stages of a Bacon essay, the form of the argument approximates a syllogism—those who are strong tell truth; dissemblers lie; therefore dissemblers are weak. In short, we seem to have a happy union of ethics and practical wisdom; for once, good morals is good business and vice versa, or so it will seem to a reader who has allowed himself to be swept along toward the waiting conclusion. But en route there are at least two indications of the direction the essay will eventually take: the "or" in "policy or wisdom" has the faintest suggestion of "it doesn't matter which" about it, and more tellingly, the emphasis in the "for" clause of the first sentence is on the proper, or timely, *use* of truth rather than on truth itself. Knowing when to tell the truth doesn't necessarily involve a regard for the truth you tell. Is morality really morality if it is only an instrument of policy and not the cornerstone of it? But while questions like this are certainly warranted by the sense of the sentence, they are not encouraged by its form, which hurries the reader past the equivocating "know when" and deposits him on the heavily stressed final phrase: "and to do it." Strictly speaking, "it" could refer to either or both of the preceding infinitive clauses, but the more available clause is the second, "to tell truth," and it is to this that the reader, taking the path of least resistance, will naturally look. As a result, strength of wit and heart is equated with telling the truth (although no such equation is made in the text), the moral tone of the paragraph is preserved (although there is little finally to support it) and the reader enters the second paragraph committed to assumptions and distinctions that will not survive the experience of the essay.

Presumably the references to Tacitus are intended to support the formula implied in the preceding sentence—dissembling and good politics are inversely related—but the examples do not fit the formula as well as one might have expected. The distinction between "arts or policy" and "dissimulation" is less firm than that between dissimulation and telling the truth; and the presence of Livia is troublesomely complicating; for her ability to adjust to the behavior of either man seems more important than the differences between them. The moral focus of the discussion is somewhat blurred, and the blurring continues when the "judgment" of Augustus and the "caution or closeness" of Tiberius, rather than being opposed, are joined as practices against which Mucianus and Vespasian are *not* rising. In both quotations, the reader is given one more ordering principle than he can comfortably use: are we distinguishing between dissembling and truth-telling or between success and failure? Or are we making no distinctions at all, but merely cataloguing the opinions of those who have written on politics? When Bacon, for his part, opines that "arts or policy" and "dissimulation or closeness" should be distinguished, his audience is more than willing to agree.

The form of the following sentence suggests a more pointed opposition than is actually forthcoming. While "penetration of judgment" is contrasted with "dissimulation," the description of what constitutes "penetration of judgment"—the judicious use of secrecy, the showing of things in "half lights"—softens the contrast considerably, and once again the reader finds himself uncertain of his footing, although the prose, assured in tone, makes no acknowledgment of his difficulty. At this point all that remains of the clear and comfortable demarcations of the opening statement is the conviction that dissembling is the mark of an inferior man. But even this last support is removed in the second half of the paragraph. The man who in one sentence is a dissembler because lack of ability leaves him no other course ("it is left to him") is, in the next, dissembling because it is the "safest" way. Not only that, but "it is good." Although "good" is qualified by the context—it is again a procedural rather than a moral "good"—it is nevertheless a movement away from the wholly negative attitude toward dissembling that has been assumed since the beginning. And in the long concluding sentence, whatever basis there had been for the making of moral distinctions, or any distinctions at all for that matter, is swept away. For a moment it seems that Bacon is returning to the sharper (and simpler) focus of the first paragraph: "Certainly the ablest men that ever were have had all an openness and frankness of dealing." Once again practical ability and moral probity are joined and seemingly equated, but their union has hardly been reestablished before it is disturbed by the phrase "and a name of certainty and veracity." The effect of "name" is retroactive and disconcerting, for if the ablest men have only the "name" of veracity, perhaps their open- ness and frankness is also a name rather than a reality. There is a word for this—dissimulation—but it has not yet surfaced, either in the text or the reader's consciousness. The drift of the sentence is still in the direction indicated by "Certainly," although, charac- teristically, certainty is less and less an adequate word for the attitude the prose encourages. (In fact "certainty," tainted as it is by "name," seems almost to mock "Certainly.") For a while, the reader's attention is drawn away from the unsettling implica- tions of "name" by the introduction of the horse simile—"they [the ablest men] were like horses well managed"—until, unex- pectedly, "well managing" is said to include "dissimulation," a practice especially available to able men who, because they man- age things so well and have a reputation ("name") for "good faith" and "a clearness of dealing," dissemble without being sus- pected or detected. This is nearly a description of Bacon's dealings with his reader: pretending to be a conventional moralist, he first proposes a comforting view of the relationship between good morality and good business, and then proceeds, "almost invisibly," to undermine it and to reveal himself as something of a Machiavel. In his *Francis Bacon: A Selection of His Works* (Toronto, 1965), Sidney Warhaft glosses "clearness" as "openness (p. 58)," a read- ing that has the advantage of emphasizing how completely the sentence (and the essay) has turned around. The ablest man emerges finally as the best dissembler, the man who can best feign "openness" (as Bacon does in his stance toward the reader), and the first part of the sentence, as well as the entire first para- graph, becomes a comment on the reader's readiness to take at face value whatever is offered him, especially if it is comforting. Obviously, the "weaker sort of politics" are not the great dis- semblers. In fact, the reverse now seems to be true. As the para- graph ends, the reader has no basis at all for making a distinction between truth-tellers and dissemblers and is not even sure that he can tell the difference. The only standard left is the completely relative one of "what the case requires." This is situation ethics minus the ethics.

The essay continues in the same pattern. Having disabused the reader of his confidence in one set of distinctions, Bacon offers him another:

> There be three degrees of this hiding and veiling of a man's self. The first, Closeness, Reservation, and Secrecy; when a man leaveth himself without observation, or without hold to be taken, what he is. The second, Dissimulation, in the negative; when a man lets fall signs and arguments, that he is not that he is. And the third, Simulation, in the affirmative; when a man industriously and expressly feigns and pretends to be that he is not (387–388).

These are fine distinctions indeed, more a matter of technique than principle. What happens to them in the rest of the essay is almost predictable, although the predictability does not prevent the reader from falling once again into Bacon's trap. According to the received definition, secrecy is less culpable than either simulation or dissimulation, because it is passive; but the description of the secret man—one whose apparent circumspection results in his receiving confessions and confidences—implies a future action and therefore an active intention. Bacon carries on with his division (*partitio*) as if its hard lines were still intact—"For the second, which is Dissimulation"—but then he immediately collapses his own structure by defining dissimulation as that which follows upon secrecy, for "he that will be secret must be a dissembler to some degree (388)." The paragraph, whose purpose, supposedly, was to sequester secrecy from dissimulation, ends by equating them: ". . . no man can be secret, except he give himself a little scope of dissimulation; which is, as it were, but the skirts or train of secrecy (388–389)."

In the third paragraph, which belongs to Simulation—Bacon continues to follow his outline, even though the distinctions it supports have long since broken down—there is a momentary return to the moral focus of the earlier part of the essay: "But for the third degree, which is Simulation and false profession; that I hold more culpable, and less politic (389)." But this new, or newly revived, distinction does not survive the next word— "except": "except it be in great and rare matters." As is so often the case, the qualification robs the main statement of most, if not all, of its force. The requirements of morality are to be overridden if the exigencies of the situation ("what the case requires") demand it, and of course that decision is the individual's. True, Bacon does go on to conclude "therefore . . . simulation . . . is a vice," but the conclusion hardly follows from what precedes it, nor is it supported by the sentence that opens the last paragraph: "The great advantages of simulation and dissimulation are three (389)."

As he brings the essay to a close, Bacon rings some changes on the pattern he has established. Instead of following a sententious commonplace with a qualification that undermines it, he does the reverse, first delivering the "good shrewd proverb," "*Tell a lie and find a troth*," and then recoiling from it in apparent horror, "As if there were no way of discovery but by simulation (389)." But while their positions are reversed, the irony (if that is the word) is still at the expense of the moralism. If the three previous paragraphs have been asserting anything, it is that "there is no way of discovery, but by simulation." As this point, the speaker's mock piety is a vestigial reminder of an innocence the essay has taken from us. Nor can we take seriously the third disadvantage of dissimulation and simulation—"it depriveth a man of one of the most principal instruments for action; which is trust and belief (389)"—since, in the world the experience of this essay creates, trust and belief hardly exist, except as signs of weakness.

In the concluding sentence, Bacon returns to his more usual order: "The best composition and temperature is to have openness in fame and opinion; secrecy in habit; dissimulation in seasonable use; and a power to feign, if there be no remedy (389)." For the last time, distinctions suggested by the form of the presentation are dissolved by the reader's experience of it. "Openness in fame" is no openness at all, but a dissembling secrecy, that is, "dissimulation in seasonable use"; and a "power to feign" is not so much a separate category as it is a rubric under which all the supposedly diverse practices discussed in these paragraphs can be grouped. As he lets us out of the essay, Bacon permits himself a last flick of his satiric lash. The understated deadpanned cynicism of "if there be no remedy" is devastatingly effective, coming, as it does,

at the end of an experience in the course of which every remedy
that might have occurred to a reader, especially a reader whose
morality has been "as he would," is systematically eliminated.
(This is, as we shall see, the controlling mechanism, in Burton's
*Anatomy of Melancholy*.)

UNLIKE ELEMENTS JOINED

The movement characteristic of this essay, the uneasy and
unsettling juxtaposition of "ethical" and "practical" or "realistic"
perspectives, has not gone unnoticed by the critics who, for the
most part, regard it as a by-product of Bacon's revisions:

> . . . compositions which were originally pervaded by an
> atmosphere of clear moral stimulation were overlaid with
> considerations of immediate practical utility, till their
> primary inspiration became altogether obscured (Zeitlin,
> 514).
>
> In the later editions . . . although the ligatures are
> good, unlike elements are joined and chronology is ignored
> (A. W. Green, *Sir Francis Bacon*, 84).

The assumption is that the presence in a single work of "unlike
elements" is regrettable, and in some sense, unintentional—Bacon
either lost control of his form in the successive editions or un-
wittingly allowed the essays to become a battleground for the
warring elements of his personality. But "Of Simulation and Dissimulation" is a late and unrevised essay, as are others in which
the same pattern can be seen. The "accidents-of-revision" theory
will not hold water, any more than will Vickers's assertion that
Bacon is without a plan: "Bacon . . . added new material at any
moderately suitable point, without much thought to the overall
development (132)." These statements are further evidence of a
general failure to see that the coherence of the *Essays*—singly and
as a whole—inheres in the experience they provide. A study of the
revisions, with a view to the changes effected in the reader's response, will, I think, reveal a determined effort to make the
*Essays* the kind of experience I have been describing.

Let us turn once again to the essay "Of Love," but this time in its 1612 guise, a perfectly straightforward piece of conventional moralism:

> LOVE is the argument alwaies of *Comedies,* and many times of *Tragedies.* Which sheweth well, that it is a passion generally light, and sometimes extreme. Extreame it may well bee, since the speaking in a perpetuall *Hyperbole,* is comely in nothing but *Loue.* Neither is it meerely in the phrase. For whereas it hath beene well said, that the *Arch-flatterer* with whom al the petty-flatters haue intelligence, is a Mans selfe, certainely the louer is more. For there was neuer proud Man thought so absurdly well of himselfe, as the louer doth of the person loued: and therefore it was well said, that it is impossible to loue, and to bee wise. Neither doth this weakness appeare to others only, and not to the party loued, but to the loued most of all, except the loue bee reciproque. For it is a true rule, that loue is euer rewarded either with the reciproque, or with an inward and secret contempt. By how much the more men ought to beware of this passion, which loseth not onely other things, but it selfe. As for the other losses, the Poets relation doth wel figure them: That hee that preferred *Helena,* quitted the gifts of *Iuno* and *Pallas.* For whosoeuer esteemeth too much of amorous affection, quitteth both riches and wisdome. This passion hath his flouds in the verie times of weakenesse; which are great prosperity, and great aduersitie. (though this latter hath beene lesse obserued) Both which times kindle loue and make it more feruent, and therefore shew it to be the childe of folly. They doe best that make this affection keepe quarter, and seuer it wholly from their serious affaires and actions of their life. For if it checke once with businesse, it troubleth Mens fortunes, and maketh Men, that they can no waies be true to their own endes (*Sp.,* VI, 557–558).

This admirably structured paragraph answers to the idea most people (who have not read them) have of Bacon's *Essays.* The argument moves smoothly from one point to the next; the prose is pithy and aphoristic; the moral vision clear and unambiguous.

The first two sentences seem almost to generate what follows: Comedy and Tragedy are used to specify the two chief character- istics of love, its excessiveness and its triviality ("lightness"). This division is then expanded into an indictment of love as an unworthy passion which interferes with the "serious affaires and actions of . . . life." The example of Paris is brought in to "prove" Bacon's thesis and the essay ends with a predictable and unexceptionable exhortation: avoid love, especially when it threatens to make you forsake your "own endes."

Much of this is retained in 1625, but the additional materials work a profound change in the tone of the essay and completely transform the phrases and sentences that have been carried over from the earlier version. The nature of this change can be seen by a comparison of the two openings:

> Love is the argument alwaies of *Comedies,* and many times of *Tragedies*. Which sheweth well, that it is a passion gen- erally light, and sometimes extreme (*Sp.,* VI, 557).
> The stage is more beholding to Love, than the life of man. For as to the stage, love is ever matter of comedies, and now and then of tragedies; but in life it doth much mis- chief; sometimes like a syren, sometimes like a fury (*Sp.,* VI, 397).

In place of the easy correspondence between life and the stage, we now have a clear separation of the two, and a suggestion that the view of love projected on the stage is an oversimplification. This implied criticism extends to the whole of the earlier essay which, like other presentations whose coherence is merely formal, excludes more of the truth than it contains.[18] Bacon's additions operate to break that coherence, and to substitute for the almost physical satisfaction of a closed experience the greater satisfac- tion of a fuller understanding. Specifically, the emphasis is shifted from the prescriptive moral—avoid love—to the difficulty, if not impossibility, of doing so. This is clearly the effect of the passage analyzed at the beginning of this chapter (p. 81). The first sen-

---

[18] In the *Novum Organum,* those "received systems" which prevent men from inquiring further are termed "so many stage plays, representing worlds of their own creation after an unreal and scenic fashion (*Sp.,* IV, 55)."

tence holds out the promise of an easy and formulaic distinction between wise men and mad lovers; but, as exceptions to it are admitted, that formula becomes less and less reliable, until the phrase "if watch be not well kept" discards it altogether by transferring the responsibility from the labels to the individual. Wise man or fool, austere man or voluptuary, it doesn't seem to matter; love can always find entrance into a heart that is not constantly on guard against it. Later, when the two versions of the essay coalesce, sentiments that had seemed unexceptionable in the tightly controlled framework of 1612 now ring somewhat hollowly in the looser, but more inclusive, framework of 1625. This is particularly true of that most familiar of proverbs, "it is impossible to love and be wise," which in the earlier essay is accepted without qualification or reservation as the inevitable conclusion to the arguments preceding it; but in 1625, with the examples of Marcus Antonius and Appius Claudius fresh in our memories, the response to that same *sententia* is made up of equal parts of skepticism and wonder. It may indeed be "well said" that "it is impossible to love and be wise," but is it true? After all, Bacon's original assertion, that "amongst all the great and worthy persons . . . there is not one that hath been transported to the mad degree of love" was also "well said," as was, presumably, the "poor saying" of Epicurus. Not that the reader will flatly reject this "saying"; the conflicting evidence is itself too inconclusive for anything so drastic. The effect of Bacon's revisions is never to cancel out what had been asserted previously, but to qualify it: something assumed to be true on the basis of what now appears to be inadequate evidence is not declared false (necessarily); rather, something else is declared to be true also. And if the fact of the two "true things" poses difficulties for the logically oriented consciousness, well, that's life. And that is also the experience of a Bacon essay.

In addition to inserting new material and (as a consequence) repositioning the old, Bacon achieves his complicating effects by slightly altering the phrasing of individual sentences. In 1612, the reader is advised that "they doe best that make this affection keep quarter, and sever it wholly from their serious affaires." In 1625 a single clause is added, but it makes all the difference in the world: "They do best who, *if they cannot but admit love,* yet make it keep quarter and sever it wholly from their serious affairs." In the light of the revised essay's emphasis on the difficulty of keeping love out, the parenthetical qualification is more than a gesture. The sentence, in its expanded form, reflects the delicate and shifting relationship between the absoluteness of a moral imperative ("morality as one would") and the realities of a difficult world, and serves as a further reminder to the reader that there are no easy answers.

As is often the case, the later essay is given a new conclusion, one which reveals more baldly than anything else the transformation that has been wrought in the vehicle:

> I know not how, but martial men are given to love: I think it is but as they are given to wine; for perils commonly ask to be paid in pleasures. There is in man's nature a secret inclination and motion towards love of others, which if it be not spent upon some one or a few, doth naturally spread itself toward many, and maketh men become humane and charitable as it is seen sometime in friars. Nuptial love maketh mankind; friendly love perfecteth it; but wanton love corrupteth and embaseth it (398).

A statement like "I know not how" would have been unthinkable at the beginning of the essay. The posture usually assumed by the moral essayist does not allow for an admission of ignorance. But by this time, a more assertive stance would be out of place. Both the speaker and the reader have long since given up the illusion that love could be easily defined or contained; all we can do for the present is note the operation of this strange passion. It is a fact that martial men are given to love, but aside from a hardly serious reference to an old wives' tale, there is no explanation for the fact. Bacon must resort to the evasion of positing a "secret inclination" whose visible effects are the actions we group under the rubric "love." In this penultimate sentence love becomes a kind of disease spreading of its own volition into every corner of our varied lives. So powerful is this force that it literally overwhelms the qualitative distinctions we usually make between its manifestations. "Humane" and "charitable" love lose their positive associations and become just two more instances of this "spreading"; the religious life is less a noble and chosen calling than it is an involuntary response to an irresistible urge. An essay that began by identifying a "mad degree" of love and implying the existence of other, more manageable degrees, concludes by suggesting that all love is uncontrollable and, perhaps, mad. In the end, Bacon does return to the pointed prose and neat schematizations of the opening paragraph, but the familiar and comforting labels—"nuptial," "friendly," "wanton"—are here nothing but the skeletal remains of a simpler vision that is no longer ours.

"Of Love" is an unusually "pure" example of the changes effected in the course of Bacon's revisions. Rarely are the earlier and later versions of an essay so markedly different. More often, the unsettling complications that surface in 1625 have been there all the while, in embryo; the additions and alterations merely make it impossible to ignore or suppress them. The opening sentences of "Of Goodness and Goodness of Nature (1612)," for instance, are potentially far less innocent than a superficial reading would indicate:

> I take *goodnesse* in this sence, the affecting of the *Weale* of men, which is, that the *Græcians* call *Philanthropia;* for the word *humanitie* (as it is vsed) it is a little too light, to expresse it. *Goodnesse* I call the habite; and *goodnesse of Nature,* the inclination. This of all vertues, is the greatest: being the character of the *Deitie;* and without it, man is a busie, mischeuous, wretched thing: no better then a kind of vermine. *Goodnesse* answers to the *Theologicall* vertue *Charity,* and admits not excesse, but error. The *Italians,* haue an vngracious prouerbe, *Tanto buon, che val niente; So good, that he is good for nothing.* And one of the Doctors of *Italie, Nicholas Machiauel* had the confidence to put in writing, almost in plaine termes; *That the Christian faith had giuen vp good men in prey, to those that are tyrannicall and vniust;* which hee spake, because indeed there was neuer law, or sect, or opinion, did so much magnifie goodnes, as the *Christian religion* doth. Therefore to

auoid the scandall, and the danger both; it is good to take
knowledge of the errors of an habite so excellent (*Sp.*, VI,
545).

The primary thrust of this passage seems to be the excellence of
goodness or charity, but there are hints of a less generous vision
just below the smooth surface. The description of man as a "busie,
mischevous, wretched thing, no better then a kind of vermine"
has a force that is not fully canceled out by the larger structure
of the sentence. (Was Swift reading this, perhaps, when he was
writing the second book of *Gulliver's Travels*?) The Italians'
proverb and Machiavelli's "almost plaine termes" are dismissed
rhetorically, but they have, after all, been given a hearing and
presumably have had some effect. There are also questions: Is
the Christian religion's magnification of goodness as satisfactory
an explanation of Machiavelli's indictment as the phrase "because
indeed" implies? Why is the word "humanitie" a little too "light"
to express "goodnesse"? Is it because "humanitie" ("as it is
used") is not really an honorific term? If so, then perhaps man
is in fact a "busie, mischevous. . . ." And, in turn, if this is so,
how answerable to the theological virtue of charity is the "goodnesse" of "humanitie," after all? The text itself certainly justifies
asking these and other questions, and yet the experience of the
text is such as to call attention away from them: The "vermine"
image has barely registered on the reader's consciousness before
it is (more or less) pushed aside by the return, in the next word,
to the subject of "goodnesse"; the attitude of the cynical Italians
does make an impression and may even occasion some uneasiness,
but all is "salved over" in the end by Bacon's praise of "an habite
so excellent."

In 1625, it is all quite different, for a considerable chunk of
new material has been inserted just before we are introduced to
the Italians:

> The desire of power in excess caused the angels to fall; the
> desire of knowledge in excess caused man to fall; but in
> charity there is no excess; neither can angel or man come
> in danger by it. The inclination to goodness is imprinted
> deeply in the nature of man; insomuch that if it not issue

towards men, it will take unto other living creatures; as is seen in the Turks, a cruel people, who nevertheless are kind to beasts, and give alms to dogs and birds; insomuch as Busbechius reporteth, a Christian boy in Constantinople had like to have been stoned for gagging in a waggishness a long-billed fowl. Errors indeed in this virtue of goodness or charity may be committed (*Sp.*, VI, 403).

At first these additional sentences are decidedly reassuring. The combination of anaphora and isocolon lends force to the opposition of charity to power and knowledge. Apparently, the "inclination to goodness" is so deeply imprinted that it is more powerful than any other desire or instinct; and with "insomuch" we settle down, expecting to hear some pretty tale which makes just that point. Instead we become increasingly *un*settled, as the succeeding clauses give rise to a number of problems that are not solved but compounded. The idea of a "goodness" that is not directed toward men is somewhat disturbing; nor is it comforting to learn that cruel people are kind to animals (the promise of "nevertheless" is certainly not fulfilled by the observation that follows it), especially when Busbechius' report reveals that this kindness manifests itself at the expense of men. This little story finally redounds to no one's credit. While the Turks are obviously the objects of the surface irony, their victim is not exactly a sympathetic figure; he was after all strangling a helpless animal, and, for fun ("in a waggishness"). The vaunted "inclination to goodness" which introduced this sequence seems less and less verifiable and the subsequent admission that "errors . . . may be committed" in this "virtue of goodness" is a particularly fine example of Bacon's deadpan understatement.

It is after all this that we meet with the Italians' proverb and Machiavelli's "plaine termes," and their dismissal is hardly as effective as it was when the main argument was presented without benefit of "supporting" examples. Ungracious to say that some men are so good that they are good for nothing? "Generous" might be a better word in the light of the "good men" whose actions have been reported to us so far. And Machiavelli's indictment is much more to the point, that is, more than "almost" plain, now that we have encountered the Turks and the Christian boy. When Bacon announces that he will now turn to the "errors of an habite so excellent," the response is likely to be something of a double take. "Errors" are all that we have been seeing; there has been no mention, strangely enough, of those whose "inclination to goodness" issues in "virtuous deeds." Later, Bacon refers again to this "habite of goodness," but only to preface a consideration of "the other side," men of "natural malignity," who "do not affect the good of others (404)." The "other side," however, is the only side the essay has been surveying. Like "Of Friendship" and "Of Truth" and "Of Fortune," "Of Goodness and Goodness of Nature" seems to be asserting the illusoriness of its subject.

More than that, although "goodness" (as it is defined by the biblical injunction "Be Ye Perfect") is at first the standard of judgment, it is finally a questionable standard, given the truth about "what men do." "The example of God teacheth the lesson truly," declares Bacon (404), but in what follows, the example of God is subtly (and not so subtly) altered to conform to the actions of men:

> *He sendeth his rain, and maketh his sun to shine equally upon the just and unjust;* but he doth not rain wealth, nor shine honour and virtues, upon men equally. Common benefits are to be communicate with all; but peculiar benefits with choice. And beware how in making the portraiture thou breakest the pattern. For divinity maketh the love of ourselves the pattern; the love of our neighbors but the portraiture. *Sell all thou hast, and give it to the poor, and follow me:* but sell not all thou hast except thou come and follow me; that is, except thou have a vocation wherein thou mayest do as much good with little means as with great; for otherwise in feeding the streams thou driest the fountain (404).

There is more than a hint here that the lessons and sayings of the Bible may be too "high" for its intended pupils who are for the most part naturally malign. That is, of course, regrettable—"Such dispositions are the very errours of human nature (404)"—and yet it is fact, and fact must be taken into account and not ignored, for "they are the fittest timber to make great politiques of; like to knee timber, that is good for ships, that are ordained to be tossed (404–405)." We are all, of course, such "knee timbers," for we are all ordained to be "tossed." The "errours" of human nature are also the essence of human nature. Once again Bacon has passed from "theological and philosophical" truth to the truth "of civil business," and once again theological and philosophical truth has been compromised and to some extent dismissed.

In the concluding paragraph (which was written for the 1625 edition), Bacon finally does turn to the "parts and signs of goodness (405)," but they are signs in potential rather than existent signs, and they come to us weighed down with the qualification of conditionals:

> The parts and signs of goodness are many. If a man be gracious and courteous to strangers, it shews he is a citizen of the world, and that his heart is no island cut off from other lands, but a continent that joins to them. If he be compassionate towards the afflictions of others, it shews that his heart is like the noble tree that is wounded itself when it gives the balm. If he easily pardons and remits offences, it shews that his mind is planted above injuries; so that he cannot be shot. If he be thankful for small benefits, it shews that he weighs men's minds, and not their trash. But above all, if he have St. Paul's perfection, that he would wish to be an *anathema* from Christ for the salvation of his brethren, it shews much of a divine nature, and a kind of conformity with Christ himself (405).

*If* a man "be gracious and courteous"; *if* he "be compassionate towards the affliction of others"; *if* he "easily pardons and remits offences (405)." The last "if"—"*if* he have St. Paul's perfection . . . and a kind of conformity with Christ himself"—is particularly damaging to the surface argument, since it posits an ideal no man, and especially not the men who have been seen in this essay, can live up to. "Goodness" is indeed, it seems, the "character of the deity" and man, for the most part *is* "without it" and therefore "a busie, mischievous, wretched thing; no better than a kind of vermin." Here, as in other essays, the added material has the effect of making the reader go back to the opening sentences which now mean quite differently than they did at first.

It is important to note what Bacon is not doing. He is not rejecting the *ideal* of goodness, but pointing out how far from it are the practices of men. It is this that distinguishes him from Machiavelli, or at least from the Machiavelli of popular reputation, a cynic who counsels self-interest at the expense of morality. Bacon is neither immoral or amoral, but *pre*moral. He accepts the moral ideal as a point of departure, and measures everything against it. The conclusions that follow, then, are conclusions to matters of fact, not directives for future action. When Bacon has finished, the ideal remains; what does not remain is any illusion we may have had about the ease of living up to it. And without illusions, Bacon would argue, our chances of doing just that are much better. That is, an understanding of the difficulty of controlling love or of the near impossibility of conforming to the goodness of Christ will serve us in better stead than all the proverbs and "witty imprecations" man formulates in order to hide from himself the complexity of the real world.

So, too, with the world of "business." The first version of the essay "Of Ambition" ends by advising against employing those who evidence this character trait: "let Princes and States chuse such ministers, as are more sensible of duty, then of rising (*Sp.,* VI, 568)." Bacon does allow that ambitious men can be used if they are well "handled," but since such men are commonly too "busie" when they are advanced and "secretly discontent" when they are "checked," "it is good not to use such natures at all."

In 1625, however, this simple rule is followed by a complicating "But": "But since we have said it were good not to use men of ambitious natures, except it be upon necessity, it is fit we speak in what cases they are of necessity (466)." Bacon reaffirms his admirably moral conclusion, but then allows it to be swallowed up by its exception. Despite the suggestion to the contrary, there has been no previous mention of "necessity"; but the mere repetition of the word is sufficient to create a memory of it in the reader's mind; and from this point on, considerations of "necessity" dominate the essay. (The extent to which this involves an arbitrary reversal of direction is obvious if the transition sentence is read without the parenthetical "except it be upon necessity.")

> But since we have said it were good not to use men of ambitious natures, except it be upon necessity, it is fit we speak in what cases they are of necessity. Good commanders in the wars must be taken, be they never so ambitious; for the use of their service dispenseth with the rest; and to take a soldier without ambition is to pull off his spurs. There is also great use of ambitious men in being screens to princes in matters of danger and envy; for no man will take that part, except he be like a seeled dove, that mounts and mounts because he cannot see about him. There is use also of ambitious men in pulling down the greatness of any subject that overtops; as Tiberius used Macro in the pulling down of Sejanus. Since therefore they must be used in such cases, there resteth to speak how they are to be bridled, that they may be less dangerous.

From "it were good not to use men of ambitious natures," we move in a few lines to "there is . . . great use of ambitious men" and finally to "therefore they must be used." The one example Bacon brings in—"Tiberius used Macro in the pulling down of Sejanus"—reinforces the note of uncompromising utility, and the earlier strictures against ambition and ambitious men seem forgotten.

But the conclusion to the 1612 essay, high-minded and highly moral, is retained in 1625. It, of course, has less force than in 1612 —one cannot help but wonder how "generally" princes do in fact choose ". . . ministers . . . more sensible of duty then of rising"—but nevertheless it is there, and the judgment that informs it exerts a pressure that is not wholly canceled out by the more practical urgings of "necessity." Again we see that the unique quality of Bacon's late essays inheres in the accommodation within them of disparate and contradictory visions. The magistral moralisms which open and often close an essay are severely qualified by what transpires in the interim, yet they are never abandoned; they are qualified as "fact," as an accurate description of what men do, but not as a *desideratum,* as an accepted statement of what men ought to do. And the result is an experience characterized by backing and filling, considering and rejecting, an experience in which the mind is often asked to go in two (or more) directions at once.

This experience can be described variously as "demanding," "stimulating," "anxiety creating," "mind expanding," or simply "scientific." Some of the words that will not do are "comfortable," "satisfying," "restful"; and indeed the smallest of Bacon's changes is designed to assure their continuing inapplicability. In 1597 and 1612 the first sentence of "Of Suitors" displays all the virtues and vices of an extreme Senecanism:

> Manie ill matters are undertaken, and many good matters with ill mindes (*Sp.,* VI, 528).

This is a veritable handbook of schemes and iterative figures— alliteration, antimetabole (ill-matters: matters-ill), anaphora, isocolon—which all combine to lock the reader in, organizing the thought for him and leaving him very little, if anything, to do. In 1625 the neat points have been dispersed; the prose is looser and the rhythms less compelling and directing:

> Many ill matters and projects are undertaken; and private suits do putefry the public good. Many good matters are undertaken with bad minds; I mean not only corrupt minds, but crafty minds, that intend not performance (495).

The doubling of "matters" to "matters and projects" adds nothing to the sense; its only effect is negative, the extra three beats rob the utterance of some of its conciseness. This is not to say that the prose is unpatterned—the two members of the period are of equal length and the alliteration in the second member is heavy and noticeable—but the patterns do not lock together as they did in 1612 and consequently they are finally not controlling. "Many good matters" provides an obvious "point" to "Many ill matters," but the substitution of "bad minds" for "ill minds" dissipates the force of the figure; the contrast now seems to be between "public good" and "bad minds," but this opposition is, in terms of the thought, "pointless," and it remains undeveloped. In general, the verbal patterns we can discern by stepping back from the prose do not register strongly in the act of reading, in part because they are obscured by larger rhetorical movements. A student of Bacon's earlier essays might expect him to hang everything on the triple repetition of "minds"—"bad minds," "corrupt minds," "crafty minds"—but, in fact, that pattern is hardly noticed by a reader who is busy attending to Bacon's *correctio,* ("I mean . . ."); the form of the thought demands a stress on the final clause—"that intend not performance"—and consequently the mind does not even take in "bad minds," "corrupt minds," and "crafty minds" as a unit.

Vickers has remarked on Bacon's "willingness," in the later essays, "to jettison a neat structure (223)," but he attributes this to a concern for objective truth:

> In some cases an expansion or correction of an idea may not fit into a symmetrical mould, and . . . we find Bacon deliberately abandoning a balanced structure in order to deepen meaning . . . . Another form taken by this triumph of meaning over mere patterning is the addition of important new quotations or historical examples, which are also allowed to disrupt a pattern (222–223).

It seems to me, however, that Bacon's disrupting of patterns is reader- rather than information-oriented. It would have been entirely within his literary resources to have built symmetrical structures large enough to accommodate "new quotations or historical examples." That he did not choose to do so is, I think, evidence of a more critical attitude toward such structures than Vickers would allow. Symmetry and balance are mnemonic devices, facilitating recall and subsequent reexpression; they fix things in the mind and tend to give things so fixed the status of absolute truths. In other words, they encourage the intellectual complacency Bacon continually inveighs against, and, conversely, a prose free of them, or at least free of their tyranny, is more likely to encourage further inquiry. Very little of the meaning is deepened in the revised version of this sentence from "Of Suitors." Very little, if any new information has been added. Instead the old meaning and the old information now seem less final and complete than they did in 1612, because the changes in the form enclosing them has changed the way in which they are received. That is, a neat and satisfying conciseness has been replaced by something at once laxer and less enervating. There are no coincidences of sound and sense stress to rest in; no "chiming points" demand our unthinking assent; and consequently, we do not feel, as we did in 1612, that the matter has been settled, but rather that we are moving, with Bacon, toward some future settling and therefore toward a more settled form.

Nor is it accurate to say that Bacon abandons balanced structures in the later essays; what he abandons is the tight control such structures can exercise over a reader's thought processes; and he does this by upsetting the perfect correspondence between them and what they contain. The result is an experience that is neither constricting nor completely (and irresponsibly) open, an experience that is the product of a tension between what we can call the inner and outer forms of an essay. The dynamics of this tension can be seen clearly if we place side by side two versions of a sentence from "Of Marriage and Single Life":

| | |
|---|---|
| Certainly, Wife and Children are a kinde of Discipline of humanity; and single men<br><br><br><br><br>                    are more cruell and hard hearted good to make severe Inquisitors. | Certainly, wife and children are a kind of discipline of humanity; and single men, though they be many times more charitable, because their means are less exhaust; yet, on the other side, they are more cruel and hardhearted (good to make severe inquisitors) because their tenderness is not so oft called upon.[19] |

In 1612, the expectations aroused by "Certainly" are more than fulfilled: everything in the sentence is tied to the central opposition of married and single men; the balanced rhythms of the two members lead the reader's eye to places of obvious point and con-

---

[19] The arrangement is taken from Arber, *A Harmony,* pp. 268–269.

trast—those with wife and children, single men; humanity,
cruell and hard hearted—and the extra clause—"good to make
severe Inquisitors"—serves as a restful and cadenced close to an
assertion that is not in any way qualified. In 1625 nothing is de-
leted, and despite the addition of more than half again as much
material, the outlines of the original structure remain clearly visible. But that structure and the argument it processes no longer
have the reader's undivided attention because they no longer constitute the whole of his experience. That is, while the rhythmic
pattern of the sentence is retained, and along with it the central
opposition of married to single men, the reader's experience of
that pattern, and therefore of that opposition, is interrupted as he
makes his way through the qualifying clauses that now follow
"and single men." As a result, the distinction on which the sentence
ultimately rests loses much of its firmness: for a moment single
men seem more humane than those with wife and children; but
then that humanity is revealed to be the accidental by-product of
an economic difference ("their means are less exhaust") and the
pendulum swings back in the direction of married men. At this
point, the phrase "yet, on the other side," is more confusing than
directing. What exactly is the other side? What side are we turning from? As in 1612, there are only two sides, but in the course
of explaining them, Bacon has brought them closer together, so
that at this late date in the sentence the reader is less sure of his
ground than he might like to be. Of course the confusion is only
momentary, and the larger outlines of the argument soon come
into focus again; but the damage has been done, and however
firmly the sentence concludes, those few moments when the reader
is side-tracked in a cul-de-sac have occurred and they do contribute to the total effect.

As a matter of fact, the sentence does not conclude firmly at all,
but tails off into still another qualification of the main point:
"because their tenderness is not so oft called upon." This implies
that if single men were called on to be tender, they would respond
in such a way as to weaken further the basis for distinguishing
between them and men with wives and children. In 1612 the fitness
of single men to be Inquisitors provided a witty conclusion to a
univocal argument; now however that observation is relegated to

parenthetical status and the emphasis of the sentence finally falls on the reserves of tenderness such men probably have within them.

What we have, then, are two discursive structures in a single space, and to the extent they pull against each other or point in different directions, the reader's experience of them is strenuous and, what is more important, inconclusive. Not that one cancels the other out; rather, neither finally carries the day, with the result that the reader remains suspended between the conclusions each of them is separately urging, and ends by asking a question instead of assenting to an argument. In 1612 the distinction between married and single men is absolute and unchallenged; in 1625, that distinction is blurred; but, because the structure that carried it is retained (although it is no longer controlling), the possibility of someday arriving at such a distinction remains a part of the sentence's assertion. That is, the presence in the new sentence of the old structure, including the introductory "Certainly," asserts the continuing relevance of Bacon's goal—the specifying of the relationship between married and single men—while the material that strains against that structure and resists its organizing pressure tells us the task is not yet complete.

I have made much of Bacon's insistence that the form of a presentation not suggest more finality than the state of knowledge presently warrants; but there is another side to his strictures. Excesses in systems, he explains in the *Novum Organum,* are of two kinds: "the first being manifest in those who are ready in deciding, and render sciences dogmatic and magisterial; the other in those who deny that we can know anything, and so introduce a wandering kind of inquiry that leads to nothing (lxvii)." One school begins with general laws to which all particulars are referred for judgment; the other believes the discovery of general laws to be beyond the powers of man and so proceeds haphazardly from isolated particular to isolated particular. One school "is so busied with the particles that it hardly attends to the structure [of both the world and the inquiry]; while the others are so lost in admiration of the structure that they do not penetrate to the simplicity of nature [they ride roughshod over distinctions that do not sort well with their preconceptions] (lvii)." The twin dangers, then, are complacency and despair, the facile assumption that everything is known and the equally facile (and debilitating) assumption that nothing is (or can be) known: and by refusing either to sacrifice the observable facts to his structure or to wholly abandon that structure when some of the observable facts will not be accommodated within it, Bacon avoids both, fostering hope and a healthy skepticism at the same time. In its 1625 form, then, this sentence from "Of Marriage and Single Life" is a kind of promissory note, assuring the reader that a more perfect knowledge awaits him in the future, while preventing him from resting too comfortably in the knowledge he has attained in the present.

What is true of this one sentence—an example that has perhaps been asked to assume a greater burden than it can bear—is true also of whole essays, and accounts for what has troubled so many critics, the simultaneous presence in the 1625 edition of an insistent formal organization and a body of material that does not always sit easily within its confines. R. S. Crane posed the problem succinctly in 1923:

> The real problem is not to account for the persistence of the aphoristic style, but rather to explain the gradual emergence alongside it, in the essays of 1612 and 1625, of a style in which "discourse of illustration," "recitals of examples," and "discourse of connexion and order" were no longer "cut off," but on the contrary multiplied until they became the most striking elements in the general effect (101).

Crane's explanation, that Bacon merely adopted more and more completely the style which he had used in the *Advancement of Learning* (103), begs the question, while Brian Vickers's contention that "the increased use of *partitio*" or "singling out of parts" points to "an overwhelming desire for clarity (220)" has no relation at all to the experience of these latter essays. Curiously enough the most helpful comments come from those who wish that Bacon had left well enough alone. A. W. Green, while admitting that in the 1612 and 1625 editions "transitions are better," complains of a "lamentable loss of coherence and power"; essays "end weakly," "simple balance and antithesis . . . is destroyed through excessive verbiage," "unlike elements are joined and chronology is ignored (81–84)." Despite its negativity, this is good criticism simply because it is a response to what is actually there: there *is* in 1625 a loss of the tight coherence that characterizes some of the earlier essays; endings *are* weak, trailing off into anticlimactic and almost irrelevant aphorisms; the simple balance and antithesis *are* made less simple and directing, if not "destroyed"; and, of course, "unlike elements" *are* joined to produce the strenuous and disquieting reading experience I have been describing. Even more penetrating, although similarly negative, are these remarks by Jacob Zeitlin:

> Subjects which in the earlier editions were treated from the purely moral point of view become strongly tinctured with worldly considerations. Trains of ideal injunctions are tagged with maxims of questionable integrity. Solemn reflections give way to baldly analytic or coldly intellectual consideration of the same topics. Time and again the whole feeling of an essay is transformed (512).
>
> When he came to read over one of his essays, new thoughts would suggest themselves directly from his immediate experience, and these he would insert, often without reference to their incongruity in spirit with what he had already written. In this way compositions which were originally pervaded by an atmosphere of clear moral stimulation were overlaid with considerations of immediate practical utility, till their primary inspiration became altogether obscured (513–514).

The seeds of my own argument are obviously present in Zeitlin's observations. We see much the same evidence but draw opposite conclusions from it, both with respect to the total effect of the revisions and the degree of Bacon's control. Most importantly, I cannot agree that the "primary inspiration" of the earlier essays "became altogether obscured." A truer description of what happens is (potentially) available in Zeitlin's own vocabulary. Words like "tincture" and "overlay"—the noun is sometimes used to designate a sheet laid over a map to add or emphasize certain features—suggest a mutual highlighting of contradictory perspectives rather than the total eclipse of one by the other. There is, I

think, a split between Zeitlin's responses, which accord perfectly
with my own, and the interpretation he builds on them, and this is
particularly evident when he turns to specific essays:

> *Of Cunning* was in 1612 distinguished for the uniform
> clarity of its moral attitude. In 1625 it is three times as long,
> the additions consisting of instruction in all the arts and
> tricks of cunning use . . . . There are about a score of
> such maxims, for which the original essay serves merely as
> a kind of ornamental framework (512–513).

The most revealing phrase in this piece of criticism is "ornamental
framework," for it implies that whatever remains of the original
essay somehow does not count; but Zeitlin's own discomfort
points in the opposite direction; the juxtaposition of the original
"framework" and the maxims of cunning throws both into sharper
relief and, more importantly, forces the reader to think about the
relationship between them, as Zeitlin is so obviously doing in this
passage.

Nor is the moral attitude of the 1612 version so uniformly
clear as all that. In fact, there is more than a hint in this brief
paragraph of what the essay will become in 1625:

> Wee take *Cunning* for a sinister or crooked *Wisdome:*
> and certainely there is a great difference betweene a cun-
> ning man, and a wise man: not onely in point of honesty,
> but in point of ability. There be that can pack the cards
> and yet cannot play well. So there are some, that are good
> in canuasses and factions, that are otherwise weake men.
> Againe, it is one thing to vnderstand persons, and another
> thing to vnderstand matters: for many are perfect in mens
> humors, that are not greatly capable of the reall part of
> business; which is the constitution of one, that hath studied
> men more than bookes. Such men are fitter for practise,
> then for counsell, and they are good but in their owne
> Alley; turne them to new men, and they haue lost their
> aime. So as the old rule to know a foole from a wise man;
> *Mitte ambos nudos ad ignotos & videbis;* doth scarse hold
> for them. Euen in businesse there are some that know the

resorts and fals of busines, that cannot sinke into the maine
of it: like a house that hath conuenient staires and entries,
but neuer a faire roome. Therefore you shall see them finde
out pretty looses in the conclusion, but are no waies able to
examine or debate matters: and yet commonly they take
aduantage of their inability, & would be thought wits of
direction. Some build rather vpon abusing others, and as
wee now say, putting trickes vpon them, then vpon sound-
nesse of their owne proceedings. But *Salomon* saith, *Prudens aduertit ad gressus suos: stultus diuertit ad dolos.*
Very many are the differences betweene cunning and wisdome: and it were a good deed to set them downe: for that
nothing doth more hurte in state then that cunning men
passe for wise (*Sp.*, VI, 546–547).

The oppositions established in the opening sentence—between
cunning and wisdom, deceitful men and honest men, men of poor
abilities and able men—promise a comfortable, almost self-orga-
nizing reading experience; and nothing in the two following sentences suggests that this promise will not be kept. But with the
word "Againe," the sharp lines of Bacon's argument begin to
blur; for while the pattern of opposition ("one thing"–"another
thing") is continued, the components within that pattern are not
related in all the ways we have come to expect. Understanding
persons and understanding matters are certainly different things,
but are they as different as packing the cards and playing well?
One does not distinguish between them in "point of honesty,"
and in "point of ability" they would seem to be equally necessary.
The second half of the sentence is even more problematical. Does
the "which" on which the last member pivots refer to those who
are, or to those who are not, "capable of the reall part of businesse"? If the former, then perfection in "mens humors" is
being contrasted to the study of men, a distinction, it would seem,
without a difference; if the latter, then the real part of business is
to study books, a sentiment one hardly associates with Bacon.
The ambiguity directly affects the interpretation of the following
sentences. Who exactly are the men "fitter for practise, then for
counsell"? And for that matter, what do "practise and counsell"

have to do with cunning and wisdom, the large contraries on which the essay is supposedly based? Being fit for practice is hardly a disadvantage in "point of ability," and in "point of honesty" there seems no way to choose between them. If the "old rule" is of no help in distinguishing "a foole from a wise man," neither is this essay, despite the suggestion to the contrary in the opening and closing sentences.

Still, one can see how Zeitlin finds the essay uniformly clear; in this early version the unit of meaning that calls attention to itself is the sentence; and for the most part each sentence taken by itself (and the aphoristic form into which they are cast encourages this) seems perfectly coherent. The inconsistencies and non-sequiturs which reveal themselves when one steps back from the prose go largely unnoticed because there is no larger structure or formal organization pressuring the reader to look to the connections (or lack of same) between sentences; and the dominant impression is, as Zeitlin maintains, of a consistently "moral" attitude.

In 1625, on the other hand, the essay has been given a visible and insistent superstructure—an introduction, a conclusion, and a middle whose "points" are apparently set down in some order; yet strangely enough, the result is not more "clarity," but a clearer, that is, sharper, sense of the confusions and tensions that exist in potential in 1612. The first paragraph incorporates most of the old essay except for a few sentences that are left out (they will surface later), so that Bacon can go directly from the "old rule," which scarcely holds, to a statement of intention: "And because these cunning men are like haberdashers of small wares, it is not amiss to set forth their shop (428)." Whatever doubts the reader may have had about the straightforwardness of the essay should now be laid to rest, since Bacon has taken him into his confidence by laying out the plan of what is to follow. This is the technique of "division" or *"partitio,"* designed, as Vickers points out, to produce "a curious feeling of recognition as the development conforms to its preordained shape, a sense of inevitability (44)." The psychological advantage, especially to one who has a thesis to prove, is explained by Bacon himself in "The Case *De Rego Inconsulto":* "before I deduce, I will give you at the first entrance a form or abstract of them [the part of his argument] that fore-thinking what you shall hear, the proof may strike upon your minds as prepared (*Sp.,* VII, 689)." But however faithfully Bacon keeps this promise in his legal writings, in the *Essays* he uses *partitio* much as he uses example and *sententia,* to wean the reader away from his "forethinkings" and from whatever his mind had been prepared to accept—in this case the essay's distinction between cunning and wise men. What we expect as "the small wares" of this shop are set out is further support for the indictment of "cunning," both as a policy and a point of morality. What we get is something quite different: "It is a point of cunning to wait upon him with whom you speak, with your eye; as the Jesuits give it in precept: for there be many wise men that have secret hearts and transparent countenances. Yet this would be done with a demure abasing of your eye sometimes, as the Jesuits also do use (428–429)." On the surface, this is a continuation of the previous paragraph: the attribution of the precepts of cunning to Jesuitical practice is not likely to recommend them to an English audience; but almost imperceptibly the direction of the argument shifts; as the "point" is opened, it detaches itself somewhat from the preceding statement and no longer seems to be the exclusive property of the Jesuits. In fact it seems to be Bacon himself who remarks that "there be many wise men that have secret hearts and transparent countenances," an observation that represents a reversal of the relationship previously established: "wise men" are now the victims of "cunning men" rather than their superiors. At the same time, the distance between those who deal in these wares and the reader is narrowed by the repeated use of the forms of the second person pronoun: "you speak," "your eye," "your eye." Technically this is an impersonal, third person "you," but the effect is to place the reader in the position of one who is receiving advice, where before he had been encouraged to assume the role of judge. In this (almost subliminal) context, "would be done," referring back to the Jesuits, becomes something close to *"should* be done."

At this point the word "cunning" disappears; the reader must supply it in the third paragraph which opens with an elliptical, "Another is" and in the succeeding paragraphs there is no reason for him to recall it at all. Without it, the survey of strategies becomes a series of commands: "when you have anything to obtain . . . you entertain and amuse the party with whom you deal with some other discourse (429). If a man would cross a business . . . let him pretend to wish it well (429)." This change in the relationship between the material and the reader is accompanied by a shift in emphasis from what is moral or admirable to what works. At first, the causal basis for a precept is specified only after the situation has been set up:

> entertain and amuse the party with whom you deal with some other discourse; *that he may not be too much awake to make objections* (429, emphasis mine).
>
> If a man would cross a business . . . let him pretend to wish it well, and *move it himself in such sort as may foil it* (429, emphasis mine).
>
> The breaking off in the midst of that one was about to say . . . *breeds a greater appetite in him with whom you confer* (429, emphasis mine).

But in the seventh paragraph (sixth point), the sequence is reversed as if Bacon were now openly acknowledging the new priorities that he has established surreptitiously: "*And because it works better* when any thing seemeth to be gotten from you by question, than if you offer it of yourself, you may lay a bait for a question (429, emphasis mine)." And the transformation from moral essay to a handbook for would-be intriguers is complete, when the seventh precept is prefaced by the words "it is *good* (429)." The world of the opening sentences, where "there is a great difference betweene a cunning man and a wise" is now only a dim memory.

But that world is recalled, unexpectedly, by the reintroduction of the operative phrase: "it is a point of cunning" ("to borrow the name of the world"). Of course the phrase has a somewhat different ring than it did when the burden of the essay appeared to be the weakness of such practices, but it does serve to remind us of that stage in our understanding. Once again, we see Bacon forcing his reader to be aware of two perspectives on a given subject and aware, too, of the difficulties of reconciling them. From here on, the moral view (what men ought to do) and the practical view (what men do) proceed in tandem, vying for the reader's allegiance. On balance, the latter exerts the greater pressure, especially since Bacon (uncharacteristically) fleshes it out with some personal (but strangely impersonal)[20] reminiscences: "I knew one that"; "I knew another that"; "I knew two that were competitors for the secretary's place in queen Elizabeth's time." This last anecdote illustrates its point (of cunning) at the reader's expense:

> one of them said, That to be a secretary *in the declination of a monarchy* was a ticklish thing, and that he did not affect it: the other straight caught up those words, and discoursed with divers of his friends, that he had no reason to desire to be the secretary in the declination of a monarchy. The first man took hold of it and found means it was told the Queen; who, hearing of a *declination of a monarchy,* took it so ill, as she would never after hear of the other's suit (430).

By the time the reader reaches the end of the story he is almost as much in the dark about the true source of the statement as was Elizabeth, and when Bacon observes that "it is not easy, when such a matter passed beyond two, to make it appear from which of them it first moved and began (430)," the difficulty is something we can attest to from experience.

The apogee in the ascendancy of the "cunning ethic" is reached with the words: "It is a good point of cunning" ("for a man to shape the answer he would have in his own words"). Here is no "sinister or crooked wisdom," no "weak" policy, but a piece of worldly advice tendered by one interested party to another. The image of the cunning man suddenly takes on something of the heroic: his labors require "great patience"; one of his ploys is described as "bold"; we last see him in the act of discovering (laying open) the identity of one who had changed his name (431); he is the exposer of deceit rather than a deceiver.

---

[20] The *Essays* are remarkable for the *absence* of a personal voice. This is not surprising however when one remembers that Bacon is not interested in the individual mind (it is the enemy, the house of idols), but in the harnessing of all minds to the method of disinterested observation.

It is from this height that we are brought down by the penultimate paragraph: "But these small wares and petty points of cunning are infinite, and it were a good deed to make a list of them; for that nothing doth hurt in a state more than that cunning men pass for wise (431)." A reader of the 1612 edition of the essays might recognize this as the last sentence of "Of Cunning," somewhat altered and slightly expanded. But in 1625 the effect is totally different; rather than a promise of future action ("it were a good deed to make a list of them") this is an ironic comment on an action that has already been taken. The list *has* been made in the course of this very essay with the result that the reader has become aware, through his own responses to the prose, of just how successfully cunning men do, in fact, pass for wise. If nothing "doth hurt in a state more," then the state whose affairs have occasioned Bacon's observations and the reader's nods of recognition is in bad shape indeed. In 1612 it was suggested that a fuller consideration of "cunning" would yield us some measure of protection against it; but now that we have that consideration, our only gain is a sharper (and felt) sense of the complexity of the problem. This is still another of the essays whose conclusion sends us back with new eyes to its opening. Upon rereading, the important words in "Wee take Cunning for a sinister or crooked wisdome (428)" are "Wee take"; for the thrust of the expanded essay is toward a reassessment of everything we take cunning (or anything else) to be, and especially of the simple and sharp distinctions—in point of ability, wisdom, and honesty— that are put forward in the first few sentences.

It is to these distinctions that Bacon returns in the final paragraph, and specifically to that portion of the earlier essay he had omitted in the first paragraph of this one:

> But certainly some there are that know the resorts and falls of business, that cannot sink into the main of it; like a house that hath convenient stairs and entries, but never a fair room. Therefore you shall see them find out pretty looses in the conclusion, but are no ways able to examine or debate matters. And yet commonly they take advantage of their inability, and would be thought wits of direction.

Some build rather upon the abusing of others, and (as we now say) *putting tricks upon them,* than upon soundness of their own proceedings. But Salomon saith, *Prudens advertit ad gressus suos: stultus divertit ad dolos* [The wise man taketh heed to his steps: the fool turneth aside to deceits] (*Sp.,* VI, 431).

Of course these sentiments, while they are unexceptionable, are of questionable value in the light of Bacon's anatomy of cunning. Specifically they will be of little help to anyone (including the reader) who is concerned to avoid the hurt the actions of cunning men can occasion. In 1612 Solomon's proverb seemed an adequate rejoinder to those who "build . . . upon the abusing of others," but now it strikes us as ineffectual and naively simplistic, an "old rule" that "doth scarcely hold," a "poor saying." In fact, the entire paragraph is merely a collection of "old rules" whose inadequacies are painfully apparent in the context of the reader's new knowledge.

One can see, I think, that Zeitlin's phrase "ornamental framework" does not really describe the role played by the original essay in its expanded form. "Envelope" might be a better word since the bifurcated essay physically surrounds and holds in (with some difficulty) the new material. Or perhaps the relationship between the two versions might be clarified if we think of the essay as a sentence, the beginning and end of which are now separated by a long parenthesis whose effect is to profoundly alter and complicate the significance of the whole and all of its parts. But the terms in which we conceive of the relationship are unimportant so long as we realize that in the conflation everything is gained and nothing is lost, except the momentary satisfaction involved in listening to the recital of commonplaces that support the illusions men hold about the ways of the world.

"OF FRIENDSHIP"

Anyone who writes on the development of Bacon's *Essays* must come to terms, sooner or later, with "Of Friendship." For here is the most radical of the revisions Bacon undertakes and a finished product that speaks to every one of the issues raised in this chapter. The 1612 version of this essay is a single paragraph in which the joys of friendship are (apparently) celebrated:

> There is no greater desert or wildernes then to bee without true friends. For without friendship, society is but meeting. And as it is certaine, that in bodies inanimate, vnion strengthneth any naturall motion, and weakeneth any violent motion; So amongst men, friendship multiplieth ioies, and diuideth griefes. Therefore whosoeuer wanteth fortitude, let him worshippe *Friendship*. For the yoke of *Friendship* maketh the yoke of *fortune* more light. There bee some whose liues are, as if they perpetually plaid vpon a stage, disguised to all others, open onely to themselues. But perpetuall dissimulation is painfull; and hee that is all *Fortune,* and no *Nature* is an exquisite *Hierling.* Liue not in continuall smother, but take some friends with whom to communicate. It will unfold thy vnderstanding; it will euaporate thy affections; it will prepare thy businesse. A man may keepe a corner of his minde from his friend, and it be but to witnesse to himselfe, that it is not vpon facility, but vpon true vse of friendship that hee imparteth himselfe. Want of true friends, as it is the reward of perfidious natures; so is it an imposition vpon great fortunes. The one deserue it, the other cannot scape it. And therefore it is good to retaine sincerity, and to put it into the reckoning of *Ambition,* that the higher one goeth, the fewer true friends he shall haue. Perfection of friendship, is but a speculation. It is friendship, when a man can say to himselfe, I loue this man without respect of vtility. I am open hearted to him, I single him frō the generality of those with whom I liue; I make him a portion of my owne wishes (*Sp.,* VI, 558–559).

The first sentence is typical both in its declarative directness and its unambiguity of attitude: "There is no greater desert or wildernes then to bee without true friends." Only a captious reader would pause to note that the negative cast of this sentence turns us away from friendship to its opposite. It is after all perfectly good

strategy to exalt a good by pointing out the disadvantages of being without it. Moreover, there are, in the paragraph, a number of
straightforwardly commendatory statements: "friendship multi-
plieth joies and diuideth griefes." "It will unfold thy vnderstand-
ing; it will euaporate thy affections; it will prepare thy businesse."
"It is friendship when a man can say to himselfe, I love this man
without respect of vtility. I am open hearted to him, I single him
frō the generality of those with whom I liue; I make him a portion of my owne wishes." The cadenced force of such declarations
is sufficient to account for Green's characterization of this two
hundred-and-seventy word piece as "a masterpiece of simplicity,
good taste, and restrained unity (83)." One should be wary, however, of attributing simplicity, even of an attractive sort, to Bacon.
There is here, as in so many of the *Essays,* more than meets the
casual eye or strikes the inattentive ear. Where Green sees a
"restrained unity," I see a rhetorical or spurious unity which succeeds (if that is the word) by not calling attention to the discordant elements it fails to harmonize. The source of this spurious
unity is the series of logical connectives—"for," "so," "therefore,"
"but"—whose presence creates the illusion of a running argument.
The reader acquiesces in the illusion partly because the single sentences of the essay are individually coherent and rhythmically
self-contained; they bear the burden of the reader's attention and
the connectives become the means of getting from one discretely
satisfying experience to another. In short, the form of the presentation works against the impulse to further inquiry which Bacon
so values.

As critics rather than readers, however, we have the option of
pausing where the prose would encourage us to move on; and
when we do so pause, the strains and ambivalences which the reading experience tends to obscure become more readily discernible.
"Whosoever wanteth fortitude, let him worshippe *Friendship*"
seems (sounds) a fine sentiment until one realizes that it equates
a need for friendship with weakness; and in the following sentence—"For the yoke of *Friendship* maketh the yoke of Fortune more light"—the play on words ("yoke" as a joining and
"yoke" as burden) faces both directions. The advice to "take

some friends with whom to communicate" sounds more like a medical prescription than an encomium and the advantages of following that advice are frankly utilitarian: "It will unfold thy understanding; it will evaporate thy affections; it will prepare thy businesse." Zeitlin argues that in the 1625 version of this essay, "the note of generous feeling is lost" and in its place there is an emphasis on the "uses of friendship (513)"; but the note of generous feeling is hardly sounded at all in 1612, and considerations of utility are very much in evidence, if one stops to look for them. In this light, the final sentences of the essay take on an irony they do not have in isolation. It may be friendship when a man can say to himself I love this man without respect of utility, but there are no reports of such men or such friendships in this short paragraph. The negative cast of the opening sentence is a harbinger of what is to come, and one might argue that the true center of the essay is not the smoothly rounded period that concludes it, but the less sanguine sentiments that period finally overwhelms: "the higher one goeth, the fewer true friends he shall have. Perfection of friendship, is but a speculation."

The preceding paragraph is not true to the experience of the essay as we have it. Rather it is an account of what the essay would be like were it so constructed as to allow a more self-consciously analytical response; and it is thus a perfect introduction to the longer and more elaborate version of 1625. This essay is, on its surface, one of the most conventionally and obviously organized of the entire collection. An introductory paragraph which announces the theme is followed by a discussion of three carefully distinguished "fruits of Friendship" and by a summarizing closing statement: "I have given the rule, where a man cannot fitly play his own part; if he have not a friend, he may quit the stage." The effect of this very simple and very obvious organization is to make the reader aware of the author's efforts to order his material and therefore more alert to the failure of such efforts. The chief difference between the two versions, then, is not their respective lengths (although this too is important), but the demands each makes on its reader; in one case the experience is passive, requiring little more than a succession of perfunctory (and unrelated) assents; while in the other, the reader joins with the speaker in an attempt to make manageable sense of a formidable body of information.

This difference can be nicely illustrated by the opening sentences of the two essays:

> There is no greater desert or wilderness then to bee without true friends.

> It had been hard for him that spake it to have put more truth and untruth together in few words than in that speech, *Whosoever is delighted in solitude is either a wild beast or a God* (*Sp.*, VI, 437).

The first of these is strongly declarative and, since it is unqualified, the reader's response is more or less directed. This is knowledge delivered "in such form as may be best believed." The second and later sentence, on the other hand, is not a declaration, but a puzzle, and the solving of the puzzle becomes the reader's business as well as the speaker's. Where, exactly, are the truth and untruth in "that speech" to be located? (Aristotle's status as an authority is an almost unnoticed casualty of the sentence; we are scarcely aware of his dislodgement, but it has been effected.) The reader who asks this question (and every reader does) will half presume an answer—a lover of solitude can be said to resemble a beast, but never a God—and this presumption is confirmed by the first part of the following sentence: "For it is most true that a natural and secret hatred and aversation towards society in any man hath somewhat of the savage beast, but it is most untrue that it should have any character at all of the divine nature. . . ." Unfortunately (and typically) the sentence does not stop there, but continues with a series of complicating qualifications:

> except it proceed, not out of a pleasure in solitude, but out of love and desire to sequester a man's self for a higher conversation, such as is found to have been falsely and feignedly in some of the heathen, as Epimenides the Candian, Numa the Roman, Empedocles the Sicilian, and Apollinius of Tyana; and truly and really in divers of the ancient hermits and holy fathers of the Church (*Sp.*, VI, 437).

Here again is the familiar pattern of the Baconian experience; a comfortably clear assertion, followed by the enumeration of exceptions which have the effect of taking away both the comfort and the clarity. In this case that effect is even more pronounced because the logic of the argument demands one adjustment too many. Just as the reader has taken in the fact of the exception and is preparing to consider supporting examples, those examples are discredited. "Such as is found to have been falsely and feignedly" is a particularly nasty piece of Baconian business. The alliteration affirms the continuity of the argument, but the sense requires that we *oppose* "found" and "falsely." In "good" (that is, clear) expository prose, sound and sense support each other; here they point in opposite directions and contribute to the reader's disorientation. As a result, the "easy" opposition between heathen philosophers and holy fathers is welcomed, even though it brings us to a point one hundred-and-eighty degrees from the general rule with which the sentence began.

A great deal happens in this first paragraph, but what happens is not what we had expected. The truth and untruth mixed together in Aristotle's statement are not separated out, but further confused so that the reader becomes increasingly less sure of his ability to distinguish them. In this context, the repeated appearances of the word "true" (and its cognates) begin to mock us. In the second sentence alone, we have "it is most true," "it is most untrue," and "truly and really," phrases which in their spacing suggest a progressive clarification, but which, in fact, mark the stages of a progressive blurring of focus. The surface rhetoric of the essay is continually implying a degree of coherence and neatness which the experience of the essay belies, thus calling attention to the disparity between what is promised and what is (finally) forthcoming. So that when the concluding sentence of this first paragraph begins, "But we may go further," the reader well may ask whether we have gone anywhere at all. The sentence itself is of little help: "But we may go further and affirm most truly that it is a mere and miserable solitude to want true friends, without which the world is but a wilderness; and even in this sense also of solitude, whosoever in the frame of his nature and affections is unfit for friendship, he taketh it of the beast and not from humanity (437)." The trouble with this latest "most true" affirmation is that it is both negative and ambiguous. Its negativity points up what may have gone unnoticed in the strenuousness of the reading experience: very little has been said about friendship, which has yielded to solitude as the subject of the essay; and its ambiguity is (potentially) operative precisely because the essayist's attitude toward friendship is as yet unclear. Are we to read "it is a mere and miserable solitude to feel the need of true friends" or "it is a mere and miserable solitude to be without true friends"? In one reading true friendship is highly desirable; in the other, the desire for true friends is itself a sign of some inner weakness. The rest of the sentence really doesn't settle anything; for the world may indeed be without true friendship ("Perfection of friendship, is but speculation"), leaving those who inhabit it to look elsewhere for consolation and help. I do not mean to suggest that the reader consciously considers these alternative readings, but that the absence in the essay of a firm line of direction prevents him from resting too easily in any one of them and makes it possible that the ambiguity will be reactivated with a more precise force at a later point. Meanwhile, the paragraph ends with a gesture back toward its problematic beginning, but the assertion that the man who is unfit for friendship "taketh it of the beast and not from humanity" does not solve the puzzle of the opening sentence; rather it introduces a new term—"humanity"—which constitutes a challenge to the facile polarization that sentence assumes. Somewhere in between "wild beast" and "god" is the condition with which we should be concerned ("The proper study . . ."); and it is to this concern that the movement of the paragraph has been directing us, however obliquely. For what the experience of the paragraph has yielded is not an answer, but more questions, questions which help to shift the center of interest from what Aristotle or anyone else *says* about friendship and solitude to what is empirically and observably true. Some of these questions are: is the world a wilderness? are love and true friends to be found in it? is solitude a state to be lamented and abhorred, or an inevitability with which we must come to terms? what exactly are the characteristics of this thing men call friendship? Of course these questions are posed here only indirectly and the reader does not ask them with any urgency, if, indeed, he consciously asks them at all; but both the asking and the urgency will follow as Bacon continues to refuse us "present satisfaction" for the sake of "expectant inquiry."

The main body of the essay begins as if all the loose ends of its opening paragraph were to be neatly tied up: "A principal fruit of friendship is the ease and discharge of the fulness and swellings of the heart, which passions of all kinds do cause and induce (437)." Here, at last, is a straightforward statement which answers to the expectations raised by the title: the subject is friendship, the tone is celebratory, and the method is demonstrative; but the comfort this sentence provides does not survive the examples brought in to support it: "We know diseases of stoppings and suffocations are the most dangerous in the body, and it is not much otherwise in the mind; you may take sarza to open the liver, steel to open the spleen, flower of sulphur for the lungs, castoreum for the brain, but no receipt openeth the heart but a true friend (437–438)." Rhetorically, this period is a machine designed to glorify friendship by allying it with a number of well-known and effective remedies, but these remedies are so notably painful and unpleasant that by the time the full weight of the preceding clauses falls on "but a true friend," the praise is at least ambiguous. One might think that this effect is unintentional and that Bacon was unaware of the multidirectional properties of his comparisons; but when he turns in the next paragraph to the "high . . . rate great kings and monarchs do set upon this fruit of friendship (438)," it becomes impossible to avoid the conclusion that he is deliberately subverting both his formal structure and the structure of his rhetorical assumptions. The slight uneasiness we may feel on reading that the wisest princes and their servants have ofttimes joined and "called" themselves friends, "using the *word* which is received between private men," flowers into full amazement when several instances of such unions are recalled: Pompey and Sylla, Decimus Brutus and Caesar, Augustus and Agrippa, at once a capsule history of the dark side of Rome and a catalogue of classic betrayals, climaxed by an account of the relationship between Tiberius and Sejanus: "With Tiberius Caesar, Sejanus had ascended to that height as they two were termed and reckoned as a pair of friends. Tiberius in a letter to him saith, *Haec pro amicitia nostra non occultavi;* and the whole senate dedicated an altar to Friendship, as to a goddess, in respect of the great dearness of friendship between them too (439)." The impact of this passage is all the greater because Bacon tells only half the story, leaving the reader to supply the second half (as he surely will) and thus to complete the pattern of rise and fall that unifies these famous friendships. Sylla "raised" Pompey to a height so great that it gave him a surname only to be told by that same Pompey that *"more men adored the sun rising than the sun setting* (438)." Decimus Brutus "lifts" Caesar up out of his chair, so that he may "draw him forth to his death ('no receipt openeth the heart but a true friend')." Augustus "raised" Agrippa to "that height" and by so doing circumscribed his own sphere of action to the point where *"he must either marry his daughter to Agrippa, or take away his life; there was no third way, he had made him so great* (439)." The words "great" and "friends" walk together through these two paragraphs, ringing more hollowly each time they appear, until, when the senate dedicates an altar "in respect of the great dearness of friendship," the irony ("dearness" indeed) is almost painful. The irony, of course, belongs to the reader rather than to the speaker, who proceeds as if his declared intention—to praise friendship by enumerating its "fruits"—were still intact and controlling, but while he may refuse to acknowledge the unsettling implications of his examples, we have no such option. The reader who is told not to forget "what Comineus observeth of his first master, Duke Charles the Hardy; namely that he would communicate his secrets with none (439)," will certainly remember that when Duke Charles did finally "open his heart" to Comineus, that worthy promptly betrayed him to his second master, Louis the Eleventh. We are continually being asked to supply a dimension of meaning of which the speaker seems unaware and as a result we end by writing a companion essay to the essay on the printed page. This second essay, which is a product of our inability to remain within the confines (structural and conceptual) of the first, grows more and more dominant, until by the time the conclusion to this "first fruit" of friendship is reached, every word looks in (at least) two directions:

> Certainly, if a man would give it a hard phrase, those that want friends to open themselves unto are cannibals of their own hearts. But one thing is most admirable (wherewith I will conclude this first fruit of friendship), which is that this communicating of a man's self to his friend works two contrary effects, for it redoubleth joys and cutteth griefs in halfs (440).

This is a summary statement of a kind usually intended to recall a rhetorical promise that has now been fulfilled; but we are likely to receive it with less equanimity than the speaker. Friendship may "cutteth griefs in half" (a phrase taken over from the 1612 essay), but the image is uncomfortably literal in the light of Caesar's fate. ("No receipt openeth the heart but a true friend.") And while it may be "hard" to say that those who want (another ambiguity?) friends to open themselves unto are cannibals of their own hearts, the alternative—to expose one's heart to the cutting edge of a friend—seems equally unattractive. There are also retroactive ironies if the reader turns back to the beginning of this section: "It is a strange thing to observe how high a rate great kings and monarchs do set upon this fruit of friendship. . . . they raise some persons to be *as it were* companions and almost equal to themselves, which many times sorteth to *inconvenience* (438, emphasis mine)." One wonders whether Sylla, Caesar, Augustus, or either Tiberius or Sejanus would accept "inconvenience" as a description of their situations. Surely we cannot, any more than we can now accept, without qualifications, the traditionally sanguine attitude toward the abstraction (is it chimera?) that gives this essay its title.

Analysis inevitably results in distortion, and the preceding paragraphs have put too much emphasis on what is negatively debunking in this essay. Even as Bacon takes away the comfort and consolation the word "friendship" traditionally offered, he is preparing us to recognize the availability of something more solidly real:

> Now if these princes had been as a Trajan or a Marcus
> Aurelius, a man might have thought that this had pro-
> ceeded of an abundant goodness of nature, but being men
> so wise, of such strength and severity of mind, and so ex-
> treme lovers of themselves, as all these were, it proveth
> most plainly that they found their own felicity (though as
> great as ever happened to mortal men) but as an half piece,
> except they mought have a friend to make it entire (439).

Although the burden of this sentence (both in its straightforward
and ironic "lives") falls on the "men so wise" and on the questionable "comfort of friendship," Trajan and Marcus Aurelius do
appear briefly to hint at values the surface rhetoric determinedly
ignores. In the popular imagination, these men are linked not only
by their abundant goodness of nature, but by an identification with
the Stoic doctrine of self-sufficiency; presumably their felicity was
not felt to be "but an half piece" because they were sustained by a
reserve of inner strength which made them independent of outward supports, including the dubious support of "true friends."
(Marcus Aurelius himself raised his son to the throne, with di-
sastrous results.) For a brief moment the submerged suggestion
(heard several times) that friendship is sought only by the weak-
willed surfaces again, and there is some slight pressure in the
direction of reversing the essay's negative judgment on those who
delight in solitude; but the speaker hurries right on past this
point (he does not acknowledge its pressure at all) and returns
to the closed security of his formal outline: "The second fruit of
friendship is healthful and sovereign for the understanding, as the
first is for the affections (440)." Once again we are graced with a
sentence that makes the maximum claims for the essay's coherence
and sincerity, but in the context of our previous experience, the
assertion that this second fruit is as healthful as the first is not
likely to be reassuring. It is something less than a surprise, therefore, when the succeeding paragraphs call into question the very
existence of the benefits they supposedly celebrate. The thesis
is clear enough: "For friendship . . . maketh daylight in the understanding out of darkness and confusion of thoughts (440)," but
the substantiation of the thesis turns out to be a triumph of di-

versionary obfuscation. The strategy is brilliantly simple: twice within the space of a few sentences the speaker announces that he will defer a consideration of the main point: "Neither is this to be understood only of faithful counsel, which a man receiveth from his friend; but before you come to that . . . (440). Neither is this second fruit of friendship, in opening the understanding, re-strained only to such friends as are able to give a man counsel; (they indeed are best), but even without that . . . (440)." Un-fortunately, however, we never do "come to that" and remain forever "without" it. That is, we never hear anything at all of "faithful counsel" or of "such friends as are able to give" it (they may be "best," but they don't seem to be available). The idea of a "true friend" whose advice is wholly reliable becomes something the reader pursues through these two paragraphs, a will-o'-the-wisp, glimpsed fleetingly in the form of the speaker's promises, but never realized either in theory or example.

> And now, to make this second fruit of friendship complete, that other point which lieth more open and falleth within vulgar observation, which is faithful counsel from a friend (441).
> . . . the best preservative to keep the mind in health is the faithful admonition of a friend (441).
> . . . the best receipt (best I, I say, to work, and best to take) is the admonition of a friend (441).
> . . . when all is done the help of good counsel is that which setteth business straight (441).
> . . . it is a rare thing, except it be from a perfect and entire friend, to have counsel given, but such as shall be bowed and crooked to some ends which he hath that giveth it (442).

This last at least acknowledges what the experience of the essay everywhere suggests, that counsel from a "perfect and entire friend" is the exception; the general rule is counsel "bowed and crooked" to the giver's ends. The true structure of this section (and of the essay as a whole) is the reverse of what it seems. The nominal subject is "faithful counsel," but that chimera appears (verbally) just often enough to sustain our belief in it, and to keep alive the hope that it will finally materialize. Meanwhile, Bacon is busily at work, subverting his arguments even as he presents them. "There is" he says "as much difference between the counsel that a friend giveth, and that a man giveth himself, as there is between the counsel of a friend and of a flatterer (441)." What the sense of this gives, the sound takes away; we are told of a difference, but in the alliteration and assonance of "flattery" "self" and "friend" we hear an assertion of sameness. At every point we are directed away from the conclusion that is being formally urged. The proposition that friendly counsel is helpful in business is supported (hardly the word) by the dismissal, at too great length, of all sentiments to the contrary:

> As for business, a man may think, if he will, that two eyes see no more than one; or that a gamester seeth always more than a looker-on; or that a man in anger is as wise as he that hath said over the four and twenty letters; or that a musket may be shot off as well upon the arm as upon a rest; or such other fond and high imaginations, to think himself all in all. But when all is done, the help of good counsel is that which setteth business straight.

The man who is thinking of these "fond and high imaginations" is, of course, the reader who, when "all is done," will remember them rather than the flat and over-general praise of good counsel. ("Reading good books of morality is a little flat and dead.") It is the negative thesis that is finally "proved," if not on the printed page, where the pretense established by the essay's title is always maintained, then in the reader's mind. In that context, where meanings either ignored or suppressed by the speaker flourish, the warning against taking counsel from too many is finally a warning against taking any counsel at all:

> And if any man think that he will take counsel, but it shall be by pieces; asking counsel in one business of one man, and in another business of another man; it is well, (that is to say, better perhaps than if he asked none at all;) but he runneth two dangers; one, that he shall not be faithfully counselled; for it is a rare thing, except it be from a perfect

and entire friend, to have counsel given, but such as shall
be bowed and crooked to some ends which he hath that
giveth it. The other, that he shall have counsel given, hurtful and unsafe, (though with good meaning,) and mixed
partly of mischief and partly of remedy; even as if you
would call a physician that is thought good for the cure
of the disease you complain of, but is unacquainted with
your body; and therefore may put you in way for a present
cure, but overthroweth your health in some other kind; and
so cure the disease and kill the patient. But a friend that
is wholly acquainted with a man's estate will beware, by
furthering any present business, how he dasheth upon other
inconvenience. And therefore rest not upon scattered counsels; they will rather distract and mislead, than settle and
direct (441–442).

Once again Bacon allows his main point to be overwhelmed by its
exceptions. As it is introduced, the discussion of the dangers attendant upon resting in scattered counsels is preliminary to the
case for resting in the counsel of a perfect and entire friend. But
that case is never made, and no such friend ever appears, except
in the contrary-to-fact context of a subordinate subjunctive clause.
What the reader takes away from this passage is a montage of
negative impressions—"hurtful," "unsafe," "mischief," "disease,"
"kill," "inconvenience"—all of which are attached to the taking
of counsel of whatever kind, even though the injunction specifies
"scattered" counsel. The concluding sentence of the paragraph,
and of this "second fruit," returns to the original limited assertion—"therefore rest not upon scattered counsels"—but in the
absence of a positive alternative, or of one positively urged, it is
difficult not to take the speaker's advice more inclusively than
he intends it. The true moral of this section is perhaps buried in a
parenthesis: "better perhaps . . . if he asked none at all."

The distance between the two essays, the one we are reading,
and the one we are (in a sense) writing, is never greater than in
the opening sentence of the final paragraph: "After these two
noble fruits of friendship (peace in the affections, and support of
the judgment), followeth the last fruit, which is like the pome-

granate, full of many kernels; I mean aid and bearing a part in all actions and occasions (442)." For the last time we are alerted to the integrity of the essay's organization: the promise implied in the opening paragraphs has been precisely fulfilled. Friendship has been "opened" and its parts enumerated according to the principles of *partitio* or "division"; and at this point the speaker invites us to look back to the unfolding of his structure and to anticipate its completion. But any sense we may have of the essay's organizational clarity is complicated by the impossibility of taking its "points" seriously; "peace in the affections" and "support of the judgement," however they are rhetorically intended, serve largely to recall how little peace friendship finally yields and how untrustworthy is the support one friend is likely to receive from another. If there is anything "noble" about these first two "fruits," the evidence is certainly not to be found in these paragraphs.

The third fruit is less noble still, for the actions in which a friend may bear a part turn out to be those one would not wish to claim as one's own: "How many things are there which a man cannot with any face or comeliness, say or do himself? A man can scarce allege his own merits with modesty, much less extol them; a man cannot sometimes brook to supplicate or beg; and a number of the like (442)." In short, a man may rely on a friend to do those things that might better have been left undone. The only exception is the aid one can be rendered posthumously by a friend who attends to uncompleted projects, "the bestowing of a child, the finishing of a work, or the like"; but even here, when at last there is something to be said for friendship, Bacon will not allow us any "present satisfaction": "If a man have a true friend, he may rest almost secure that the care of those things will continue after him (442)." The positive statement in this sentence is so hedged about with qualifications that its force is barely felt. In the light of what has preceded it, the first clause alone ("*If* a man have a true friend") is enough to cancel out whatever follows; and as for resting "almost" secure, a more uncomfortable state can scarcely be imagined. Like its predecessors the third "fruit" is bitter to the taste.

The final sentence of the essay is very similar to this one, both in its provisionality and in its negativity: "I have given the rule, where a man cannot fitly play his own part; if he have not a friend, he may quit the stage (443)." Again the "if" clause is controlling simply because the hypothesis it contains has proved to be the case. That is, everything in the essay points to the probability of a man's not having a friend to supply the several offices of friendship, and therefore the attentive reader is left with but two alternatives; either he can fitly play his own part, in the self-reliant manner of a Trajan or a Marcus Aurelius, or he can quit the stage, retiring perhaps into the solitude of the desert (a making literal of the veritable desert we all inhabit in society). There is a third possibility, if Bacon's metaphor is taken with a deadly seriousness, the ultimate Stoic remedy against the buffets and betrayals of a hostile world, a quitting of the stage which precludes any reappearance on it. In other words, if there is a message in this essay, it may be one a twentieth-century reader could translate into his own idiom: "Either shape up or ship out."

We can now return to the problem first raised by Crane, "to explain the gradual emergence . . . in the essays of 1612 and 1625, of a style in which 'discourse of illustration,' 'recitals of examples,' and 'discourse of connexion and order' were no longer 'cut off,' but on the contrary multiplied until they became the most striking elements in the general effect." By "general effect," I take Crane to mean the effect of stepping back from an essay and noting the prominence in it of examples and "discourse of connexion and order." I would argue, however, that this effect is not only general but superficial, and that, while it is certainly true that these "elements" are multiplied in the later essays, the most "striking" thing about them is their incompatibility. In "Of Friendship" and "Of Cunning" (among others), the examples that are brought in to "supply" the discourse instead subvert it. If this were a scientific experiment of the kind Bacon describes (and prescribes) in the *Novum Organum,* the course and direction of the investigation would be altered to take this new and unsettling evidence into account; but the "moral" scientist who gives us these "counsels" feels no such obligation; he continues to be true to his announced intention long after the assumptions that sustain it have become questionable; and he completes the scaffolding of his orderly and well-connected discourse seemingly unaware that it holds together disparate and unlike elements. The reader, however, cannot help but be aware, if only because Vickers's account of Bacon's practice is, in its reductive way, perfectly accurate: "Outlines are clear and easily grasped, the argument proceeds firmly through each section, and each topic is covered with thoroughness and precision (30)." "It is impossible," declares Vickers, "not to admire the structure of Bacon's works." It is impossible, I would emend, not to *notice* the structure of Bacon's works, and once noticed, it becomes impossible (at least in the case of the *Essays*) not to notice how inadequate these structures are to the materials they contain. Indeed one might say that these *Essays* display not one, but two structures, which point in different directions and make conflicting demands on their single reader.

The explanation for this double structure will not be found where Crane seeks it, in the style of the *Advancement of Learning,* or where Zeitlin locates it, in the changing focuses of several revisions, but in the experience an essay so ordered or disordered provides. What does the reader of the essay "Of Friendship" carry away with him? The answer, like the experience, is complex: (1) an overwhelming sense of the integrity of its organization; and (2) an equally overwhelming sense of the intractability of the material supposedly being organized. Together these two effects combine to generate (1) a critical awareness of the tendency to facility of all methodical schemes, and (2) a genuine (that is, felt) desire for an arrangement of the material which would more perfectly accord with the facts. In other words, knowledge "broken" so as to avoid the impression of more completeness than has been achieved, but not so broken as to make us despair of ever achieving that final completeness. The reader of this essay does not feel that he knows the whole truth about friendship; indeed he is probably wondering whether friendship as "the word . . . is received" really exists; yet he has learned a great deal about what men call friendship and this knowledge, although it is negative, exerts a pressure in the direction of "further inquiry." It is the received body of opinion concerning friendship, not the abstraction itself, which is the casualty of the reading experience, and the effect of its discrediting should be to initiate a search for something better.

In a way, all I am saying is that "Of Friendship" and essays like it are unfinished; but they are unfinished with a purposefulness that makes the bestowing of the adjective less a criticism than a compliment. Everywhere in his writings Bacon insists on the provisionality of all stages of investigation preliminary to the final one.[21] In these late essays he communicates that provisionality by letting the information he has collected spill out of an organizational scheme that remains visible and compelling despite its obvious failure. That is, the "discourse of connexion and order" continues to stand for something—a future possibility, a promise not yet redeemed—even though its present claims to full adequacy must be disallowed. George Williamson has observed that "the form of the essays remains an index to the state of their wisdom"[22]; the same form prevents the reader from overestimating the state of his own. For the style of the essays, their manner of presentation, simultaneously gestures toward Bacon's goal—the orderly disposition of everything in the universe—while acknowledging his (and our) distance from it. In their incompleteness and unresolved complication, the *Essays* reflect the genuine, if paradoxical, humility of a man who could hope that what he began would end someday in "the discovery of all operations and possibilities of operations from immortality (if it were possible) to the meanest mechanical practice."[23]

## METHOD AND DIALECTIC

We are now in a position to consider precisely the relationship between Bacon's method (in the *Novum Organum* and the *Essays*) and the tradition of Platonic-Augustinian dialectic. There are many points of contact (some of which will have already occurred to my readers), but they find a single source in a shared

---

21 See for example *The Advancement of Learning* (III, 366): "And generally let this be a rule, that all partitions of knowledge be accepted rather for lines and veins than for sections and separations." As Brian Vickers notes of this and other passages, Bacon sees his divisions as "a temporary highlighting of a branch within the fundamental unity of the sciences (58)."

22 *The Senecan Amble,* p. 181.          23 *Sp.,* III, 222.

distrust of the human mind. Like Plato, Bacon deplores the tendency of the mind to equate its immediate horizons with the horizons of reality, and, again like Plato, he devises a mode of proceeding that prevents the mind from resting too easily in the satisfaction of closed and artificial systems. They are alike, too, in what they oppose. Where Plato turns away from rhetoric (at least in its sophistic guise), Bacon turns away from the syllogism, and for the same reasons. The conclusions processed by a syllogism are true only with the circle of its own order ("The syllogism commands assent to the proposition, but does not take hold of the thing—xii"); in the larger context that circle excludes they are neither authoritative nor (necessarily) helpful. The deliberations of a syllogism are defensive rather than exploratory; it is committed from the beginning to something that is assumed to be true (as the rhetorician is committed to popular belief) and will admit evidence only in support of it. Rather than challenging received notions, a syllogism builds on them (syllogisms do not permit examination of their basic premises) and therefore confirms the mind in the opinions it already holds. In short, the syllogism is a conservative form which (like rhetoric) induces complacency rather than encouraging change.[24]

It is change, of course, that is promoted both by dialectic and by the method of induction, change not only in the discernment of what is true and real, but in the mind that is to be the instrument of the discerning. Dialectic and the method of induction are refining processes and what they refine (in their early stages) is the understandings of their users; they clear away debris, remove film, expose error, prevent sloppiness, encourage rigor, sharpen perception. In the words of Milton, they "purge with sovrain eye-

---

[24] As Rossi points out (*Francis Bacon: From Magic to Science,* p. 151), the syllogism, like other forms of discursive logic, is "a delicate precise instrument patiently fashioned by man for predetermined ends." That is to say, discursive reason is an instrument of "science as one would" and its procedures are answerable to the disposition of things in the mind rather than to their disposition in reality. The absence of discursive reason in Bacon's method is (like the absence of imagination) further evidence of his determination to wean the mind away from the false security of its own procedures. See Karl Wallace, *Francis Bacon on the Nature of Man* (Urbana, 1967), for the distinction in Bacon's philosophical psychology between "reason" (by which Bacon usually means the syllogism) and "understanding." See especially pp. 118–126, 162–164.

salve that intellectual ray which *God* hath planted in us," making it once more "fit and proportionable to Truth the object, and end of it." [25]

But it is precisely here, where the two operations are most similar, that they must be sharply distinguished. The Truth to which the understanding will be made "fit and proportionable" is for Plato, Augustine, and Donne a truth above the phenomenal world, while for Bacon it is a truth about the phenomenal world. In the light of this one difference (which makes all the difference) the points of similarity become points of opposition. While Bacon's insistence on rigor and precision and on the making of finer and finer distinctions is directly related to his goal—the accurate and exhaustive description of the empirically verifiable—in Plato's dialogues and Donne's sermons the making of distinctions is only a preliminary stage, a clearing away of the ground before the mind prepares to transcend the empirical. And, although the movement of inductive method is, like the movement of dialectic, irregular and uneven (positions that have been reached must often be abandoned when new evidence is uncovered), this is merely a condition of a present imperfection in our knowledge. The way of proper "rejections and conclusions," of trial and error, will in the end establish a succession of related certainties, and when the big picture is complete, the entire body of knowledge will be capable of a tabular representation which will, at a glance, specify temporal and spatial relationships of cause and effect: "A method

[25] *Complete Prose Works of John Milton,* Vol. I, p. 566. Indeed, Bacon's attack on the "schoolmen" might well have been taken from *The Reason of Church Government* (although the influence, if there is any, would flow of course from the philosopher to the poet): "as in the inquiry of the divine truth their pride inclined to leave the oracle of God's word and to vanish in the mixture of their own inventions, so in the inquisition of nature they ever left the oracle of God's work and adored the deceiving and deformed images which the unequal mirror of their own minds or a few received authors or principles did represent unto them (*Sp.* III, 287)." There is one difference, however, and it is crucial: where Milton's emphasis would fall on the pride of those who prefer their own inventions to the revealed word, Bacon is concerned chiefly with the failure of men to submit themselves to nature, that is to disinterested empirical observation. Of course this concern is "baptized" by referring to nature as "God's work" and authorized by the verbal echo ("God's word"—"God's work"); but as always Bacon brings in the theological context only so that he may more gracefully (no pun intended) set it aside.

rightly ordered leads by an unbroken route through the woods of experience to the open ground of axioms (lxxxii)." In Plato's dialogues and Donne's sermons there is no "unbroken route"; the moment of insight is a moment of revelation, and when it comes, if it comes, it does not follow directly from the discursive gestures that precede it. And though it would seem that the tension in Bacon's *Essays,* between the "discourse of connexion and order" and the observations that do not fit comfortably inside it, parallels the tension in the Anglican sermon, between the logical superstructure and the problems it is unable to solve, they are finally not to be equated; for while Bacon uses this tension as a "caution" against assuming too easily that the job is done, the sermonists use it to insist that the job can *never* be done, at least not by rational means or rational beings. In short, while the dialogues of Plato and the sermons of Donne are self-consuming, Bacon's *Essays* are merely self-regulating; his words may be, as he terms them, seeds, living not so much in their references as in their effects, but they will flower in other words rather than in a vision, and in words which do have the referential adequacy that is presently unavailable. For all their provisionality the *Essays* are finally objects; they are not used up in the reading but remain valuable as source material for future consultation, for they reflect quite accurately the partial (not irrelevant) understanding of the mind that fashioned them and of the minds that read them.

It is, of course, the disposition toward the mind that finally distinguishes method from dialectic. Although the object of both is to change the mind, one works a profound, the other a superficial, change. Method provides "helps" to the mind, protects it from itself, neutralizes its distorting tendencies, prevents it from concluding prematurely, and makes of it an unprejudiced reporter or mirror of the way (earthly) things are. The effects of method, however, are negative and temporary, for while it fits the mind to perform certain mechanical operations, it does so at the expense of a personal point of view (the first person is, after all, one of the idols that method filters out) and therefore at the expense of a personal commitment.[26] Method, in short, bypasses the soul, in-

[26] Wallace (*Francis Bacon on the Nature of Man*) points out that unlike others of his time, Bacon did not posit a "common sense" faculty which "assumed a first

stituting controls rather than demanding a reorientation. Dialectic, on the other hand, is soul-centered; the response it requires is decisional (in the religious or existential sense) and its effects are long-lasting because the changes they work are basic. Dialectic asks not for reform or restraint, but for revolution; it does not polish, but purges; it does not delay, but extirpates self-satisfaction; it does not make the mind capable, but unmakes the mind. Method reduces all minds to a common level, the level of empirical observation. Dialectic raises the level of the mind, and raises it to the point where it becomes indistinguishable from the object of its search, and so disappears.

This is what happens in Herbert's poetry.

---

level of organization immediately after sensory experience. . . . For Bacon a common sense faculty was unnecessary (155)." For Bacon, a common-sense faculty was *undesirable* because it would give the mind a role in the organizing, rather than the simple receiving, of reality, whereas "Bacon . . . appears to have assumed that there were ultimate modes of being . . . and that they organized man's object world quite apart from him (155)." This elimination of a common-sense faculty is of a piece with the devaluing of discursive reasoning in favor of a procedure that does not indulge, but hobbles, the natural processes of the mind. In short, the method of induction is designed to filter out a variable, and that variable is *you*.

III

# Letting Go: The Dialectic of the Self in Herbert's Poetry

THY WORD IS ALL

In the third stanza of "The Flower," George Herbert gives voice to an article of faith which is itself a description of the action taking place in many of his poems:

> We say amisse,
> This or that is:
> Thy word is all, if we could spell
>                                   (19–21).[1]

The point of doctrine is, of course, a seventeenth-century commonplace: the distinctions—of times, places, objects, persons—we customarily make as we move about in the world are the illusory creations of a limited perspective; if our visions were sufficiently enlarged, we would see that all things visible were not only framed by (Hebrews 11:3) but are informed by (are manifestations of) the word that is God: "Thy word is all."

Herbert's poems characteristically ask us to experience the full force of this admission in all its humiliating implications. If God is all, the claims of other entities to a separate existence, including the claims of the speakers and readers of these poems, must be relinquished. That is, the insight that God's word is all is *self-*

---

[1] *The Works of George Herbert*, ed. F. E. Hutchinson (Oxford, 1941). All citations are to this edition.

destructive, since acquiring it involves abandoning the perceptual and conceptual categories within which the self moves and by means of which it separately exists. To stop saying amiss is not only to stop distinguishing "this" from "that," but to stop distinguishing oneself from God, and finally to stop, to cease to be. Learning to "spell" in these terms is a self-diminishing action in the course of which the individual lets go, one by one, of all the ways of thinking, seeing, and saying that sustain the illusion of his independence, until finally he is absorbed into the deity whose omnipresence he has acknowledged (thy word is *all*).

There is nothing easy about the "letting go" this poetry requires of us. We are, after all, being asked to acquiesce in the discarding of those very habits of thought and mind that preserve our dignity by implying our independence. Naturally (the word is double edged) we resist, and our resistance is often mirrored in the obstinate questionings and remonstrations of the first-person voice. The result is a poetics of tension, reflecting a continuing dialectic between an egocentric vision which believes in, and is sustained by, the distinctions it creates, and the relentless pressure of a *re*solving and *dis*solving insight. That dialectic takes many forms, but its basic contours remain recognizable: the surface argument or plot of a poem proceeds in the context of the everyday world of time and space, where objects and persons are discrete and independent; but at the same time and within the same linguistic space, there is felt the pressure of a larger context which lays claim to that world and everything in it, including speaker, reader, and the poem itself:

> *Lord, my first fruits present themselves to thee;*
> *Yet not mine neither: for from thee they came,*
> *And must return* ("The Dedication").

The return of these fruits and of everything else to the God of whose substance they are is the self-consuming business of these poems, which can be viewed as a graduated series of "undoings" and "letting go's": (1) the undoing of the perceptual framework in which we live and move and have our (separate) beings. This involves the denying of the usual distinctions between "this" and "that"—a *"making of one place everywhere"*—and the affir-

mation of a universe where God is all. An inevitable consequence of this undoing is the gradual narrowing (to nothing) of
the distance between the individual consciousness (of both speaker
and reader) and God; that is, (2) the undoing of the self as an
independent entity, a *"making of no thine and mine"* [2] by making
it all thine, a surrender not only of a way of seeing, but of initiative, will, and finally of being (to say "I am" is to say amiss). To
the extent that this surrender is also the poet's, it requires the
silencing of his voice and the relinquishing of the claims of authorship, and therefore (3) an undoing of the poem as the product
of a mind distinct from the mind of God. This undoing, or letting
go, is an instance of what it means, in Herbert's own words, to
*"make the action fine"* [3] (by making it not mine). And finally, and
inevitably, Herbert's poems are undone in still another sense when
(4) the insight they yield ("thy word is all") renders superfluous
the mode of discourse and knowing of which they themselves are
examples. These poems, as they ask their readers to acknowledge
their complete dependence, act out that acknowledgment by calling attention to what they are not doing, and indeed could not do.
In their final radical modesty, they perform what they require of
us, for as they undermine our reliance on discursive forms of
thought, and urge us to rest in the immediate apprehension of
God's all-effective omnipresence, they become the vehicles of their
own abandonment. "God only is," writes Thomas Browne, "all
others . . . are something but by a distinction." [4] To read Herbert's poems is to experience the dissolution of the distinctions by
which all other things are.

MAKING ONE PLACE EVERYWHERE

The preceding is a summary statement that raises as many
questions as it answers. If the insight of God's omnipresence is
violated by the very act of predication ("This or that is"), how
does a poet who is committed to that insight practice his craft?
How does one avoid saying amiss if language is itself a vehicle

2 "Clasping of Hands," 1. 20.  4 *Religio Medici*, I, 35.
3 "The Elixir," 1. 20.

for the making of invidious distinctions? How can God's prerogatives be preserved if one produces sentences which automatically
arrange persons and objects in hierarchical relationships of cause
and effect? Answering these questions will be the burden of this
chapter, but we can begin by noting that Herbert baptizes
language by making it subversive of its usual functions. In his
poetry words tend to lose their referential fixity, and syntactical
patterns often obscure the relationships they pretend to establish.
In short, Herbert avoids saying amiss in an ultimate context by
deliberately saying amiss in the context of a perspective he would
have us transcend.

The peculiar force of a Herbert poem, then, often depends on
our awareness that the terms in which we are being encouraged
to formulate a concept are inadequate to it. In some poems, this
awareness is only a momentary thing, the (by)product of a single
phrase:

> Subject to ev'ry mounter's bended knee
> ("The Holy Scriptures, I," 1.14).

To read this line is to experience the insufficiency of its mode of
discourse. It is a miniature exercise in epistemology. "Mounter's"
involves the reader in the most conventional of homiletic practices, the figuring forth of a spiritual distinction by a spatial
image; but "bended" undermines the simple formula (up-good,
down-evil) on which the analogy depends, forcing the reader to
let go of the image and of the way of thinking that has generated
it, and calling into question the very possibility of comprehending
spiritual matters in spatial forms. It is called into question in a
more substantive way in "The Temper I":

> How should I praise thee, Lord! how should my rymes
> Gladly engrave thy love in steel,
> If what my soul doth feel sometimes,
> My soul might ever feel!
>
> Although there were some fourtie heav'ns, or more,
> Sometimes I peere above them all;
> Sometimes I hardly reach a score,
> Sometimes to hell I fall.

If, as Arnold Stein has argued, the " 'plain intention' " of this poem is "to transform its initial attitude into its concluding one," [5] that transformation is the result of exchanging one way of looking at the world for another. The "initial attitude" is one of complaint: Herbert's inability to praise God as he would like to is a condition, he maintains, of his inability to sustain the occasional moment of perfect joy ("Sometimes I peere above them all"); and that, in turn, is a condition of God's fitful presence. The stated wish to praise God, then, is a thinly disguised accusation of him. Were he more faithful, more constantly in attendance, the poet's lines and rhymes would flow easily and everlastingly. (God here has the role assigned to inspiration in the laments of secular poets). Of course this (hidden) argument holds only if one limits God to times and places, and that is exactly what Herbert is doing in the extended image of the second stanza. Presumably God resides in that fortieth heaven to which the poet occasionally ascends; lower levels receive proportional shares of his emanations and in hell there is (literally) no trace of him at all.

But while this localization of God's presence is consistent with certain Neoplatonic systems and even with the three-tiered universe of popular tradition, it will hardly do for the deity of whom Augustine speaks when he says "He came to a place where He was already".[6] This statement (if it is a statement) illustrates the Christian solution to the problem of thinking and talking about God in terms whose frame of reference he transcends. One uses the terms (no others are available), but simultaneously acknowledges their insufficiency, as Herbert does in the concluding and, in view of his earlier complaint, triumphant, stanza of this poem:

> Whether I flie with angels, fall with dust
> Thy hands made both, and I am there:
> Thy power and love, my love and trust
> Make one place ev'ry where (25–28).

The speaker's dilemma, both as would-be praiser and God-seeking man, exists only in his formulation of it, and its solution is effected when that formulation is abandoned or let go. The process

---

[5] Arnold Stein, *George Herbert's Lyrics* (Baltimore, 1968), p. 28.

[6] *On Christian Doctrine,* trans. D. W. Robertson (New York, 1958), p. 14.

of letting go is set in motion in the first line: the pointing of the "whether–or" construction (one supplies the "or") suggests that Herbert is still committed to the divided worlds of the opening stanzas, but at the same time the alliteration of "flie" and "fall" is pulling us in a different direction, toward the dissolving of the distinctions—between angels and dust, heaven and hell—the syntax is supporting. By the end of the following line, "ev'ry where" has been made one place through the agency of the precisely ambiguous "there," which refers neither to the earth ("dust") nor to the ("fourtie") heavens, but to God's hands, the framers, supporters, and therefore, in a real sense, the location, of both. The point of doctrine is, as always, a commonplace—since all things were made by God (John, 1:3) and by him all things consist (Colossians, 1:17), everywhere in his "there"—but the peculiar value of its appearance here resides in the process through which Herbert makes his readers approach it. The reader who negotiates the distance between "Whether" and "there" passes from a (syntactical) world where everything is in its time and place to a world where specification of either is impossible, to a *uni*verse.[7] This same movement is compressed into an even smaller space in the final line, where "one place" actually does become "ev'ry where" in the twinkling of a reading eye. And, of course, the ease with which we take in the paradox is a direct result of the experience of the preceding lines.

As is often the case in a Herbert poem, the resolution of the spiritual or psychological problem also effects the resolution of the poetic problem. For when the speaker is able to say "Yet take thy way; for sure thy way is best (21)" he removes the obstacle to his singing of God's praises; that obstacle is not his uneven spiritual experience, but his too easy interpretation of that experience as a sign of God's desertion. Once he gives up that reading of his situation, he is free to see in it a more beneficent purpose:

> This is but tuning of my breast,
> To make the musick better (23–24).

[7] See on this point Helen Vendler, "The Re-invented Poem," in *Forms of Lyric: Selected Papers From the English Institute,* ed. Reuben A. Brower (New York, 1970), p. 32.

Thus the very condition the speaker laments finally yields the praise he thought himself debarred from making, and itself becomes the occasion for, because it has been the stimulus to, praise.[8] That is, the sense of heaven's desertion leads to the mental exertions which produce the poem which generates the intuition that God's way is best. What begins as a complaint against God ends with the realization that the supposed basis of the complaint, when properly seen, is something to be thankful for. The poem's movement in effect anticipates the counsel of Sir Thomas Browne, who advises us "so to dispute and argue the proceedings of God as to distinguish even his judgements into mercies (*Religio Medici*, I, 53)."

Just how great a mercy God affords Herbert here can be seen in the poem's penultimate line:

> Thy power and love, my love and trust (27).

What this does is give the poet a part in the action of the concluding line—making one place everywhere ("make" has a multiple subject). God's power and love, His continuing presence in the world, are of course the final cause of this effect, but the poet's love and trust in that other love are necessary for its perception since the perceiving consciousness he was born with suggests something else altogether (that "this" or "that" is).

Making one place everywhere, in contradiction to the appearance (or illusion) of a multiplicity of places, is also the action and the experience of "Even-Song." As in "The Temper I," the opening lines suggest a distinction, in some part spatial, which does not survive the reading experience:

> Blest be the God of love,
> Who gave me eyes, and light, and power this day,
>   Both to be busie, and to play.
>   But much more blest be God above,
>     Who gave me sight alone (1–5).

[8] See on this point Fredson Bowers, "Herbert's Sequential Imagery: 'The Temper,'" *Modern Philology* (February, 1962), p. 212. "The reconciliation is then complete when he sees that, in truth, the joy and the pain he feels in extremes are tempering him to write better poetry on his subject."

Apparently the poet prays to two Gods, the "God of love," and that more powerful and more to be thanked "God above," the God, presumably, of the higher regions. This halving of the world's empire is immediately suspect and is already being challenged by the unifying force of the rhyme "love–above." By the time the reader takes in the pun in line 8—"But I have got his sonne, and he hath none"—the two deities have become one, or, what is in effect the same thing, two coequal and coidentical members of a trinity, and for the remainder of the poem the speaker addresses his remarks unambiguously to a second person singular.

The dividing and distinguishing tendencies of the human consciousness, however, are irrepressible, and they reassert themselves toward the end of the poem:

> I muse, which shows more love,
> The day or night (25–26).

The answer is implicit in what has gone before; since they are both God's they show equally his love; and moreover as manifestations of that love they lose their separate identities, which is exactly what happens to them in this stanza:

> I muse, which shows more love,
> The day or night: that is the gale, this th' harbour;
> That is the walk, and this the arbour;
> Or that the garden, this the grove (25–28).

The speaker muses in the (submerged) context of a familiar proverb: "as different as day and night." At first this sense of difference is reinforced; the "gale and harbour" image is made up of easily separable components, distinct in time and place; the gale *brings* one to the harbour. The distinctness of "walk" and "arbour" however is less immediately striking; either they are adjacent or one encloses the other. The third pair of substitute coordinates actually works against the argument it is supposedly supporting; for while "garden" and "grove" are distinguishable, distinguishing between them requires more of an effort than the heavily alliterative verse ("gale," "garden," "grove"; "harbour," "arbour," "garden") encourages. In the very process of (supposedly) expanding an opposition, Herbert has led us surreptitiously and by degrees to a sense of sameness, and it is this experience that gives force to the triumphant assertion of the following line:

My God, thou art all love (29).

Here the poet admits that the question he had posed three lines earlier was based on assumptions (that "this" day, or "that" night, is) that are found to be invalid when our perspective on "things" is sufficiently enlarged, as it has been in the course of the poem. Of course, that invalidated perspective is the one we must live with (or in), even after its insufficiency has been demonstrated or experienced, and the speaker returns to it, and to the logical language which is an extension of it, in the final lines:

> My God, thou art all love.
> Not one poore minute scapes thy breast
> But brings a favour from above;
> And in this love, more then in bed, I rest (29–32).

Once again God is "above" (the rhyme of the opening stanza reappears) and man "below," but this formulation is now less dangerously distorting than it might have been at the beginning of the poem because we know now (what we always knew, but less self-consciously) that this way of thinking and verbalizing is an accommodation. That is, we know, even as we read line 32, that resting in bed or anywhere else, we are always resting in God's love which makes one (any) place everywhere.

Examples of this kind could be multiplied indefinitely, but the point, I think, has been made: to read many of Herbert's poems is to experience the dissolution of the lines of demarcation we are accustomed to think of as real. Perhaps the most spectacular of the poems in this mode is "Church Monuments," which has been brilliantly analyzed by Joseph Summers:

> The dissolution of the body and the monuments is paralleled by the dissolution of the sentences and stanzas.
>
> The movement and sound of the poem suggest the "falls" of the flesh and the monuments and the dust in the glass. The fall is not precipitous; it is as slow as the gradual

fall of the monuments, as the crumbling of the glass, as the descent of the flesh from Adam to dust . . . . With the cluster of consonants, it is impossible to read the poem rapidly. The related rhymes, with their internal echoes and repetitions, both give phonetic continuity to the poem and suggest the process of dissolution . . . . The sentences sift down through the rhyme scheme skeleton of the stanzas like the sand through the glass and the glass itself has already begun to crumble.[9]

To this obviously authoritative description of what is happening in the poem I would add a description of what is happening in (and to) the reader; for the dissolution of sentences and stanzas and of the objects within them produces a corresponding dissolution, or falling away of, the perceptual framework a reader brings with him to the poem and indeed to life. Thus, in the opening lines the firm sense of time and place, which at first allows us to distance ourselves from objects and processes, is progressively eroded:

> While that my soul repairs to her devotion,
> Here I intombe my flesh that it betimes
> May take acquaintance of this heap of dust;
> To which the blast of deaths incessant motion,
> Fed with the exhalation of our crimes,
> Drives all at last. Therefore I gladly trust (1–6).

The first three lines are replete with distinctions, distinctions of times, persons, objects, spaces, and actions. The body is distinguished from the soul and both from the heaps of dust with which they are bid take acquaintance. The words on which the syntax pivots are "While" and "Here," time and place markers respectively. Even less essential words, like "repairs" and "betimes," contribute to the strong impression of local identities, separable objects, discrete and specifiable moments. Yet no sooner have these demarcations been established and assumed a kind of reality in the reader's mind, than the process of undermining them begins. If it is "impossible to read the poem rapidly" it is also impossible to read the poem in stages because it affords us no natural resting

[9] Joseph Summers, *George Herbert* (Cambridge, Mass., 1954), pp. 134–135.

places. Units of meaning that seem complete in themselves are unexpectedly revealed to be only the introductory clauses in a larger utterance, an utterance whose scope finally expands to include the whole poem.[10] It is, in Herbert's own words an "incessant motion," and it proceeds by blurring the distinctions it momentarily establishes. This process begins with "To which (4)," a transition that forces the reader to keep one eye on the three preceding lines at the same time that he is a witness to, and to some extent the agent of, the melting into one another of the objects that fill those lines. Initially, the referent of "which" is assumed to be "dust," but as the "blast" of the verse's "incessant motion" drives us toward the full stop in line 6, the possibilities widen to include, first, "this heap of dust" and then, when we reach the climactic "all," that other "heap of dust," "my flesh." That is to say, the word "all" operates retroactively to make earlier words and phrases mean differently. As the poem opens, "intombe my flesh" seems merely a fancifully witty way of referring to the speaker's immobility while at prayer. Now we see that the witticism is a tautology: his flesh *is* its own tombe, one more heap of dust, exactly like those that are the objects of its contemplation. To take acquaintance of *this* heap of dust is to follow (with a vengeance) the Socratean injunction, "know thyself." It is an injunction to which we too must respond for the simple "our" of line 5 does not allow us, as readers, to exempt ourselves from the statement the poem is making. In the first two lines we are insulated from this shock of recognition by the objects that literally stand between us and "this heap of dust"—the church, its monuments, and the speaker—but by the end of line 6 (which, of course, ends nothing), these have all become one ("at last") and that oneness has been extended outward to embrace us too.

Thus when Herbert declares "Therefore I gladly trust," we await the identification of the object of his trust with more than a syntactical interest, and for a moment we are surprised by what we find:

> My bodie to this school, that it may learn
> To spell his elements, and finde his birth

[10] *Ibid.*, p. 133.

Written in dustie heraldrie and lines;
Which dissolution sure doth best discern,
Comparing dust with dust, and earth with earth.
These laugh at Jeat and Marble put for signes

(7–12).

The body would seem to be a questionable repository of trust given the prediction in the first stanza of its imminent dissolution; and, of course, as the line continues the sense changes, forcing us to replace "my bodie" with "this school" as the object of "trust," a grammatical adjustment which mirrors perfectly the life adjustment the poem is urging us to make. In the school to which both the reader and the body are sent the lessons are strangely self-defeating. One *spells* correctly when one *discerns* the indecipherability of the text; discerning is *"sure"* only when the object of discernment dissolves; *"signes"* signify properly only when they become indistinguishable from their surroundings (a word that itself has little meaning at this point); *"comparing"* becomes an exercise in tautology, "comparing dust with dust." The words I have emphasized all receive both a metrical and a sense stress and together, that is, in isolation, they strongly suggest a process by which some measure of phenomenal clarity can be achieved; but between them and surrounding them are other words, which finally mock the pretensions of this clarifying vocabulary. Consider, for example, lines 9 and 10: The stressed words taken by themselves piece out a strong declarative statement "Written . . . lines/Which . . . sure . . . discern." But for a reader, the firmness of the past participle "written" is severely qualified by the adjective "dustie" which in its forward movement makes it impossible to take the word "lines" literally; in addition, the noun itself has so many possible referents—the lines of body, the genealogical lines of the body's heraldry, the lines of the epitaph (no longer there), the lines of the poem (which are themselves becoming progressively more "dustie")—that "which" is more a question than a pronoun. The question becomes academic with the next word "dissolution." Whatever "which" was, it is no more, having dissolved; only that dissolution is "sure" and, as the line ends, the verb "discern" completes an irony of which it itself is a victim.

The syntactical structures of this poem are no more successful at discerning or distinguishing than are the monuments they so unclearly present. Indeed, the forms of both (syntax and monuments) collapse simultaneously before the reader's eye, and with them collapses the illusion they together perpetuate, the illusion that the world of time and space—where "this or that is"—to which they have reference is permanent or even real. That is to say, discursive linguistic forms, no less then jeat and marble, are extensions of an earthbound consciousness, and, like jeat and marble, they become true (accurate) hieroglyphs only when their pretensions are exposed. Thus in lines 14–16 the imminent failure of the monuments to point out (isolate, individuate) the heaps they have in "trust" (what an irony in *that* word) is imitated in the failure of the syntax to keep separate (point out) its own components:

> What shall point out them,
> When they shall bow, and kneel, and fall down flat
> To kisse those heaps, which now they have in trust?

The fact that Hutchinson feels compelled to provide a full gloss of these lines—"What shall distinguish tomb and bodies, when all are, sooner or later, commingled in one heap of dust (499)?"—is a nice comment on the success of Herbert's strategy. Where his editor obligingly provides the distinguishing specificity of "tombs" and "bodies," the poet gives us only an obfuscating series of pronouns and demonstratives—"what," "them," "they," "those," "they"—with the result that the larger structure of the utterance is progressively undermined. "Them," "they," and "those" become one, not in the future of Herbert's "shall," but in the present of his question. And that question is as much the object of irony as are the markers whose dissolution it predicts; for the very basis for asking a question—for rational predication in general—is taken away when the phenomena to which the question would direct our attention will not stay put and are, in fact, in the process of disintegrating. In other words, this self-consuming question convinces us not only of the insubstantiality of monuments, but of the final irrelevance and insufficiency of the way of thinking (spatially and temporally) the act of questioning assumes.

The same use of language—not to specify, but to make specification impossible—is on display in the final lines, where to monuments and bodies and sentences and questions is joined time, as one more earthly mold whose form dissolves in the context of a more inclusive vision:

> That flesh is but the glasse, which holds the dust
> That measures all our time; which also shall
> Be crumbled into dust. Mark here below (20–22).

As before, the referents of the relatives expand so that for the second "which" the reader understands not only "time," but "glasse," "flesh" (one hears an echo of the biblical "all flesh is grass") and even "measures," all of which have been crumbled into dust. With this in mind, the final gesture of the first-person voice is more than a little suspect:

> Mark here below.

Mark where? and with what? and in what? "Mark" follows immediately upon "dust" (the heavy stresses of the Lydgatian, or "humpbacked," line pushes them up against each other) and the juxtaposition of the two words undermines the pointing motion of the imperative, leaving the reader to look at one more example of "dustie heraldrie." In this context, the final distich—"How tame these ashes are, how free from lust,/That thou mayst fit thy self against thy fall"—can hardly be taken as seriously as its alliterative neatness would suggest. There is finally something facile about the stance of the speaker, who lectures his body as if he were not implicated in either its pride or its fall. The poem laughs not only at the pretensions of jeat and marble, but at its own pretensions, and also at the facility of those readers who thought to escape from it with an easy and pious conclusion. Summers tells us that the hieroglyphic form of "Church Monuments" serves "to reinforce the message," [11] but that message itself crumbles just as we are about to carry it away.

Isabel MacCaffrey has written of Milton that his "worlds all fit exactly inside each other," [12] an observation that also fits Herbert. In fact it might be a description of the action of "Church

---

[11] *Ibid.*, p. 135.
[12] Isabel MacCaffrey, *Paradise Lost As "Myth"* (Cambridge, Mass., 1959), p. 142.

Monuments," where a succession of worlds or containers, at first separate and discrete, are discovered finally to be perfectly congruent, not only fitting inside each other, but filled with the same substance, dust. Yet in some important respects, this is not a representative poem. More typically the vessels and boxes (a favorite word) of Herbert's poetic landscape, when opened, are found to contain not dust, but Christ. This is uniquely true of the poem "Sepulchure," whose ostensible plot is the search for a lodging suitable to hold Christ's body:

> O Blessed bodie! Whither art thou thrown?
> No lodging for thee, but a cold hard stone?
> So many hearts on earth, and yet not one
> > Receive thee (1–4)?

The speaker's questions depend on two assumptions that do not survive the experience of the poem: (1) that stone and heart are separate and opposed entities, and (2) that the initiative in this situation rests with the heart. The first assumption is challenged even as it is taking form; for while the argument of the stanza distinguishes between heart and stone, their juxtaposition cannot help but bring to mind the biblical characterization of the heart as hard and stony. The second assumption will be overturned when we realize that Christ's entry into the heart is not conditional on its disposition to receive him, and that, in fact, he is already in residence. That realization, however, is still several stanzas away, and for a time we continue to move within the context of the speaker's complaint:

> Sure there is room within our hearts good store;
> For they can lodge transgressions by the score:
> Thousands of toyes dwell there, yet out of doore
> > They leave thee.

> But that which shews them large, shews them unfit.
> What ever sinne did this pure rock commit,
> Which holds thee now? Who hath indited it
> > Of murder (5–12)?

These lines apparently confirm and extend the opposition of heart and stone: not only is the latter more hospitable than the former ("out of doore/They leave thee"), but it is the more fitting receptacle. Again, however, the two objects are brought closer together, even as they are distinguished: both are now regarded as sepulchures, one for the body of Christ, the other for the body of sin, and, more significantly, both are drawn into the complex of associations evoked by the charged phrase, "this pure rock":

> for they drank of that spiritual Rock
> that followed them: and that Rock was
> Christ (I Corinthians 10:4).

> Behold I lay in Sion a chief corner
> stone, elect, precious: and he that
> believeth on him shall not be confounded
> (I Peter 2:6).

In the context of these allusions (and they are hardly recondite), the stanza receives a double reading. The rock of line 10 is simultaneously the stone that holds Christ's body and Christ himself, the sinless rock on which his church (another rock) and all its members ultimately rest. As in "Church Monuments," the components of the poem's scene are beginning to collapse into one another and, as they do, the sense made by the syntax becomes problematical. Literally, "Which holds thee now" is a relative clause, but in the multiple perspectives now available to the reader, it becomes a question. Which sepulchure holds thee now, now that supporter and supported, container and contained, have become one? "Oh blessed body! Whither art thou thrown?"

The answer to these questions is given in the penultimate stanza:

> And as of old the Law by heav'nly art
> Was writ in stone; so thou, which also art
> The letter of the word, find'st no fit heart
> To hold thee (17–20).

Every reader will recognize this as a near paraphrase of II Corinthians 3:2–3: "Ye are our epistle written in our hearts . . . not with ink, but with the Spirit of the living God; not in tables of stone, but in fleshly tables of the heart." Once more, however,

the allusion works against the literal sense of the argument, undermining its urgency; for while in the surface rhetoric the problem
remains the finding of a fit heart, II Corinthians tells us that the
heart has been made fit by the very person who occupies it. That
is to say, "this pure rock" has already made pure the rock which
holds it *now,* not the actual stone sepulchure, which, after all, is
empty—"And they entered in, and found not the body"—but the
sepulchure of our once stony hearts, softened so by the Word
inscribed upon them that they are able to produce laments and
self-accusing poems.

Reading "Sepulchure," then, is like the experience of reading
the Scriptures—"This verse marks that, and both do make a mo-
tion/Unto a third, that ten leaves off doth lie"—and with each ex-
pansive motion, the lines of demarcation with which we began
seem less and less real. The answer to the question "O Blessed
bodie! Whither art thou thrown?" is finally discovered to be
"everywhere" (now made one place), but especially in the inhos-
pitable heart which by virtue of its occupation has become what it
is so often termed in another galaxy of biblical allusions—the
temple of God. The solution of the problem that was the poem's
occasion ("No lodging for thee?") coincides with the *dis*solution
of its phenomenal distinctions, and both solution and dissolution
are confirmed in the final stanza:

> Yet do we still persist as we began,
> And so should perish, but that nothing can,
> Though it be cold, hard, foul, from loving man
>                   Withhold thee (21–24).

In these lines the poem's two arguments finally converge, one
asserting plainly what the other has all the while been suggesting:
the active force in this situation, as in every other, is not the heart
but Christ. Paradoxically, this plain point is underlined by the
ambiguity of the concluding line and one-half. Is it that nothing
(either stone or heart or stony heart) cold, hard, and foul can
keep Christ from loving (adjective) man? or that nothing cold,
hard, and foul can keep Christ from loving (participle) man? [13]

---

[13] One should note also the ambiguity of "should" which is to be read both as a
future condition that has now been forestalled and as a statement of just dessert,
"ought to" or "deserves to."

The pressure to resolve the ambiguity is minimal, because the distinctions that would make one reading better than the other—between loved and loving man, between the heart as agent and Christ as agent, between letting in and forcing entry—are no longer operative. In a world where Christ occupies every position and initiates every action, ambiguity—of place, of person, of agency—is the true literalism. His word is all.

MAKING NO THINE AND MINE

> O be mine still! still make me thine!
> Or rather make no Thine and Mine
>              ("Clasping of Hands," 11.19–20).

In the previous section, I began by making one point—that to read Herbert's poetry is to experience the dissolution of the lines of demarcation we are accustomed to think of as real—and ended by making another—that in the course of this dissolution Christ is discovered to be not only the substance of all things, but the performer of all actions. The two are, of course, related; for a vision which denies to created matter an existence apart from God, also denies the separate existence of free and autonomous agents. The tension between the two visions in Herbert's poetry—one dividing and specifying, the other resolving and unifying—is a tension between the "I" of the speaker and reader and the "all" of God; and the moment of recognizing and entering into this wider, sacramental vision is also a moment when the "I" surrenders its pretence to any independent motion and even to an independent existence. Thus the affirmation of an all-informing reality, as opposed to the separate and distinct realities ("this's" and "that's") validated by our senses and our reason, is a supreme and total act of humility; not so much a reversal of values, but a giving up of the responsibility for valuing, and for everything else, to an acknowledged superior power. "For in him we live and move and have our being." This is the most difficult of all actions because, as Summers remarks, it requires that "the individual should abandon the pretense that he *can* act in any way (61)"; and the extent of the difficulty becomes clearer when we understand that this abandoning is itself an act for which the individual must disclaim responsibility, and that this disclaiming is itself an act . . . and on and on. In some sense, then, the putting away of the self is an impossibility, since every success is simultaneously a defeat. The problem is implicit in many of Herbert's poems, including those we have examined here, but a number of them take it up explicitly. In these poems the speaker directly confronts the fact of Christ's sacrifice and realizes, by degrees and stages, exactly at what price he is its beneficiary. It is a price he is usually reluctant to pay and his recalcitrance is the shape of the poem's plot, a shape that is particularly well defined in "The Holdfast":

> I Threatned to observe the strict decree
> > Of my deare God with all my power & might.
> > But I was told by one, it could not be;
> Yet I might trust in God to be my light.
> Then will I trust, said I, in him alone.
> > Nay, ev'n to trust in him, was also his:
> > We must confesse that nothing is our own.
> Then I confesse that he my succour is:
> But to have nought is ours, not to confesse
> > That we have nought. I stood amaz'd at this,
> > Much troubled, till I heard a friend expresse,
> That all things were more ours by being his.
> > What Adam had, and forfeited for all,
> > Christ keepeth now, who cannot fail or fall.

The question that lies behind this poem is the central question of the Christian life. What must I do to be saved? The speaker answers it by declaring his intention to act in a certain way, only to be told that God has reserved that particular action to himself. In response he accepts a series of lesser roles only to be informed that each one of them also belongs to God. In amazement he falls silent and hears another voice supply the one answer the implicit question would seem to have excluded—"Nothing!" Of course that was always the answer, and the fact of the poem is a testimony to the speaker's unwillingness to consider it. That is, he will agree to anything so long as some sphere of responsibility remains to him. What he will not do is admit that nothing is required of him, for to do so would be to give up his sense of personal worth, the feeling that he was in some way "needed." His persistence, his reluctance to let go, his *holding fast,* is reflected in the structured sequence of concessions. First, he surrenders the arena of actual physical action, the observance of strict decrees, and resolves to perform an act of the will ("Then will I trust"); discovering that this arena too is preempted, he resolves to acquiesce in its preemption ("Then I confesse"); but even this least spectacular of mental actions is denied him, and he withdraws in confusion. The voluntary narrowing of the space in which he will operate has not been enough and he is unable to take the final step and narrow it to nothing. Yet, paradoxically, what he will not do, he does in spite of himself. That is, the unacceptability of each of his resolutions leads finally to silence and inaction—"amaz'd" here suggests both paralysis and a debilitating perplexity—and thus to an involuntary admission that the solution of the dilemma is beyond him. In short, he *gives up.* This prepares the way for the revelation from without, the revelation that the solution, and indeed all else, is beyond him, but that it is well within the capacity and inclination of another. The proper response to the dilemma the poem poses is discovered to be not action, mental or physical, but humility and self-abnegation.

The reader's experience of "The Holdfast" is similarly humiliating because it is similarly a discovery of personal insufficiency. The poem is constructed in such a way as to allow the reader to assume at several points that he is in control of its argument and can predict that argument's direction; but this seemingly firm ground keeps shifting under him and it becomes increasingly difficult to specify even what the poem is about. At first it seems to be about the opposition between faith and works, between what is required under the New Dispensation and the Old. This is an assumption the reader falls into easily, in part because the quatrain is so self-contained. It is, in fact, a little poem, complete with a full "plot"—statement-objection-resolution—and a rhyme scheme which provides a strong sense of closure. The opening line of the second quatrain serves as a coda to this small action, and it appears that what follows will be in the nature of elaboration or commentary. But with line 6 the poem opens up again. Nothing has, in fact, been settled, and as the speaker prepares to deal with a new objection, the reader is forced to revise his understanding of the issues. Once again, the patterned rhymes and the one-to-one ratio of thought to line combine to give the impression (actually an illusion) of manageability, an impression that is strengthened by the firm conclusiveness of line 8: "Then I confesse that he my succour is." At this point, however, the reader is likely to be wary of accepting this or any other conclusion too easily, and the brusque "but" of line 9 is probably less of a surprise than it would have been earlier. But the other side of this new caution is a new passivity. Where the reader began by asserting his control over the poem, he now allows the poem to control him as he waits for some indication of the direction *it* will take. He is thus exactly in the position of the speaker; in unison they give up their respective pretensions and put their trust in an exterior power, and the final and true conclusion—"all things were more ours by being his"—is for both of them something revealed or given rather than earned. (They get it by giving up trying and even that is an action they are forced into.)

In many ways "The Holdfast" is the quintessential Herbert poem: it poses directly the question posed more obliquely by other poems (not what man ought to do, but what man can do); it answers that question by first entertaining and then disallowing answers that would leave man with some measure of independence and efficacy; and it proceeds in stages which correspond not only to the evasive strategies of the speaker, but to the interpretative evasions that are made available to the reader. The extraordinary thing about these evasions is that they are moral. The speaker of "The Holdfast" wants nothing more than to do good, but he is frustrated in his resolve by the supererogatory goodness of God which is so extensive that it finally claims responsibility not only for the deeds that are done but for the impulse to do them. One cannot even take credit for the act of loving God, and it is this last refuge of the independent will to which the speaker of "The Pearl" holds fast:

> The Pearl. Matth. 13. 45.
> I Know the wayes of Learning; both the head
> And pipes that feed the presse, and make it runne;

What reason hath from nature borrowed,
Or of it self, like a good huswife, spunne
In laws and policie; what the starres conspire,
What willing nature speaks, what forc'd by fire;
Both th' old discoveries, and the new-found seas,
The stock and surplus, cause and historie:
All these stand open, or I have the keyes:
                  Yet I love thee.

This is another poem that encourages a premature identification of
its mode and therefore a too-easy assumption that its issues are
"fully understood." As we listen to the first-person voice document his proficiency in "the wayes of Learning," the suspicion
grows that this is a performance and that the ostentatious boast-
ing is merely preliminary to some other gesture. Moreover, that
gesture is likely to be anticipated (not perhaps in the precise form
it takes) by the reader who recalls the verse alluded to in the
title:

      . . . the kingdom of heaven is like unto
      a merchant man, seeking goodly
      pearls: Who, when he had found one pearl
      of great price, went and sold all that he
      had, and bought it.

Thus when the stanza concludes with a rejection of the intellectual glories it had been celebrating—"Yet I love *thee*"—the reader
is neither surprised nor disconcerted. More probably he wel-
comes what is, in effect, a confirmation of his suspicions, and he is
likely to be a little pleased with himself for having tumbled so
quickly to the point Herbert is making: "Ah, yes, this poem is
affirming the necessity of giving up the kingdoms of the world
('keyes') in favor of the kingdom of Heaven." I do not mean that
every reader formulates this exact sentence or any other in his
mind, but that the response of every reader will include something of the feeling the sentence expresses, and as one example I
cite Mary Rickey, who writes *"The Pearl* . . . is 'about' what
the title implies—the giving up of all that one has in order to
purchase the kingdom of Heaven." [14]

[14] *Utmost Art: Complexity in Herbert's Verse* (Lexington, Ky., 1966), p. 45.

But with the repetition of the same formula in the second and third stanzas, the performance, including the climactic affirmation, begins to wear thin and another suspicion obtrudes itself: the speaker's piety is a thinly disguised form of pride; the ringing declaration "Yet I love thee" is not so much a praise of God as it is a praise of the self for having had the good sense to recognize superior merchandise when he saw it; that is, the line becomes self-congratulatory and its emphasis changes from "Yet I love *thee*" to "Yet *I* love thee." At this point the poem seems to be exhibiting a standard variation of the Herbertian "double motion": the speaker and the reader part company and the latter becomes a critic and corrector of the former's words and thoughts. This new sense of the poem's structure is strengthened by the first six lines of the final stanza.

> I know all these, and have them in my hand:
> Therefore not sealed, but with open eyes
> I flie to thee, and fully understand
> Both the main sale, and the commodities;
> And at what rate and price I have thy love;
> With all the circumstances that may move
>
> (31–36):

These lines constitute a nearly exhaustive catalogue of the various forms intellectual pride can take. The speaker's assertion that he has "all these [wayes]" in his hand displaces God as the source and bestower of all things; one cannot properly give up what is another's. His claim to full understanding and open eyes is silently denied by one of the most familiar of Scriptural passages: "For now we see through a glass darkly . . . now I know in part." The verb "flie" suggests that ascent is his proper motion and makes no acknowledgment at all of the debilitating effects of original sin. And, worst of all, he misinterprets the parable of the Pearl, making himself the purchaser of the kingdom of heaven and forgetting that the great price and rate has been paid not by him, but by Christ. (It is we who have been bought and he is the buyer.)

In line 37, however, the speaker recovers himself and acknowledges the dependence he had seemed to be denying:

Yet through these labyrinths, not my groveling wit,
But thy silk twist let down from heav'n to me,
Did both conduct and teach me, how by it
                    To climbe to thee.

This "yet" works against the previous three "yets" by declaring
the action they introduce—"Yet I love thee"—to be illusory, at
least insofar as the "I" is taken to be the agent. Not only is God
the proper object of love, but it is he who is responsible for any
man's properly loving him. What we have, then, is another poem
of three stages: the first (it is short-lived) celebrates the value of
certain things in the world, the second (represented by the refrain
line "Yet I love thee") recognizes and asserts the superiority of
another value, and the third assigns to that superior value the responsibility for its own recognition ("not my groveling wit, /
But thy silk twist"). The experience of the poem, for both speaker
and reader, involves the successive passing from one stage to
another, and therefore a successive relinquishing of the prerogatives they had reserved for themselves at each prior stage. The
speaker begins by declaring his willingness to give up all that he
has for God and he ends by giving up the giving up.

Is this, however, the end? Isn't there yet a yet to the speaker's
fourth "Yet," and doesn't the satisfaction we feel at the resolution he achieves exactly parallel the satisfaction we felt earlier,
before the self-congratulatory tone of his refrain became obtru-
sive? What I am suggesting is that the mechanism by which the
reader is asked to penetrate to deeper and deeper levels of the
poem is still operative and pressuring when it is formally complete.
And moreover, that mechanism is infinitely self-perpetuating, for
if one must give up the giving up of the world, then one must, per
force, give up the giving up of the giving up, and so on in an infinite regress. Like "Church Monuments," "The Pearl" is finally
a *profoundly* unsatisfactory poem, for there is no position one
can assume in relation to it without compounding and extending
the error it exposes.

The case is clearer, although no more comfortable, with the
poem "Miserie":

Lord, let the Angels praise thy name.
      Man is a foolish thing, a foolish thing,
   Folly and Sinne play all his game.
His house still burns, and yet he still doth sing

(1–4).

In the Williams manuscript "Miserie" bears the title "Publican" and it is likely that Herbert was thinking of the parable of the Pharisee and the publican, Luke 18: 9–14:

9   And he spake this parable unto certain which trusted in themselves that they were righteous and despised others:
10  Two men went up into the temple to pray; the one a Pharisee, and the other a publican.
11  The Pharisee stood and prayed thus with himself, God I thank thee, that I am not as other men *are,* extortioners, unjust, adulterers, or even as this publican.
12  I fast twice in the week, I give tithes of all that I possess.
13  And the publican, standing afar off, would not lift up so much as his *eyes* unto heaven, but smote upon his breast saying, God be merciful to me a sinner.
14  I tell you, this man went down to his house justified *rather* than the other: for every one that exalteth himself shall be abased; and he that humbleth himself shall be exalted.

For seventy-seven of "Miserie's" seventy-eight lines we are listening to the voice of a Pharisee, self-righteous and critical of others. The self-righteousness is communicated by an absence: nowhere in the body of the poem does the speaker acknowledge his complicity in the sins he is indicting. The stance he assumes is that of a third person who speaks to God of the inadequacies of others. The object of his criticism is either man in the generic sense—"Man is a foolish thing, a foolish thing (2)"—or a generalized "he"—"What strange pollutions doth he wed, / And make his own (13–14)?"—or a pointedly self-excluding "they"—"They quarrel thee, and would give over / The bargain made to serve thee (25–26)." In a way, the most prominent word in the poem is one that does not appear, although it is implied in every accusation: man, not I; he, not I; they, not I. "How shall infection /

Presume on thy perfection?" the speaker asks, even as he presumes by disassociating himself from the infection he is documenting. He stands not with his fellows ("I am not as other men"), but with his God, and after line 49 he stands alone, pronouncing in his own voice the judgment for which he had been petitioning:

> Oh foolish man! where are thine eyes?

The judgment the preceding paragraph makes on the speaker is not made in the poem. There is nothing wrong with what he says (as doctrine his statements are unexceptionable); it is just that he is wrong in claiming for himself the right to say it, and it is this claim that the reader is asked first to recognize and then to deny. The poem, then, is a test for the reader, but it is a test so constructed that to pass it is simultaneously and necessarily to fail it. That is to say, however the reader responds to the poem, he cannot help but repeat the speaker's error: either he condones that error by failing to discern it (by accepting as doctrine what he should be criticizing as presumption) or by discerning it he places himself in the untenable position of judging the speaker for judging others. Thus in one of two ways the reader and the speaker walk together through the poem in a lockstep of self-congratulation until they are brought up short by the dramatic reversal of the concluding stanza:

> But sinne hath fool'd him. Now he is
> A lump of flesh, without a foot or wing
>     To raise him to a glimpse of blisse:
> A sick toss'd vessel, dashing on each thing;
>         Nay his own shelf:
> My God, I mean my self (73–78).

The impact of this stanza and of the entire poem depends on the final line, which is three-ways ambiguous: (1) My God (exclamation) I've really been talking about myself as well as others (2) My God (form of address) I deserve as little from you as do those I have been criticizing (3) I have been saying "My God," but meaning by that title myself. Each of these readings corresponds to successively realized levels of interpretation: in the first, the basic error of the "suppressed I" is acknowledged and corrected, in the second, that error is confessed to God, and in the third, the blasphemy it has involved is specified. At each level the speaker and reader are further dislodged from their position of moral privilege and are made the objects of the poem's indictment. That indictment, of course, still stands; what does not stand is the speaker's distance from it or the reader's distance from him. The questions he had asked of others (Oh foolish man! where are thine eyes?) are now asked of himself—the poem detaches itself from his proprietary claims and turns on him—and, along with the reader, he is reduced to the relative silence of the publican: "God be merciful to me a sinner."

In their unfolding, "Miserie," "The Pearl," and "The Holdfast" act out the dilemma of the man who would enter into a proper relationship with God. Every withdrawal from a prideful claim only reconstitutes it on the other side of a gesture. Every moral stance entails a presumption that must be disavowed, and every disavowal immediately reestablishes the presumption. It is an insoluble problem, or at least one that cannot be solved by forever retreating from one position to another or by vowing to follow the paths of righteousness. Moreover it is Christ who is the source of the problem, for it is his love, expressed in the redemptive act of the crucifixion, that makes it impossible to assume a stance for which he is not responsible. Christ is so good a friend that he becomes an adversary. "I will revenge me on thy love," cries the speaker of "The Thanksgiving," as he specifies the complaint heard in so many of Herbert's poems:

> Oh, King of wounds! how shall I grieve for thee
> Who in all grief preventest me (3-4)?

The answer is implicit in the question, but in an attempt to avoid it the speaker threatens a series of actions which correspond to the successive resolutions of "The Holdfast":

> Surely I will revenge me on thy love,
>   And trie who shall victorious prove.
> If thou dost give me wealth, I will restore
>   All back unto thee by the poore.

> If thou dost give me honour, men shall see,
>     The honour doth belong to thee.
> I will not marry . . .
> I'le build a spittle . . .
> The world and I will quarrell
>                 (17–23, 33, 37).

The strategy, then, is to imitate Christ, to match him deed for deed, and so prove victorious in a contest of love; but on one point the speaker falters:

> As for thy passion—But of that anon,
>     When with the other I have done (29–30).

But when with the other he has done, the passion remains to be dealt with, and it defeats him:

> . . . I will reade thy book and never move
>     Till I have found therin thy love,
> Thy art of love, which I'le turn back on thee:
>     O my deare Saviour, Victorie!
> Then for thy passion—I will do for that—
>     Alas, my, God, I know not what (45–50).

The first person continues to be assertive even in the final line, but what it asserts is its own failure—"I know not what"—and with this admission the victory the speaker had prematurely claimed is forfeit. The good works he had threatened to perform are included in the one action he cannot match. Having found the art of love, he finds that its perfection in Christ has left him with nothing to do.

He discovers what he can do in the following poem:

>                     though I can do nought
> Against thee, in thee I will overcome
>                 ("The Reprisall," ll.14–15).

Or, in other words, if you can't beat him, join him, which is precisely what happens in "The Crosse," a poem that begins where "The Thanksgiving" ends, with a speaker for whom the taste of victory has become ashes:

What is this strange and uncouth thing?
To make me sigh, and seek, and faint, and die,
Untill I had some place, where I might sing,
    And serve thee; and not onely I,
But all my wealth and familie might combine
To set thy honour up, as our designe.

And then when after much delay,
Much wrastling, many a combate, this dear end,
So much desir'd, is giv'n, to take away
    My power to serve thee; to unbend
All my abilities, my designes confound,
And lay my threatenings bleeding on the ground (1–12).

The terrible ambiguity symbolized by the cross is reflected in the shifting emphases and small surprises of lines 7–10. The piling up of short clauses combines with the "suspended" syntax ("when . . .") to create a sense of impending climax, and for a moment the upward sweep of the lines finds a terminal point in the firmness of "is giv'n." The sequence of "end . . . desir'd . . . giv'n" forms a closed unit which is both rhythmically and dramatically satisfying, or so it seems until the words "to take away" change the direction of the entire utterance. As a result, line 9 now pivots uncertainly around "giv'n" which looks both backwards and forwards, performing two (contradictory) actions at once. It is not too much to say that the verb enacts (in the experience of the reader) the familiar commonplace: the Lord giveth and the Lord taketh away. What the Lord taketh away in this instance is revealed immediately—"my power"—and while this phrase stabilizes the syntax of the stanza, it also reveals the true nature of the speaker's concern, and makes clear the subordinate position occupied by God in his scheme of things. In that scheme, service means an opportunity to exercise personal power rather than an admission of dependence or an acknowledgment of weakness, and this is mirrored in the syntax itself where "My power" controls not only "to serve," but also "thee." It is this (implied) assertion of control that is countered by the cross, or, more properly by what it signifies, an action so totally efficacious that it leaves its beneficiaries with nothing at all to do; it unbends our abilities, confounds our designs, and makes of our threatened resolutions to do good one grand self-deception.

These lines establish a pattern that is repeated in subsequent stanzas. Along with the speaker, the reader experiences a series of reversals and anticlimaxes, momentary triumphs that last only so long as the time it takes to report or read them—"Taking me up (22)," "To have my aim (25)," "the fee/Of all my woes (27–28)"—before they turn again into defeats—"to throw me down (22)," "and yet to be/Further from it then when I bent my bow (25–26)," "another wo (28)." The impasse that is worked out in the course of other poems is the occasion of this one, and for thirty lines the speaker rings its variations:

> One ague dwelleth in my bones,
> Another in my soul (the memorie
> What I would do for thee, if once my grones
>     Could be allow'd for harmonie):
> I am in all a weak disabled thing,
> Save in the sight thereof, where strength doth sting.
>
> Besides, things sort not to my will,
> Ev'n when my will doth studie thy renown:
> Thou turnest th' edge of all things on me still,
>     Taking me up to throw me down:
> So that, ev'n when my hopes seem to be sped,
> I am to grief alive, to them as dead.
>
> To have my aim, and yet to be
> Further from it then when I bent my bow;
> To make my hopes my torture, and the fee
>     Of all my woes another wo,
> Is in the midst of delicates to need,
> And ev'n in Paradise to be a weed (13–30).

His will may be turned in the right direction (studying thy renown), but he cannot even take credit for the turning. This is the woe that is the fee of all his other woes, the reason why he is cast down by being taken up, why his hopes when they are sped become griefs—because they are sped not by him, but by the figure on the cross—why the strength which now fills him "doth sting"—because it is borrowed and therefore diminishes him. The sense of stalemate, of irreconcilable antipathies, intensifies with every word, creating a pressure that is relieved only in the final stanza:

> Ah my deare Father, ease my smart!
> These contrarieties crush me: these crosse actions
> Doe winde a rope about, and cut my heart (31–33):

To the demands Herbert's poetry characteristically imposes are now added the demands created by a proliferation of perspectives so rapid that the verse threatens to leave the mind's eye far behind. Line 31 is easily taken in and placed: it is a cry for help from someone who has just spent five stanzas complaining that he has been helped too much. In other poems the speaker deals with a problem by realizing, finally, that its solution has been effected by someone else; here that realization is precisely the problem, and still the only recourse is to turn to the very person whose action is the problem's cause. "Ah my deare Father. . . ." So much is clear and within the mental grasp of any reader who, like Louis Martz, has for some time been aware of the "note of personal willfulness" and "scarcely covert pride." Such a reader, as Martz notes, anticipates the collapse of "the whole edifice of self will." [15] What he does not anticipate, however, is the sudden opening up of linguistic and conceptual vistas which begins with the words "crosse actions." This phrase refers immediately and most obviously to the "contrarieties" of the previous stanzas, that is, to all the smaller paradoxes that make up the large paradox of a victory whose reward is total *self*-defeat. "Crosse actions" also refers to the burden this paradox represents for him; that is it "crosses" his will. And finally, and also ultimately, "crosse actions" specifies the great action whose precise meaning is the puzzle that has been the poem's occasion:

> What is this strange and uncouth thing?

When this question is finally answered, the negative connotations of "crosse actions" will have been absorbed into a full comprehension of the significance for the individual sinner of heavenly

---

[15] Louis Martz, *The Poetry of Meditation* (New Haven, 1954), p. 135.

love. Meanwhile the multiple reverberations of the phrase pull the reader forward into the following line, where presumably he will find a fuller and more specifying context for it. The context he finds, however, is too full, for included in it is still another expansion of the significance of "crosse actions"; the cross-cutting of his heart is the inscribing on its fleshly tablets of the Law of Love. These woes and griefs, then, these death throes of the self, are but the working in him of the Holy Spirit, a "tuning of [his] breast,/To make the musick better" ("The Temper I"). In this case, the music is the poem itself and its lines and phrases are the groans that are now "allowed for harmonie"; but a harmony for which not the speaker, but the Spirit playing upon him, is responsible. (Underlying this confluence of associations are the two conceits whose histories Miss Tuve has documented, the conceit of "man as God's music" and the conceit of the crucified Christ as lyre upon whom is played the music of love—"Oh Father, forgive them. . . .")

Of course, no reader pauses to spell out the implications of "crosse actions" so neatly as this, but every reader whose ear is attuned to the resonances of the verse and to Christian doctrine will be aware (at some level of consciousness) of what is happening: the speaker and his God, at odds for so much of the poem, are beginning, literally, to come together. The distance between them has been narrowing as the contexts of "crosse actions" have been expanding; for in this expansion (of the Word into all), the positions of the two figures (on and before the cross) become less clearly, that is adversarily, defined, until finally, when the distance has been narrowed to an identity and the context expanded into an all-inclusiveness, they become indistinguishable:

> And yet since these thy contradictions
> Are properly a crosse felt by thy Sonne (33–34),

The extraordinary impact of these lines is attributable in large part to the precise ambiguity of the words "thy Sonne." Do they refer to the speaker who is, as we all are, a son of the Father? And is the cross "properly" felt the burden of sin left to each of us as a legacy by Adam? Or is this the first explicit reference in the poem to the crucified Christ? One is forced by the verse to ask the questions, but Herbert is careful to provide no basis for an answer; and, as a result, all the hitherto separate (but related) significances that have been attached to the word "crosse"—the crossing of the speaker's will, the cross-cutting of the Law of Love on his heart, the actual cross of the crucifixion—meet in the (possible) double reference.

The ambiguity, and the pressure for its resolution, are carried over into the final line:

> With but foure words, my words, *Thy will be done.*

The experience of this line is a succession of "double takes." "With but foure words" leaves open the question raised by "thy Sonne" and raises a related question: whose words? "My words," the speaker obligingly answers, and for a split second the line and its meaning are stabilized. But then we hear the words—*"Thy will be done"*—and they are not his words but the words of Christ in the garden. This revelation not only reopens the old questions (who is "thy Sonne"? whose words are these?), but creates a new one: whose pronoun is "my"? It was at first assigned to the speaker, but now it would seem to belong "properly" to Christ. These questions are never answered, because it is by forcing us to ask them that Herbert makes his point (or has us make it): the specifying of ownership (of "mine" and "thine") is unnecessary because the words of Christ (words, not incidentally, of submission) are simultaneously and by right the words of those who accept Him as their Savior. For "in him we live and move and have our being" and "all things are more ours for their being his." These are commonplaces of Christian doctrine, but they come alive here in the shifting relationships of this final couplet. Reading these lines is like looking at a gestalt figure in which first one and then another pattern emerge from the same physical (here verbal) components—My words, thy words, thy Son, I Son, thy cross, my cross—until finally there is only one pattern made up of two declarations which, if they were laid side by side, would be perceived as mutually contradictory, but here, occupying the same linguistic space, they constitute a triumph over discursive language. It is also a triumph of humility, since in the total merging of the two voices in the poem, the figure before the cross *becomes* the figure on the cross and finds himself by totally losing himself.

The problem posed in so many of Herbert's poems—what can I do if you have done everything?—is finally solved by *dis*solving the distinction (between thine and mine) that occasioned it.

## MAKING THE ACTION FINE

It is not difficult to see why a poem whose subject is the countermanding and gradual stilling of the individual will would end in what is for the speaker a virtual moment of silence. Speech, after all, no less than action (it *is* an action) is the vehicle of self, and it is entirely appropriate that the realization of total dependence coincides with the disappearance (at least as a separable and identifiable entity) of the first-person voice. (This is exactly what happens, you will recall, in *Death's Duell*). This, however, raises the question of a larger appropriateness, one which must be put to Herbert himself. Is not the poet who describes and requires (of his speakers and his readers) a progressive and relentless self-diminishing open to the charge of hypocrisy? What, after all, could be more egregiously *self*-assertive than the writing of poetry? Sidney speaks for all his fellows in the *Apology* when he glorifies the poet's imagination, "lifted up with the vigour of his own invention . . . freely ranging within the zodiac of his own wit." Short of silence, how is one to give up these claims, inseparable as they are from the act of speech itself? A declaration of dependence is no solution; it simply reintroduces the problem by producing something else that must be disclaimed. (Winnie-the-Pooh: "There must be somebody there, because somebody must have *said* 'Nobody.' ") Herbert's speakers can fall silent (as they frequently do) and his readers can be teased out of thought (as they frequently are), but the poem would seem to be irreducibly there, an intransigently visible manifestation of the self the poet would extinguish. The dilemma is not the invention of twentieth-century critical ingenuity. Herbert himself gives eloquent voice to it in "Jordan II" when he admits the failure of his attempt to achieve a poetic humility:

So did I weave my self into the sense (14).

The question, simply, is, how does a poet (or anyone else) weave himself *out* of the sense?

The question can be answered, at least provisionally, if we glance for a moment at "The Elixir." In this poem the speaker asks that God teach him to act in such a way as "to make thee prepossest (7)," or as Hutchinson glosses the line "to give thee a prior claim." Any action done "as for thee (4)" we are told is "bright and clean (16)," and for "clean" we may read "unpolluted by self-regard or self-assertion." The point is made explicitly in the first two lines of a canceled stanza: "He that doth ought for thee,/Marketh that deed for thine." By acting not in one's own, but in God's name, one transfers the responsibility and the credit to him, makes him "prepossest" and gives the action "his perfection":

> Who sweeps a room, as for thy laws,
>   Makes that and th' action fine (19–20).

If we return from these lines to "Jordan II" we can see that one way for the poet to weave himself out of the sense is to make God "prepossest" and so make the action fine; but this is simply to introduce a new question: how does one make the action fine in the sense specified by "The Elixir"?

Herbert's answer is to make it "not mine" by making the experience of his poems the discovery of their true authorship. That is, the insight to which a particular poem brings us is often inseparable from the realization that its source is not Herbert, but God. In some sense, which is verifiable on the reader's pulse (and available, I think, to analysis), Herbert writes himself out of his poems (weaves himself out of the sense) and leaves them to the prior claim of another. In short, he lets his poems go, so that both they and the consciousness whose independence they were supposedly asserting give themselves up to God, exchanging their separate identities for a share in his omnipresence. Rather than affirming (and therefore denying) that God's word is all, these poems become, literally, God's word.

This is, however, a final stage in a long and arduous process, the earlier stages of which are represented in *The Temple* by a series of poems corresponding in their progression to the progressive surrendering of initiative in "The Holdfast," "The Pearl," "Miserie," "The Thanksgiving," and "The Crosse." In those poems, as we have seen, the speaker struggles to understand and then accept the implication for his sense of individual dignity of Christ's act; and in response to the total efficacy of that act, he retreats, claiming for himself a smaller and smaller sphere of action. But at each stage he discovers that he must withdraw further; the pressure exerted by the insight "Thy word is all" is relentless and in the end it leaves him no room at all. The "plot" of the poetry poems is similar in shape. For the question "what shall I do" (or "what *can* I do"), there is substituted the question "what shall I write" (or "what *can* I write") and again the answer takes the form of a succession of retreats and structured concessions in the course of which the poet tries to reserve for himself some small part of the action of writing; but again this voluntary withdrawing is not enough, and he is forced to give up more and more of the resources (and claims) of his art until in the end he is reduced to silence, and disappears.

We may begin with the sonnets from Walton's *Lives,* which represent a level of intuition roughly parallel to that of the refrain line in "The Pearl," "Yet I love thee":

> My God, where is that ancient heat towards thee,
> Wherewith whole showls of *Martyrs* once did burn,
> Besides their other flames? Doth Poetry
> Wear *Venus* Livery? only serve her turn?
> Why are not *Sonnets* made of thee? and layes
> Upon thine Altar burnt? Cannot thy love
> Heighten a spirit to sound out thy praise
> As well as any she? Cannot thy *Dove*
> Out-strip their *Cupid* easily in flight?
> Or, since thy wayes are deep, and still the same,
> Will not a verse run smooth that bears thy name?
> Why doth that fire, which by thy power and might
> Each breast does feel, no braver fuel choose
> Than that, which one day Worms may chance refuse?
>
> Sure, Lord, there is enough in thee to dry
> Oceans of *Ink;* for, as the Deluge did
> Cover the Earth, so doth thy Majesty:
> Each Cloud distills thy praise, and doth forbid

> *Poets* to turn it to another use.
>     *Roses* and *Lillies* speak thee; and to make
>     A pair of Cheeks of them, is thy abuse.
> Why should I *Womens eyes* for Chrystal take?
> Such poor invention burns in their low mind
>     Whose fire is wild, and doth not upward go
>     To praise, and on thee, Lord, some *Ink* bestow.
> Open the bones, and you shall nothing find
>     In the best *face* but *filth,* when, Lord, in thee
>     The *beauty* lies in the *discovery.*

In these two poems Herbert resolves to use his poetic gifts to glorify God, and distinguishes himself from those lesser poets who take as their subject matter the inferior things of this world. The tone is self-congratulatory, and, as Miss Tuve rightly says, the sonnets might be entitled "Of Myself." [16] They do, however, have some interest in that they point, if only negatively, to some of the concerns that will inform Herbert's tougher-minded considerations of such matters. A line like "Will not a verse run smooth that bears thy name?" looks forward to a much harder question: *does it matter* whether or not a verse that bears thy name runs smooth? And the contrast in the second sonnet—between the "invention" to which the praisers of earthly beauty have recourse and the simple act of discovering the beauty of the Lord—anticipates that moment in "Jordan II" (originally titled "Invention") when "invention," everything that issues from the creative imagination, is declared unnecessary and the poet is told simply to "copie." "Invention" carries its full Herbertian weight in "Love I" and "Love II":

> How hath man parcel'd out thy glorious name,
> And thrown it on that dust which thou hast made,
> While mortall love doth all the title gain!
>     Which siding with invention, they together
>     Bear all the sway, possessing heart and brain,
> (Thy workmanship) and give thee share in neither
>                         ("Love I," 3–8).

[16] *A Reading of George Herbert* (Chicago, 1952), p. 192. See also, Stein, *George Herbert's Lyrics,* pp. 2–6.

. . . kindle in our hearts such true desires,
As may consume our lusts, and make thee way.
　　Then shall our hearts pant thee; then shall our brain
　　All her invention on thine Altar lay,
And there in hymnes send back thy fire again
　　　　　　　　　　　　　　　　　("Love II," 4–9).

In *"Love I"* man's wit finds out—invents—the beauty of created things, and his praising of them becomes a praise of his perceptual successes ("beautie raiseth wit"). Meanwhile no mention is made of the source of both the wit and the beauty. Quite another account of the process is offered in "Love II," one in which God is acknowledged to be playing all the parts: He teaches us to see in the beauty of created things evidence of his glory, and thus what ever issues from this perception, although it may appear to be the invention of our brains, is in fact the result of his "kindlings." "Hymnes" which celebrate God's fire are the products of what they celebrate. The illusoriness of human participation is most strikingly insisted upon in the substitution of "our hearts pant thee" in place of the more conventional "our hearts pant *after* thee." The deletion of the preposition makes "thee" the agent as well as the object of the panting.

Still, however suggestive these poems are of the directions Herbert's thought will eventually take, they are themselves primarily a plea for a poetry dedicated to God rather than to his creations: "and though thy glorious name/Wrought our deliverance from th' infernall pit,/Who sings thy praise?" [17] (The answer to this question is distressingly obvious.) In this context the idea that such a poetry would be God's in more than one sense is simply another rhetorical club with which the poet beats his wrongly inspired brethren. What he does not yet seem to realize is that in these terms, the critique of secular poetry is implicitly a critique of poetry per se (that is, of its presumption), irrespective of its impulse or rationale.

That realization is closer in "Jordan I," where the resolution to apply the riches of poetic language to their proper object is undercut by the suggestion that their proper object has no need of them:

[17] "Love II," ll. 11–13.

Who sayes that fictions onely and false hair
Become a verse? Is there in truth no beautie?
Is all good structure in a winding stair?
May no lines passe, except they do their dutie
Not to a true, but painted chair?

Is it no verse, except enchanted groves
And sudden arbours shadow course-spunne lines?
Must purling streams refresh a lovers loves?
Must all be vail'd, while he that reades, divines,
Catching the sense at two removes?

Shepherds are honest people; let them sing:
Riddle who list, for me, and pull for Prime:
I envie no mans nightingale or spring;
Nor let them punish me with losse of rime,
Who plainly say, *My God, My King*.

The surface argument of "Jordan I" continues Herbert's indictment of secular poetry, but only slightly beneath that surface there has been spied the rather bare bones of a Platonic-Christian anti-aesthetic: "Drawing upon this famous illustration of imitation, then, Herbert arraigns the poetic copyists of his own time. All poets whose inspiration derives from Helicon, who write of Human love, have chosen a subject removed from the truth, which is God Himself. . . . For Herbert, whose wellspring is Jordan, and who will try to write of truth, not fable, the most beautiful words are *My God, My King* (Rickey, *Utmost Art*, p. 32)." But Herbert, I think, is more rigorous than Miss Rickey's account suggests. If *"My God, My King"* are the most beautiful words, they are so in a sense that makes the standard of beauty, as we are accustomed to apply it, irrelevant. These words are beautiful by virtue of their being true, not true *and* (also) beautiful. The point is made by Augustine in *On Christian Doctrine* where eloquence is declared to be attendant on wisdom, rather than a quality separable from it. The criterion of eloquence, of "beautiful words," is not aesthetic, but moral-philosophical, and it is this that Herbert hints at when he asks: "Is there in truth no beauty?" A harder question, one which the poem stops just short of asking, is, "Is there in beauty, insofar as it can be abstracted from content or commitment, any truth?" The answer given by a succession of Platonically inclined Christians in the Middle Ages and Renaissance was a thundering "No!" And more often than not that "no" is accompanied by an attack on those who, in their response to beauty, physical or verbal, betray an idolatrous attachment to the projections of their own imaginations. The most impressive contemporary voice is, as usual, Milton's:

> he that will cloath the Gospel now, intimates plainly, that the Gospel is naked, uncomely . . . Do not, ye Church-maskers, while Christ is cloathing upon our barenes with his righteous garment . . . doe not, as ye do, cover and hide his righteous verity with the polluted cloathing of your ceremonies to make it seem more decent in your eyes.[18]

Herbert is less harsh and peremptory than this, but there is something of the Miltonic scorn for "corporeal resemblances and cloathings" in the words "fictions," "false," and "painted"; and in their insistence on the sufficiency of naked truth, the two poets are one. This aesthetic—if it can be called that—leaves the would-be celebrant with very little to do but affirm his allegiance in the most direct and unspectacular way, perhaps by saying "plainly," *"My God, My King."*

By thus enrolling himself in the ranks of plain-style poets, Herbert indicates a willingness to give up a large part of those very resources with which he had proposed, in the sonnets from Walton's *"Lives,"* to glorify his God. "Jordan I," then, represents an advance in the dialectic of the consuming of the poetic self; for to the restriction on subject matter imposed in the earlier poems, it adds a restriction on language; and to the question "Why don't we dedicate our abilities as poets to God," it provides an answer which "unbends" some of those abilities. But if the "immolation of the individual will" [19] is the *desideratum* here as elsewhere, the poem fails, since its effect is to call our admiring attention to the very individual will of the speaker. Nearly every line is an overt or implied request for applause. "Who sayes that fictions onely

---

[18] *Complete Prose Works,* Vol. I, p. 828.     [19] The phrase is Miss Tuve's.

and false hair/Become a verse?" The response obviously required is "certainly not this poet," and to the criticism of romancers and courtly versifiers in the second stanza the reader is expected to supply a counterpoint of praise for the poet who has let go of such toys. Even the relinquishing of the graces of art is so artfully done as to elicit our aesthetic approval. He does not lose his rhyme by simply saying *"My God, My King,"* but gracefully and care-lessly recovers it (from an approving God, one assumes). This is one poet who has his humility and his private triumph too, and once again Miss Tuve's comment is exactly to the point: "Herbert makes a personal dedication of his imagination to Heavenly Love; but the dedication is made not without a touch of defiance and pride, and the problem is simply seen and simply solved." [20]

The problem is less simply seen, and, in one sense, not solved at all in "Jordan II":

> When first my lines of heav'nly joyes made mention,
> Such was their lustre, they did so excell,
> That I sought out quaint words, and trim invention;
> My thoughts began to burnish, sprout, and swell,
> Curling with metaphors a plain intention,
> Decking the sense, as if it were to sell.
>
> Thousands of notions in my brain did runne,
> Off'ring their service, if I were not sped:
> I often blotted what I had begunne;
> This was not quick enough, and that was dead.
> Nothing could seem too rich to clothe the sunne,
> Much lesse those joyes which trample on his head.
>
> As flames do work and winde, when they ascend,
> So did I weave my self into the sense.
> But while I bustled, I might heare a friend
> Whisper, *How wide is all this long pretence!*
> *There is in love a sweetnesse readie penn'd:*
> *Copie out onely that, and save expense.*

"Jordan II" is a reprise of its predecessor, but with a difference. The pose is not dramatically assertive, but retrospective. In place

[20] *A Reading of George Herbert,* p. 188.

of those poets who are wrongly inspired or presumptuously artful, Herbert puts himself, precisely and openly documenting his failure to praise God properly. In other poems, the speaker is the unwitting victim of ironies which arise when he says more than he knows; here the ironies are self-directed and the speaker is no less aware of them than we are. There is a "double motion" in the poem, but it is a motion the speaker controls, and he is also in control of the ambiguities which in this case reinforce the plain sense of his argument. That argument turns on the confusion in his thought of a concern for God with a concern for the art he would offer to God; and it is a confusion we share (momentarily) in the second line when the pronouns "their" and "they" refer indiscriminately to "heav'nly joyes" and "my lines." The displacement in his poetry of the object of praise by the act of praising is here recreated in the verse, which moves away from any "mention" of "heav'nly joyes" (they do not reappear until the last line) to the self-absorbing problems of composition, to questions of diction, structure, and figure.

It is not, however, Herbert's strategy (as it is elsewhere) to draw us into the error of his former ways. We are to recognize rather than share the misplaced emphasis of his verbal narcissism, and he distances us from its appeal by supplying his *ars poetica* with a built-in commentary. The words he sought (the past tense is important) were "quaint," that is, curiously and conspicuously artful; his thoughts first "swelled" (with pride) and then moved, "curling" and snakelike, further and further from a "plain intention" which was more and more obscured by the covering ("decking the sense") of cosmetic metaphors. In the second stanza, words, thoughts, and metaphors are replaced by their source—the brain itself—which is also the true recipient of the "service" they offer; the poetic process takes the form of a closed circuit of self-worship "running" from brain to language and back again to the "I," which now occupies the position held in the first stanza by "heav'nly joyes." The original title of "Jordan II" was "Invention" and it is invention that is here anatomized and labeled, so that we know it for what it always was, the attempt of the individual consciousness to reserve to itself a role in the chorusing of divine harmonies and so gain a share of the praise it pretends to bestow. The point is made explicitly in line 14 (the climactic line in a sonnet) which confirms the moral we have been encouraged to draw from these two stanzas: "So did I weave my self into the sense."

To this point, the experience of "Jordan II" is more even and assured than is usually the case in a Herbert poem and, as a result, we feel able to predict the direction the argument will finally take. The solution of the poet's dilemma, it would seem, is to weave himself out of the sense, to return to the "plain intention" with which he began, by removing from it the overlay of painted language, burnished thoughts, and curled metaphors. The implied injunction of "Jordan I" ("who plainly say, *My God, My King*") will, perhaps, be reinvoked but with a new awareness of how far Herbert himself was from obeying it. This is more than a reasonable expectation; it is almost directed by the univocal thrust of the poem's first fourteen lines; and yet it is disappointed, not once, but twice. The adversative "But," which signals the turn in the argument, belongs clearly to the speaker, but it is not the speaker who supplies the poem's resolution. Instead, a "friend" (Herbert's special word for Christ) enters the poem to take possession of it, and because he enters in mid-line, we experience exactly the sense of sudden and peremptory intervention the poet recalls. Moreover, since the friendly voice is introduced by a construction that is ambiguously tensed ("I might heare a friend"), its "Whisper" sounds in the present, and in the context not only of the speaker's bustling but of the bustling reader who is busily anticipating the poem's conclusion. That conclusion remains a possibility, even though its source will obviously not be the speaker. The exclamation of line 16 could well be preliminary to a statement that would accord with our expectations: "undeck the sense, do not presume to clothe the sun, return to a plain intention." What we hear, however, is something very different and very much less comfortable:

> *There is in love a sweetnesse readie penn'd:*
> *Copie out onely that, and save expense.*

This couplet reaches out (as many have noted) to the first and most famous of the sonnets in the *Astrophel and Stella* sequence, but the effect is to point up the radical difference in the two poems. Sidney, oft turning others' leaves, is bid by his muse to "look in thy heart and write." Herbert, absorbed in his own inventions, is bid by *his Lord* to "look in thy heart and find what I have *already written* (in its fleshly tables)." The speaker in one poem learns in the end what it is that he should do; the speaker in the other is told by an authoritative voice that he neither can nor need do anything; one is advised to call on his own resources; the other is reminded that his resources are not his own. Rather than a "plain intention," the speaker in "Jordan II" is left with the fulfilled ("readie penn'd") intention of another, and it is that other who now directs him to it (he both makes and mends our eyes). The price of this saving of expense is very high, for the expense saved is the effort that would allow the self to justify its pretensions to independence and efficacy. This is why the resolution, made so neatly in "Jordan I," to become a plain-style poet, is finally no solution to the problem of weaving oneself out of the sense; for while the plain style limits the area in which the poet operates, it is a *self-imposed,* or voluntary, limitation for which he and his art can take credit. The solution imposed (not chosen) by this poem, or by the voice that enters to preempt it, is more radical, not the plain style, but no style at all and, in a way, silence. By copying out what is already there one speaks in the words of another, and therefore, to the extent that speech is an assertion of self, does not speak. And so the self-diminishing progress of the poet's career continues, from the limiting of subject matter, to the restricting of language, to the disallowing of even the least spectacular of linguistic options. To the question, so often asked in these poems, "how shall I praise thee?" "Jordan II" answers, "by doing nothing," and so unbends *all* the poet's abilities.[21]

"A True Hymne" goes even further by denying to him not only the action of praise, but the impulse behind it:

[21] Here I depart from the consensus view in which Herbert is held to be a poet of the plain style. In his aesthetic, or anti-aesthetic, the plain style is not a solution, but a temptation, the last infirmity of the noble poetic mind. By failing to see this, the commentators oversimplify exactly at the point where Herbert's rigor and clearsighted toughness are most remarkably in evidence. See for recent examples, William H. Halewood, *The Poetry of Grace,* (New Haven, 1970), pp. 110–111, and Coburn Freer, *Music for a King* (Baltimore, 1972), pp. 234–240.

My joy, my life, my crown!
My heart was meaning all the day,
    Somewhat it fain would say:
And still it runneth mutt'ring up and down
With onely this, *My joy, my life, my crown.*

Yet slight not these few words:
If truly said, they may take part
    Among the best in art.
The finenesse which a hymne or psalme affords,
Is, when the soul unto the lines accords.

He who craves all the minde,
And all the soul, and strength, and time,
    If the words onely ryme,
Justly complains, that somewhat is behinde
To make his verse, or write a hymne in kinde.

Whereas if th' heart be moved,
Although the verse be somewhat scant,
    God doth supplie the want.
As when th' heart sayes (sighing to be approved)
*O, could I love!* and stops: God writeth, *Loved.*

Like "The Holdfast," "A True Hymne" proceeds in stages,
and again like "The Holdfast," its stages represent levels in the
reader's understanding as well as plateaus in the spiritual history
of the speaker. In the first stanza that speaker betrays the debilitating *self*-concern that characterizes the early career of Herbert's
poet-protagonists. The impulse to "mean," to seek out "quaint
words and trim invention," is born less of a desire to praise God
(who is not mentioned) than of a need to validate the worth of
his own imagination. The muttered litany of "My joy, my life,
my crown" has too little of the poet woven into its sense to satisfy
him.

The shallow self-centeredness of this complaint is apparent
even to the speaker; and in the second stanza he moves beyond it
(too easily perhaps) to a gesture of resignation. The strict and
objective standards of art are replaced by the warmer if less verifiable standard of sincerity ("when the soul unto the lines

accords"). While "My joy, my life, my crown" may fall short of what God deserves and be less than art would approve, it is nevertheless valuable ("Among the best") as a sincere expression of a desire to praise.

This is a traditionally pietistic resolution of the problem posed in the opening stanza. The poet declares his willingness to forego the self-satisfaction of producing fine phrases for the greater satisfaction of having his poor, but well-meant, efforts graced by the acceptance of God. The poem could well end here, with this firm subordination of art and its flourishes to the plain statement of a loving faith. It does not end, however, and the complacency of this premature conclusion will be more and more disturbed by the succeeding lines. In the third stanza, the neat antithesis of art and sincerity is complicated by an ambiguity. It is not at all clear whether the "He" who craves "all the minde,/And all the soul" and "justly complains" if the words "onely ryme" is God or the poet. The imprecision of the pronoun reference suggests that the confusion between what belongs to God and what the speaker would reserve to himself—the rights of requiring and judging—remains. Moreover, the words of this stanza rhyme very nicely and the insistence of the rhymes and near-rhymes mock its surface argument. Where is the sincerity here? Exactly what does "in kinde" mean? The reader who had accepted the easy coherence of the first two stanzas may now be moved to ask some of the questions raised by Arnold Stein: "the problem of how the words are to be 'truly said' or how the accordance of the soul is to be achieved remains unexplained (7)." In other words, as the poem draws to a conclusion, the issues it had supposedly left behind are once again open and vexing.

Initially, the final stanza moves to restore the stability and equilibrium of the poem's earlier moments. The first three lines form a concisely aphoristic unit which reinstates the easy distinction between art and sincerity; but, rather than supporting that distinction, the final couplet collapses it. At first we tend to read *"Loved"* as "you are loved by me," but the immediate context ("O, could I love") demands an alternate reading: "I decree that I am loved by you." The two readings (they are not ambiguous, but simultaneous) make God responsible not only for finishing the poem, but for the emotion (love for Him) that was (*"Loved"* is in the past) its occasion. By writing *"Loved"* then, God supplies not only the want of a scanty verse, but the want of a scanty heart. His love for us is so great that He makes up the deficiency of our love for Him, moving us to praises which He then graciously accepts (*"Loved"*). The point is made quietly when the rhyme ("moved"–*"Loved"*) joins the actions of lines 16 and 20. The influence of the rhyme is retroactive, and the reader who had assumed that the poet himself was the agent of the moving must now revise his understanding. As in "The Holdfast," reader and speaker retreat together to a new position, only to find that it, too, is held by God. It is not enough to give up art, to fall silent and claim only the interior action of sincerity; for even this lesser claim (of a heart self-moved) leaves the poet a larger sphere of action than he is finally allowed. The poem's last word leaves him nothing, except the knowledge that the source of his every breath, thought, word, poem, is the God who animates him: "for we know not what we should pray for as we ought: but the spirit itself maketh intercession for us with groanings which cannot be uttered (Romans 8:26)."

I can imagine an unsympathetic reader who would object that the conclusion of "A True Hymne" is only a trick. It is, after all, Herbert, not God, who writes "Loved." On one level, of course, this is an unanswerable objection, but on another, it is beside the point. The crucial question is, where exactly does a poem live, on the page or in its experience? If one answers "on the page," the fact of heavenly intervention has no more authority than any other formal feature in the poem, and in these terms "Inspiration" is unprovable; but it is provable if one turns from the form of the poem to the form of the reader's experience; for if, in that experience, a sense of God as maker displaces our awareness of Herbert, then it is not too much to say that the poem is no longer his, or ours. This is, I believe, what happens in many of Herbert's poems. The retroactive understandings of which other critics have spoken involve the reassigning of responsibility for the poem and for its effect away from Herbert to God.

It is in this light that we should consider what is for some the most troublesome fact about Herbert's poetry, the presence in

*The Temple* of so many curiously wrought forms, the "Acrostic Land" of Dryden's criticism. If the thrust of Herbert's art is in the direction of its own self-consumption (and therefore in the direction of the consuming of the self) what are we to make of "Altar," "Easter Wings," "Deniall," and other poems which ostentatiously declare the wit and ingenuity of their author? I would answer this question with another—who *is* their author?— and assert further that the two questions are intimately related; for it is characteristic of these poems that at precisely those points where we are most aware of them as formal structures, we are aware of them as formal structures that have been mended or completed or given meaning by God. The moment of highest artfulness always coincides with the identification of the true source of that art; the wit and ingenuity are referred to that source rather than to the poet, who in losing title to his poem also loses (happily) the presumption of its invention, and is known for what he always was, a discoverer, one who copies out.

Consider, for example, "Coloss. 3.3":

*Coloss. 3.3.*
*Our life is hid with Christ in God.*

*My* words & thoughts do both expresse this notion,
That *Life* hath with the sun a double motion.
The first     *Is* straight, and our diurnall friend,
The other       *Hid* and doth obliquely bend.
One life is wrapt     *In* flesh, and tends to earth:
The other winds towards *Him,* whose happie birth
Taught me to live here so,     *That* still one eye
Should aim and shoot at that which     *Is* on high:
Quitting    with daily    labour all     *My* pleasure,
To    gain at     harvest    an    eternall    *Treasure.*

The two motions of "Coloss. 3.3"—one issuing from the self ("wrapt in flesh") and bounded by space and time ("our diurnall friend"), the other issuing from Him who "*Is* on high"—are represented by the linear and vertical patterns of the verbal object, and as a result the reader is himself involved in a double motion. For at whatever point (and it will vary) he becomes aware of the operation of the italicized words, he will be performing two (reading) actions, one linear ("straight") and sequential, the other vertical and episodic. Moreover, as the poem proceeds he will come more and more to regard the linear experience merely as a way of getting to the next component of the vertical experience; that is, sequence, rather than the generator of meaning, is more and more a conveyor to a meaning that is independent of it.

In this way the reader is led to adopt the grotesque physical posture of the "walleyed" man of lines 7 and 8, moving forward in time and space but responding within that framework to "that which *Is* on high" or, as the italics imply, to that which really is. He reads with one eye on the syntax and the other on the developing pattern imbedded, in some sense accidentally, in it. The significance of this "double motion" is clearer when we remember that the imbedded pattern is the word of God (or at least a paraphrase of it). Thus the dual commitment the reader must make— to the linear movement and the vertical unfolding—is a model of the dual commitment he must make in his life—to the things and processes of the world and to the spirit that gives them meaning and value. He has been led by the demands of the verse to proceed in time, traveling from point to point but for (the sake of) the eternal word, to move within the confines of a time-space experience but to use that experience in order to catch a glimpse of a reality which, while it may be revealed *in,* is not bounded *by,* time and space.[22]

Of course, this means that the reader's attention is gradually drawn away from the first-person voice. In the opening lines, the

[22] If this seems to be making too much of the simple fact that reading "Coloss. 3.3." involves one simultaneously in two "eye-actions," I would cite as supporting and extending evidence the poem's primary image: *"Life* hath with the sun a double motion./ The first *Is* straight, and our diurnall friend,/ The other *Hid* and doth obliquely bend." Always present in the seventeenth century as a possibility, the pun on "sun"–"Son" is here unavoidable, especially since the description of the planetary double motion parallels so exactly the double motion of a God who, in Milton's words, "also went/ Invisible, yet stay'd" (*P.L.,* VII. 588–589). The son descends to become our "diurnall friend" and here he performs actions that "obliquely" effect not only his but our return to the prospect high where there is only one eternal day. In short, he moves simultaneously in time and in eternity, the perfect example of the man who lives here so *"That* still one eye/ Should aim and shoot at that which *Is* on high." The poem displays not one but (at least) four "double motions"—its own, and those of the sun, the Son, and the reader, whose experience in this context can be said to approximate an imitation of Christ.

speaker's personal pronoun (*"My"*) dominates, and only within the motion of his words is the hidden word of God discerned; but in the end the hidden word is triumphant and the personal pronoun is dismissed along with all its pleasure. The very act of assertion is transformed into an act of self-abnegation, and this transformation is complete when we find ourselves unable to assign the final word, *"Treasure,"* to either of the two motions. That is, the speaker's voice becomes indistinguishable from that of God's, and the intuition that serves as the poem's psychological occasion —"in him we live, and move and have our being"—finds a perfect formal and experiential expression. By finding the *"Treasure"* that awaits him at the end of the poem—now no longer his—the poet loses himself, at least insofar as he is able to claim (pridefully) an existence apart from God.

As in so many of Herbert's poems, the moment of resolution, which is also a moment of revelation, retroactively illuminates the preceding lines, even to the extent of changing the direction of their meanings. In this case the reader is almost certain to turn back to the beginning of the poem and when he does so he will find that everything is different. On a first reading the least emphasized word in line 1 is *"My."* The initial word of a poem is often italicized, and there is no reason, when we are innocent of its final significance, to linger over a typographical detail. In the light of our new knowledge however, *"My"* receives a special emphasis, not only because we are aware of its position in an unfolding significance, but because our awareness includes the knowledge that the possessive pronoun belongs not to the speaker's words and thoughts, as the line apparently asserts, but to the (literally) revealed word. In a second reading the preeminence of that word is known at once, rather than at the end of a dialectical process; the poem is acknowledged to be God's from the very beginning, and within the influence of His motion the oppositions on which the logic of the plot turns are no longer operative. The distinction between our "diurnall friend" and "Him" who is "on High" is collapsed, since the "sun" of line 2 is now understood as Christ. Our life is indeed "wrapt *In* flesh," but in the flesh the Word became, the flesh of the living God who tended to earth so that He might become our "diurnall friend." These differences between the first and second readings are exactly reflected in what is required of us as we negotiate the verse. While in the first reading, it is our business to distinguish and follow the two motions which are the poem's ostensible subject, in the second, the "one" and the "other" (words now literally meaningless) "wind" in the same direction, toward (and from) *Him,* and we are asked not to distinguish, but to conflate them. In the very act of conflation, however, we reaffirm their distinctness, simply by making the effort. Even more than "The Crosse," "Coloss. 3.3" operates like a Necker cube figure, now looking one way ("My words"), now another *("My* words"), asserting simultaneously the loss of the self and the finding of its greater glory in a union with divinity.

Of course a poem like this may fail by succeeding too neatly, leaving the poet with the credit and with the self of which he had hoped to be free. It would have been simpler and safer, perhaps, if Herbert had burned his poems or not written them at all; but he takes this way because he knows that if the obligation is to send God's fire back again, that obligation cannot be met by withholding his energies (which, at any rate, are not his); they must be expended, and expended in such a way as "to make thee prepossest." Only then will the self realize the hope expressed in "Easter Wings," to "imp my wing on thine" and so grow more strong by growing less. This, not incidentally, is a description of what happens in that poem. The pivotal line in both stanzas—"With thee" —looks in two directions and unites the two motions the poem describes and imitates. Becoming "most poore with thee" is also, and simultaneously, rising "with thee" (the effect is similar to that in the last line of "The Crosse," "With but foure words, my words, *Thy will be done"*) and to become "thinne/with thee" is also to "With thee/combine" and be no longer "thinne." In the acts both of understanding the poem and tracing out its shape the reader's attention is always centered on the line "With thee," and therefore on God who receives credit for the process the poem describes and for the shape it takes.

The intention, then, is not merely to give up art, but to give up art to God by sending it back clearly labeled as His, a making of the action fine by making it not mine. It is a literally unimaginable venture (to sign someone else's name to your poems and

make the attribution stick), one that involves the risk of holding
fast to everything of which the poet would let go, and I will not
presume to judge his successes or failures; but as one (and that
a supreme) example of Herbert's glorious inglory, I offer this
analysis of "The Altar":

> A broken ALTAR, Lord, thy servant reares,
> Made of a heart, and cemented with teares:
>> Whose parts are as thy hand did frame;
>> No workmans tool hath touch'd the same.
>>> A HEART alone
>>> Is such a stone,
>>> As nothing but
>>> Thy pow'r doth cut.
>>> Wherefore each part
>>> Of my hard heart
>>> Meets in this frame,
>>> To praise thy Name:
>> That, if I chance to hold my peace,
>> These stones to praise thee may not cease.
> O let thy blessed SACRIFICE be mine,
> And sanctifie this ALTAR to be thine.

The most notable and noticeable feature of the poem is, of
course, its shape. In fact, one might say that the first thing the
poem does, even before we take in any of its words, is call attention to itself as something quite carefully made; and at the same
time attention is called also to the skill and ingenuity of the maker,
who is presumably the poet. This is important because it indicates
one path Herbert chose not to follow. He might have striven for
the art that hides art and in this way kept himself, as the artificer,
out of sight. Instead, he chose to throw the fact of authorship and
of "wit" or "invention" in the reader's face. The moment the poem
is spied, it seems to be saying, "Look what I've been clever enough
to do" and to the extent that this (silent) boast registers, the
poem, simply as a visual object, is already introducing us to what
will become its central issue, the question of agency. Who is doing
what and how? Herbert is always asking this question and his
answer is always the same: whatever the appearances, all effects

belong to God, just as all things are informed and supported by his spirit ("thy word is all"). If this generalization is to apply to "The Altar," both as an object and an action, it will be the business of the poem to reverse its first impression. That is, at first sight (literally), "The Altar" makes certain claims for itself and, by extension, for its author; but when the last word has been read, these claims will have been unmade or undone, that is, let go.

As readers, we share in these claims; for, as has often been remarked, the action of reading a shaped poem is imitative of, and analogous to, its writing. The poet builds the altar on the page and this feat is recreated by the reader as his eye moves from word to word and line to patterned line. The experience a poem of this kind provides or promises is uniquely self-satisfying, involving first the anticipatory pleasure of surveying, at a glance, the task to be completed and then the even greater pleasure of completing it, according to a plan that is finally as much ours as it is the poet's. In the case of "The Altar," however, that satisfaction and the sense of control in which it is rooted are subverted and the poem becomes the discovery, by both the speaker and reader, of how little their efforts or even their understandings are their own.

For the reader, this discovery begins in the first line where a surfeit of interpretative possibilities interferes with his leisurely completion of the foreseen pattern:

A broken ALTAR, Lord, thy servant reares,

The delaying of the verb momentarily suspends the sense and leaves us uncertain of the relationship of the three noun phrases, altar, Lord, servant. Is one subject and the other object? If so, which one, and what of the third? Or are all three (or perhaps two) in apposition to one another? Obviously I do not expect an answer to these questions, nor am I suggesting that any reader asks them consciously; but they do represent syntactic and semantic options which are available, and in their availability, pressuring, until the verb appears. In its position, then, "reares" performs a number of related actions: (1) it unmixes "ALTAR," "servant," and "Lord" by arranging them in syntactical relationships which are also temporal-spatial relationships of cause and effect ("I, thy servant, O Lord, rear this broken altar"); (2) it reaffirms the claims made by the poem for the ingenuity of its author by specifying "thy servant" as agent;[23] and, as a consequence of (1) and (2), (3) it allows the reader to feel once again that he is in control of his experience, in both its present and future contours.

These several effects of "reares" are all manifestations of the way language serves us by putting things (words, concepts, persons, actions) in their (that is, *our*) place. The difference between one's sense of the line before and after the verb is supplied is the difference between inhabiting a world where objects are floating and undifferentiated and a world where they are tied down and distinguished; and the satisfaction (almost relief) we feel at the completion of the line is the satisfaction of having our ordinary habits of thought confirmed. In what follows, however, this satisfaction is disturbed, and we are returned, in stages, to the state of "confusion" that existed before "reares" appeared to clear things up. Indeed, in the end, the very possibilities that are here rejected —that the altar is the Lord, that the altar is the servant, that altar, servant, and Lord are one and the same—will finally be affirmed.

Meanwhile, we enter the second line with a rather precise understanding of what is happening, and in the context of that understanding, "made" is an extension of "reares": same agent, same object. But this identification of the poet-servant as the maker (both of the altar in the poem and the altar that is the poem) is called into question, if not imperiled, by the phrase "made of a heart." In what sense can an altar or a poem be said to be made of a heart by a human artificer? In no sense if one remains within the terms established (finally) by the first line; and at this juncture, the reader is forced, as he will be again, to expand the frames of reference within which his understanding is moving. (As a result he experiences less and less of the satisfaction inherent in reading a shaped poem). There seem to be two possibilities: either the poet is taking metaphorical liberties and we are to add "heart" to the list of referents for "ALTAR"; in this case the line would read, "the poem represents the inner shape of my

---

[23] Of course there remains the possibility that "broken ALTAR" could be the subject of "reares." Inanimate objects, however, take action verbs only when a more "natural" reading is unavailable, which is not the case here.

heart and its structure is held together by my tears." Or, perhaps the line in its puzzling ambiguity, is alerting us to the presence of another agent, one who would then have some claim to the rearing of the altar-poem. To the extent that he is aware of these possibilities, the reader will probably lean toward the first, since it supports the view of the situation (both inside and outside the poem) to which he is committed even before he begins to read. Moreover, the alternative interpretation is uncomfortably complicating, creating more problems than it solves. One might wonder, for instance, "whose teares"? and the reader who asks this question, at whatever level of consciousness, will hear himself echoed by the first word in the following line:

> Whose parts are as thy hand did frame;

Whose parts indeed? The line itself answers the question and any others the reader may have been asking, but at the expense both of his assumptions and of his privileged position. The parallel structures of this and the first lines direct us to the large difference between the world pictures they project. While the force of the verbs ("reares," "frame") are the same and their objects (altar, poem, heart) are, in some sense not yet specified, identical, "thy hand" is substituted for "thy servant." The poet is not the framer of his altar-poem and we are not coparticipants in an independent and autonomous act of creation. Instead, both the shape we see on the page and the experience it provides are generated by a power whose presence has only now been fully revealed.[24] It is as if a curtain had been drawn back during the presentation of a puppet show, and the hidden springs of the players' actions were suddenly visible.

To this point, I have ignored the biblical commonplaces that give the poem its peculiar resonance, although as Joseph Summers observes, "There is hardly a phrase in 'The Altar' which does not derive from a specific passage." [25] In these first three lines, however, the reader's awareness of these passages, and of their rele-

---

[24] One hears in line 3, I think, an echo of Job 38: 4–6: "Where wast thou when I laid the foundations of the earth? . . . or who laid the corner stone thereof?"

[25] *George Herbert,* p. 142.

vance, is subordinate to his difficulties with the plain sense of the poem. It is only at line 4, after the relationships of agent and object, cause and effect, have been unambiguously established, that the biblical context becomes insistent and explicit.

> No workmans tool hath touch'd the same.

This is a direct and directing reference to Exodus 20:25 and Deuteronomy 27:2–5.

> And if thou wilt make me an altar of stone, thou shalt not build it of hewn stone; for if thou lift up thy tool upon it, thou hast polluted it.
> And it shall be on the day when ye shall pass over Jordan unto the land which the LORD thy God giveth thee.
> . . . And thou shalt write upon them all the words of this law, when thou art passed over . . .

These verses, as Summers explains, reach out to others in the New Testament, and together they make plain the connection between the poem's multiple frames of reference:

> The Mosaic sacrifices were considered types of the one true Sacrifice, in which Christ had shed blood for the remission of sins once for all time. . . . The Hebrew altar which was built of unhewn stones was a type of the heart of man, hewn not by man's efforts but by God alone. The engraving on those stones with which "all the words of this Law" were written "very plainly" (Deut. xxvii.8) was a type of the "Epistle of Christ," the message of salvation engraved on the Christian heart (2 Cor. iii.3).

This is where most readings of the poem begin, with the information that supposedly directs us to its interpretation. But that information is not really available until the fourth line, and it comes too late to save the reader the trouble of puzzling out the syntactical and phenomenal relationships of line 1–3.[26] What it

---

[26] This is a mistake made often by the practitioners of a naive historical criticism, to proceed *at once* on the basis of what the seventeenth-century (eighteenth-century, nineteenth-century) reader knew. It is usually forgotten that he didn't know it all the time. In this case the informed reader necessarily doesn't

does do is provide a confirmation and expansion of the intuition for which the verse has made us struggle: the poem itself is just such an altar as we find in Deuteronomy and Exodus, unpolluted by any human tool (pen, mind) because its true artificer is God, who is also, through it, the artificer of our understanding. This is not something we know when we begin to read; rather it is an insight we acquire in the act of reading, and it is purchased at the expense of the expectations and assumptions we carry with us into the poem, expectations and assumptions that support the sense we have of ourselves as independent and efficacious agents. For while each line adds to the pattern whose unfolding we had foreseen (and therefore, to some extent, controlled), the progress of our understanding is such that the value the pattern originally had for us, its promise of *self*-satisfaction, is greatly diminished. What we do with our eye—that is, trace out the shape of the altar—is being undone by the eye of the mind, which is not only reading but understanding; and what it understands is its own superfluousness to this or any other activity. Although we (literally) put the poem and all its related contexts together, our reward is the discovery that it was really done by someone else. The more the altar completes itself on the page, the less we are able to claim a share in its rearing.

There is, then, a "double motion" to the reader's experience of "The Altar," one in which he performs an action, and another in which he discovers how little of that action is properly his own. And this same motion is realized, too, in the career of the poet-speaker, who begins by asserting his agency and control, and then gradually relinquishes his claims to both the form and the effects of his art. Not only the altar-poem on the page, but the "altering" (the pun is not beyond Herbert) the poem may effect in the reader's heart, the true altar, is the work of God:

———

know from the title that the poem should be read in the light of Exodus and Deuteronomy. Rather, what distinguishes him from less able readers is the ability to put clues together when they come to him and discover (as part of his reading experience) the full biblical context. The fact that he could produce that context on demand doesn't mean that he has it in mind when he begins to read the poem (why should he?), for it is only in the fourth line that it is, in some sense, demanded of him.

> A HEART alone
> Is such a stone,
> As nothing but
> Thy pow'r doth cut.

Significantly, the two possible readings of these four lines are indistinguishable in their emphasis. Whether we take them as an assertion of the heart's uniqueness—only a heart is the kind of stone that requires for its cutting "thy pow'r"—or of the heart's dependence—a heart uninformed by your spirit ("alone") is merely a stone until it is cut by "thy pow'r"—they direct us to acknowledge "thy pow'r" as the force responsible for the finished (regenerated) heart's shape, and, by extension, for the shape of the altar in nature and the altar in print. The power of "thy pow'r" extends, literally and syntactically, into the following lines where it is the only available source of energy:

> Wherefore each part
> Of my hard heart
> Meets in this frame,
> To praise thy Name.

Within this self-enclosed unit, "Wherefore" is more a question than a specification of cause, for there is no agent supplied for the actions of meeting and praising; but an agent is so obviously required that the reader is moved to search for one, and finds— "Thy pow'r." God is revealed to be responsible even for the poem's psychological occasion, the desire to praise, and is simultaneously the object and the bestower of praise.[27] (Because of *thy* power, each part of my hard heart meets in this frame to praise *thy* name.) The necessity of reaching backward to find a

[27] The poem thus enacts in its syntax the fulfillment of the wish Herbert expresses in "Love II":

> And kindle in our hearts such true desires,
> As may consume our lusts, and make thee way.
>> Then shall our hearts pant thee; then shall our brain
>> All her inventions on thine Altar lay,
> And there in hymns send back thy fire again (4–8).

"The Altar" is God's fire sent back, an identity it claims by subverting its status as a man-made artifact.

subject for "meets" and "praise" underlines the change that has taken place in the status of the poet-speaker: a "rearer-maker" in the first line, he now has disappeared from (what was at first assumed to be) his own poem; and when he returns, it is to admit openly what his syntactical absence from the verse has already told us, that the activities to which the poem refers and of which it is the product—rearing, building, making, writing, praising— proceed independently of his efforts and/or participation. Indeed, they would continue, even if he were to stop here, in midpoem:

> That, If I chance to hold my peace,
> These stones to praise thee may not cease.

I am aware that these two lines are usually read differently, as a hedge against mortality: if I should die, these stones (words, lines, poem) would continue to praise thee in my name. Herbert is assumed to be ringing a witty change on a familiar common-place of courtly poetry: my lines will live eternally, or, as in the sonnets of Shakespeare, my lines will give you eternal life. The import of "The Altar," however, is exactly the reverse. If these lines have any value, it is because eternity, in the form of God's active presence, has (literally) graced them. Herbert does echo the claims of other poets, but only in order to impress us with their radical absence in his, that is, God's, poem. He trusts not in his art, but in the appropriation of that art by God, to whom he relinquishes all the rights of authorship, to the extent even of declaring that the poem is perfectly capable of completing itself without him. Indeed, as we discover in the final couplet, "The Altar" was complete even before he set pen to paper:

> O let thy blessed SACRIFICE be mine,
> And sanctifie this ALTAR to be thine.

Each of these lines expresses a wish that has already been granted, and the granting of the first entails the fulfillment (in all cases) of the second. That is, Christ died for us all—he is the "broken ALTAR" of line 1—and his blood ("cemented with teares") washes away all our sins and makes us, as his re-generated creations, capable of virtuous action, of rearing altars, writing poems, singing praises, in short, of "sending back his fire."

This "Altar," then, since it is the product of that sacrifice, was written at the moment of the crucifixion; and the poet and the reader are merely tracing out, with pen and eye respectively, a pattern that stood complete before they came to it. The final couplet is superfluous in exactly the same way and for the same reason that the efforts of the poet-speaker (and the reader) have been superfluous from the beginning. One cannot ask for what has already been given; nor can one do what has already been done. Christ's sacrifice has always been ours, and the altars we seemingly raise have always been his, and yet ours too, because "all things are more ours for their being his." In their mutual dependence of sense and logic these two lines are interchangeable; they imply each other, as do, finally, the possessive pronouns which provide their rhyme and alert us to still another making in Herbert's poetry of no mine and thine.

In its unfolding, then, this extraordinary poem manages to free itself from the pollution of its putative proprietors, the speaker and the reader, and to identify its true author. Appropriately, this freedom is fully realized and the identification made plain (by signature, one might say) in the last word, which is really the first word. That is, the reader whose experience of the poem is as I have described it may remember at this point what the first sight of the poem helped him to forget—that altars are raised from the ground up. Even on the most basic procedural level the notion that the poet is doing the work will not stand up. He is building backwards and we are reading backwards, so that in the end we reach, both physically and in our understandings, the poem's sole support, its first stone, its origin—"thine."

I observed earlier that if "The Altar" were not to fly in the face of Herbert's self-sacrificing aesthetic, the impression it makes as a verbal object would have to be reversed. And that, of course, is exactly what has happened. The poem concludes exactly as it began, by calling attention to its shape, but in the interim the responsibility for that shape and for the art that produced it has been shifted to God and away from Herbert. In losing the poem Herbert also loses, happily, the prideful claims it made silently in his name, and in this way he makes of its writing an act no less self-diminishing than the experience it records and provides.

LETTING GO

The reader will perhaps have noted that the climactic poem in the order of my analyses is the first poem in "The Church." This in itself should qualify any suggestion of too easy or regular a progression (even of dissolutions) in Herbert's poetry. His Jordans, as Miss Tuve has reminded us, never stayed crossed, and in the sequence of *The Temple* every successful crossing is followed by the reintroduction of the problems that were supposedly left behind. In its unfolding, then, *The Temple* is determinedly inconclusive; it refuses to yield a portable truth, or to be contained within a formula, even the formula put forward at the beginning of this chapter. Indeed, insofar as the analyses of individual poems have challenged or compromised the neatness of my Herbertian paradigm, the chapter is itself a self-consuming artifact. Not that I am here repudiating that paradigm which is, I believe, an accurate description of Herbert's poetic program. It is just that the poetry itself is less an enactment of that program than an exploration of its problematics. Letting go is finally not what Herbert's poems do (except for an occasional and therefore suspect success) but what they try to do. The difference is crucial and it is the subject of "The Forerunners," a poem that reopens much I may at times have seemed to close:

> The harbingers are come. See, see their mark;
> White is their colour, and behold my head.
> But must they have my brain? must they dispark
> Those sparkling notions, which therin were bred?
>      Must dulnesse turn me to a clod?
> Yet have they left me, *Thou art still my God*.
>
> Good men ye be, to leave me my best room,
> Ev'n all my heart, and what is lodged there:
> I passe not, I, what of the rest become,
> So *Thou art still my God*, be out of fear.
>      He will be pleased with that dittie;
> And if I please him, I write fine and wittie (1–12).

These two stanzas recapitulate the entire action of "Jordan I." The "sparkling" notions that issue from the brain in the form of "beauteous words" are declared to be less valuable finally than the simple repetition of a true "formula." The source of this formula is, as in "Jordan I" the Psalms, and in both poems the simple word of God or (what is the same thing) of God's inspired is preferred to all the embroidered and embellished effusions of the merely human imagination. What is different in "The Forerunners" is the situation of the speaker. Rather than choosing, in the privacy of his study, perhaps, to do without certain tools of his craft (much as one might give up some minor pleasure for Lent), the poet is here confronted dramatically with the realization that time's winged chariot has made that same choice inevitable, and therefore no choice at all. As a result, the gesture of renunciation, basic to both poems, is placed in a context that emphasizes the great cost involved if it is made sincerely. In one case there is a conscious decision to accept a limitation on the use of language; in the other the narrowing of linguistic options is inseparable from the extinguishing of consciousness itself. It is this larger dimension to the problem that the smooth surface of "Jordan I" allows us to ignore.

The tension in the dramatic situation is reflected in the ambivalent implications of the imagery. In Neoplatonic terms (which are certainly operative) the absence of color, the "whiteness," marks the moment when the mind's eye catches a glimpse of the ultimate reality, which is, we are told in the *Phaedrus*, "without shape or color"; but in purely personal terms the poet's white hairs point to the imminent dissolution of the mind and of everything else into a "clod." Of course, that word also looks in two directions; it is both descriptive of the speaker's deepest fears, and an allusion to that place in Scripture where the proper response (if not the antidote) to those fears is to be found: "Dust thou art and unto dust . . . ." This feature of the speaker's language—its "double motion"—is not something of which he is unaware. In fact, it is awareness, so full that at times it shades into self-mockery, that distinguishes him from other first-person voices we have listened to. One need only contrast the complacent solemnity of "Who plainly say, *My God, My King*" with the quiet and self-directed humor of a couplet whose jingling feminine rhyme joins two verses that do not at all "run smooth," a rejection of wit so egregiously witty that the gesture becomes a comment on its own inadequacy. It is as if the Herbert of "The Forerunners" were calling across to his alter ego in "Jordan I" and asking, "Is it so easy as all that?"

The answer of course is, "No" and it is given in the succeeding stanzas where parting is such sweet sorrow that what begins as a leave-taking turns very quickly into an entreaty to stay:

> Farewell sweet phrases, lovely metaphors.
> But will ye leave me thus? when ye before
> Of stews and brothels onely knew the doores,
> Then did I wash you with my tears, and more,
>          Brought you to Church well drest and clad:
> My God must have my best, ev'n all I had.
>
> Lovely enchanting language, sugar-cane,
> Hony of roses, whither wilt thou flie?
> Hath some fond lover tic'd thee to thy bane?
> And wilt thou leave the Church, and love a stie?
>          Fie, thou wilt soil thy broider'd coat,
> And hurt thy self, and him that sings the note

(13–24).

The movement of these stanzas is adumbrated in line 13. "Farewell" is just what one would expect, given the direction of lines 1–12; but what is given up with one word is taken back with the next, "*sweet* phrases, *lovely* metaphors," and suddenly the rhetoric becomes that of the forsaken lover: "But will ye leave me thus?" This is a distortion of the facts of the matter as they were acknowledged in the opening stanzas. It is he who is leaving, albeit involuntarily, and this show of concern for the phrases and metaphors that will soon no longer be his to command is really a concern for the poetry-writing self whose silencing he had supposedly welcomed. That welcome was predicated on the acceptance of certain hard truths about the ultimate value of "lovely enchanting language" and even of the brain itself; and it is this acceptance that is now gainsaid as the speaker pursues a strategy of evasion designed to hide from himself (and from the reader) something he has already acknowledged. There are two prongs to his strategy: he sets out to seduce himself with sound (*he* is the "fond lover" of line 21) by gradually intensifying the sensual appeal of his language "sugar-cane,/Hony of roses" and at the same time he gilds the seduction with a veneer of "respectable" philosophical commonplaces, most of which are borrowed wholesale from the arguments put forward in the sonnets from Walton's *Lives* and rejected in "Jordan I":

> Let foolish lovers, if they will love dung,
> With canvas, not with arras, clothe their shame:
> Let follie speak in her own native tongue.
> True beautie dwells on high: ours is a flame
>           But borrow'd thence to light us thither.
> Beautie and beauteous words should go together
>                          (25–30).

One measure of the success of this ploy is the number of readers who have fallen to it, and especially to its overtly Neoplatonic climax (lines 28–30). Arnold Stein is only the latest victim:

> Here Platonic solution is emphasized, rather than Platonic division. The statement is handsome and, as well as we can judge from the context and other poems, heartfelt—a major poetic belief. . . . As the Visible Church stands truly, beautifully, but imperfectly for the Invisible Church, so the "sweet phrases, lovely metaphors" express imperfectly the "True beautie on high" (*George Herbert's Lyrics,* pp. 17–18).

One can account for the persuasiveness of these lines on purely formalistic grounds. Two alliterative patterns—"*b*eautie . . . *b*ut *b*orrow'd . . . *b*eautie . . . *b*eauteous; *T*rue . . . *th*ence . . . *th*ither . . . *toge*t*h*er"—virtually carry the reader to the waiting conclusion; in fact the words "should go together" are superfluous as argument, since the argument has already been made, subliminally but effectively, by the alliterative patterns, which, in every sense, "go together." This is just the kind of pre-

sentation Bacon has in mind when he speaks of knowledge delivered in a manner "as may soonest be believed, and not easiliest
examined," and as a statement it is, as Stein says, "handsome."
It is also "heartfelt," but not because it is a "major belief" of the
poet's but because it is something the poet's fictional surrogate
would very much like to believe. The context here is not autobiographical, but rhetorical, and in that context we hear the voice
of someone who is exercising all his powers in a *heartfelt* attempt
to avoid admitting that he must let them go. One should note that
the speaker and the literary critic (or any lover of poetry) share
a common interest in this respect; both are reluctant to assent to
a position that hits at the very practice of their professions. Stein
goes out of his way in this section of his book to assure us (and
himself) that Herbert really doesn't mean it when he devalues
art and language, and in this he is a spokesman for all those
readers who recognize, as Herbert intended them to, how much
of a stake they have in the extenuating justifications that are rehearsed here in "The Forerunners." The self-seduction of the
speaker is also a seduction of the reader; and it succeeds because,
for both, the bait is the rehabilitation of everything they would
like to think valuable.

If one steps back from these lines for a moment, the fallacy
in their argument becomes immediately apparent: what begins as
a contrast between heavenly (true) and earthly beauty ends in a
virtual identification of the two, or at least in the narrowing of
the focus to earthly beauty alone. The image in line 30 is of
beauty and beauteous words ascending together to their source
on high, whereas in most formulations of the doctrine the ascent
involves the *discarding* of lesser beauties as their source is ap-
proached; the only support for the argument is the literary em-
broidery that adorns it. This, however, is beside the point, since
nothing encourages us to step back. On the contrary, this and the
preceding two stanzas are constructed so as to secure our active
participation in what is essentially a (mental) act of *self*-justifica-
tion. The speaker and the reader together ransack philosophy and
aesthetics for refutations of the familiar Platonic and Christian
anti-aesthetic, and together they sweep to triumph in this "handsome" conclusion. But that triumphant line is an engine of its own

reversal, for two very different readings of the phrase "go to-gether" are possible: either "belong together" in the sense that they are complementary and mutually dependent, or "go *away* together" in the sense that they are to be let *go* of simultaneously. One reading accords with the dramatic thrust of the poem at this point, the other would return us to the opening stanzas and to the acceptance of a necessary and even joyful farewell. There is little doubt, I think, as to the reading we are likely to follow (the criticism is my best documentation); in fact, as the line is read for the first time the ambiguity is not even felt, since everything immediately preceding has directed us away from it. What acti-vates it is the first line of the concluding stanza:

> Yet if you go, I passe not; take your way:

This second "go" retroactively complicates our experience of the first, and, as a result, the firm conclusiveness of "Beautie and beauteous words should *go* together" is irreparably compromised. And compromised, too, is the entire structure of rationalizations of which that assertion was a chief support. The effect is similar to that achieved by the word *"Child!"* in "The Collar"; in both poems a "line" of wit is allowed to play itself out until, at its furthest extent, the line draws taut and then, suddenly, snaps back, returning speaker and reader together to the simple truth they had been trying so desperately (and wittily) to avoid:

> For, *Thou art still my God,* is all that ye . . .

For the moment that it takes to read this line, the poem appears to have turned its final corner and the reader prepares to rest in the completion of a conventionally satisfactory meditative pattern: resolution, doubt, reresolution. But "The Forerunners" refuses to end so neatly and, in fact, for a time it seems unwilling to end at all. Any tendency on the reader's part to relax will certainly be checked by the first word of the following line:

> *Perhaps* with more embellishment can say.

With this single word, "so emphatically placed," [28] the poem leans back in the direction of the self-serving extenuations of the middle

[28] Martz, *Poetry of Meditation,* p. 314.

stanzas, and it is itself ambiguous. Does it qualify "all that ye can say" or "with more embellishment"? In one reading, the claims made for lovely language are revived, in the other, they are further diminished since even the *ornamental* value of language is questioned. The point is a small one and the ambiguity does not exert much pressure, if indeed it exerts any pressure at all, but it is one more indication of the poem's unwillingness to declare unequivocally for any one of the attitudes that alternately possess it. This is why the third and final "go" is felt to be such a release:

> Go birds of spring: let winter have his fee . . .

Even here, of course, the firmness of "go" is qualified by "birds of spring," as once again the speaker caresses what he is relinquishing; but the resignation of "let winter have his fee" seems firmly conclusive, especially since it reenacts the sequence of the opening lines where the harbingers are first welcomed ("See, see their mark") and then resisted ("but must they have my brain?") and then accepted ("I passe not"). The image of winter reaches back to the image of the speaker's white hairs and together they suggest a finality that is reinforced by the penultimate line:

> Let a bleak palenesse chalk the door . . .

By repeating the gesture of resignation, the line stabilizes it and we feel sure that the mental drama of the poem has been played out. The rights of the harbingers have been recognized and the king of whose visit they warn is now precisely identified by the allusion to Revelations 6:8: "And behold a pale horse: and his name that sat on him was Death." Once again, however, the assumption of closure is premature; for in the course of establishing one context, the line reaches out to another, by reminding us of an occasion when the visit of Death was forestalled: "Your lamb shall be without blemish, a male of the first year. . . . And they shall take of the blood, and strike it on the two side posts and on the upper door post of the houses. . . . And when he seeth the blood the Lord will pass over the door and will not suffer the destroyer to come in unto your houses to smite *you* (Exodus 12: 5, 7, 23)." My point is not that the situation of the speaker and the situation of the Israelites are collapsed into one another, but that the pattern of their similarities and differences complicates

our response to the line by once again giving the poem two interpretative directions. In one the harbingers mark for Death,
who will soon arrive to occupy the rooms they have requisitioned;
in the other they mark for life—they once again become the birds
of spring—and the houses so marked are passed over. We are
not asked to choose between these two interpretations, but rather
to affirm their separate *and* related relevances. The link between
them is typological—the unblemished male lamb whose blood
preserves the Israelites from physical death is a type of Christ
who, by shedding his blood, preserves us from the death of the
spirit—and since typology is simultaneously a way of distinguishing between and linking two levels of reality, we end the poem
with a complex and double view of the speaker's situation. Death
will, in fact, come to claim what *his* harbingers (of winter) have
marked—the speaker will grow old and decline into senility—but
because one room, and that the best (once again the poem reaches
back to an earlier context) is already host (in several senses) to
another king—to the Lamb who has marked us for his with his
blood—Death's possession will be only temporary, and after a
time, all (both body and spirit) will be livelier than before:

> Let a bleak palenesse chalk the door
> So all within be livelier than before.

That time, however, is not yet come; although the poem ends
by opening up onto a vision of everlasting life, the more immediate
future will bring the reality of Death; and the bleak paleness of
his inevitable presence has been too strongly asserted to be effaced by either an allusion or a promise. As an experience, then,
"The Forerunners" is no more conclusive than the debate it records between lovely language and the language of religious
formula. The rhythm of regret and renunciation is sustained until
the very end; the values which compete in the poem are still
competing when the last word is read; and we remain the un-
settled center of its contending impulses, unable to let go of them
because they will not let go of us. In its resolute uneasiness "The
Forerunners" is a powerful comment on the difficulty, if not impossibility, of the self-consuming enterprise of Herbert's art.

In *The Pilgrim's Progress* the enterprise is impossible not for
the author but for the hero, who is therefore doomed to success.

IV

# *Progress in* The Pilgrim's Progress

This book will make a traveller
of thee (Bunyan, "Author's Apology").

About a man that left his family,
it didn't say why (Huckleberry Finn).

### "I AM THE WAY"

Recently U. Milo Kaufmann has suggested that *"The Pilgrim's Progress* presents a conspicuous superimposition of stasis
and linear development," for, as he points out, "in a pilgrimage
that is in large measure the exfoliation of a Word once and for
all delivered, events only seem to be happening." [1] In other words,
the linear and sequential movement of the work exists in a state of
tension with the vision that informs it, and in Kaufmann's reading this tension reflects the irreconcilability of aesthetic and doctrinal demands. "Prevenient grace, like prevenient knowledge, if
too evident in the springs of the narrative, is likely to destroy the
illusion of a dynamic career (116)." Bunyan, Kaufmann believes,
is aware of this "danger" and moves to neutralize it by drawing
the reader's attention away from the "problematical dynamics"
of the narrative (107, 116–117). It will be my contention, however, that exactly the reverse is true. The illusory nature of the
pilgrim's progress is a large part of Bunyan's point, and the
reader's awareness of the problematics of the narrative is essential

[1] *The Pilgrim's Progress and Traditions in Puritan Meditation* (New Haven,
1966), pp. 107, 112.

to his intention, which is nothing less than the disqualification of his work as a vehicle of the insight it pretends to convey. It will take the following pages (and more) to document this thesis, and I would like to begin by examining an episode, which, in its unfolding, can serve as a model for the whole.

> Now as *Christian* went on his way, he came to a little ascent, which was cast up on purpose, that Pilgrims might see before them: up there therefore *Christian* went, and looking forward, he saw *Faithful* before him, upon his Journey. Then said *Christian* aloud, Ho, ho, So-ho; stay, and I will be your Companion. At that *Faithful* looked behind him, to whom *Christian* cried again, Stay, stay, till I come up to you: but *Faithful* answered, *No,* I am upon my life, and the Avenger of Blood is behind me. At this *Christian* was somewhat moved, and putting to all his strength, he quickly got up with *Faithful,* and did also overrun him, so the *last was first.* Then did *Christian* vain-gloriously smile, because he had gotten the start of his Brother: but not taking good heed to his feet, he suddenly stumbled and fell, and could not rise again, until *Faithful* came up to help him.[2]

This episode unfolds in two stages and in the course of the first stage, the reader is directed to an interpretation that reflects and extends the implications of Bunyan's title. That is to say, we are at first invited to measure the *progress* the two pilgrims are making by noting the positions they occupy on the graduated scale of a linear and shared "way." The sequence of events allows, indeed encourages, the assumption of one to one correlation of physical and spiritual place, and in the context of that assumption the point of the episode coincides with what seems to be its conclusion:

so the *last was first*

This "sense of an ending" is reinforced by the unmistakable allusion to one of the most familiar of biblical passages: "And

[2] *The Pilgrim's Progress,* ed. James Wharey, rev. by Roger Sharrock (Oxford, 1960), p. 66.

every one that hath forsaken houses, or brethren, or sisters or father, or mother, or wife or children, or lands, for my name's sake, shall receive an hundredfold, and shall inherit everlasting life. But many *that* are first shall be last; and the last shall be first (Matthew 19: 29–30)." The fit between Christian's situation and these verses is perfect, and as a result we are invited, indeed directed, to employ them as an interpretative key and to draw the obvious moral: Christian, who was last, has overrun his fellow pilgrim and is now first.

This is certainly the moral Christian draws (it is the reason for his smile), and had he stood, it would have stood too; but when he falls (for the apparent conclusion is a false one) it falls; or rather it becomes the subject of *re*interpretation, since it is suddenly an open question as to who exactly is "first" and "last." It is at this point that the reader is likely to recall Christ's rebuke to his contentious disciples: ". . . by the way they had disputed among themselves, who should be the greatest. And he sat down, and called the twelve, and saith unto them, If any man desire to be first, the same shall be last of all (Mark 9: 34–35)." In the light of this passage, which now replaces the light of the merely physical evidence (the evidence of things seen), Christian's desire to be first is a desire for precedence among his fellows. What moves him, literally, is pride of place, and it is this that puts him behind in the race ("run that ye may obtain," "run with patience the race that is set before us"), despite his apparent triumph. If the last is first, the first is Faithful, who is never more ahead of Christian than when he is overrun by him.

We have here two complementary and interdependent experiences. The reader is forced to give up a premature interpretation just when Christian is forced to give up the self-confidence and self-reliance of his vainglorious smile. Not only do hero and reader stumble together, they are picked up together, and in the same way, by an agent from without. Christian could not have risen, we are told, "until *Faithful* came up to help him," and without the second, and *revelatory*, stage of the episode, we would have remained the captives of a literal and incorrect reading. As it is, we are finally not allowed to infer anything from the physical circumstances of the pilgrim's situation (although for a time such inferences are encouraged) and in the end we can only distinguish between them on the basis of intention. Faithful's refusal to "stay" is finally understood as an assertion of the primacy of salvational over social concerns ("No, I am upon my life"), and although he and Christian change places, their relative spiritual places remain the same. The moral here, if there is one, is "it's not whether you are first or last, but how you run the race."

The moral I would draw is even more far-reaching. If the unfolding of this scene disallows Christian's claims to be first, it also disallows the mimetic claims of the spatial image in which he and the reader momentarily believe, the image of the journey with its attendant promise of the pilgrim's progress. Indeed one could say that Christian's initial error (and it is the reader's too) is to take seriously and literally the title of his story, and this is an error he has himself censured in an earlier episode:

> *Chr.   Why came you not in at the Gate which standeth at the beginning of the way? Know you not that it is written, That he that cometh not in by the door, but climbeth up some other way, the same is a thief and robber . . .*
>
> *Form. & Hyp.* They told him . . . so be we get into the way, what's matter which way we get in; if we are in, we are in: thou art but in the way, who, as we perceive, came in at the Gate; and we are also in the way that came tumbling over the wall: Wherin now is thy condition better than ours?
>
> *Chr.* I walk by the Rule of my Master, you walk by the rude working of your fancies. . . . You come in by yourselves without his direction, and shall go out by yourselves without his mercy (39–40).

The distinction between the two positions put forward here is finally a distinction between two senses of the word "way"; and it is one the reader makes for himself when the repetitions of the prose pressure him to ask seriously the question Formalist and Hypocrisy ask defensively: after all, what does being in the way mean? It is clear that for them the "way" is any way which finds them in an external conformity with the directions they have been given. We are, they say to Christian, in the same *place* as you; are we not therefore in the same way? Christian answers by internalizing the metaphor within which they are (self) confined; for him, the "way" refers to an inner commitment of the spirit (a road, as Augustine says, not from place to place, but of the affections), a commitment to the rule of his master, and as long as he walks by *that,* any road he literally walks in is *the* way. Being in the way, then, is paradoxically independent of the way you happen to be in, for you will be in the way only if the way is in you. The point is made silently (and by the reader) when the dreamer reports on the conclusion of this conversation. "Then I saw that they went on, every man in his way." Literally, this makes no sense at all; the three pilgrims are, after all, walking side by side; but it makes perfect sense if the word "way" is understood as Christian understands it, for then the proximity that joins the pilgrims is of less significance than the disparity of spirit that places them on different roads.

To the extent that he makes this distinction (between "way" and "way") the reader attests to his awareness of a dimension that is not available in the visible configurations of the scene or in the language that describes it. Indeed, in order to affirm the primacy of that dimension he must (like Christian) interpret the language of spatial configuration in such a way as to deny its claims to referential adequacy. The pressure to so interpret or *de*interpret (we are, after all, asked to *cut off* meanings) is basic to our experience of *The Pilgrim's Progress,* and the issues are always more than linguistic or literary. When Formalist and Hypocrisy restrict themselves to a literal "reading" of the way, they not only betray an inability to think symbolically, they perform an act of willful self-worship. This is what Christian means when he declares "you walk by the rude working of your fancies." The assessment they make of their situation is based on the physical and available evidence ("Wherin now is thy condition better than ours?") which defines the boundaries of their belief. They believe only in what they see, and since it is what *they* see, they believe in themselves. Christian, on the other hand, believes in (and walks by) the "rule" of his master.

This rule is nowhere given, but the several scriptural allusions in the passage point us unmistakably to it:

I am the way, the truth and the life; no man cometh to
the Father, but by me (John 14: 6).

*I* am the way. This is an absolute and unqualified assertion which
defines both the obligations and the dangers of the pilgrimage.
The many temptations set in the path of Christian and his fellows
are essentially one, the temptation to substitute for the way of
Christ the way of the self, either by presuming to come alone,
without His intercession, or by presuming to come by an external
way, and not by the inner way of belief (the example of Ignorance
is pertinent here). And yet these are precisely the presumptions
that are inherent in the title, *The Pilgrim's Progress,* and in the
metaphor which literally carries us through the story. What this
suggests is that the form of *The Pilgrim's Progress,* because it
spatializes and trivializes the way, is as great a danger as any the
pilgrims meet within its confines; so that if we are to read the
work correctly, we must actively resist the pressure of its temporal-spatial lines of cause and effect.


PROGRESS IN *The Pilgrim's Progress*

Curiously enough we are helped to resist by the prose itself
which consistently disappoints the expectations generated by
the title. These include (1) the negotiation by one or more pilgrims of a fixed and graduated set of obstacles (2) a direct and
progressive relationship between the number of obstacles negotiated and the piling up of spiritual "points" toward a definite
goal (3) a growing sense of accomplishment and self-satisfaction
(in the reader as well as in the characters) which accelerates as
the pilgrims draw nearer to the Heavenly City. What we find,
however, are (1) a route whose landmarks and dangers vary with
the inner state of those who travel it (2) no direct relationship at
all between the point (in space and time) one has reached and
the attainment of the ultimate reward, and (3) a pattern of backslidings and providential rescues that works to subvert the self-
confidence of pilgrim and reader alike.

In short, *The Pilgrim's Progress* is antiprogressive, both as a
narrative and as a reading experience. To be sure the illusion of a
progress and of a fixed and external way is often present, but it is

just as often undermined. Thus, when Faithful and Christian compare notes, we discover that there is not one but an infinity of ways, each of which shapes itself to the inclinations of its single traveler. Christian's doubts lead him to fall into the Slough of Dispond and later make him vulnerable to the despair-inducing arguments of Apollyon. Faithful's firmness neutralizes these dangers (he avoids one and is never confronted by the other), but the forms of *his* weakness find their own visible and threatening expression. Accosted by Wanton, he escapes her net, but not, as he admits, "wholly (69)." Some part of him has responded to the lure of "carnal and fleshly content (68)" and it is this part that Adam the First lays hold of: "I turned to go away from him: but . . . I felt him take hold of my flesh and give me such a deadly twitch back, that I thought he had pull'd part of me after himself (70)." Faithful manages to tear himself away, but within a few minutes he is overtaken by Moses who falls to beating him "because of [his] secret inclining to *Adam the first*." Rescued from a certain end by one with "holes in his hands, and his side," Faithful is next tempted by Shame who whispers to him of "the base and low estate of . . . Pilgrims (72)." The entire sequence, which has no parallel in Christian's adventures, can be subsumed under a single rubric: the temptations of the world or "The lust of the flesh, the lust of the eyes and the pride of life (I John 2:16)." The enemy wears many faces, but his appeal is always the same; and it is an appeal which fits itself, like a glove, to the individual flesh:

> *The tryals that those men do meet withal*
> *That are obedient to the Heavenly call,*
> *Are manifold and suited to the flesh,*
> *And come, and come, and come again afresh;*
> *That now, or sometime else, we by them may*
> *Be taken, overcome, and cast away* (74).

Now, or sometime else, or someplace else, it doesn't really matter. A trial is never further away than the next step or thought, for the perils of the way are generated by a pilgrim's weakness, and they persist as long as it persists. Fleeing from place to place is no way to escape a foe who lives within. Thus Faithful moves

from the wiles of Wanton, to the "delights" that are the wages
offered by Adam the First, to Shame and *"that which is highly
esteemed among Men* (73)," that is, to the wiles of Wanton.
Christian's experience is similarly homogeneous, but his exterior-
interior landscape is crowded with an entirely different cast of
characters (he renounces the pleasures of the world in the opening
pages) and the comment he makes at the end of Faithful's story
speaks for itself:

> *I am sure it fared far otherwise with me* (74).

It fares far otherwise with everyone.

Not only does the way vary according to the inner landscapes
of its travelers, but it is static in its variety, since each traveler
simply meets himself, over and over again. From the beginning,
the sense of a progression, of events following one another and
causing one another, is countered by a deepening conviction that
every crisis along the way is discrete and total. Although we move
with Christian and the others from scene to scene and adventure
to adventure, we (and they) are always in the same place. Within
minutes (seconds in reading time) of his rescue from the Slough
of Dispond, Christian falls to the arguments of Mr. Worldly-
Wiseman, and when Evangelist discovers him, their conversation
follows the pattern established by the opening scene:

> *Are not thou the man that I found crying, without the
> walls of the City of* Destruction?
> *Chr.*   Yes, dear Sir, I am the man.
> *Evan.   Did not I direct thee the way to the little Wicket-
> gate?*
> *Chr.*   Yes, dear Sir said *Christian.*
> *Evan.   How is it then that thou art so quickly turned
> aside, for thou art now out of the way* (20)?

Christian's explanation, of course, is woefully inadequate, and
Evangelist's admonitions soon bring him to tears: "Then *Christian* fell down at his foot as dead, crying, Woe is me, for I am
undone: at the sight of which *Evangelist* caught him by the right
hand, saying, All matter of sin and blasphemies shall be forgiven unto men; be not faithless, but believing; then did *Chris-*

*tian* again a little revive, and stood up trembling, as at first, before *Evangelist* (22)." "At first" refers not only to Christian's posture as Evangelist begins to speak ("So he stood trembling"), but to his first appearance on our stage: "I looked, and saw him open the Book, and Read therin; and as he read, he wept and trembled: and not being able longer to contain, he brake out with a lamentable cry; saying, *what shall I do* (8)?" We discover Christian paralyzed by fear, lacking a basis for direction, and crying in despair, "What shall I do?" And when Evangelist appears before him for the second time, he is paralyzed by fear, lacking a basis for direction, and wondering, "what shall I do?": "Christian was afraid to venture further, lest the *Hill* should fall on his head: wherefore there he stood still, and wotted not what to do (20)." Directed by Evangelist to the Wicket-gate, he knocks and asks "tell me what I must do (25)." Instructed by Interpreter and Good-Will, he proceeds confidently on his way, only to be caught up once again in the familiar cycle of crisis and paralysis: "he felt in his bosom for his Roll: that he might read therin and be comforted; but he felt, and found it not. Then was *Christian* in great distress, and knew not what to do. . . . Here therefore he began to be much perplexed, and *knew not what to do* (43)."

The only consistent spatial pattern Christian's actions trace out is cyclical, for whenever a new opportunity to fall into an old error presents itself, he invariably seizes it. A contrite Christian, "greatly ashamed to think that this Gentlemans [Mr. Worldly-Wiseman] arguments . . . should have that prevalency with him as to cause him to forsake the right way," listens attentively to Evangelist's warning, "take heed that thou turn not aside again (24)"; but a later scene finds him hearkening to one "Flatterer" and explaining to another rescuer, "we did not imagine . . . that this fine-spoken man had been he (134)." The last difficulty encountered on the way is the bridgeless River of Death, which is "deeper or shallower," Christian is told, *"as you believe in the King of the place* (157)." Christian's response is distressingly familiar: *"Christian* began to dispond in his mind." We have returned full circle to the beginning of the journey and the Slough of Dispond whose depth varies in direct proportion to the doubts and fears of the sinner (15). Christian sinks into one and is in danger of sinking into the other; the depth of both is the measure of his little faith; and in both scenes only the intervention of an agent of grace saves him from himself. Although he is within sight of his goal, in some sense Christian has not advanced at all. Nor have we: the refusal of the narrative to trace out a progress frustrates the reader's desire to follow one. There is, it would seem, no progress in *The Pilgrim's Progress*.

This is, of course, only a half-truth. After all, distances are traveled, milestones are passed, and the Heavenly City is reported to be nearer and nearer. Moreover, Christian enjoys a number of successes and these at least would seem to justify the idea of a progress for which he is, in some part, responsible. But it is precisely at these moments of apparent self-assertion that Christian's dependence is most clearly and forcefully revealed; so that if we do think in terms of a progress, it is never felt to be the pilgrim's.

The famous victory over Apollyon is a case in point:

> Then did *Christian* draw, for he saw 'twas time to bestir him; and *Apollyon* as fast made at him, throwing Darts as thick as hail; by the which, notwithstanding all that *Christian* could do to avoid it, *Apollyon* wounded him in his *head,* his *hand* and *foot;* this made *Christian* give a little back: *Apollyon* therefore followed his work amain, and *Christian* again took courage, and resisted as manfully as he could. This sore Combat lasted for above half a day, even till *Christian* was almost quite spent. For you must know, that *Christian,* by reason of his wounds, must needs grow weaker and weaker.
>
> Then *Apollyon* espying his opportunity, began to gather up close to *Christian,* and wrestling with him, gave him a dreadful fall; and with that *Christian's* Sword flew out of his hand. Then said *Apollion, I am sure of thee now;* and with that, he had almost prest him to death; so that *Christian* began to despair of life. But as God would have it, while *Apollyon* was fetching of his last blow, thereby to make a full end of this good Man, *Christian* nimbly reached out his hand for his Sword, and caught it, saying,

*Rejoyce not against me, O mine Enemy! when I fall, I shall arise;* and with that, gave him a deadly thrust, which made him give back, as one that had received his mortal wound: *Christian* perceiving that, made at him again, saying, *Nay, in all these things we are more then Conquerours, through him that loved us.* And with that, *Apollyon* spread forth his Dragons wings, and sped him away, that *Christian* [for a season] saw him no more (59–60).[3]

The seemingly irreversible movement of the action is in the direction of Christian's defeat. Apollyon's successful advances alternate with statements of Christian's inadequacy: "notwithstanding all that Christian could do," "as manfully as he could." The result is a sense of inevitability that is perfectly captured in the final sentence of the first paragraph. The two "musts" leave no room for any outcome other than the one pointed to by the repetition of "weaker," and when Apollyon cries in triumph, "I am sure of thee now," his confidence would seem to be wholly justified.

This is, of course, a reading from Apollyon's point of view, and it is not a point of view we are likely to share. *The Pilgrim's Progress* is, after all, Christian's story, and the reversal that follows is not unexpected. What may be unexpected, however, is the manner of the reversal, for when Apollyon is routed, it is not by Christian, but by a phrase, "as God would have it." In effect, these words take away the independence of the two actors, shifting the focus from the thrusts and parries of the battle to the unseen force that is responsible for them. "As God would have it" exerts a syntactical as well as a real control over everything that falls within its sphere (this includes even Apollyon's actions or pseudo-actions); so that, while in the immediate context of the isolated clause "nimbly" is Christian's adverb, in a larger and more inclusive context (both of syntax and reality), it belongs to God. The structure of the sentence thus imitates the double struc-

---

[3] Here I depart from the Wharey-Sharrock text and include the phrase "for a season." It appears in the first edition on which Sharrock bases his text. I can only assume that he deletes it because Apollyon is not seen again, *in this form;* but of course Apollyon has as many forms as there are temptations to forsake the way, and therefore Christian meets him again and again.

ture of reality: a surface level on which cause and effect are matters of sequence and contiguity, and a deeper level where the accidents of time and space are seen to be incidental to true causality.

That is to say, the placing of "as God would have it" results in a double perspective for the reader (much like the perspective he enjoys in the "footrace" scene *after* it unfolds); he is responding simultaneously to the moves and countermoves of the antagonists and to the revelation that they are controlled by an influence less immediately visible. Apollyon, on the other hand, is in the position the reader would occupy were the first part of the sentence withheld. He is unaware of any heavenly presence—"as God would have it" is nowhere *in sight*—and in his eyes Christian's recovery is not only unexpected but inexplicable. Apollyon's strategy and expectations are grounded in the calculation of probable and measurable effects; there is no room in his reasonings for something he cannot see; and within the confines of this radically empirical vision, the conclusion can be none other than the victory he prematurely claims. "As God would have it" gives the lie to this vision by countermanding, and indeed, including, Apollyon's "thereby" ("thereby to make an end of this good man"). In this battle (and in every battle) the issue is not determined by the relative strength and position of the combatants, but by the absolute strength of a deity who occupies *all* positions.

Christian's victory (insofar as it is his) is achieved precisely because he trusts in that deity and resists the interpretative pressure of the evidence of things seen. Pressed almost to death, with no remedy *in sight,* he reaches out nevertheless and finds not only a sword, but the Word (the syntax joins them): "and caught it, saying." When he gives Apollyon a thrust "with that," "that" is a verse from the seventh chapter of Micah. The battle is really a battle of words, for the syntax is continually shifting the responsibility from verbs of physical action to a quotation. Apollyon fights with the word of *self*-confidence ("I am sure of thee now"); Christian's word is the word of his confidence in another; indeed it is *another's* word. When he cries, "Rejoyce not against me, O mine Enemy: when I fall I shall arise," we are meant to recall the words that follow: "I will look unto the Lord; I will wait for the God of my salvation: my God will hear me." In the face of danger, Christian relies not on himself, but on his God, and when he makes no claim to the victory soon to be his—"Nay in all these things we are more than conquerors through him that loved us"— Apollyon is completely routed: "And with *that* [again the Word] *Apollyon* spread forth his Dragons wings, and sped him away." The glory is God's and because Christian rejoices in that knowledge, it is also his, "for a season," that is until the weakness which made him vulnerable to Apollyon's assault reasserts itself, as it surely will, "for you must know, that *Christian,* by reason of his wounds [original sin] must needs grow weaker."

"For a season" militates against the conclusiveness of the battle and, along with "as God would have it," prevents the reader from experiencing the full satisfaction that usually attends a hero's triumph. One wonders if this is indeed a triumph when the enemy lives to fight another day, and one knows that whatever it is, it is not (except in a very special sense) the hero's. As Christian gives thanks to his deliverer, "there came to him an hand with some of the leaves of the Tree of Life, the which *Christian* took, and applyed to the wounds that he had received in the Battel (60)." The appearance of this hand, unbidden and unattached to anything in the visible landscape, is a dramatic validation of the lesson we have learned, or, to be more precise, experienced, in the course of the episode: cause and effect are independent of the sequence of events and the operation of visible forces. I say "experienced" because in the process of discounting those forces we are ourselves made independent (at least for the moment) of the discursive forms that reflect and validate them. In other words, what we learn here—and not only here, but in the episode of the footrace and in the conversation with Formalist and Hypocrisy—is how not to read *The Pilgrim's Progress:* one must not read *The Pilgrim's Progress* as a progress, as the record of one man's step-by-step advance toward an appointed goal; one must not read *The Pilgrim's Progress* as a sequence of causally related events, for the true agency can at any time reverse the direction generated by a sequence, although he will rarely manifest himself so spectacularly as he does here ("there came to him an hand"); one must not, in short, read *The Pilgrim's Progress* in the way that every reader will certainly be tempted (a word precisely intended) to read it.

This leads me naturally to a question some of *my* readers will have been asking. If so much of *The Pilgrim's Progress* is given over to the subverting of its basic figure, why does Bunyan employ it at all? Why does he make the metaphor of the journey the vehicle of his narrative and then ask us to turn away from the interpretative direction it affords? The answer is to be found in the correspondence between reading and wayfaring, and the complementary obligations they confer. The truth about the world is not to be found within its own confines or configurations, but from the vantage point of a perspective that transforms it. It is Christian's duty to meet his trials in terms of that perspective, and it is the reader's duty to perform his acts of interpretation in the same way. ("This book will make a traveller of thee"—"Author's Apology"). In both contexts the source of danger and of potential error is to be located in the world as it usually appears, and, more precisely, in the perceptual habits that yield and create it; and in both contexts the danger is complicated by the fact that the shape of the two experiences—the pilgrimage and the flow of print— is an extension of those habits. The natural tendency of every reader to interpret the events of the narrative as if their springs were visible and rational, as if sequence were the *generator* rather than simply the *bearer* of meaning, is exactly equivalent to the tendency of every erring pilgrim to forsake the way of Christ for the rude workings of his own fancy. For the reader as well as for the pilgrim, to believe in the metaphor of the journey and in the *pilgrim's* progress, is to believe in himself, to prefer the operations of his discursive intellect to the revealed word of God. (*I* am the way.) It is Bunyan's method alternately to encourage and then disallow this prideful self-reliance by encouraging and then disallowing the interpretative pretensions of his prose. In this way he makes the subversion of the "dynamics of the narrative" the subversion of the reader's understanding (that is, of his *faith* in it); for every time he is turned away from the narrative context to a revelation, every time he draws lines of cause and effect prematurely, and every time he is asked to *de*signify the vocabulary of spatial direction, the reader is that much less a prisoner of his own mental processes. We may be unavoidably confined within temporal-spatial forms of thought, but we can at least learn to move within them with a consciousness of their ultimate insufficiency and therefore of the insufficiency of our merely human ways. (I am the way.)

What I am suggesting is that the issues in *The Pilgrim's Progress* (for both hero and reader) are always interpretative and that their resolution always involves a turning away from the context (the literal way, the flow of print) in which they are raised. Thus, in order to interpret correctly one must resist the interpretative pressure of the immediate landscape in favor of something (the revealed Word) or someone (Christ) it cannot contain. The rule of interpretation, the rule Christian walks by, is given properly in the House of the Interpreter:

> things present, and our fleshly appetite, *are . . . near Neighbours one to another;* and again . . . things to come, and carnal sense, are such strangers one to another: therefore it is, that the first of these so suddenly fall into *amity,* and that *distance* is so continued between the second (32).

The experiences of both the reader and the characters are continually enforcing this inverse relationship by enforcing a distinction between what appears to be happening, in the scene and on the page, and what is really happening: that distinction is realized in any number of ways, but most often by a delayed revelation, which has the effect of widening a perspective that had been assumed to be full and adequate; and once again the paradigm instance occurs in the House of the Interpreter:

> Then I saw in my Dream, that the *Interpreter* took *Christian* by the hand, and led him into a place, where was a Fire burning against a Wall, and one standing by it always, casting much Water upon it to quench it: Yet did the Fire burn higher and hotter.
> *Then said* Christian, *What means this?*
> The *Interpreter* answered, This fire is the work of Grace that is wrought in the heart; he that casts Water

upon it, to extinguish and put it out, is the *Devil:* but in that thou seest the fire, notwithstanding, burn higher and hotter, thou shalt also see the reason of that: So he had him about to the back side of the Wall, where he saw a Man with a Vessel of Oyl in his hand, of the which he did also continually cast, but secretly, into the fire. Then said *Christian, What means this?* The *Interpreter* answered, This is *Christ,* who continually with the Oyl of his Grace, maintains the work already begun in the heart; by the means of which, notwithstanding what the Devil can do, the souls of his people prove gracious still. And in that thou sawest, that the Man stood behind the Wall to maintain the fire; this is to teach thee, that it is hard for the tempted to see how this work of Grace is maintained in the soul (32–33).

Even before Christian speaks, the reader is asking and answering his question, "What means this?" for anyone within hearing (or seeing) of a riddle is naturally provoked to attempt its solution. In this case there would seem to be help in the explanation given but a moment ago of another of the Interpreter's puzzles: "The *dust,* is his Original Sin. . . . He that began to sweep it first, is the Law; but She that brought water and did sprinkle it is the Gospel . . . even as thou sawest the Damsel lay the dust by sprinkling the Floor with Water, so is sin vanquished and subdued . . . through the Faith (30)." Even without this information, we would be likely to take "water" as a symbol of grace; and fire as a figure for the hot fires of hell. Both the local and traditional contexts, then, would seem to be pointing us to a directed interpretation: despite the infusion of grace, the influence of sin in man persists and grows strong. The correct interpretation, however, is exactly the reverse of this, although it is unavailable to us until we literally go behind the scenes ("So he had him about to the back side of the Wall"). The motion required here— interpretation imposed on rather than generated by the *visibilia* —is exactly equivalent to the motion forced on us whenever we yield too easily to the interpretative pressure of the prose (which is, itself, one of those "things present" that are too closely allied

with "our fleshly appetite"); in both contexts the light afforded
by natural signs is to be disregarded in favor of a light that is not
immediately available.

Indeed, there is in *The Pilgrim's Progress* an inverse relationship between visibility and reliability, and Christian's first conversation with Evangelist not only establishes this relationship,
but implicates the reader in it:

> Then said *Evangelist,* pointing with his finger over a very
> wide Field, Do you see yonder *Wicket-gate?* The Man
> said, No. Then said the other, Do you see yonder shining
> light? He said, I think I do. Then said *Evangelist,* Keep
> that light in your eye, and go up directly thereto, so shalt
> thou see the Gate; at which when thou knockest, it shall be
> told thee what thou shalt do.
>
> So I saw in my Dream, that the Man began to run;
> Now he had not run far from his own door, but his Wife
> and Children perceiving it, began to cry after him to re-
> turn: but the Man put his fingers in his Ears, and ran on
> crying, Life, Life, Eternal Life: so he looked not behind
> him, but fled towards the middle of the Plain (10).

The entire scene is built on the metaphor of sight. As Evangelist
points assuredly to yonder "Wicket-gate," the reader naturally
assumes that the gate in question can be seen, and he allows an
image of it to form in his mind. But when Christian answers with
devastating brevity—"No"—that image blurs and perhaps even
disappears. (Now you see it, now you don't.) As a result, Evangelist's next question—"Do you see yonder shining light?"—
draws a more cautious response; we don't know whether it's going to be there or not; and the quality of our relationship to the
light is mirrored perfectly in Christian's reply: "I think I do."
In the circumstances, Evangelist's exhortation—"Keep that light
in your eyes, and go up directly thereto"—seems almost perverse.
How can we (Evangelist speaks to us as well as to Christian)
follow a light only faintly and intermittently visible; and with
such an uncertain light as our lodestar, how can we expect to go
directly to a gate whose existence we know of only by hearsay?

Christian and the reader are now joined by a shared uncer-

tainty, which places them in a hierarchy of vision somewhere below Evangelist. As the scene continues, that hierarchy is expanded
to include other figures. The narrator intrudes himself into the
narrative to say that he, too, sees. "So I saw in my dream"—
what? the light? the gate? Only the man running. Apparently his
perceptions extend no further than ours. And this is true also
of Christian's wife and children; they stand by the door of their
house, "perceiving it"; but the "it" they perceive is only the inexplicable sight of their provider and protector leaving them for
they know not what. The neighbors also "see" and they occupy
the lowest rung on our ladder, for their only concern is the spec-
tacle Christian is making of himself. They come out *just* to "see
him run."

What we have, then, is a tableau arranged almost like an
emblem. In the center is a man running. Behind him stand a
variety of personages: the mysterious stranger who alone knows
the reason for his action; the reader and the narrator whose insight into the situation is, at best, partial; a wife and children
who understand only that they are being deserted; and a crowd
of men who are reacting to the absurdity (if not insanity) of
someone who would leave everything that is solid and real for a
phrase: "Life, Life, Eternal Life." In their relationship these
figures measure out the distance between "carnal sense" and
"things to come." It is this distance that the reader experiences
when the momentary solidity of the Wicket-gate is taken away
from him, and he is left with only a dim and fitful light, shining
somewhere "yonder"; and the same reader bears personal witness
to the appeal of "things present" in proportion to the sympathy he
almost certainly feels for Christiana and her children. The claims
of "Eternal Life" are made at the expense of this life—its pleasures, its values, its loyalties, and, above all, its point of view.
Christian's family and friends judge him to be insane when he
complains of a burden they cannot see and turns his back on
them to run into a large and formless nothing; but this judgment
is made on the basis of "carnal sense" which rigorously excludes
from consideration anything so insubstantial as a promise ("I am
the way"). The moral is provided by Bunyan's marginal comment,
which is again not so much an imposition from the outside as a

confirmation of the *felt meaning* his art has created in us: *"They that fly from the wrath to come, are a Gazing-Stock to the world."*

Christian's obligation, then, is to follow a light which has no correlative in the world of fixed objects, and to ignore the less real, but more congenial, lights that serve as beacons for his fellowmen. That is, he must willfully refuse to credit the evidence of his senses; he must put fingers in his ears and blinders on his eyes and move in response to a voice no one else hears, and walk by a light not even he sees.

Christian discovers how difficult this is when he replays this same scene with another interlocutor. Persuaded by Mr. Worldly-Wiseman to seek out Legality, *"a very judicious man . . . that has skill to help men off with such burdens as thine* (19)," Christian asks, as he had asked before, to be directed on his way:

> *Chr.*  Sir, which is my way to this honest man's house?
> *Worl.*  *Do you see yonder high hill?*
> *Chr.*  Yes, very well.
> *Worl.*  By that *Hill* you must go, and the first house you come at is his.
>
>   So Christian turned out of his way to go to Mr. *Legality's* house for help: but . . . (19–20).

Do you see yonder high hill? Rather than a disconcerting "No," the answer here is an immediate and assured "Yes, very well." Unlike the Wicket-gate or the shining light whose existence must be taken on faith, the hill is unmistakably there and it does not go away as Christian and the reader approach it by a route that is both direct and easy. On the surface, then, the two scenes contrast the quixotism of a venture that sets people to run after "they know not what (18)" with a remedy that is "at hand," *"not quite a mile from this place* (19)," but the real contrast is exactly the reverse, for it is the visible and near object that constitutes the clear and present danger. It is, therefore, entirely appropriate that the hill be identified in the margin as Mt. Sinai: for on Mt. Sinai was given the Law, a written body of prescriptive and explicit directions that offers itself as a "way" to salvation, but actually commits its adherents to the error of legalism. In short, the Law, like the literal way and the available hill, is visible and external and therefore a temptation to an outward conformity. As readers, we come to know this not by reasoning from the name, Mt. Sinai, to the hill, but by transferring our experience of what the hill means *in context* to the name, Mt. Sinai. The marginal note is not offered as a key to the episode; rather the episode points the reader to an understanding of the marginal note.[4]

That understanding finally has less to do with hills and houses than with the self, for, as Evangelist observes when he appears to rescue Christian, he who hearkens to a Worldly-Wiseman rejects the counsel of God for the counsel of his "own consenting (22)," that is, for the rude workings of his own fancy. The model for this self-worship in *The Pilgrim's Progress* is Atheist, who declares of the Heavenly City, "there is no such place as you Dream of, in all this World (135)." This is, of course, the literal truth (the only truth Atheist is capable of recognizing); there is no such place in all the world, both because all the world, when seen in the proper light, *is* that place, and because, as Christian insists, that place is a promise, a *"World to come."* To this, Atheist can only oppose his empirically derived conclusion: "Had not I, when at home, believed, I had not come thus far to seek: But finding none, (and yet I should, had there been such a place to be found, for I have gone to seek it further then you) I am going back again, and will seek to refresh my self with the things that I then cast away, for hopes of that, which I now see, is not (135)." Or, in other words: If there were such a place, it could be seen; I have traveled far and wide and have not seen it; therefore, there is no such place. Atheist refuses to consider the existence of anything that cannot be confined within the structures of time, space, and reason. These are the measure of his belief, and since they are coextensive with the dimensions of his own mind, his belief in them is a belief in himself, in the things *he* can see. Against this

---

[4] Here I again take issue with U. Milo Kaufmann, who tends to regard the didactic materials in the work as evidence of Bunyan's fear that he will be misunderstood. See *The Pilgrim's Progress and Traditions in Puritan Meditation*, pp. 7, 19–21, *passim*. In Kaufmann's view, the commentary clarifies the event. My view is exactly the reverse. It is the didactic (and usually commonplace) commentary that is being clarified, or, to be more precise, illuminated, by our experience of the event.

kind of evidence the insubstantiality of "hopes" counts for nothing. Christian remarks that Atheist is *"blinded by the God of this World* (136)." What he is blinded by is the apparently self-sufficient light of his own worldly-wise understanding.

Paradoxically, Christian comes to terms with this delusive light when it goes out, in the Valley of the Shadow of Death. The darkness prevents him from seeing anything but "the flame and smoke" which "come out in . . . abundance"; he hears only "hideous noises" and "doleful voices" and imagines "a company of *Fiends* coming forward to meet him (63)." Not surprisingly, the concerted pressures of the situation result in paralysis and a return of the old familiar problems: what to do? where to go? how to decide? "he stopt; and began to muse what he had best to do."

Christian's decision, when it comes, follows, but does not issue from a survey of the options open to him:

> Sometimes he had half a thought to go back. Then again he thought he might be half way through the Valley; he remembered also how he had already vanquished many a danger: and that the danger of going back might be much more, then for to go forward; so he resolved to go on. Yet the *Fiends* seemed to come nearer and nearer, but when they were come even almost at him, he cried out with a most vehement voice, *I will walk in the strength of the Lord God;* so they gave back, and came no further (63).

As Christian moves back and forth between the obvious alternatives, the reader moves with him. On the surface that movement is ratiocinative and discursive, a sequence of "yets" and "buts" whose end (supposedly) will be a clarification of the issues and a reasoned program of action. But the experience of the passage, for both Christian and the reader, is anything but clarifying and its issue is not action but indecision. The qualification that attends each "yet" or "but" or "then" is made at the expense of Christian's momentary resolves: "he had half a thought to go back, *then again* . . ."; "so he resolved to go on. *Yet.* . . ." The more fully the problem is explored in the light of the physical evidence, the further away we seem from a satisfactory conclusion. This little interior dialogue finally communicates a profound sense of impasse.

Christian is released (or releases himself) from this impasse when he reaches a decision that has nothing to do with the rational and empirical considerations that have preceded it. His action is not taken because of his analysis of the situation, but in spite of it. *"I will walk in the strength of the Lord God"* is an instance of what Kaufmann finely calls "the saving non sequitur of faith (198n)." It is a non sequitur because on the basis of a projection of eventualities, moving forward is no more reasonable a motion than retreating or standing still; and it is saving, because it signifies a turning away from such projections, and from the appearances which yield them, to a *blind* trust in God. As Kaufmann remarks in another context: "the only escape from the dilemma was a resolute act of faith wholly discontinuous with the morass of verification (198)," and it is as such an act that we receive his declaration, because the experience of the prose is too determinedly inconclusive to allow us to predict it.

Once again it is the obligation of both hero and reader to affirm *against* the available evidence (of things seen), to refuse to accept as final the perspective that validates a problem, and once again the doctrine underlying a scene is given immediately after our experience of it. As Christian walks in the strength of the Lord, he hears a voice saying *"Though I walk through the valley of the shadow of death, I will fear none ill, for thou art with me,"* and this makes him glad, "For that he perceived, God was with them, though in that dark and dismal state; and why not, thought he, with me, though by reason of the impediment that attends this place, I cannot perceive it (64)." Superficially, the two "perceives" that stand at the beginning and the end of the paragraph present a paradox; he perceives though he cannot perceive. But the paradox is merely the familiar formula for spiritual seeing. Perceiving correctly in spiritual terms means ignoring what is plainly there, and responding, instead, to a reality that is not verifiable either by the senses or by the light of an unillumined reason; perceiving correctly means rejecting the counsel of the worldly wiseman who resides in each of us, in our carnal understanding (of objects, ideas, values, courses of action) in favor of the all-inclusive counsel of the revealed word ("I am the way"). Christian never more surely perceives than when he refuses to be paralyzed by his inability to perceive and affirms his faith in a presence for which there is, in his field of perception, no evidence. The "impediment" that attends this place is darkness, both the literal darkness of the narrative situation and the metaphorical darkness of man's clouded intellect; but it is no longer an impediment to Christian who now walks by an inner light. "Why not . . . with me" he declares, even though everything in the immediate context, that is everything he *sees,* points to a different conclusion.

When the morning comes, Christian, we are told, sees "more perfectly" and "more clearly" the "hazards he had gone through" because "the light of the day made them more conspicuous to him": but this distinction, between the light of faith and the light of day, does not survive the account of his journey through the second part of the Valley. "About this time," the dreamer reports, "the Sun was rising," and already the latent pun is beginning to operate on our consciousness, especially since this physical phenomenon is called a "mercy (65)." The description of the new dangers that await Christian—"Snares, Traps, Gins, . . . Nets . . . Pits, Pitfalls, deep holes"—serves to emphasize his need of this light, and when it is followed by a repetition of the key phrase—"as I said, just now the Sun was rising"—we are hardly able to ignore the reference to Christ. Should there be any doubt on the point, it is resolved by Christian himself who says *"His candle shineth on my head, and by his light I go through darkness."* His candle, the sun, and the light with which he illuminates men's hearts, the day-star, are one and the same in this formulation. Once again, the limited and limiting significance of physical objects gives way to the larger significance of those objects as manifestations of an all-informing reality; and when the next paragraph begins, "In this light . . . he came to the end of the Valley," we know that by "this light," Bunyan intends us to understand the light Christ's presence in the world affords us, no matter what form it takes (or doesn't take). In fact "this light" is "that light" to which Evangelist pointed at the beginning of Christian's journey; and it is here, in the Valley of the Shadow of

Death, that he obeys Evangelist's injunction and keeps "that light" in his eyes.

Not that Christian's success here assures his subsequent successes. Bunyan does not mean us to substitute a progressive clearing of vision for the more literal progress he denies his pilgrims. Much later, Christian and Hopeful are taken "to the top of an high Hill called *Clear* (122)" and invited to look through a "perspective Glass" at the Gates of the Celestial City. But even with this aid, they are unable to free themselves from their *own* perspective, and the account of their failure returns us to the first scene and Evangelist's question: "Do you see yonder shining light?": "Then they essayed to look, but the remembrance of that last thing that the Shepheards had shewed them, made their hands shake; by means of which impediment they could not look steddily through the Glass; yet they thought they saw something like the Gate, and also some of the Glory of the place (122–123)." The tentativeness of "they *thought* they saw *something*" echoes Christian's original response to Evangelist: "I think I do." The "last thing that the Shepheards had shewed them" was the "by-way to Hell" and this specter is enough to shake their confidence in the fact of their salvation, that is, in the efficacy of the promise. (This, as Bunyan tells us in the margin, is the *"fruit of slavish fear."*) Even at this late date Christian's faith is not firm enough ("they could not look *steddily*") to enable him to keep "that light" *continually* in his eyes.

That light is deliberately withheld from those who will not even strain after it and their reward, appropriately, is a kind of blindness in which actions are performed in perfect ignorance of their true significance. This is especially true of the jurors who preside over the death of Faithful:

> Then went the Jury out, whose names were Mr. *Blindman,* Mr. *No-good,* Mr. *Malice,* Mr. *Love-lust,* Mr. *Live-loose,* Mr. *Heady,* Mr. *High-mind,* Mr. *Enmity,* Mr. *Lyar,* Mr. *Cruelty,* Mr. *Hate-light,* and Mr. *Implacable,* who every one gave in his private Verdict against him among themselves, and afterwards unanimously concluded to bring him in guilty before the Judge (96).

In the sequence that follows, the reader is a witness to two actions, one planned and executed by the townspeople of Vanity Fair, who believe it to be final and conclusive, and another authored by God. Ultimately, of course, the two are one, and they are both God's. The only distinction to be made is a distinction of perspectives, between what appears to be happening and what is really happening; and the realization of this distinction, so basic to the design of *The Pilgrim's Progress,* is the main business of the passage.

At first, Bunyan's language operates to restrict us to the point of view assumed by Faithful's persecutors:

> therefore he was presently Condemned, To be had from the place where he was, to the place from whence he came, and there to be put to the most cruel death that could be invented.
>
> They therefore brought him out, to do with him according to their Law; and first they Scourged him, then they Buffeted him, then they Lanced his flesh with Knives; after that they Stoned him with Stones, they prickt him with their Swords, and last of all they burned him to Ashes at the Stake. Thus came *Faithful* to his end (97).

The movement of the prose is relentlessly linear, locking us into the sequence of events that has been set in motion by the pronouncements of the jury, and preventing us from looking any further than the significances that appear on the surface. The lines of cause and effect are built into the syntax, which itself proceeds "according to their Law," a series of legal phrases joined together in logical and sequential relationships by words like "therefore," "first," "then," "after," "last," and "thus." This is not only the language of execution, it is self-executing language, for its unfolding on the page seems to generate and make inescapable the act it directs. As a result, a strong sense of inevitability and completion is communicated to the reader who is inclined to accept the conclusiveness of the sentence announcing Faithful's demise: "Thus came *Faithful* to his end."

But this is not the end, either of Faithful or of the episode

("Thus came Faithful to his end" is, like "so the first was last" a
premature conclusion), although it would be were "their Law"
the final court of appeal. Behind the crowd that has ordained and
(or so it thinks) effected his death, there stands "a Chariot and a
couple of Horses, waiting for *Faithful,* who (so soon as his adversaries had dispatched him) was taken up into it, and straight-
way was carried up through the Clouds, with the sound of
Trumpet, the nearest way to the Cælestial Gate." Where did this
chariot come from? How long has it been there? (Bunyan is
careful *not* to say, "suddenly, there appeared"). How can Faithful be taken anywhere or for that matter any longer be a "who,"
if he is ashes? Far from clearing away the confusion this
new information has created, Bunyan's parenthesis (so soon as
his adversaries had dispatched him) merely raises another question. How soon was that? Surely Faithful was (literally) dead
before he was burned? Perhaps after he was scourged? or buf-
feted? or lanced? or pricked? The impossibility of specifying the
moment results in the superimposition of one action on the other.
That is, rather than watching two events separated in time, the
reader now sees the killing of Faithful and his subsequent (if it
was subsequent) rescue occurring simultaneously. Even as the
townspeople are busily (and blindly) implementing their collective will, the will of another is countermanding them and trans-
porting the object of their actions to a realm of which they are
not even aware.

Once the reader has been afforded the experience of this double perspective, it controls his responses to the surface of the
narrative. When Christian is said to have some "respite," in that
he "was remanded back to prison," the literal statement is received ironically in the light of what the reader now knows. Christian's respite is a respite from the everlasting bliss Faithful now
enjoys, and his reprieve from death is more of an imprisonment
than anything his captors could devise; for he has been remanded
back to the prison of this life. In short, a correct reading of
Christian's situation involves an inversion of the appearance it
presents in the context of earthly assumptions and values; and
to the extent that the experience of Bunyan's prose directs us to

that inversion by directing us *away* from its literal meaning, we have learned in the act of reading what it means to see with the eyes of faith.

Christian's escape from prison is as anticlimactic and inconclusive as his victory over Apollyon: "But he that over-rules all things, having the power of their rage in his own hand, so wrought it about, that *Christian* for that time escaped them, and went his way (97)." "He that over-rules" is exactly equivalent in its effect to "as God would have it," for what it overrules is the conventional force of "escape," preventing us from granting to Christian the initiative he may appear to be taking ("his way" is nicely and pointedly ambiguous). And "for that time," like "for a season," prevents us from regarding the escape as anything more than a mechanism. As a result, we enter the next scene with no hostages, that is, with no interpretative dependence on the apparent causality of sequence and physical agency. Our experiences, like Christian's, continue to be discrete and repetitive, even though we move with him from place to place and page to page.

REMEMBER THE PROMISE

To this point we have discovered three experiential patterns: (1) the subversion of the interpretative direction afforded by the prose and especially by the metaphor of the journey (2) the reassigning of the responsibility for cause from visible forces to a force not immediately available in the landscape (3) the discrediting of the light of the evidence of things seen in favor of the inner light of faith. The effect of these patterns is antiprogressive: they provoke the reader to look upward rather than forward and they help him to resist the pressure of local contexts and respond instead to the pressure of a relentless and exclusive rule, "I am the way."

The fourth and final pattern I will discuss subsumes all the others. It is the recurrence of the theme of memory. Memory is the repository of the master's rule, the source of the inner light, the pulpit that the Holy Ghost preaches in. It is only memory that enables us to impose the correcting perspective of what is distant on what is near. Only by remembering can we resist the temptation to read causality into the mere sequence of events. Only memory can affirm against both the appeal and the fear of things present by bringing to mind the promise of things to come.

The first specific reference to memory is made by Interpreter, who teaches Christian how to use the sights he has been shown: "Let this mans misery be remembered by thee, and be an everlasting caution to thee (35)." Memory in this formulation is simply the application of the knowledge gained from previous experiences (one's own or another's) to present situations. Interpreter's warning is a warning against allowing history to repeat itself. Later, when Hopeful warns Christian against Atheist, he makes exactly the same point in the same terms: "Take heed, he is one of the *Flatterers;* remember what it hath cost us once already for our harkning to such kind of Fellows (135)." As Bunyan remarks in the margin: *"A remembrance of former chastisements is an help against present temptations."*

But remembering past chastisements (or anything else) is not so simple or mechanical a matter as this one scene would suggest. Hopeful recognizes Atheist as a flatterer only because his most recent experience has immunized him against the appeal Atheist makes, and if we learn anything from reading *The Pilgrim's Progress,* it is that the effects of such immunizations do not last. Memory is an act of the will in which the consciousness calls on something that is not literally there in order to interpret correctly what is (or seems to be) there; and it is an act whose difficulty increases with the distance in time from the event (mental or physical) to be remembered. Remembering, then, is directly analogous to faithful seeing (or reading) in that it involves a rejecting of the meanings conferred on things and situations by immediate contexts. Deeds of memory and deeds of faith are based on the same formula—an inverse relationship between what is seen and what is to be relied upon. Every crisis in *The Pilgrim's Progress* is a crisis of memory.

Hopeful's small success with Atheist follows upon a series of disasters all of which are attributable, in large measure, to a failure of the pilgrim's memory. The sequence begins, appropriately enough, when Christian and Faithful come upon "an old Monument" which "seemed to them as if it had been a *Woman* transformed into the shape of a Pillar (108)." For a moment they do not know what to make of this strange sight; but then Hopeful spies some writing on the head of the pillar, and Christian, "for he was learned," puzzles out the meaning:

> *Remember Lot's Wife*

This discovery provokes a fit of moralizing—"Ah my Brother, this is a seasonable sight," "Let us take notice of what we see here, for our help"—and the reader settles into what appears to be another of the doctrinal interludes that fill the space between the more dramatic encounters. But as the exchange of pieties continues, the conversation takes an unexpected turn and the reading experience becomes less comfortable and less automatic. Christian and Hopeful begin by expressing gratitude for the new mercy God has afforded them, but they end by congratulating themselves for paying attention to the object lesson so many others have ignored:

> *Hope* . . . above all, I muse at one thing, to wit, how *Demas* and his fellows can stand so confidently yonder to look for that treasure, which this Woman, but for looking behind her, after (for we read not that she stept one foot out of the way) was turned into a pillar of Salt; specially since the Judgment which overtook her, did make her an example, within sight of where they are: for they cannot chuse but see her, did they but lift up their eyes (109–110).

Hopeful's words betray an insensitivity to the difficulty of keeping to the way (even if the roadsigns are clear) and suggest a complacent faith in his ability to avoid the errors less watchful men have fallen into. The implication is that with such clear examples before him, a pilgrim should find it easy to maintain his righteousness; and the further implication, that any failure would be inexcusable, is made explicit by Christian's conclusion: "And it is most rationally to be concluded, that such, even such as these are, that shall sin in the sight, yea, and that too in despite of such examples that are set continually before them, to caution them to

the contrary, must be partakers of severest Judgments (110)."
This is a rational conclusion with a vengeance, for it excludes the
possibility that justice might be tempered by mercy. While Christian and Hopeful have been discussing the importance of remembering—the scene ends with another reference to the lesson of
the pillar, "always . . . remember Lot's wife"—they have forgotten the cornerstone of their faith and the promise of their
salvation. This may seem of little consequence at the moment;
indeed a reader may not even notice the omission since the surface pieties slide so easily into the mind; but later, when the
Pilgrims are languishing in the Dungeon of Doubting Castle, the
true significance of what they say here will become evident. In
this sequence, each scene operates to expose the limitations of
the perspective assumed in the preceding scene, and therefore, of
the reader's perspective too.

Some time and many miles are said to have gone by before
Christian and Hopeful meet their next trial, but the distance
traveled by the reader amounts to less than a page, and in his
experience, the temptation of By-Path-Meadow follows immediately upon the slighting of Lot's wife:

> *So the soul of the Pilgrims was much discouraged, because
> of the way.* Wherefore still as they went on, they wished
> for better way. Now a little before them, there was on the
> left hand of the Road, a *Meadow,* and a Stile to go over
> into it. . . . Then said Christian to his fellow. If this
> Meadow lieth along our way side, lets go over into it.
> Then he went to the Stile to see, and behold a Path lay
> along by the way. . . . 'Tis according to my wish, said
> *Christian,* here is the easiest going (111).

Only two paragraphs ago, the pilgrims were remarking on the
strictness of the judgment visited upon Lot's wife, "for we read
not that she steps one foot out of the way"; yet now they are
considering stepping out of the way altogether. Hopeful demurs,
*"how if this Path should lead us out of the way?"* but Christian
brushes his objection aside: "That's not like [likely]; look, doth
it not go along by the way side?" Once again Christian has forsaken the way of the Lord for the way which recommends itself

to his senses ("look") and his reason ("That's not like"), and this misplaced confidence is compounded when he asks directions of another pilgrim: "so they called after him, and asked him whither that way led? he said, To the Celestial Gate." This is enough to confirm Christian in his opinion—"Look, said Christian, did I not tell you so? By this you may see we are right." Unfortunately, by "this" (merely carnal authority) they may see no further than their own noses; and, not surprisingly, Christian's vain confidence (the character is a projection of his cast of mind) leads to disaster: "Now Christian and his fellow heard him [Vain Confidence] fall. So they called to know the matter, but there was none to answer, only they heard a groaning (112)." The pilgrims respond to their plight with an outpouring of self-recriminations (*"Oh that I had kept on my way"*) and in the episode that follows they become the prisoners of their own guilt. That is, in their eagerness to condemn themselves, they forget about the merciful inclinations of a higher tribunal, and the redemption promised to them as the beneficiaries of Christ's sacrifice; and, paradoxically, this forgetfulness has its roots in the harshness of the judgment they make on those who fail to remember Lot's wife.

The relationship between Giant Despair's power and the psychology of his captives is made clear immediately:

> They told him, they were Pilgrims, and that they had lost their way. Then said the *Giant,* You have this night trespassed on me, by trampling in, and lying on my grounds and therefore you must go along with me. So they were forced to go, because he was stronger than they. They also had but little to say, for they knew themselves in a fault. The *Giant* therefore drove them before him, and put them into his Castle (113–114).

Two reasons are given for the docility of the pilgrims, but only the second is finally controlling. The first is a simple statement of cause and effect: "He was stronger than they"; but the apparent afterthought—"They also had little to say, for they knew themselves in a fault"—is itself a deeper analysis of the physical fact.

The reader is alerted to this by the word "therefore" ("The *Giant* therefore drove them") whose force is naturally attributed to the clause nearest it. Once again, we enjoy a double perspective; that of the surface action and that of the inner landscape which generates its events. So that when, in the next paragraph, Despair proceeds to beat Hopeful and Christian "without any mercy," we realize, with a shock of recognition, that his action is at once a self-definition and a function of their state of mind. That is, they contrive to turn remembering Lot's wife into a forgetting of mercy and therefore when they lead themselves out of the way, they have no mercy left for themselves; having no mercy for themselves, they become the partakers of their own severest judgment, which then leaps outside their minds, picks up a club and beats them—*without mercy.*

The central question of the episode, then, is, will they remember? And the crucial scenes are structured so as to emphasize the irrelevance to memory of external signs and contexts. Christian establishes the dimensions of the problem when he asks the familiar question—"what shall we do?"—and cites the life they now live as reason for following the Giant's advice, "forthwith to make an end of themselves (115)." But Hopeful, while admitting that *"our present condition is dreadful,"* refuses to accept that condition as necessarily final, and it is his insistence on taking a larger view than the situation warrants that opens the way for their eventual escape. This first day's counsel is largely negative: *"But yet let us consider, the Lord of the Country to which we are going, hath said, Thou shalt do no murther. . . . And moreover, my Brother, thou talkest of ease in the Grave; but hast thou forgotten the Hell whither, for certain, the murderers go (115)?"*

Christian has forgotten more than that, but at this stage the incompleteness of Hopeful's argument is less important than the fact that it has been hazarded and that memory (this is what considering means) has been put forward as a part of the answer to Despair's urgings. The key words in this passage are its first words—"but yet"—for they signify the recognition of the existence of possibilities other than those that are immediately available. The experience of this speech is the experience of "butyetness" and as Hopeful continues, his language more and more reflects his unwillingness to put on the blinders Despair has fashioned for him:

> *Others, so far as I can understand, have been taken by him, as well as we; and yet have escaped out of his hand: Who knows, but that God that made the world, may cause that* Giant Despair *may die; or that, at some time or other he may forget to lock us in; or, but he may in short time have another of his fits before us, and may lose the use of his limbs; and if ever that should come to pass again, for my part, I am resolved to pluck up the heart of a man, and to try my utmost to get from under his hand* (115–116).

Hopeful's resolution is made even before he announces it; once he rejects the either-or formulation (either die or remain here forever) within which Despair seeks to confine them (*that* is their prison) and replaces it with the openness of "may" and "if," he is already halfway out "from under his hand." At this point the reading experience becomes somewhat frustrating, for while the direction of everything that Hopeful says leads us to expect a final and redeeming step, that step is not taken. Instead, Hopeful continues to counsel patience and to remind Christian of past trials which presented no less fearful an aspect than the present one: *"My Brother, said he, remembrest thou not how valiant thou hast been heretofore;* Apollyon *could not crush thee, nor could all that thou didst hear, or see, or feel in the Valley of the Shadow of Death* (116)?"

These references to Apollyon and the Valley are especially tantalizing, since the issues in these episodes and the issue here are exactly the same. In fact, Apollyon's arguments are Despair's arguments: he confronts Christian with a résumé of his sins and transgressions and implies that because of them he has been deserted by God. As we recall this incident, we remember Christian's reply and wait for him to remember it too: "The prince whom I serve and honour is *merciful,* and ready to forgive (58, emphasis mine)." But Christian says nothing and the pilgrims remain sitting in their dungeon, preparing themselves for whatever new tortures the Giant may have in mind.

As a result, when the breakthrough does come, we are both prepared for it and surprised. We are prepared because so much in the conversation between Christian and Hopeful has pointed to it; yet we are surprised because they have so far been unable to follow their own remarks to a conclusion we have already reached. And at the crucial moment, the exasperation we may have been feeling at the pilgrims' failure to remember is voiced by Christian himself:

> Now a little before it was day, good *Christian*, as one half amazed, brake out in this passionate speech, *What a fool, quoth he, am I, thus to lie in a stinking Dungeon, when I may as well walk at liberty?* I have a *Key* in my bosom, called *Promise,* that will, (I am perswaded) open any lock in *Doubting-Castle.* Then said *Hopeful,* That's good news (118).

The promise is, of course, the promise of salvation, and it is theirs for the taking if they will only reach for it, that is, remember. The sense of anticlimax, of "so that's all there is to it," is exactly right, for remembering is simply the bringing to mind of what has always been there, something at once ridiculously easy ("the door flew open with ease"), and, until it occurs, impossibly difficult. Both the ease and the difficulty are part of our experience of the scene: Bunyan lets us know from the first how close at hand the pilgrims' deliverance is, but then he leaves us dangling and anxious as they look everywhere but in the right place.

In this way we are led, through our experience, to an important insight: memory is an exercise of the will rather than the end of a process. It must affirm against, not as a consequence of, the sequence of events, and it is therefore *antiprogressive.* "I am perswaded" says Christian. By what? by Hopeful's arguments? If so, we never see them determining his decision. By something he recalls during prayer? perhaps, but we are never told what it is. All we see is the act itself preceded by deliberations which are never linked to it directly. Remembering the promise (the "good news" as Hopeful so accurately labels it) is something one does despite, not because of, the available evidence. We are given the evidence and then made to experience its irrelevance as once again the dramatic potential of a scene is dissipated. Christian's persuasion, like his decision to walk forward in the Valley of the Shadow, is an "act of faith wholly discontinuous with the morass of verification," and that is exactly how we receive it.

Memory continues to be the mainspring of the episodes that follow. After escaping from Doubting Castle, Christian and Hopeful are entertained by the Shepherds of the Delectable mountains, who send them on their way with gifts and advice: "When they were about to depart, one of the Shepherds gave them a *note of the way*. Another of them, *bid them beware of the flatterer*. The third *bid them take heed that they sleep not upon the Inchanted Ground*. And the fourth, *bid them God speed* (123)." These parting instructions follow one another so quickly that no one of them has any particular force. There is something disarmingly casual about the whole sequence, and whatever urgency the Shepherds' injunctions generate is dissipated by the conventionality of "God speed." In short, the style and positioning of this paragraph operate to minimize probability of the reader's remembering it. And the pages immediately following are not likely to recall it to him. The story of Little Faith, while it contains much of interest, has nothing to do with notes of the way or with flatterers. In retrospect, its telling is somewhat ironic, since there is much talk of Little Faith's failure to remember his jewels; but a reader is no more aware than the pilgrims of the (potential) ironies, and with each passing moment any impression the Shepherds' words may have made is being effaced.

What this means is that when Christian and Hopeful are confronted with two ways, each of which "seemed straight before them," the reader is as much at a loss as they are, and while he may be suspicious of the "man black of flesh" whom the pilgrims decide to follow, he has no alternative course of action to recommend. It is Christian finally, after they have been led "within the compass of a Net," who suddenly remembers; "Did not the Shepherds bid us beware of the flatterers"; and immediately (memory returns in a rush) Hopeful chimes in with, "They also gave us a note of directions about the way . . . but therin we have . . . forgotten to read (133)."

If my experience and that of my students is at all representative, the reader will hurriedly turn back to what he had forgotten or perhaps never fully taken in; and when the inevitable rescuer begins to cross-examine Christian and Faithful, he is no less shamefaced than they are: "He asked them . . . , If they had not of them Shepherds *a note of direction for the way?* They answered; Yes. But did you, said he, when you was at a stand, pluck out and read your note? They answered, No. He asked them why? They said they forgot (134)." The pilgrims' terse responses underscore the lesson the reader has proved on his pulse: memory, like clarity of vision and possession of the true way and perfect faith, depends on a willful holding fast to what is not (in a physical sense) there; and the difficulty of remembering points once again to the central text of *The Pilgrim's Progress:* "things present, and our fleshly appetite, *are . . . near Neighbours one to another"*; and again ". . . things to come, and carnal sense, are such strangers one to another." It is a difficulty and a strangeness we have ourselves experienced, and the episode ends with a warning in which we are explicitly included:

> *Come hither, you that walk along the way;*
> *See how the Pilgrims fare, that go a stray!*
> *They catched are in an intangling Net,*
> *'Cause they good Counsel lightly did forget:*
> *'Tis true, they rescu'd were, but yet you see*
> *They're scourged to boot: Let this your caution be* (134).

Only one more obstacle remains before Christian and Hopeful reach the gates of the Celestial City; and it, too, is a trial of memory, because it is a trial of faith. The River of Death offers "no bridge to go over," and for the last time the pilgrims look for a "way," but "no way could be found" in the context of the physical situation. They are told by men in gold raiment to look within— "You shall find it deeper or shallower, as you believe in the King of the place (157)"—but when Christian does so, he finds only "the sins that he had committed, both since and before he began to be a pilgrim." These fill his heart and crowd out all thought of Christ. Once again the evidence of things seen (or experienced) is preferred to the promise.

It is Hopeful who responds to this crisis by calling on Christian to remember (memory too is a gift of grace): "My Brother, you have quite *forgot* the Text. . . . These troubles . . . are no sign that God hath forsaken you, but are sent to try you, whether you will *call to mind* that which heretofore you have received of his goodness, and live upon him in your distresses (158, emphasis mine)." Living upon him means living upon the memory of his merciful deliverances in situations which, on their face, seem to rule out the possibility of deliverance. Hopeful adds a final word: *"Be of good cheer, Jesus Christ maketh thee whole,"* and "with that, *Christian* brake out with a loud voice, Oh I see him again! and he tells me, *When thou passest through the waters, I will be with thee, and through the Rivers, they shall not overflow thee.* Then they both took courage, and the enemy was after that as still as a stone, until they were gone over (158)." The brightening (through the agency of Hopeful) of the memory of Christ provides Christian with a light (inner, of course,) to see by, and in that light (of belief), the river of death is transformed into the waters of baptism, the river Jordan, the fount of (and *way* to eternal life. This is the power of memory, because it is the power of faith, not only to move mountains, but to *re*move them, to see through the significances they bear in earthly contexts to the significances they bear in the light (memory) of God's infinite love and mercy.

AND BEHOLD IT WAS A DREAM

For Christian and Hopeful, the journey is over, but *The Pilgrim's Progress* ends not once, but five times, and with each successive ending much of the satisfaction we experience at the first is taken away. At precisely the moment when our full sympathies should be with the pilgrims as they are welcomed into the Celestial City, we are suddenly made aware of the Dreamer, who is left outside the Gate:

Now just as the Gates were opened to let in the men, I looked in after them; and behold, the City shone like the Sun, the Streets also were paved with Gold, and in them walked many men, with Crowns on their heads, Palms in their hands, and golden Harps to sing praises withall.

There were also of them that had wings, and they answered one another without intermission, saying, *Holy, Holy, Holy, is the Lord.* And after that, they shut up the Gates: which when I had seen, I wished my self among them (162).

The poignancy of this is something we not only appreciate, but share; for Christian and Hopeful are walking away from our perspective, leaving us, with the Dreamer, on the outside looking in, knowing that it will possibly be a long time before we are welcomed into the Heavenly City. Scarcely has this disappointment registered, than the specter of a far greater one arises in the person of Ignorance, whose story is the third ending of *The Pilgrim's Progress:*

When he was come up to the Gate, he looked up to the writing that was above; and then began to knock, supposing that entrance should have been quickly administred to him: But he was asked by the men that lookt over the top of the Gate, Whence came you? and what would you have? He answered, I have eat and drank in the presence of the King, and he has taught in our Streets. Then they asked him for his Certificate, that they might go in and shew it to the King. So he fumbled in his bosom for one, and found none. Then said they, Have you none? But the man answered never a word. So they told the King but he would not come down to see him; but commanded the two shining Ones that conducted *Christian* and *Hopeful* to the City to go out and take *Ignorance* and bind him hand and foot, and have him away. Then they took him up, and carried him through the air to the door that I saw in the side of the Hill, and put him in there. Then I saw that there was a way to Hell, even from the Gates of Heaven, as well as from the City of *Destruction* (162–163).

Ignorance is merely another in the long line of pilgrims whose great error is to believe too literally in the image of the journey; but as the last of that line his appearance (and disappearance) has an extraordinary impact, if only because it constitutes a warning of what may yet happen to us if we ignore the light of the revealed word for the light of our own understandings. As always Bunyan's warnings stimulate us to a rehearsal of the kind of behavior that constitutes our best defense against the dangers of wayfaring. For the last time we perform the act of *re*interpreting and *de*signifying that has so often been required of us, affirming the irrelevance of the position Ignorance occupies in the linear form of the narrative and turning the pressure away from the evidence of physical and discursive (progressive) processes to the inner evidence of a truly saving faith. In short, we once again read *The Pilgrim's Progress* correctly by denying the pilgrim's progress and thereby practice our reading of the world we will reenter when the book is closed.

The fourth ending is the narrator's: "Then I saw that there was a way to Hell, even from the Gates of Heaven, as well as from the City of *Destruction*. So I awoke and behold it was a dream." The note of personal discovery in *"Then* I saw . . ." is an admission of something we may well have suspected earlier: the dreamer-narrator is also a wayfarer and he is no less fallible in that profession than either Christian or the reader. Indeed at those points where we become aware of him, he is almost always making an observation or asking a question that indicates a limited understanding of the action he is reporting. As the journey begins and Christian falls, along with Pliable, into the Slough of Dispond, the dreamer responds not with a moralization (he almost never plays that role), but with a question: Why is *"this* Plat . . . not mended that poor Travellers might go thither with more security (15)?" The answer (given by Help) is that each traveler carries (or doesn't carry) his security within him, and by asking the question the dreamer reveals himself to be as much a believer in the literal way as Formalist or Atheist. Later, when Christian and Hopeful talk "more in their sleep than ever they did in all their Journey," the dreamer stands "in a muse," and again the proper "reading" is provided (somewhat testily) by a more reliable interpreter than he. "Wherefore musest thou at this matter? It is the nature of the fruit of the grapes . . . as to cause the lips of them that are asleep to speak (156)." Of course, the primary function of moments like this is to provide instruction for the reader, but their secondary effect is to undermine the authority and prescience of the narrator; and this is certainly the effect here when he sees belatedly what we have been seeing all along, that the idea of a progress which is measurable and irreversible is not answerable to the realities of spiritual trial.

The narrator, then, is not our guide, but our fellow. The events of his dream happen to him just as they happen to us and to Christian, and in the end he is unable even to place himself in his own landscape ("I wished myself among them"). In this context, his final words, "and behold it was a dream," are more than conventionally literary, for they constitute a relinquishing of any claim either to the content or the effects of his narrative. This is not merely a dream, it is a dream vision, a *visio,* and in that genre the dreamer is not the author, but the vehicle of the experience he recalls. (His rational faculties are, literally, asleep.) In this case, the true author is not specified, but he is surely to be identified with the better interpreters who appear along the way to correct and rescue erring pilgrims and they, in turn, are surely to be identified with Christ. The same overruling agency who bears responsibility for everything that happens in the story is also responsible for the story itself and for the lessons it has taught us.

These lessons have been, by and large, interpretative and they are rehearsed for the last time in the fifth and final ending, a verse *Conclusion* addressed directly to the reader:

> *Now Reader I have told my Dream to thee*
> *See if thou canst Interpret it to me,*
> *Or to thyself or Neighbour, but take heed*
> *Of misinterpreting: for that instead*
> *Of doing good, will but thyself abuse:*
> *By misinterpreting evil insues.*
> *Take heed also that thou be not extreame*
> *In playing with the outside of my Dream* (164).

Together with the promise in the "Author's Apology"—"This book will make a traveller of thee"—this *Conclusion* is an authoritative description of the "dynamics of the narrative" which are finally the dynamics of the reading experience. To play "extremely" with the outside of the dream is to take its linear form seriously by failing to pierce through it to the truth it cannot itself image or contain; it is then that misinterpreting and evil ensue. Of course misinterpreting is often what Bunyan provokes when he overgenerously provides us with information or withholds the one piece of information that would enable us to interpret correctly; but whenever we are thus caught in his "intangling net," he is careful to extricate us and send us on our way (as Christian is sent on his) chastened and instructed in the wisdom of self-distrust. By "self-distrust" I mean not only distrust of ourselves, that is of our untutored interpretative abilities, but distrust of *it*-self, of the interpretative direction afforded by the linear configurations of the prose. *The Pilgrim's Progress* is the ultimate self-consuming artifact, for the insights it yields are inseparable from the demonstration of the inadequacy of its own forms, which are also the forms of the reader's understanding.

That understanding is the real subject of Milton's *The Reason of Church Government*.

V

# *Reason in* The Reason of Church Government

John Milton begins his *Reason of Church Government* by rehearsing a distinction which asserts the superiority of rational persuasion to peremptory or "lordly" commands:

> In the publishing of humane lawes, which for the most part aime not beyond the good of civill society, to set them barely forth to the people without reason or Preface, like a physicall prescript, or only with threatnings, as it were a lordly command, in the judgement of *Plato* was thought to be done neither generously nor wisely. His advice was, seeing that persuasion certainly is a more winning, and more manlike way to keepe men in obedience then feare, that to such lawes as were of principall moment, there should be us'd as an induction, some well temper'd discourse, shewing how good, how gainfull, how happy it must needs be to live according to honesty and justice, which being utter'd with those native colours and graces of speech, as true eloquence the daughter of vertue can best bestow upon her mothers praises, would so incite, and in a manner, charme the multitude into the love of that which is really good as to imbrace it ever after, not of cus-

> tome and awe, which most men do, but of choice and pur-
> pose, with true and constant delight.[1]

The advice is Plato's, but it is clearly (or so it would seem) approved by the present author. Indeed, in the course of the long and complex second sentence, the presence of Plato is less and less felt (he is represented only by a pronoun), and in the end his words are received by the reader as if they were Milton's.

None of this is surprising. The invoking of an authority and the assumption of his mantle is good rhetorical practice. The sentiments expressed (and apparently endorsed) are thoroughly conventional, and they give rise to a number of conventional expectations:

1. The expectation of a mode of procedure. What follows, presumably, will be an instance of the "well tempered discourse" that aims at a rational persuasion—the title is, after all, the *reason* of church government—and this, in turn, entails

2. the expectation of a formal logical structure, complete with propositions, counterpropositions, the arraying of evidence, and the drawing of conclusions concerning a matter in doubt. Together, 1 and 2 generate

3. an expectation of what will be required of the reader, the careful weighing of the arguments put forward by those who advocate one or the other of the forms of church government.

There is, too, the immediate expectation of a proportional argument of the form; if it is the case in X (in the publishing of laws which aim not beyond the good of civil society), so much more will it be the case in Y (in the publishing of laws which aim at the good of religious society); and it is the disappointment of this expectation that first alerts us to the imminent disappointment of all the others:

> *Moses* therefore the only Lawgiver that we can believe to
> have been visibly taught of God, knowing how vaine it was
> to write lawes to men whose hearts were not first season'd
> with the knowledge of God and of his workes, began from
> the book of Genesis, as a prologue to his lawes; which
> *Josephus* right well hath noted. That the nation of the

[1] *Complete Prose Works,* Vol. I, p. 746. All references are to this edition.

Jewes, reading therein the universall goodnesse of God to all creatures in the Creation, and his peculiar favour to them in his election of *Abraham* their ancestor, from whom they could derive so many blessings upon themselves, might be mov'd to obey sincerely by knowing so good a reason of their obedience (747).

As they unfold, these two sentences (Or are they one? Exactly what constitutes a sentence in *The Reason of Church Government* is not always clear) seem to make exactly the point we have been allowed to anticipate: Moses, knowing, as Plato did, how important it is to persuade men before commanding them, was careful to preface his laws with reasons. But this ready and easy sense is complicated (if not threatened) by the ambiguity of reference in the phrases "his workes" and "his lawes"; for, in fact, Moses has no more title to the one than to the other, and by pressuring the reader to assign responsibility for the two phrases (which, after all, are more alike than they are different) the prose makes it possible that he will go further and see that the question of responsibility is deeper than the structure of the surface argument suggests. Indeed, it requires only a slight shift in emphasis to reveal a quite different structure, one in which the illusion of human agency is countered at every point by a reference to the truer agency of God ("taught of God," "season'd with the knowledge of God," "the universall goodnesse of God"); for if they are his laws as well as his works, it is also he who begins from the book of Genesis to season men's hearts with *his* knowledge. From this point of view (which finds syntactic support in the possibility of substituting God for Moses as the subject of "knowing": "taught of God [*who*] knowing . . .") God plays all the parts— *he* perceives the obdurateness of the heart which *he* then softens by infusing into it a knowledge of himself after which he presents himself to it in the form of *his* laws—and his preeminence is asserted at the expense not only of Moses (who disappears after the first word), but of the rhetorical and reasonable arts which were supposedly to have effected the persuasion of the Jews. Indeed, in this reading (which is, at the very least, available) the values attached in the opening lines to "winning persuasion"

("persuasion certainly is a more winning . . .") and "lordly commands barely set down" ("to set them barely forth . . . as it were a lordly command") are being reversed—"Lordly" now takes on a different meaning—and the reversal is complete at the end of the sentence when reason, another form of persuasion, is absorbed into obedience: "That the nation of the Jewes, reading therein the universall goodnesse of God . . . might be mov'd to obey sincerely by knowing so good a reason of their obedience." The "reason" which moves the Jews to obey is the goodness of God, which, while it may be a reason *for* obeying, is certainly not a reason in the sense suggested by the title *The Reason of Church Government.*

There are, then, in this sequence two anatomies of persuasion, one in which discursive or reasonable processes play a prominent part, and another in which persuasion is to be attributed solely to the influence of God; and while the implications of their uneasy juxtaposition are at this stage only slightly pressuring (the uneasiness may be more a product of my analysis than of the reading experience), they will in time become unavoidable and unavoidably subversive, not only of the claims made for the tract by its title, but of the complacency of the reader:

> If then the administration of civill justice, and under the obscurity of Ceremoniall rites, such care was had by the wisest of the heathen, and by *Moses* among the Jewes, to instruct them at least in a generall reason of that government to which their subjection was requir'd, how much more ought the members of the Church under the Gospell seeke to informe their understanding in the reason of that government which the Church claimes to have over them: especially for that the church hath in her immediate cure those inner parts and affections of the mind where the seat of reason is; having power to examine our spirituall knowledge, and to demand from us in Gods behalfe a service intirely reasonable (747–748).

The most prominent feature of this sentence is the repeated appearance in it of the word "reason." Of course one might well expect "reason" to appear often in *The Reason of Church Gov-*

*ernment;* what one does not expect, however, is to find the word used in such a way as to take from it much of the force it usually carries, and in this sentence what is taken away from reason is also taken away from us. First we are "instructed" (with Milton's Jews) in a "generall reason," and presumably in any situation to which those terms would be appropriate our participation would be important; "government" is a slight dissonance, moving, as it does, almost imperceptibly in the direction of a reason imposed, or no reason at all; with "subjection" we are rudely and unceremoniously (the adverb is carefully chosen) shown our true position vis-à-vis the government God would have us accept; and "required" takes away any suggestion that the initiative, or for that matter the choice (for reason is but choosing), is ours. Only fifteen words separate "instruct" from "required," but the reader who has negotiated the distance between them has exchanged one way of looking at the world for another, moving from a context in which rational processes have some place in the consideration of matters spiritual to another, in which reason and the assent of a reasoning mind are somehow superfluous. And this journey is retraced when the reader is brought from the circumlocutory blandness of "seeke to informe their understanding" to the nakedness of "demand." The phrase "intirely reasonable" is finally mocking.

The mockery has two objects, the forms of rational discourse, and those who have recourse to them; at this point the reader may begin to suspect that Milton is toying with him. Any such suspicion becomes a certainty as the preface draws to a close:

> Let others therefore dread and shun the Scriptures for their darknesse, I shall wish I may deserve to be reckon'd among those who admire and dwell upon them for their clearnesse. And this seemes to be the cause why in those places of holy writ, wherein is treated of Church-government, the reasons thereof are not formally, and profestly set downe, because to him that heeds attentively the drift and scope of Christian profession, they easily imply themselves, which thing further to explane, having now prefac'd enough, I shall no longer deferre (750).

Here the subversion of discursive reasoning, and therefore of the reader's position, is obvious and even insulting. The argument (if that is the word) is grounded in two interdependent distinctions, one between formal reasoning (reasons formally set down) and reasons whose force is independent of any chain of inferences ("they easily imply themselves"), and a second between those who look for proofs in Scripture and those for whom God's word itself constitutes a proof. The concluding sentence acts as a "multiple choice question," pressuring the reader to place himself in one of these two categories.[2] The choice, however, is no choice at all, at least as the sentence offers it: either agree that the truth of the matter is self-evident, or admit that you have not heeded "attentively the drift and scope of Christian profession." (Heads I win, tails you condemn yourself.) This is a brilliant piece of strategy (one might call it the "emperor's clothes" ploy) and it has the effect of "predeciding" the question which was supposedly to have been settled in the body of the tract. Earlier Milton had declared his intention to "prove" that the responsibility for the "faithful feeding" of the ministerial order belongs to "no other" than the Presbyters and Deacons (749). Now we discover that proof, in the conventional and expected sense, is unnecessary, except for those of little faith. (Who me?) The reader who is bullied into agreeing that the truth is self-evident, commits himself to the Presbyterian position, a decision that is an almost accidental byproduct of a self-defensive gesture ("Of course I see!"); and moreover, having conceded the major point, he preconcedes all subsequent points, since he has acquiesced in the devaluing of the very faculty from which later counter-arguments might be expected to arise—reason.

The implications of this remarkable sequence extend far beyond the local discomfort of the reasonable reader to fundamental questions about the tract itself. If deliberation is superfluous to the validation of the truth, and if clearness is a condition of perception rather than of presentation, what is the point of going on? Presumably, to bring those of his readers who have not heeded attentively the drift and scope of Christian profession to their senses. But the status of that group remains always what it is

---

[2] I borrow this phrase from Joan Webber who uses it to characterize Burton's sentences in her brilliant study of seventeenth-century prose, *The Eloquent "I"* (Madison, 1968), pp. 101–102.

here, a convenient designation, a limbo as it were, for those who differ with Milton,[3] and a pretext, transparently specious, for continuing an argument which never progresses beyond its original assertion: church government by Presbyters and Deacons is commanded by God; church government by prelates is an invention of man. (As K. G. Hamilton observes, "Milton, as a dialectician, is at times given to jumping up and down in one place.") [4]

In short, *The Reason of Church Government* is something of a joke, which functions at the expense of the expectations its title encourages, and therefore at the expense of the reader who becomes their captive. But it is a serious joke, which in the course of discrediting one kind of logic, makes use (almost surreptitiously) of another, a logic of association. For while the irrelevance of reason to the question of record is everywhere insisted on—it is a matter, Milton says, "of eye sight, rather then of disquisition (775)"—neither the word "reason" nor the structures characteristic of rational discourse disappear from the pages of the tract. The continued presence of an excrescent logical apparatus in conjunction with a sustained attack on a certain group of men results, in time, in the linking of the one with the other. That is, the dismissal of reason as a means of validating the truth and the attack on the prelates, who find their truth in "the rare device of mans braine (781)" rather than in the word of God, come to be perceived as one. This association—it is eventually an identity —is already present in embryonic form in the concluding sentences of the preface, where in addition to the surface argument (itself circular) there is a covert argument made by the pairs of opposing and coordinate terms, which emerges if one glances down the printed page:

[3] See, for example, *Complete Prose Works,* p. 779: "Yet because it hath the outside of a specious reason, & specious things we know are aptest to worke with humane lightnesse and frailty, even against the solidest truth, that sounds not plausibly, let us think it worth the examining for the love of infirmer Christians, of what importance this their second reason may be." Again the reader is put in the position of having either to claim fellowship with Milton—it is offered to him, ever so casually, in the phrase "let *us*" (emphasis mine)—or to accept the description of himself as someone inclined by frailty to be impressed by specious, plausible-sounding reasons.

[4] "Structure of Milton's Prose," in *Language and Style in Milton,* ed. Emma and Shawcross (New York, 1967), p. 329.

| | |
|---|---|
| darknesse | clearnesse |
| reasons formally set down | reasons that imply themselves |
| those who have not heeded | those who have |
| the drift and scope of | |
| Christian profession | |
| Prelacy | Presbyterianism |

These opposing pairs together form one large opposition which turns outward to face the reader, asking him, in effect, "where do *you* stand?" (Milton gives *his* answer loudly) although, as we have seen, the answer is more directed than the question would imply.

What is true of the preface is true of the pamphlet as a whole. In every unit of *The Reason of Church Government,* there coexist two structures, an outer structure which promises rational deliberation, progressive clarification, and encapsulated knowledge, and an inner structure whose points are made at the expense of the other's promises and at the expense, too, of the readers who believe in them. The argument projected by the first is consistently circular and tautologous, while the real argument inheres in the reinforcing and expanding of the oppositions and associations established in the preface, especially the opposition of reason to intuition and the linking of one with the Prelates and of the other with the clear-eyed adherents of Presbyterianism.

In other words, reason is very much the subject of *The Reason of Church Government,* but it is an *anti*subject (almost an anti-Christ) whose proportions grow larger as the dimensions of the danger it poses are sketched in. The discrediting of reason and of her attendant machinery continues at every level, even when the word itself is not present:

> Whether therefore discipline be all one with doctrine, or the particular application thereof to this or that person, we all agree that doctrine must be such only as is commanded (761).

Here the very form of the syntax generates all the expectations that in other places are raised by the direct invocation of "reason." The juxtaposition of "whether" and "therefore" generates two sets of related expectations: "whether" leaves us awaiting an "or," and, of course, with this kind of construction, the alternatives are assumed to be something on the order of contradictories. "Therefore" reinforces the promise of logicality without delimiting it. Whatever the content of the sentence is to be, we feel that it can be organized and placed, that is, explained, within the rational framework of which this syntax is one manifestation. "Discipline," with its strong suggestion of order and regularity, does nothing at all to upset the reader's complacency; while the nicely lilting alliteration of "discipline" and "doctrine" lends a slight, but not unfelt, stylistic support to the assumptions the sentence has been encouraging. In the next clause, two new and complementary contexts are alluded to: the opposition of "all" to "particular" is faintly scholastic; and the rather stiff formality of "thereof to this or that person" is decidedly legalistic. (The echo of "therefore" in "thereof" makes its own small contribution.) When the sentence begins its downward motion with "we all agree," we all anticipate a conclusion that accords perfectly with what has gone before. Instead, we are brought up hard against "commanded" (the impetus of the rhythm virtually deposits us on it) and with that word whatever claims had been made, silently, in the names of reason, logic, and law, are peremptorily swept away, by a "lordly command." The "whether . . . or" construction must now be read as "it-doesn't-matter-which"; the force of "therefore" is blunted by a verb that overrides all "therefores"; and the illusion of choice that is projected by "we all agree" fades before the acknowledgment of a power whose commands make agreement unnecessary.

This sentence and others like it [5] give indirect support to the more explicit assertions of an intimate connection between reason and Prelacy. In the second chapter of the second book, Milton opposes the presumptuousness of Prelatical "fleshly pride and wis-

---

[5] See, for example, *Complete Prose Works,* p. 761: "since Church-government is so strictly commanded in Gods Word, the first and greatest reason why we should submit thereto, is because God has so commanded." The form of the syntax describes a logical sequence—since X, therefore Y—but the logic, if we can call it that, is circular, not linear: we should obey because it is commanded. The middle clause works to give the illusion of an argument, especially since its force is centered in the word "reason"; but the true force of the sentence resides in the antimetabole formed by "commanded . . . Gods"–"God . . . commanded."

dom" to the "pure simplicity of saving truth," and in the ringing indictment that follows, "fleshly pride" is more precisely identified as "mans reasoning":

> Instead of shewing the reason of their lowly condition from divine example and command, they seek to prove their high pre-eminence from humane consent and autority. But let them chaunt while they will of prerogatives, we shall tell them of Scripture; of custom, we of Scripture; of Acts and Statutes, stil of Scripture, til the quick and pearcing word enter to the dividing of their soules, & the mighty weaknes of the Gospel throw down the weak mightines of mans reasoning (827).

Here, as before, reason is first invoked and then identified with the divine command; the effect, of course, is to bypass the reasoning *process* and redefine reason to mean self-validating reason. But Milton goes further; not only is the machinery of proof declared unnecessary, it is condemned as a source of authority because it is merely human. "Shewing" God's reason is one thing, seeking to prove man's is another; one is an acknowledgment of a superior wisdom, the other an exercise in solipsism, the building of a structure designed to confirm the mind in the opinions it already holds. While, in reason's terms, the word of God may appear weak (or worse), the true priorities of judgment are exactly the reverse, and it is this that the reader "proves" on his pulse when *his* reason is "thrown down" by the double paradox of "mighty weaknes" and "weak mightines." Singly, neither of these would have been especially troublesome, but together they ask for more distinctions and cross-distinctions than the mind can comfortably manage; and, just as the reader is struggling to align and match the different orders of weakness and might, the weight of the sentence's disapproval falls on the very activity in which it has involved him —"mans reasoning."

"Mans reasoning" and Prelacy are linked in earlier chapters when the sentences that characterize the Episcopal position display both the vocabulary and form of logical argument. Accept what the bishops say, warns Milton, and "it will *inferre* Popedome (773)." After denying that the king is a type, he declares

"Therfore your typical chaine of King and Priest must unlink (771)," and it is clear that what must unlink is a chain of inferences. We see "abundantly," he boasts, "the little assurance which they finde to *reare up* their high roofs"; for it is after all, "a matter of eye sight, rather then of *disquisition* (775)." The "tedious muster of citations, Sees and *successions*," he insists, are "repugnant to the plaine dictat of Scripture" and "the *arguments* of fooles (778)." These same arguments, we are told, will in time raise a Pope, for "that the *exaltation* of the Pope *arose* out of the *reason* of Prelaty it cannot be denied (782)." In all of these examples there is the suggestion of a chained and linked structure which stands (shakily) on its base and aspires to the heavens, and it is a structure both of ecclesiastical hierarchy and demonstrative reasoning. This equation is not fortuitous, but essential, for reason and Prelacy are the abstract and substantial manifestations, respectively, of the same impiety. The basic assumption made by the bishops—that the question of the true ministerial order remains open—is finally the only justification for devising systems of church government at all. If, on the other hand, the question is closed, and closed by God, that "devising" is an act of presumption in which the clear and revealed word is "patch't" and "varnish't over" with the "imbellishings of mans imagination (757)." The ascending pyramidal structure (790) of the Episcopal hierarchy is thus a mirror image of the structures reared (and formally set down) by the carnal reason; and those who submit to the one, worship the other, preferring it (and in it themselves) to the lordly command of God.

It is for this "reason" that Milton's attack on the pretensions of Prelacy involves the continual undermining of the rational pretensions of his own prose, although there is one point where the ratiocinative promise of the prose is more than fulfilled:

> When as the catholick government is not to follow the division of kingdomes, the temple best representing the universall Church, and the High Priest the universall head; so I observe here, that if to quiet schisme there must be one head of Prelaty in a land or Monarchy rising from a Provinciall to a nationall Primacy, there may upon better

> grounds of repressing schisme be set up one catholick head over the catholick Church. For the peace and good of the Church is not terminated in the schismelesse estate of one or two kingdomes, but should be provided for by the joynt consultation of all reformed Christendome: that all controversie may end in the finall pronounce or canon of one Arch-primat or Protestant Pope (783).

This is a perfect demonstration both of the dangers of reason and of the "reason" for its appropriation by the Prelates. The conclusion generated by a chain of inferences depends on its initial assumptions, but these are themselves unexamined; and, moreover, as the chain lengthens, there is less and less pressure to look closely at its first link. In the sentence immediately preceding this passage, the pattern of the High Priest is said to "set up with better *reason* a Pope" and the word "better" is not, I think, to be taken ironically. The "better" the reason, the more formally and fully it is set down, the more successful will the Prelates be in calling attention away from the falsehood on which their structure (of church government and argument) rests. On the other hand, if one simply asserts the truth the sequence is designed to hide, the entire demonstration (and with it the Prelatical organization) "unlinks" and falls to the ground. And this is precisely the effect of the following sentence: "Although by this meanes for ought I see, all the diameters of schisme may as well meet and be knit up into one grand falsehood." Knitting all "up into one grand falsehood" is exactly what these sentences have done, and by "this meanes" we are to understand the means of logical inference which simultaneously builds the argumentative structure of the prose (what Milton calls in the next sentence a "league of consequence") and the structure of Prelatical hierarchy. Later in this same chapter Milton declares "there can be no reason . . . if it [Prelaty] have lawfully mounted thus high, it should not be a lordly ascendant in . . . the Church, from Primate to Patriarch, and so to Pope (789–790)," and again the reference is simultaneously to the mounting Pope and to the rational machinery ("there can be no reason") by which, and in the name of which, he mounts. Once the basic proposition that supports Episcopacy is admitted, the proposition that there *is* a place for reason in the determining of church government, the laws of reason can be invoked with perfect (self) confidence that they will support and abet the raising of the scaffolding to whatever pyramidal heights the Prelates wish to reach. In short (and with apologies to James I), no reason, no bishops, no Pope.

### THE THINGS THEMSELVES CONCLUDE IT

We are now in a position to consider the criticism that has been leveled at Milton's prose in general and at *The Reason of Church Government* in particular. Don Wolfe compares *The Reason of Church Government* with "the patient array of argument for Episcopacy" and "the reasoned pages of Hooker's *Ecclesiastical Polity*" and finds it "a weak presentation of Presbyterian claims," an "almost irrelevant document." [6] And this judgment is given analytical support by K. G. Hamilton, who discerns in much of the prose a basic "ratiocinative emptiness," "a lack of real intellectual content":

> We can be carried along for a time by the apparent closeness of the argument, by the rhetoric, or by the imaginative force of the words and images; but, because of Milton's method which depends so much on the development of argument within the individual sentence rather than on a strong ratiocinative progress through the whole work, when a relative emptiness of dialectical content becomes characteristic of the sentence the reader inevitably begins to get the impression that nothing is being offered him beyond words, that he is getting nowhere, gaining no real illumination. Milton, as a dialectician, is at times given to jumping up and down in one place—what appears structurally to be a dynamic progress may resolve itself finally into a complex but static expression of the strength of his own conviction, rather than either a reasoned statement or an imaginative apprehension of the basis of that conviction. [7]

[6] *Complete Prose Works,* Vol. I, 199.    [7] "Structure of Milton's Prose," p. 329.

In these strictures the reader will recognize, I trust, the reverse image of my praise ("irrelevant document," "jumping up and down in one place," "complex but static expression"). Hamilton and Wolfe assume a failure in exactly the terms Milton is concerned to discredit. *The Reason of Church Government* is indeed "a weak presentation of Presbyterian claims"; it could be nothing else given Milton's central point, the irrelevance of rational presentation to the matter ("of eye sight rather then of disquisition") at hand. And the reader does "get the impression . . . that he is going nowhere," for after the initial assertion—the first and greatest reason of church government is the command of God—there is nowhere to go. The experience of reading *The Reason of Church Government* is indeed a static one, and the homogeneity of the sentences analyzed in the preceding pages is itself a confirmation of Hamilton's observations. (They are much alike, not only in form and effect, but even in phrasing, and yet they were chosen at random, from widely separated chapters and sections.) There is no "development of argument" within the work because there is no arguing, merely the unceasing repetition of a few key words— "fleshly," "pure," "clear," "carnal," "spiritual," etc.—which are themselves implicated in a limited number of set relationships. Rather than reason or reasoning, we have resonance. Of course these repetitions are imbedded in a surface rhetoric that displays (rather ostentatiously) all the signs of a logical structure: the division into two books, separated by a digression (dutifully and ingenuously labeled); the further divisions into chapters, complete with opening and concluding sentences and summarizing chapter headings. But even here, Milton gives the game away. The headings for the first two chapters read as follows:

> *That Church-government is prescrib'd in the Gospell, and that to say otherwise is unsound* (750).
> *That Church-government is set downe in holy Scripture, and that to say otherwise is untrue* (756).

The similarities in form are obvious and revealing: an assertion of the proposition to be proved is followed by what would appear to be an anticipatory refutation of the opposing party's position: the rising rhythm of "that to say otherwise" leads us to expect that

what follows will be equal in length (and force) to the clause controlled by the first "That." Instead, we are met by the sudden
abruptness of the conclusion, "is unsound," "is untrue." All the
force generated by the sequence is concentrated in these final
words. *They* are what we carry away with us, and they prejudice
us against the "otherwise" before it is even heard. In still another way, then, the proffered illusion of reasonable and rigorous
argument is subverted from within.

Even more destructive of that illusion, however, is the inter-
changeability of the two chapter headings. In Milton's lexicon,
"unsound" and "untrue" are synonyms; "Gospell" and "holy
Scripture" are synonyms in anyone's lexicon, as are "set downe"
and "prescribe." The rhythms are the same, the number of sylla-
bles more or less equal, and the force of the constructions, as we
have seen, identical. The reader who moves from chapter to chapter hasn't really moved at all, except perhaps in a circle, back to
the point of origin; although time is consumed and distances, in
print and pages are negotiated, there is no substantive advance in
the argument. The beginning of each chapter holds out the promise of a new direction, a second or third reason, a further conclusion, but within a few lines a corner is turned—perhaps in the
middle of a sentence—and waiting there are the familiar points
Milton has made again and again: the Presbyterian form of
church government is commanded by God; Episcopacy is not.
This is an obvious truth, requiring no proof. Those who rely on
the machinery of proof rather than on God's word are blind or
worse.

The effect of coming repeatedly upon these same self-evident
truths is to make the chapter one happens to be reading indistinguishable from the preceding chapter or from the chapters yet to
come. Doors keep opening in *The Reason of Church Government*,
and the reader keeps passing through them only to find himself
in the room he has just left. After a while, the relationship between the plan of the building and what is inside it is seen to be
accidental. No matter what the chapter heading says, no matter
what label is put on the container, the import of what is asserted
is always the same.

The seventh chapter of the first book is another case in point.

The heading reads, "That those many Sects and Schismes by some suppos'd to be among us, and that rebellion in Ireland, ought not to be a hindrance, but a hastning of reformation (794)." In the first sentence we are told, in effect, that the problem itself is a fabrication of those who see sects and schisms where there are none: "As for those many Sects and divisions rumor'd abroad to be amongst us, it is not hard to perceave that they are partly the meere fictions and false alarmes of the Prelates, thereby to cast amazements and panick terrors into the hearts of weaker Christians." (Once more, the "emperor's clothes" ploy; you, not being one of these weaker Christians, perceive this, don't you?) Having dismissed the issue as a fiction, Milton proceeds to the inevitable conclusion, not really a conclusion at all: "And thus I leave it as a declared truth, that neither the feare of sects no nor rebellion can be a fit plea to stay reformation, but rather to push it forward with all possible diligence and speed (800)." By "declared truth," Milton means a truth not proved, one not requiring proof. This final sentence is nothing more than a reformulation ("stay" for "hindrance," "push it forward" for "hastning") of the point originally made by the chapter heading, a point beyond which we haven't advanced at all. Of course, something must be going on in the interim—there are some five pages between the opening and closing of the chapter—but whatever it is (and we shall return to it), it is not the chain of inferences one might expect to find in a work entitled *The Reason of Church Government*.

What I am suggesting is that *The Reason of Church Government* is a grotesquely huge parody of one of its self-cannibalizing sentences. Outwardly, it presents itself as a series of carefully reasoned arguments, complete with propositions, proofs, and conclusions, and tied together in a larger logical framework by numbered chapters and books, the whole rising toward a grand and triumphant *quod erat demonstrandum*. But in terms of what the reader experiences while he is inside the tract, these highly visible ligatures have no determining force at all, and the divisions supposedly marked out by them have only a physical existence. The silent claim made by the logical superstructure is that it processes truth; but in fact, its machinery merely marks out areas within which the reader, or at least one class of reader, experiences a series of recognitions (or rememberings) of what he has always known to be true; and these recognitions occur independently of the pressure exerted by numbered chapters, divisions into books, first or second reasons, "thuses" and "therefores." Of course this pressure does exist and it reasserts itself each time a chapter begins or ends; but for the reader whose responses are answerable to Milton's vision, these moments are merely occasions for the taking of a mental breath, and not, as the surface rhetoric implies, signposts marking another stage in the building of a rational structure.

Indeed, it is precisely at these points of emphasis, where another author would call attention to the progress of his argument, that Milton returns us to the beginning (and end) of his. The penultimate sentence of the third chapter of the second book, for example, is simply a reprise of the conclusion to the preface:

> And thus Prelaty both in her fleshly supportments, in her carnall doctrine of ceremonie and tradition, in her violent and secular power going quite counter to the prime end of Christs comming in the flesh, that is to revele his truth, his glory and his might in a clean contrary manner then Prelaty seeks to do, thwarting and defeating the great mistery of God, I do not conclude that Prelaty is Antichristian, for what need I? the things themselves conclude it (850).

Here again is the now familiar double structure, the one the reader is allowed (encouraged) to anticipate, and another that reveals itself when the first has aborted. The first structure is logical and argumentative; it is a structure of expectations, based on the words "thus Prelaty both," and exhibiting the form, "A, because of B and C, is D." That is to say, it promises a conclusion that will follow naturally upon the identification of the two salient attributes of Prelaty. But the anticipated rhythm of the sentence is not carried through; rather than two attributes, we are given three, and before we have time to consider exactly what this means in relation to the very specific "both," the weight of the sentence shifts to the explanatory clause which begins at "that is." The focus of attention shifts too, from Prelaty to the "end of Christs comming"; and it is at this point, when the control

afforded by a linear and directing syntax is relaxed (or abandoned), that a new principle of organization comes to the fore.
The pivot point of the sentence is now the word "that," and on
either side of it a series of opposites face each other in a kind of
confrontation: "Prelaty," "fleshly," "carnall," "ceremonie," "tradition," and "secular" vs. "Christs," "revele," "truth," "might,"
and "clean." Whatever meaning the sentence finally has is the
product of this confrontation rather than of any sustained argument. Indeed, so strong is the figurative element, the attracting
power of associatively linked phrases, that individual words mean
independently of the syntax in which they are supposedly imbedded. Technically, "clean" is an adverb, and should be glossed
"wholly"; but the proximity of "truth," "glory," and "revele"
(which here retains its root meaning, *revelare,* to unveil or uncover) pressures us to read "clean" and "clear" or "unsullied,"
a reading that has the advantage of providing a nice counterpoint to the combined suggestiveness of "ceremonie," "tradition," and "fleshly." The words on either side of the dividing
"that" become interchangeable; together they form a single
pair of words and a single large opposition which is the sum of
the associations they share: on one hand all the false appearances
and fleshly coverings of the earthly perspective, and on the other
the simplicity and clarity of unadorned truth.

Often in *The Reason of Church Government,* a logical statement is allowed to complete itself, only to be resolved into a
tautology. Here it is simply aborted, as Milton breaks off his still
verbless sentence (so unimportant has syntax become that the
omission is hardly noted) to tell us that the chain of inferences
we had been led to expect is superfluous: "I do not conclude that
Prelaty is Antichristian, for what need I? the things themselves
conclude it." This is a perfect description of what has happened
in the prose. The responsibility for "concluding" has passed from
the logically based syntax, which is left incomplete, to a series of
single words whose argumentative force is immediate and (self)
sufficient; and this shift from rational discourse to figurative declaration is reflected in the response of the reader, who does not
wait for a formal conclusion to determine the truth about Prelacy.
In effect, the reader has been made to exchange one way of know-

ing for another: he begins by withholding judgment pending the marshaling of evidence, but in the end he is judging simply by reading or seeing and without the intermediary interposition of any evidentiary process.

One might say, in fact, that in the course of this sentence, the reader is transformed from an outsider who receives information through a filter (of language and logic) into an insider who is confronted directly with the naked thing itself. And this is perfectly consonant with the sentence's only declarative assertion. Things that "conclude themselves" are things that wear their meanings and values on their faces for all, who have eyes, to see. It follows, then, that any interposing conveyer—formal logic, rhetorical pointing, language itself—is a hindrance to close-up viewing, a hindrance that is here removed when the discursive structure first recedes and then falls away. This falling away is a spectacular instance of what is happening all the time in *The Reason of Church Government*. The prose and its forms are continually removing themselves from the reader's path of vision and leaving him face to face with Reality. This is true even when the rational framework is left standing, but with nothing to support. Sentences whose logic is circular and numbered chapters whose content is indistinguishable contribute to the pressure exerted on the reader to dispense with mediators and attend "in person" to the things that are concluding and implying themselves. At times, that pressure is literally irresistible, and the reader is given no choice:

> We shall be able by this time to discern whether Prelaticall jurisdiction be contrary to the Gospell or no. First therefore the government of the Gospell being economicall and paternall, that is, of such a family where there be no servants, but all sons in obedience, not in servility, as cannot be deny'd by him that lives but within the sound of Scripture, how can the Prelates justifie to have turn'd the fatherly orders of Christs houshold, the blessed meeknesse of his lowly roof, those ever open and inviting dores of his dwelling house which delight to be frequented with only filiall accesses, how can they justifie to have turn'd these

domestick privileges into the barre of a proud judiciall
court where fees and clamours keep shop and drive a trade,
where bribery and corruption solicits, paltring the free and
monilesse power of discipline with a carnall satisfaction by
the purse. Contrition, humiliation, confession, the very
sighs of a repentant spirit are there sold by the penny.
That undeflour'd and unblemishable simplicity of the Gospell, nor she her selfe, for that could never be, but a false-
whited, a lawnie resemblance of her, like that aire-born
*Helena* in the fables, made by the sorcery of Prelats, instead of calling her Disciples from the receit of custome,
is now turn'd Publican her self; and gives up her body to
a mercenary whordome under those fornicated arches
which she cals Gods house, and in the sight of those her
altars which she hath set up to be ador'd makes merchan-
dize of the bodies and souls of men. Rejecting purgatory
for no other reason, as it seems, then because her greedi-
ness cannot deferre but had rather use the utmost extor-
tion of redeemed penances in this life. But because these
matters could not be thus carri'd without a begg'd and
borrow'd force from worldly autority, therefore prelaty
slighting the deliberat and chosen counsell of Christ in
his spirituall government, whose glory is in the weaknesse
of fleshly things to tread upon the crest of the worlds pride
and violence by the power of spirituall ordinances, hath on
the contrary made these her freinds and champions which
are Christs enemies in this his high designe, smothering
and extinguishing the spirituall force of his bodily weaknesse in the discipline of his Church with the boistrous and
carnall tyranny of an undue, unlawfull and ungospellike
jurisdiction (848–850).

We begin with a clearly defined three-dimensional situation: a
speaker about to make a point by appealing to his audience's reason: an "I," a "thou," and an "it." With "First therefore," the
reader girds himself for a rigorous mental exercise; the mode of
discourse will be logical and the argument lengthy, moving, presumably, from first to second to third and so on. The expectation

of logical rigor is strengthened by the speaker's apparent concern to define his terms; there is a progressive clarification of "economicall and paternall," first by "that is" and the clause it introduces, and then by the "but-not" pattern within the clause itself. This is, apparently, the proposition that will be the basis of the final conclusion, and the care Milton takes with it validates his claim to the reader's (rational) attention. But with "how can the Prelates," we experience the first of two shifts in the direction of the syntax; the sudden introduction of the interrogative mode forces a revision in our expectations of what is to come. The dislocation is momentary, however, and the adjustment is made easily; the logic of the sequence will be less formal than had been anticipated, perhaps an enthymeme rather than a complete proof, but logically based it will presumably be. The repetition, within a few lines, of the "how can they" formula serves to settle the syntax in its new track and we fall easily into the anticipatory rhythm of a question. It is at this point that the sentence shifts again, and breaks away entirely from its syntactical and logical moorings. The key word is "where"; ostensibly the occasion of a slight detour in the journey toward the waiting question mark, the "where" construction instead takes over the sentence, and its influence is extended to the sentences (if they are sentences) that follow. The question mark is never reached; nor do we continue to expect it, since the force of the interrogative is less and less felt. In its place we have the thrust of a series of suspended clauses, all ruled by "where." And it is not long before these clauses break free even of "where" and present themselves to the reader directly, without sponsor and without a mediating discursive framework. For as the organizing and directing pressure of the syntax is relaxed, the sense of a voice, and of a temporal and spatial context enclosing both the voice and its audience, fades. "Where" has become here and now and there is suddenly no distance at all, physical and epistemological, between the reader and the truth. Things no longer come to him through the medium of a structured and structuring syntax, but in their essence, as they are in the structure of reality, to which he now has access; he is literally immersed in the words (and things) on the page. Now and here, not in a sentence spoken by an identifiable voice, are contrition, humiliation, and confession sold by the penny; now and here, the false semblance of the true gospel sets herself up to be adored. And the reader sees and interprets these things himself; he is, in the truest sense of the phrase, an *eye witness,* and because he is an eye witness, the sentence that ends the sequence, a sentence we have seen before, is, as it was meant to be, an anticlimax:

> And thus Prelaty both in her fleshly supportments, in her carnall doctrine of ceremonie and tradition, in her violent and secular power going quite counter to the prime end of Christs comming in the flesh, that is to revele his truth, his glory and his might in a clean contrary manner then Prelaty seeks to do, thwarting and defeating the great mistery of God, I do not conclude that Prelaty is Antichristian, for what need I? the things themselves conclude it (850).

This remarkable sequence is less a statement than a strategy. Rather than passing judgment on Prelacy, it transfers the responsibility for judging to the reader by placing the defendant before him and going away. It is, literally, an eye-opener, and is thus answerable to the hope Milton expresses in the sixth chapter of the first book: "But my hope is that the people of England will not suffer themselves to be juggl'd thus out of their faith and religion by a mist of names cast before their eyes, but will search wisely by the Scriptures and look quite through this fraudulent aspersion of a disgracefull name into the things themselves (788)." "Looking through" is the motion encouraged everywhere by *The Reason of Church Government,* whether the veil to be pierced is of its own making, or the false logic of episcopal argument, or the clothing and ceremonies that obscure the true nature of Prelaty.[8] In the act of removing itself from the reader's path of vision, the prose acts to disperse the mists that have been cast by others; and

---

[8] "Believe it, wondrous Doctors, all corporeal resemblances of inward holinesse & beauty are now past; he that will cloath the Gospel now, intimates plainly, that the Gospel is naked, uncomely, that I may not say reproachfull. Do not, ye Church-maskers, while Christ is cloathing upon our barenes with his righteous garment to make us acceptable in his fathers sight, doe not, as ye do, cover and hide his righteous verity with the polluted cloathing of your ceremonies to make it seem more decent in your own eyes (828)."

it does this by bringing the reader in, past or through the obscur-
ing element, to "the things themselves." This zoom lens effect is
achieved whenever a discursive form recedes or aborts—when, for
instance, a sentence virtually deposits us on "God's command"—
but it is particularly noticeable in those places where Milton
wishes to rub our noses in the Prelatical essence:

> Can we believe that your government strains in good ear-
> nest at the petty gnats of schisme, when as we see it makes
> nothing to swallow the Camel heresie of *Rome,* but that
> indeed your throats are of the right Pharisaical straine
> (785–786).

This rhetorical question unfolds in three stages, in each of
which there is a different relationship between the submerged
simile and the reader. In the first stage, it is we who "strain" to
make out the components of the figure, and as a result, they are
sharply differentiated. The Prelates and their government (themselves distinguished) stand in relation to the vague image of a
man straining at gnats, that is, at the petty annoyances attending
the existence of "innumerable sects." In the second stage, the
image is strengthened by the concrete visibility of "swallow." At
the same time, the distinction between the tenor and the vehicle,
between the inanimate institution and the figure of the open-
mouthed man, is also strengthened by the pointedly neuter "it."
In the third stage, however, all distinctions are collapsed: "your"
encompasses both the Prelates and their government, and tenor
is no less animate than the vehicle; in fact, the vehicle becomes
the tenor when "throats" moves from one side of the analogy to
the other.

These stages in the development of the figure produce corresponding alterations in the reader's mode of perception. At first
we are translating from vehicle to tenor, holding the components
of the comparison at arm's length in our mind's eye; in the second
clause the vehicle is well enough established for us to see the tenor
in terms of it; and finally the terms themselves are discarded and
our apprehension of the animated image is immediate. This effect
is intensified by the internal logic of the figure, which requires
that the swallowing mouth grow larger in order to accommodate

the camel heresy of Rome. Just as we gain unmediated access to the "thing itself," its proportions increase, with the result that it seems to be moving toward us, as we move *in* to it—a grotesquely huge blind mouth ready to leap from the page and devour us.[9] (The sect-gnats have disappeared in the falling away of the analogy, and we are the only potential victims in sight.)

This is not a simple case of vividly making a point. The making of a point is what is left behind when the machinery of analogy is abandoned and we are brought face to self-validating face with the object. The sequence is not a quasi-logical assertion of similarities: Prelates are like gaping throats. "Gaping throatness" *is* the essence of Prelacy and in the end we see this essence—the moral transforms the physical as in some surrealist paintings— and we see it without the distorting and distancing mediation of "like" or any other discursive formula. In another place, Prelaty's essence is whoredom and it is similarly perceived by moving inward away from analogy and toward instantaneous apprehension:

> This very word of patterning or imitating excludes Episcopacy from the solid and grave Ethical law, and betraies it to be a meere childe of ceremony, or likelier some misbegotten thing, that having pluckt the gay feathers of her obsolet bravery to hide her own deformed barenesse, now vaunts and glories in her stolne plumes (765).

At first "childe" is understood figuratively; Episcopacy is born (in a metaphorical sense) of ceremony; and the abstractness of the figure is emphasized by "thing"; but then the abstraction is personified; and given a gender; the child grows up and stands before us ("now" is a direct reference to reading time), an obscenely gowned and gesturing harlot. And with each transformation the mental action required of us is less and less, until we are asked to do nothing at all but look. (Ironically, the plumes that were stolen to hide the deformed bareness of Episcopacy become its emblem; moral truth always shines through coverings to those who have eyes to see.)

---

[9] Hell was often represented in Medieval and Renaissance iconography as a huge open mouth. See Robert Hughes, *Heaven and Hell in Western Art* (New York, 1968), pp. 175–188.

I shall not "trifle," declares Milton, "with one that will tell me of quiddities and formalities, whether Prelaty or Prelateity in abstract notion be this or that, it suffices me that I find it in his skin (824)." Finding it in his skin is what the experience of these collapsing similes (and others like them) allows us to do, simply by narrowing (to nothing) the distance between the naked eye and the object. And, as always, the bypassing or piercing of worldly "coverings," of "outsides," involves the discarding of the machinery of rational discourse, itself an "outside," a distancing screen. In these examples, not only do we see through or past robes and surplices and mitres and titles, but through analogy and simile, which as forms of discursive thought—"quiddities and formalities"—stand between us and the immediate perception of the truth.[10] The sum of our experience, here and elsewhere, is, of

[10] At times it is the prose itself that obstructs our view simply because it is difficult, and at these times the difficulty becomes, by association, a property of its subject:

> But because about the manner and order of this government, whether it ought to be Presbyteriall, or Prelaticall, such endlesse question, or rather uproare is arisen in this land, as may be justly term'd, what the feaver is to the Physitians, the eternall reproach of our Divines; whilest other profound Clerks of late greatly, as they conceive, to the advancement of Prelaty, are so earnestly meting out the Lydian proconsular Asia to make good the prime metropolis of Ephesus, as if some of our Prelates in all haste meant to change their soile, and become neighbours to the English Bishop of Chalcedon; and whilest good *Breerwood* as busily bestirres himselfe in our vulgar tongue to divide precisely the three Patriarchats, of Rome, Alexandria, and Antioch, and whether to any of these England doth belong . . . (748–749).

This sentence threatens to be as endless and intricate as the questions it reports. It is a struggle simply to get through it, and emerging from it is like emerging from a dark tunnel into the clear light of day. What we find waiting for us at the end of the tunnel are Milton and the presbyters:

> I shall in the meane while not cease to hope through the mercy and grace of Christ, the head and husband of his Church, that England shortly is to belong, neither to See Patriarchall, nor See Prelaticall, but to the faithfull feeding and disciplining of that ministeriall order, which the blessed Apostles constituted throughout the Churches: and this I shall assay to prove can be no other, then that of Presbyters and Deacons (749).

The force of this clear and simple declaration is a function of its position in the sequence; it comes to us literally out of the (syntactical) mists of prelatical obscurity, and simply by welcoming it, by preferring it as an experience to the first part of the sentence, we once again stand up for Milton and against prelacy, for the inner light and against "profound Clerks," for the immediate validation of illumined eyes and against the worldly machinery of reasons formally set down.

course, not a conclusion, or even an indictment, but an exhortation—"open your eyes." For, after all, it is a matter of eyesight, not of disquisition.

### JUMPING UP AND DOWN IN ONE PLACE

My description of *The Reason of Church Government* is a curious one by any of the standards we usually apply to controversial prose—sentences without verbs, conclusions before arguments, points made by declining to make them—but in the context of the tradition we have been following in this book, it falls perfectly into place as a work that undermines its own pretensions and repeatedly calls attention to what it is *not* doing. It does not express truth, or contain it, or process it. Indeed, its elaborate rational machinery operates only to emphasize how independent truth is of the validation that reason and rational structures can confer. At best, it turns the mind of the reader (and then only of the reader who is predisposed) in the direction of truth.

In a curious way, then, I agree with Hamilton when he implies that *The Reason of Church Government* doesn't say anything at all ("a lack of real intellectual content"), but this is not the same thing as concluding that it doesn't mean anything at all. It is simply that the locus of meaning is not the printed page, where literally nothing is happening, but the mind of the reader, where everything is happening. I make it a point to ask my students what they remember of their previous night's reading of *The Reason of Church Government;* and invariably they answer not with propositions or chains of inferences, but with words, and groups of words, that come tumbling out haphazardly, and yet arranged somehow in the patterns of relationship we have observed in particular passages. I cannot recreate their response in all its associative spontaneity, but an equivalent effect is produced simply by rehearsing, in the order of their appearance, two lists of opposing phrases and images:

gross, patched, varnished, embellishings, veil, sumptuous, tradition, show, visibility, polluted, idolatrous, Gentilish rites, ceremonies, feather, bravery, hide, deformed, plumes, pomp, flesh, outward, ceremonial law, delusions, particolored, mimic, custom, specious, sophistical, names, fallacy, mask, dividing, schismatical, forked, disfigurement, Egyptian, overcloud, scales, false, glitter, beads, art, sweet, dim, reflection, fleshly wisdom, garb, defaced, overcasting, copes, vestures, gold robes, surplices, adorn, corporeal resemblances, clothing, maskers, gaudy glisterings, delude, carnal, high, sensual, fermentations, worldly, external, flourishes, counterfeit, crafty, artificial, appearance, outward man, skin, defile, ignorance, pride, temples, carpets, tablecloth, slimy, confections, profane, faulty, false-whited, gilded, vanities, dross, scum, luggage, infection, formal outside, greasy, brazen, temporal, oil over, besmear, corrupt, shadow, darkened, obscured.

And on the other side:

plainly, clearness, eternal, invariable, inspired, open, spiritual eye, inward, plain, clear, evident, pure, spiritual, simple, lowly, internal, faith, homogeneous, even, firm, unite, truth, steadfastness, perfection, unity, seamless, unchangeable, constancy, light, sacred, illumination, luster, inspiration, revelation, eye-brightening, inward prompting, divine, bright, belief, common sense, simplicity, clear evidence, naked, inward holiness, inward beauty, bareness, lowliness, purity of Doctrine, wisdom of God, glory, enlightened, true knowledge, holy, cleansed, health, purge, God's word.[11]

What will strike the reader of these two lists at once, I think, is the presence of an argument, even in the absence of a discursive syntax. Statements of relationships form themselves unbidden simply because the words and phrases so obviously belong together; and this continues to be true even when they *are* implicated in a syntactical structure: "however in *shew* and *visibility* it may seeme a part of his Church, yet in as much as it lyes thus unmeasur'd he leaves it to be trampl'd by the Gentiles, that is to be *polluted* with *idolatrous* and *Gentilish rites* and *ceremonies* (761, emphasis mine)." The order of the underlined words is the order of their (consecutive) appearance in the list; and the im-

[11] These lists only record initial occurrences; the repeated appearance of many of these words and phrases intensifies the effect analyzed below.

pression they make in the two contexts is remarkably similar. In one, the mere fact of their contiguity suffices to generate connections; and in the other, the connections supplied by the syntax are overwhelmed by the connections they themselves generate. Were one asked to form a sentence of these words, the result would no doubt be something like this: "The show and visibility of Gentilish rites and ceremonies are evidence of the pollution of idolatry." And this is exactly the import of the sentence in which they do, in fact, appear. The organizing pressure of the "however . . . yet" construction makes little difference, for the construction is finally not the agency of relationship. Its only effect is to focus our attention on the indeterminate "it," a neutral counter which draws to itself the multiple and complementary associations of the surrounding words. They *are* the sentence at the same time that their interrelationships are independent of its structure. The source of the fellowship they so obviously (self-evidently) share is to be found outside the framework that happens, for the moment, to contain them. And what is true of these words and a single sentence is true of the full list and the entire tract.

In fact one can rewrite the entire tract by rearranging the two lists into a table of natural contraries:

| | |
|---|---|
| carnal | spiritual |
| false | true |
| sight | faith |
| varnished | plain |
| outer | inner |
| darkness | light |
| polluted | pure |
| idolatrous | holy |
| hid | open |
| covered | naked |
| earthly | divine |
| veil | clear |
| schism | unity |
| sophistical | simple |
| pride | lowliness |
| clothing | bareness |
| profane | sacred |
| slimy | clean |

This is by no means complete, and even if there were space enough to continue indefinitely, the result would still be a distortion; for not only does each term interact with its opposing fellow, it is also, by virtue of the vertical equivalences (carnal= false=polluted) implicated in all the other single oppositions. Obviously the entire complex of interrelationships could not be represented on the printed page (mine or Milton's), for it is not linear. Its true medium, because it is the only medium flexible enough to hold in solution all of the shifting patterns, is the reader's consciousness. I return, by a kind of back door, to the idea of a progress in *The Reason of Church Government;* not, of course, to the "ratiocinative progress" whose absence Hamilton deplores, but to a progressive enlargement of the understanding. Hamilton and I agree, in our different ways, that the reader who negotiates these sixty or so pages is not following an argument. And yet he must be doing something, and what he is doing, with varying degrees of self-consciousness, is accumulating and cross-referencing pairs of coordinate words and images on either side of a great divide; and as these pairs succeed one another, not on the page but in the mind, they lose their discreteness and become, in the process of (reading) time, interchangeable. That is to say, at some point (and I will not specify it), one reads "Prelacy" in (not into) the word "profane," and "profane" in the word "Prelacy," and both in the phrase "fair outsides"; and conversely "Presbyter" in the word "pure," and "pure" in the word "Presbyter," and both in "inward." The reader proceeds in space and time and from point to point, but always to find the same unchanging essences shining through their local manifestations.

Again, this is possible only because the ligatures of logical thought are binding rather than directing; they help the flow of the prose along, but they do not structure it. For another example, one longer than a single sentence, consider the opening of the second chapter of the second book:

That which next declares the heavenly power, and reveales the deep mistery of the Gospel, is the pure simplicity of doctrine, accounted the foolishnes of this world, yet crossing and counfounding the pride and wisdom of the flesh (826).

Typically, the main verb and the construction it supports make little claim on the reader's attention. The real work of the sentence is done by the sequence of phrases—"heavenly power," "deep mistery of the Gospel," "pure simplicity of doctrine," "foolishnes of this world," "crossing and counfounding," "pride and wisdom of the flesh"—and by the several patterns of relationship in which they become implicated. The first pattern forms when the conjunction "and" joins not only the verbs "declares" and "reveales" (near synonyms in Milton's lexicon), but also "heavenly power" and "deep mistery." For a moment, "pure simplicity of doctrine" makes a third in this series, before it combines with "foolishnes of this world" into a new pattern, a pattern of opposition. But almost immediately "foolishnes of this world" separates itself to enter into a fellowship with "pride and wisdom of the flesh," and this pair then stands in obvious contrast to "heavenly power," "deep mistery of the Gospel," and "pure simplicity of doctrine" (that pattern is now reestablished).

All of these patterns can operate more or less simultaneously because the pressure of the syntax is so minimal that nothing in the sentence is confined to one place or to one relationship; and the possibility of the whole dividing too neatly into halves is forestalled by "crossing and counfounding," a strongly rhythmic phrase that is not a part of the shifting configurations of contraries and correspondences. "Crossing and counfounding," however, establishes a pattern of its own, a pattern of doublets and alliteration that soon dominates the chapter. "Pride and wisdom" (made one by the "and") are drawn into it immediately to be joined in succeeding sentences by "worship and service," "presumption of ordering," "traditions and ceremonies," "defeated and counfounded," "proudest and wisest," "bulwark and stronghold":

> And wherein consists this fleshly wisdom and pride? in being altogether ignorant of God and his worship? No surely, for men are naturally asham'd of that. Where then? it consists in a bold presumption of ordering the worship and service of God after mans own will in traditions and ceremonies. Now if the pride and wisdom of the flesh were to be defeated and confounded, no doubt, but in that very

point wherin it was proudest and thought it self wisest, that so the victory of the Gospel might be the more illustrious. But our Prelats instead of expressing the spirituall power of their ministery by warring against this chief bulwark and strong hold of the flesh, have enter'd into fast league with the principall enemy against whom they were sent, and turn'd the strength of fleshly pride and wisdom against the pure simplicity of saving truth (826–827).

The ruling doublet remains "pride and wisdom." In the company of "flesh" (and derivative forms) it weaves a way in between the others, undergoing a series of permutations, from "pride of wisdom of the flesh" to "fleshly wisdom and pride" back to "pride and wisdom of the flesh," made adjectival (and superlative) in "proudest and wisest" (flesh has for a moment attached itself to "bulwark and stronghold") until finally it ends the sequence as "fleshly pride and wisdom," opposed, not surprisingly, to the "pure simplicity of saving truth."

This is also the opposition of the chapter's concluding sentence:

Thus we see again how Prelaty sayling in opposition to the main end and power of the gospel doth not joyn in that mysterious work of Christ, by lowliness to confound height, by simplicity of doctrin the wisdom of the world, but contrariwise hath made it self high in the world and the flesh to vanquish things by the world accounted low, and made itself wise in tradition and fleshly ceremony to confound the purity of doctrin which is the wisdom of God (829–830).

Here the word "opposition" itself controls the first of two polarizing motions, aligning "Prelaty" against "gospel" and "work of Christ," "lowliness" against "height," and "simplicity" against worldly wisdom. At this point the second polarizing motion is introduced by "contrari*wise*" (a pun anticipates the transformation of worldly wisdom) and the sentence winds its way through the smaller contraries of "high" and "low," "fleshly" and "purity," "ceremony" and "doctrin," before coming to rest on the cadenced rhythm of "wisdom of God." ("Wisdom" has, in the course of the chapter, been redefined and baptized.)

The first words of this sentence—"thus we see"—contain something I have spoken of before, the suggestion of a challenge to the reader who *doesn't* see. To be sure, the pressure on the reader is slight, but it is enough to place him in the action, as it were, poised somewhat uneasily between the contending parties, their modes of apprehension, and their indigenous patterns of imagery. This is a position he occupies literally in the concluding sentences of the third chapter of the first book, which are, incidentally, nearly indistinguishable from the passage we have just analyzed:

> If the religion be *pure, spirituall, simple,* and *lowly,* as the Gospel most truly is, such must the face of the ministery be. And in like manner if the forme of the Ministery be *grounded* in the *worldly* degrees of autority, honour, *temporall* jurisdiction, we see it with our eyes it will turne the *inward* power and *purity* of the Gospel into the *outward carnality* of the *law;* evaporating and exhaling the *internall* worship into empty conformities, and *gay shewes* (766, emphasis mine).

Here the syntax does not even pretend to do anything more than hold in place the words I have underlined; *they* carry the argument, moving in a kind of dance from one pattern of relationships to another; first ranging themselves formally in lines of battle, "pure," "spirituall," "simple," "lowly" against "grounded" (the metaphor becomes literal in the company of its fellows), "worldly," "temporall," and then separating into opposing pairs which engage each other in hand-to-hand combat: inward vs. outward, purity vs. carnality, internall vs. gay shewes. These smaller oppositions operate to flesh out the more abstract opposition of the Gospel to the law which, in turn, feeds into the ever-present opposition of Prelaty to Presbyterianism. And exactly in the middle of the sentence, and therefore in the middle of the smaller and larger coordinates, stands the reader or, more properly, his eyes which are declared responsible ("we see it with our eyes") for judging between the "faces" of the two ministries. The responsibility, however, is limited, since the judgment is already imbedded in the imagery and the reader can only approve it or become its object. The sentence pressures us to choose between alternatives that are implicitly self-revelatory. Are your eyes "pure," "spirituall," "inward," or are they "carnal," "worldly," and "outward"? Are they answerable to that which "most truly is" or to "gay shewes"? And, of course, the reader's response (he can hardly withhold it) not only places him in a hierarchy of vision, but commits him to a whole series of attendant positions: for the Presbyters and against Prelacy, for the inner light and against priestly ceremony, for the immediate validation of illumined eyes and against the worldly machinery of reasons formally set down.

Thomas Kranidas has observed that "a study of the prose of Milton becomes in large part a study of the way things are complexly unified or related." [12] *The Reason of Church Government* not only provides support for this statement, but, as an object, itself exemplifies the principle of unity that is, as Kranidas points out, one of Milton's "obsessions." There is a perfect and sustained correspondence between the two structures of the tract (inner and outer), the two ecclesiastical structures that are its subject, the two ways of knowing (reason and illumination) that support those structures, and the two patterns of imagery that reflect their properties. The final (and activating) links in this chain of correspondences are, of course, the two sets of readers whose differing visions are reflected in and answerable to every one of these patterned oppositions. Thus the reader who inclines to the party of the Prelates will be the reader who attends carefully to the order of the numbered chapters and to the unfolding argument they presumably carry, while to the eye of the Presbyterian (or illumined) reader, these divisions will be less pressuring than the truths that imply themselves at every point. In a way, then, *The Reason of Church Government* is nothing more (or less) than an elaborate and continuing eye test. It validates not reasons, but visions, and it is always reaching conclusions not about systems of church government (a matter closed to disquisition), but about *you.*

[12] *The Fierce Equation* (The Hague, 1965), p. 57.

Indeed, it would not be too much to say that you are finally the subject of the tract, since your discerning (or not discerning) is its only real issue, although it is not the issue of record until the concluding chapter of the second book: *"That Prelatical jurisdiction opposeth the reason and end of the Gospel and State."* Prelatical jurisdiction, the jurisdiction of courts and judgments, would impose the outward censure of a worldly authority, and it is opposed (predictably) to the inner censure of a man's "own severe and modest eye upon himselfe (842)." This is merely an extension and reformulation of the familiar correspondences and oppositions. The outward and formal censure of Prelatical jurisdiction is, like the superstructure of reasons and proofs, superfluous to those whose court of jurisdiction sits within. It is to this court and to that "severe and modest eye" that the tract has been speaking all along, and the lengthy discussion here is merely a reconfirmation in more explicit terms of everything that has gone before. It is also an additional explanation (hardly required at this point) of the absence in the tract of a sustained and coercive argument: for if the judgment of the inner eye is sufficient and necessary, any judgment rendered or urged by a body of print will be either unnecessary, if the inner eye is indeed illumined and severely modest, or inefficacious, if it is not. *The Reason of Church Government* does not pretend to correct eyes—only the inner mechanism of "honourable shame" can do that—it merely tests eyes and issues interim reports on the visions of its two sets of readers.

It reports also on Milton's vision, for the question the prose is always asking—"you see don't you?"—contains an implied declaration, *"I* do!" Milton is continually affirming the illumination of his own eyesight, indirectly whenever his independence of reasons formally set down is implied, and directly in the famous autobiographical digression, which is really not a digression at all since its argument is no more (or less) than the argument of the preceding seven chapters—those who have eyes will see. Technically these pages constitute the author's "defense for writing," but it is the writing itself that is finally put on the defensive. Rather than proclaiming (and documenting) his fitness for the task at hand, Milton declares that the business at hand is beneath him, because it is beneath the capacities he has been given by God. It is a kind of arrogant humility, in which the emphasis is not on his powers but on their source in divine inspiration. The question for Milton is "how and in what manner he shall dispose and employ those summes of knowledge and illumination, which God hath sent him into this world to trade with (801)." Immediately, the burden of proof is shifted from Milton to any reader who would challenge his credentials, which are now revealed to have been issued by God. The identification of Presbyterianism with the revealed word is here extended to the poet, but with a more literal force. The Holy Spirit has, in effect, appropriated Milton and made of him an instrument of the divine will:

> For surely to every good and peaceable man it must in nature needs be a hatefull thing to be the displeaser, and molester of thousands; much better would it like him doubtless to be the messenger of gladnes and contentment, which is his chief intended busines, to all mankind, but that they resist and oppose their own true happinesse. But when God commands to take the trumpet and blow a dolorous or a jarring blast, it lies not in mans will what he shall say, or what he shall conceal (803).

This is a conventional claim of the inspired (and reluctant) prophets to whom Milton refers and with whom he identifies himself, but it takes on added force when we recall that at crucial points in the body of the tract the sense of a personal voice recedes to be replaced by the voiceless proclaiming of a universal and self-validating truth. Of course the personal Milton is heard here, in this digression, but his tone is not exactly as commentators have described it. This is no program for a later career (although the accidents of literary history have made this misinterpretation inevitable), but a complaint, tempered by resignation, against the interruption of a career that may never be resumed. The emphasis is not on his hopes, but on their frustration. He is not concerned chiefly to tell us what he will do in the future, but what he is not doing now. He is not now writing something which "aftertimes" will not willingly let die (810); he is not now inbreeding and cherishing "in a great people the seeds of vertu (816)"; he is not now "Teaching over the whole book of sanctity (817)" or making "the paths of honesty and good life . . . appeare . . . easy and pleasant (818)." And, above all, he is not now engaged in those higher pursuits whose reward is the "beholding the bright countenance of truth (821)."

Once again, the validation of eyesight has as its reverse consequence the *in*validation of the tract. "Clubbing quotations" is not only distasteful, and far below his abilities, it is also useless and irrelevant:

> I trust hereby to make it manifest with what small willing-
> nesse I endure to interrupt the pursuit of no lesse hopes
> then these . . . to come into the dim reflexion of hollow
> antiquities sold by the seeming bulk, and there be fain
> to club quotations with men whose learning and belief
> lies in marginal stuffings, who when they have like good
> sumpters laid ye down their hors load of citations and fa-
> thers at your dore, with a rapsody of who and who were
> Bishops here or there, ye may take off their packsaddles,
> their days work is don, and episcopacy, as they think,
> stoutly vindicated (822).

With such men as these, one may wage a war of citations, and win, without effecting the chief end, the inculcation of belief. Those who believe that a system of church government can be vindicated by marginal stuffings (or formal reasons) may be forced to yield a point and still remain *inwardly* unpersuaded; and insofar as Milton enters this arena and parades this kind of learning, he commits himself to an impossible task.

Why, then, does he do it? The assumptions that dictate the strategy of *The Reason of Church Government* entail the futility of the entire enterprise. There are only two kinds of readers in Milton's audience, those for whom the reasons imply themselves, and those so unregenerate that no reason, of man or God, will convince them. When Milton asks "What need I conclude?" he might as well be asking "What need I write?" And the answer to that question is the answer to all the questions this tract raises and declines to prosecute: the first and greatest reason is because God hath so commanded, and "when God commands (803)," even though the service be inglorious and of doubtful issue, his servant obeys: "But were it the meanest under-service, if God by his Secretary conscience injoyn it, it were sad for me if I should draw back (822)." In *Paradise Lost,* the angels loyal to God evidence their faith by persevering in an action they know to be unnecessary in response to a command—drive out the rebel host—which they find themselves incapable of carrying out. That perseverance entitles them to the epithet "hero," and to the extent that his situation in *The Reason of Church Government* parallels theirs, it is Milton's epithet too, and presumably he will someday be the recipient of the praise God bestows on Abdiel:

Servant of God, well done (*P.L.,* VI, 29).

Meanwhile, however, Milton stands alone, or with those of his audience who, like him, are "eye-brightened" and the prose continues to pressure the reader to enroll himself in that number:

And if ye think ye may with a pious presumption strive to goe beyond God in mercy, I shall not be one now that would dissuade ye. Though God for lesse then ten just persons would not spare *Sodom,* yet if you can finde after due search but only one good thing in prelaty either to religion, or civil goverment, to King or Parlament, to Prince or people, to law, liberty, wealth or learning, spare her, let her live, let her spread among ye, till with her shadow, all your dignities and honours, and all the glory of the land be darken'd and obscurd. But on the contrary if she be found to be malignant, hostile, destructive to all these, as nothing can be surer, then let your severe and impartial doom imitate the divine vengeance; rain down your punishing force upon this godlesse and oppressing government: and bring such a dead Sea of subversion upon her, that she may never in this Land rise more to afflict the holy reformed Church, and the elect people of God (861).

In an important sense, *The Reason of Church Government* is a self-consuming artifact only in one direction: for while it does invalidate its own claims to process knowledge and illumination, it does not provoke the self of the reader to change, merely to acknowledge his position in the polarities it continually uncovers. The tract does not persuade or convert; rather it bullies, and in this final paragraph the basic pattern of the reader's experience is rehearsed for the last time. First he is asked to choose between two alternatives, as he was asked in the beginning to choose between two forms of church government, but no sooner is one of them proffered (and indeed urged) before its terrible consequences are visited: "with her shadow, all your dignities and honours, and all the glory of the land be darken'd and obscurd." The choice is, as it has been so many times before, no choice at all, and its rhetorical pretense is further subverted by the parenthetical "as nothing can be surer" which introduces the downward sweep of the concluding sentence. The form of that sentence is conditional ("if she be found to be malignant"), but because all the conditions have already been fulfilled, it becomes a command ("rain down your punishing force"), a command which has all the more impact because we have been implicitly included in the group in whose name it is issued, the elect people of God.

Inclusion is also the motion of Burton's prose in *The Anatomy of Melancholy,* but in his vision there are no elect, and God is prominent only by his absence.

VI

# Thou Thyself Art the Subject of My Discourse: Democritus Jr. to the Reader

### I REFER IT TO YOU

The reader who manages to make his way through the preface to Burton's *Anatomy of Melancholy* may be excused if he is unable to take its concluding sentences at face value:

> but I presume of thy good favour, and gracious acceptance (gentle reader). Out of an assured hope and confidence therof, I will begin (123).[1]

It is not simply that, given the treatment he has received, "gentle reader" is mockingly ironic, but that the same reader knows (if he knows anything at this point) that the promise Burton makes here will not be kept. The key word is "confidence." The conventional rhetoric implies the existence of a mutual and interrelated confidence in the speaker, in the reader, in the tractability of the material they confront, and in the possibility of carrying through with the proposed task. But it is precisely these confidences that have been eroded and finally destroyed by the experience of the prose, so much so that one is likely to respond with a wry and not altogether comfortable smile to the declaration, "I will begin." For beginning or ending or concluding or any of the other actions we associate with rationally discursive processes have (along with the

[1] *The Anatomy of Melancholy*, Vol. I, ed. Holbrook Jackson (London, New York, 1932).

"gentle reader") been among the chief casualties of this amazing tour de force.

The erosion of the reader's confidence, in himself and in everything else, begins on the first page, with the question, thrust on us by Burton, of the speaker's identity. "Gentle Reader," he says, "I presume thou wilt be very inquisitive to know what antic or personate actor this is . . . arrogating another man's name; whence he is, why he doth it, and what he hath to say (15)." This deference to our presumed needs and desires is short-lived, however, as Burton immediately declares his independence of the reader and, indeed, of everyone: "I am a free man born, and may choose whether I will tell; who can compel me? . . . Seek not after that which is hid . . . I would not willingly be known." Scarcely have we adjusted to this new pose before it, too, is abandoned; the speaker, it seems, will honor his traditional obligations after all: "Yet in some sort to give thee satisfaction, . . . I will show a reason, both of this usurped name, title, and subject." Of course, this does not reestablish the old relationship between speaker and reader. Too much has already happened for that. In fact, the overall effect of this opening address is to disorient the reader; he is off-balance, unable to predict the direction the speaker will next take, and this sense of disorientation is intensified by the first substantive sentence of the preface:

> And first of the name of Democritus; lest any man by reason of it should be deceived, expecting a pasquil, a satire, some ridiculous treatise (as I myself should have done), some prodigious tenent, or paradox of the earth's motion, of infinite worlds, *in infinito vacuo, ex fortuita atomorum collisione,* in an infinite waste, so caused by an accidental collision of motes in the sun, all which Democritus held, Epicurus and their master Leucippus maintained, and are lately revived by Copernicus, Brunus, and some others (15).

To a great extent the preface (and finally the whole of the *Anatomy*) is a series of false promises which alternately discomfort the reader and lead him on.[2] Here the promises are at once syn-

2 This was first suggested to me by Steven Rankin, then a student at Washington University, St. Louis.

tactical, methodological, and thematic. Our general expectation is
of an orderly defense of the name, title, and subject (after the
"first," a "second" and so on); more particularly, we expect the
"lest" clause, which appears to be dependent, to be followed by
an independent clause and a main verb ("lest any man . . . , I
will"); and within this syntactical expectation we are allowed to
assume a continuing negative attitude toward the kind of "ridiculous treatise" the speaker promises not to deliver. But as a matter
of fact, he does deliver it; for as the clauses in apposition to
"ridiculous treatise" succeed one another, they take over the
sentence which ends with an impressive list of those ancient and
modern philosophers who have, in fact, maintained this "paradox
of the earth's motion." With this shift in focus, the original direction (and promise) of the syntax is forgotten, and fortunately so,
since the main verb and its independent clause never arrive. Also
forgotten is the place of this sentence in the numbered and reasoned defense of the "name, title, and subject." In fact, the
Democritus who heads the roll call of atomists, seems strangely
unconnected with the Democritus whose identity the sentence
promised to clarify; and when a Burton (or Burton-Democritus)
gestures toward the broken thread of his discourse with "besides,"
the adverb has no clear argumentative referent. The sense of an
argument is restored, momentarily, when the observation of Gellius is cited: "it hath been always an ordinary custom, as Gellius
observes, 'for later writers and imposters to broach many absurd
and insolent fictions under the name of so noble a philosopher as
Democritus, to get themselves credit.'" But if this is "a reason
of the name (20)," it is not Burton's, who mentions it only to
disclaim it: "'Tis not so with me." (Not accidentally, this tends,
retroactively, to discredit Gellius.)

It is at this point, just as the reader may be wondering if he
will ever find out what is going on, that Burton finally tells him:

Thou thyself art the subject of my discourse (16).

This enigmatic announcement is typical of Burton's strategy. On
one hand it merely adds to the confusion; rather than a single
clearly designated subject, we apparently have three, melancholy,
Democritus Jr., and the reader (before the final word has been

spoken, we will know the many ways in which these are the same);
but on the other, it provides, if not a reason for the name, a reason
for going on. It is an appeal to the reader's "self-interest" in two
senses. He is naturally interested in hearing about himself, and he
is interested in benefiting from what the treatise may have to tell
him. The ploy is an obvious one, but it is nonetheless successful,
especially since it is followed by what promises to be a straightforward and (relatively) comfortable account of the historical
Democritus, "what he was with an epitome of his life (16)."

But this interlude of factual reporting proves to be no less
unsettling and strenuous than the paragraph preceding it, if only
because we have as many Democrituses as we have sources for his
life, and not all of them are compatible:

> Democritus, as he is described by Hippocrates and Laer-
> tius, was a little wearish old man, very melancholy by na-
> ture, averse from company in his latter days, and much
> given to solitariness, a famous philosopher in his age,
> *cooevus* with Socrates, wholly addicted to his studies at
> the last, and to a private life: writ many excellent works,
> a great divine, according to the divinity of those times,
> an expert physician, a politician, an excellent mathema-
> tician, as *Diacosmus* and the rest of his works do wit-
> ness. He was much delighted with the studies of husbandry,
> saith Columella, and often I find him cited by Constantinus
> and others treating of that subject. He knew the natures,
> differences of all beasts, plants, fishes, birds; and, as some
> say, could understand the tunes and voices of them. In a
> word, he was *omnifariam doctus,* a general scholar, a great
> student; and to the intent he might better contemplate, I
> find it related by some, that he put out his eyes, and was in
> his old age voluntarily blind, yet saw more than all Greece
> besides, and writ of every subject, *Nihil in toto opificio
> naturæ, de quo non scripsit* [there was nothing in the whole
> range of nature about which he did not write]. A man of an
> excellent wit, profound conceit; and to attain knowledge
> the better in his younger years he travelled to Egypt and
> Athens, to confer with learned men, "admired of some,

despised of others." After a wandering life, he settled at
Abdera, a town in Thrace, and was sent for thither to be
their law-maker, recorder, or town clerk as some will; or
as others, he was there bred and born. Howsoever it was,
there he lived at last in a garden in the suburbs, wholly
betaking himself to his studies and a private life, "saving
that sometimes he would walk down to the haven, and
laugh heartily at such variety of ridiculous objects, which
there he saw." Such a one was Democritus (16).

Hardly is the biography under way before the emphasis shifts
from the subject to his chroniclers. It is Democritus "as he is
described by Hippocrates and Laertius." A little further on it is
Democritus as described by Columella, and then by "some," and
finally by an undifferentiated and suspect "others." As the authorities cited become less reliable, the reader finds it increasingly
difficult to form a clear picture of Democritus. In effect, we are
offered several Democrituses, a new one appearing each time the
rhythmical cadence comes to a natural close, at "solitariness,"
"private life," "do witness," and so on. And the account of each of
these is problematical. We first meet Democritus the "famous
philosopher" who is, somewhat incongruously "a little wearish
old man." We next hear of Democritus the "great divine," but
his greatness is hardly asserted before it is questioned by the
trailing phrase, "according to the divinity of those times." A third
Democritus, the interpreter and master of nature, suffers a similar
diminution when his reputation is ascribed to what "some [un-
identified] say." At this point Burton makes a gesture toward
reconciling his sources through the agency of a generalization:
"In a word, he was *omnifariam doctus,* a general scholar"; but
when we are told, in support of this judgment, that "to the intent
he might better contemplate . . . he put out his eyes," the gro-
tesqueness of the action reflects back on everything that has been
said previously. Of course this story may be apocryphal; nothing
more is claimed for it than that it is "related by some"; but by the
same reasoning, the other, more positive reports, are equally suspect. Since the speaker gives no indication of which authorities
he considers most reliable, the reader is left with the unresolved

contradictions and incongruities. In the end, even the pretense of
accuracy and objectivity is abandoned. After a wandering life,
Democritus settled at Abdera where he was "sent for to be their
law-maker." Or was it their "recorder"? Or perhaps their "town
clerk as some will." Or was he sent for at all, but merely returning to the place where he was "bred and born"? Clearly Burton's
"ors" are to be translated "it doesn't matter which" and he tells
us as much with his next word, *"Howsoever* it was. . . ." "Such a
one was Democritus," the paragraph concludes, as if it had redeemed the promise of its introduction, to "set down a brief character of this our Democritus, what he was"; but given the number
of available Democrituses and the spectacular lack of verifiable
information about any one of them, this is less a conclusion than
a joke.

The joke, of course, is on the reader, who had been led to
expect a straightforward biographical sketch, factual and sequential, in the course of which actions and events would be linked in a
chain of cause and effect, and thereby placed in perspective. Instead, something very curious happens. The principle of organization is not the sequence of Democritus's life, but the authorities
who are responsible for its details; and since they come to us
unauthorized, or, what is worse, indiscriminately authorized, the
details they offer confuse rather than clarify. There is no perspective at all, merely a progressive softening of focus. The absence of a clear line of reportorial responsibility results in the blurring of all lines: the narrative line of Democritus's life, the outline
of his personality, and more generally, the hard lines of a universe
where a man is either blind or not, and if he is, he is not spoken
of as laughing heartily at the ridiculous objects which he *saw*.

At this point, the reader would be justified in putting the book
aside on the grounds that its author is irresponsibly playful. The
excursion into biography had been welcomed, in part because it
seemed to offer relief from the unsettling changes in tone and attitude that mark the opening sentences; but that relief has proved
illusory and we are no more sure of our ground than we were
before. The speaker disarms us, however, by conceding the irrelevance of the digression—"But in the meantime, how doth this
concern me (17)?"—before moving to repersuade us that he will,

after all, speak seriously to the original question—"upon what reference do I usurp his habit?" This is a strategy Burton will employ repeatedly, and always with success. He declares a narrow intention and proceeds for a time to adhere to it; but sooner or later (more often sooner) the original impulse of the discourse is obscured and the reader becomes confused and disoriented. It is then that Burton recovers himself and, with apologies, again promises to keep to the announced plan, and the entire sequence begins anew. As a result, although the reader is continually off-balance, he is never quite ready to give up, since a clear line of direction seems always to be just around the corner. In this case, Burton does finally give a "reason of the name." Because Democritus left "unperfect" his work on melancholy, he, Democritus Jr. will "Revive" and "prosecute" it (20). But this reason is no more authoritative than any of the others he has put forward ("to assume a little more liberty and freedom of speech"); it merely allows him to bring the discussion to a rhetorical close. "You have had *a* reason of the name," he tells us, silently making the point that in the multiple contexts of the preceding paragraphs, we cannot be sure that it is *the* reason, or even that *the* reason exists.

In succeeding sections of the preface, Burton turns away from a justification of his nom de plume to a justification of the entire enterprise. His first line of defense has often been quoted, "I write of melancholy, by being busy to avoid melancholy," and in support of it he cites the example of Tully (Cicero). Or does he? "Cardan professeth he wrote his book *de Consolatione* after his son's death, to comfort himself; so did Tully write of the same subject with like intent after his daughter's departure, if it be his at least, or some impostor's put out in his name, which Lipsius probably suspects (21–22)." At first, the point of the sentence is the warrant Tully's work lends to the present task; but then his authorship is questioned ("if it be his at least") and that question becomes the new focus of attention. Almost immediately, a third focus is found in the testimony of Lipsius, who "probably" suspects an imposture. "Probably" bears two significances here, "perhaps" or "not surely," and the more positive "with proof" or "on a probable" basis. The ambiguity works to make Lipsius's evidence as inconclusive as the example of Tully, if such an example indeed exists.

What we have here is a regressive series of supports, no one of which is firm enough to support even itself. While this may be bad logic, it is excellent strategy, for it enables Burton to transfer the burden of proof from himself to Tully and Lipsius, and by implication, to the entire body of learned tradition. Supposedly, the business of the sentence is the validation of the speaker's credentials; but by the end of it the speaker has disappeared and it is his witnesses who are on trial.

This is a rather subtle instance of a technique Burton employs more obviously as the preface unfolds. "I have only this of Macrobius to say for myself (24)," he declares a little further on, and although "I" and "myself" surround Macrobius, the assertion, when it comes, will be attributed to him, and he will be held to account for it. Later it is Erasmus who speaks for the speaker, and with the same result, "to say truth, with Erasmus (27)." Joan Webber has said that Burton's "I" assimilates his quotations.[3] It is also true that the quotations assimilate Burton. As a result, he is able to escape responsibility for whatever is said, and, moreover, the reader is deprived of a point of reference from which whatever is said can be judged.

In these examples we see Burton retreating behind the statements of one or two of his predecessors. In time, the base of responsibility (or irresponsibility) is widened until it includes everyone. He will typically reply to an objection by turning it back on the objector. You will say that I am a thief (to borrow the name and work of another)? " 'Tis most true," but, then, who is not? "A fault that every writer finds, as I do now, and yet faulty themselves, *trium literarum homines,* all thieves; they pilfer out of old writers to stuff up their new comments, scrape Ennius' dung-hills, and out of Democritus' pit, as I have done (23)." In this sentence, accuser and accused, victim and thief, change places with bewildering rapidity. All is in flux, no one stays fixed, least of all the "I" who stands syntactically with both the fault-finders and the faulty. Individuality and individual responsibility disappear along with the distinction between the speaker and his thieving brothers (including, one must assume, Democritus), and the reader is once again deprived of a point of reference. Even the idea of thievery

[3] Joan Webber, *The Eloquent "I"* (Madison, 1968), p. 84.

itself, insofar as it implies a moral judgment made by one person on another, ceases to have any force.

When the first person voice abdicates and his sources are discredited, the reader is left with only one recourse: to assert the values and standards he presumably carries within him. But here, too, he is thwarted when Burton moves to include *him* in the ever-growing list of unreliable authorities:

> 'Tis not worth the reading, I yield it, I desire thee not to lose time in perusing so vain a subject, I should be peradventure loath myself to read him or thee so writing; 'tis not *operae pretium*. All I say is this, that I have precedents for it, which Isocrates calls *perfugium iis qui peccant,* others as absurd, vain, idle, illiterate, etc. *Nonnulli alii idem fecerunt,* others have done as much, it may be more, and perhaps thou thyself, *Novimus et qui te,* etc. [we know someone who has seen you also] (26).

Again Burton defends himself not by denying the charge, but by appealing to precedents whose common guilt neutralizes his own.[4] This time, however, the guilt is extended, first in an aside ("or thee so writing") and then more directly, to the reader, effectively preventing him from judging a community of which he has been declared a member. "We cannot accuse or condemn one another, being faulty ourselves (46)."

One might suppose that this was merely good strategy, one more way of disarming criticism before it is offered; but Burton has already told us that "Thou thyself art the subject of my discourse" and in this, at least, he keeps his word. The attacks on the reader become more frequent and more pointedly challenging. "If you like not this," he declares, "get you to another inn: I resolve, if you like not my writing, go read something else. I do not much esteem thy censure, take thy course, 'tis not as thou wilt, not as I will, but when we have both done, that of Plinius Secundus to Trajan will prove true, 'Every man's witty labour takes not, except the matter, subject occasion, and some commending favourite happen to it' (28)." Even in his hostility, Burton is evasive; he throws down the gauntlet, but then lets Plinius Secundus pick it

[4] *Ibid.,* p. 199.

up, with a quotation whose length and generality depersonalizes the rhetorical situation. Nevertheless, the suggestion, "get you to another inn," has been made, and it is, at least, a possibility; or it seems to be, until, in the same paragraph, some of the other inns to which we might go are surveyed and found to be no more habitable than this one. Democritus himself has been criticized for the very sins his namesake is now committing. Not even Seneca escapes, "that superintendent of wit, learning, judgement . . . the best of Greek and Latin writers in Plutarch's opinion; 'that renowned corrector of vice,' as Fabius terms him, . . . could not please all parties, or escape censure. How is he vilified by Caligula, A. Gellius, Fabius, and Lipsius himself, his chief propugner! *In eo pleraque perniciosa,* saith the same Fabius, many childish tracts and sentences he hath . . . too negligent often and remiss, as A. Gellius observes . . . an homely shallow writer as he is (29)." As Seneca's status becomes less clear (the speaker, of course, never commits himself), the judgments of his critics seem more arbitrary. At first the "opinion" of Plutarch is authoritative, but when equally prestigious names speak for the opposition, Plutarch's "opinion" becomes just that, a personal statement, with no more weight than other personal statements. In addition, the confusion of multiple voices is compounded by the inconsistency of Fabius who appears on both sides of the question. So bewildering finally is this parade of expert witnesses, that the reader has little choice but to accept Burton's conclusion: "If Seneca be thus lashed, and many famous men that I could name, what shall I except?" It is a nice Burtonian touch that Seneca is soon rehabilitated as an authority, precisely because no one will grant him the status of one: " 'No man so absolute,' Erasmus holds, 'to satisfy all . . .' as I have proved in Seneca (29)."

"What shall I except?" This is the first appearance in the preface of a question that will be heard again in various forms: what shall I except, whom shall I except, what individual, class, nation, age, can be excepted? It is a question that implies its own answer—"Nobody"—an answer Democritus himself gives in the closing pages (117); but it is an answer the reader refuses to believe, and, for reasons we shall explore, he continues to turn the pages in search of something that will never be found. Mean-

while, Burton pursues the strategy of inclusion and the reader continues to be kept off-balance. He is alternately invited to distinguish between himself and those whose "dotages" prove the general conclusion "For we are . . . all mad," [5] and made to claim
his share of their folly. *"Mutato nomine, de te fabula narratur*
[change but the name, the tale applies to you]." [6] At one moment
he is called upon to judge and in the next placed in the dock and
declared guilty. "Say at a word, are they fools? I refer it to you,
though you be likewise fools and madmen yourselves, and I as
mad to ask the question; for what said our comical Mercury?
*Justem ab injustis petere insipientia est.* I'll stand to your censure
yet, what think you (72)?" "I refer it to you," a perfectly ordinary sentence whose syntax reflects a world in which persons (I,
you) are distinguishable from one another and from objects (it);
but that world and those distinctions are dissolved before the paragraph ends. Referred, referrer, and referee are all discovered to be
manifestations of a single essence ("foolishness"), separable only
in the artificial and distorting structure of sentences and anatomies. In this context, Burton's final gesture—"I'll stand to your
censure yet, what think you"—is as audacious as it is meaningless
(censure implies differences in authority and wisdom) and yet it
maintains just enough of a rhetorical pretense to allow us to go on.

We go on to find more of the same. Fabatus may hold that
"seafaring men are all mad," but then "He was a madman that
said it," and, lest we feel excluded, "thou peradventure as mad to
read it (116)." Burton gives us complete leave to censure him, so
long as we are ready to stand to the censure ourselves: "have I no
faults? Yes more than thou has, whatsoever thou art (119)." (In
this example the reader is silently reduced to the status of a thing,
a "what.") We are at once the observers and the observed, continually moving from the inside to the outside and back again,
from being readers to being read, until the boundaries between
these categories become as indeterminate as any other.

There are, of course, long stretches in the course of which the
reader is addressed only indirectly, if at all; but this only makes
Burton's sudden turnings outward that much more effective, and
in the final paragraphs, he assaults us with a bewildering succes-

[5] *Anatomy of Melancholy,* p. 46.          [6] *Ibid.,* p. 70.

sion of poses and reversals. At first there is a return to the defiance
of the opening lines: "If any man take exceptions, let him turn the
buckle of his girdle, I care not. I owe thee nothing (reader), I look
for no favour at thy hands, I am independent, I fear not (122),"
but immediately this posture gives way to one of total abjection:
"No, I recant, I will not, I care, I fear, . . . I have spoken fool-
ishly, rashly, unadvisedly, absurdly, I have anatomized mine own
folly . . . I will make you amends in that which is to come; I
promise you a more sober discourse in my following treatise
(122)." Were the preface to end here, as it seems to, one might
make the mistake of taking this final promise seriously; but there
is a full revolution yet to come. Tiring of apologies, Burton exclaims "But what needs all this (123)?" and for perhaps the thou-
sandth time, he disclaims all responsibility: "I'll deny all (my last
refuge), recant all, renounce all I have said, if any man except,
and with as much facility excuse as he can accuse it (123)." If this
is his last refuge, it leaves the reader with none at all, and certainly with no confidence in the "more sober discourse to follow."
What we are left with is a closing sentence, still another promise,
and the accumulated ironies of more than one hundred pages: "but
I presume of thy good favour and gracious acceptance (gentle
reader). Out of an assured hope and confidence therof, I will
begin (123)."

WHOM SHALL I EXCEPT?

The reader's skepticism concerning "the treatise to follow"
indicates more than a lack of confidence in the author. It is not
simply that Democritus Jr. seems incapable of a sober discourse,
but that sober discourse itself is an impossibility given the world
the preface reflects and describes. The strategy of inclusion, which
collapses speaker, reader, and a thousand or more "authorities"
into a single category of unreliability, extends also to every aspect
of what we usually think of as "objective reality." If, as I have
suggested, the base of irresponsibility is widened to include everyone, it also includes every *thing*, every structure, every institution,
every profession, every nation, every concept. Burton says as
much, again and again; his assertion of universal madness is un-

qualified; but the human mind is perfectly capable of assenting to generalities and then finding ways to slip out of them in its response to particulars. Burton makes use of this tendency by encouraging it, by allowing the reader to believe momentarily in the discreteness of entities (including himself) which are revealed, upon closer examination, to be infected with the general malady. There is, therefore, a "double motion" in the preface—one rational and distinguishing, in the direction of making sense of things, and the other irrational and inclusive, leading to the discovery everywhere of nonsense—and the first is prosecuted with just enough conviction and plausibility to make us forget the (literally) disillusioning implications of the second. It is, after all, entirely reasonable on Burton's part to anticipate the objection that he is a divine meddling in physic, and entirely reasonable on our part to consider his response. That response unfolds in easy stages. First he argues that there are already more than enough treatises in divinity, "so many . . . pamphlets, expositions, sermons, that whole team of oxen cannot draw them (35)"; and, moreover, this "tempest of contention (35)" so absorbs us that, "Severinus the Dane complains," we leave untouched " 'those chiefest treasures of nature . . . wherein the best medicines for all manner of diseases are to be found' (36)." And if he be thought unfit for the task, there are, as always, precedents. Physicians have forsaken their practices to write in divinity, and divines, Marsilius Ficinus for one, have taken themselves to physic. Indeed, there are many poor country vicars who "for want of other means, are driven to their shifts, to turn mountebanks, quacksalvers, empirics, and if our greedy patrons hold us to such hard conditions . . . they will make most of us . . . at last turn taskers, maltsters, costermongers, graziers . . . or worse (36)." For a moment the satiric impulse threatens to overwhelm the argument: if Burton looks to these examples for justification, he is not likely to win our confidence. He assures us, however, "I hope I shall commit no great error or indecorum (36)," and returning to the defense, he concludes with his strongest point: melancholy is the disease of both the body and soul "and who knows not what an agreement there is betwixt these two professions?":

A good divine either is or ought to be a good physician, a spiritual physician at least, as our Saviour calls Himself, and was indeed (Matt. iv,23; Luke v,18; Luke vii,21). They differ but in object, the one of the body, the other of the soul, and use divers medicines to cure: one amends *animam per corpus* [the soul through the body], the other *corpus per animam* [the body through the soul] as our Regius Professor of Physic well informed us in a learned lecture of his not long since. One helps the vices and passions of the soul, anger, lust, desperation, pride, presumption, etc., by applying that spiritual physic; as the other uses proper remedies in bodily diseases. Now this being a common infirmity of body and soul, and such a one that hath as much need of a spiritual as a corporal cure, I could not find a fitter task to busy myself about, a more apposite theme, so necessary, so commodious, and generally concerning all sorts of men, that should so equally participate of both, and require a whole physician (37).

One can see from this how persuasive an apologist Burton could have been had it suited his purposes. He appeals to the empiricist bias toward "fruitful works" and, at the same time, manages to clothe himself in all the authority of the most powerful of Christian images, the divine physician. Reconciling these two strains of seventeenth-century thought is no mean feat, and Burton moves to consolidate his position by recapitulating the arguments which support it:

But this I hope shall suffice, when you have more fully considered of the matter of this my subject, *rem substratum,* melancholy, madness, and of the reasons following, which were my chief motives: the generality of the disease, the necessity of the cure, and the commodity or common good that will arise to all men by the knowledge of it, as shall at large appear in the ensuing preface. And I doubt not but that in the end you will say with me, that to anatomize this humour aright, through all the members of this our *microcosmos,* is as great a task as . . . (38).

This is so firmly reasonable that we are likely to finish the sentence for him: "to anatomize this humour aright is as great and important a task as a man could set himself." And, in some sense, this is exactly what he does go on to say, but unfortunately his case for the "greatness" of the task is made so strongly that it argues as well for its impossibility:

> to anatomize this humour aright . . . is as great a task as to reconcile those chronological errors in the Assyrian monarchy, find out the quadrature of a circle, the creeks and sounds of the north-east or north-west passages, and all out as good a discovery as that hungry Spaniard's of *Terra Australis Incognita,* as great a trouble as to perfect the motion of Mars and Mercury, which so crucifies our astronomers, or to rectify the Gregorian calendar (38).

Even today one hears "you might as well try to square the circle," when a project is declared unfeasible; and as Burton proceeds to pile Pelion on Ossa, the implication is unmistakable: the anatomization of this humor is a grand piece of folly, he is a fool for proposing it and we are fools for reading it. The supposed justification of the undertaking—the generality of the disease—has suddenly become the strongest argument against it. The speaker, however, seems unaware of the double edge his comparisons carry and he continues as if the smooth surface of his narrative were undisturbed: "And as that great captain Zisca would have a drum made of his skin when he was dead, because he thought the very noise of it would put his enemies to flight, I doubt not but that these following lines, when they shall be recited, or hereafter read, will drive away melancholy (though I be gone) as much as Zisca's drum could terrify his foes (38)." This is ambiguous praise indeed since it depends wholly on one's estimate of the effectiveness of Zisca's drum, a point the prose carefully leaves in doubt. Zisca *thought* the noise of it would put his enemies to flight; he may have been wrong, and to the extent that he was, the comparative "as much as Zisca's drum" is deflating. But before the reader has time to react to these equivocations (Burton's prose never allows you to stop) his attention is diverted by a new and very personal issue:

Yet one caution let me give by the way to my present or future reader, who is actually melancholy, that he read not the symptoms or prognostics in this following tract, lest by applying that which he reads to himself, aggravating, appropriating things generally spoken to his own person (as melancholy men for the most part do), he trouble or hurt himself, and get in conclusion more harm than good. I advise them therefore warily to peruse that tract; *Lapides loquitur* (so said Agrippa, *de occ. Phil.*), *et caveant lectores ne cerebrum iis excutiat* [he discourses stones, and the readers must beware lest he break their heads]. The rest I doubt not they may securely read, and to their benefit. But I am over-tedious, I proceed (38).

Joan Webber has written that Burton's sentences function as multiple-choice questions.[7] Here the choice is between two categories, those who are melancholy and those who are not, but the idea of a class of *non*-melancholics, for whom much of the book is intended, undermines the line of defense Burton has been pursuing and we have been following. If the only people who can read the *Anatomy* are those who don't need it, how can it be medicinal, in either a physical or a spiritual sense? My question shows how easy it is to engage Burton at one level and walk into his traps at another. Every reader is "actually melancholy" (just as he is necessarily both future and present), for "we are all mad." By offering the empty category, Burton makes certain that we will read the interdicted sections, if only to prove to ourselves that his warning was meant for others. The ruse is transparent, but it is enough to overcome our sense of the absurd when Burton announces, "But I am over-tedious, I proceed."

This sequence, from the original rhetorical question "What have I to do with physic?" to the transitional, "I proceed" establishes a pattern that recurs so often that it is finally controlling: a declaration that distinctions between persons, times, professions, nations are invalid because all are mad, and melancholy is followed by a return to the supposedly discredited task of distinguishing, and the asking of the question "Whom shall I

[7] *The Eloquent "I,"* p. 101.

except?" The sequence is less remarkable than the fact that we negotiate it so often without finally balking at it, and we do not balk at it precisely because its renegotiation represents another opportunity to ask the question, which is, at least potentially, an opportunity to disassociate ourselves from the general indictment of a world gone mad. The mechanism that keeps shutting off avenues of escape also keeps opening them; the determined inconclusiveness of the prose, its refusal to stop, protects us from the negative conclusion it is continually, but never finally, reaching.

Thus when Burton promises to "make a brief survey of the world," we know, because he tells us, what that survey will uncover—melancholy; yet in the course of it, we will believe, if only momentarily, in persons, times, professions, nations that have escaped the general infection. Indeed the very assertion of universal madness is often made in such a way as to allow us to deny it in the act of reading it:

> That men are so misaffected, melancholy, mad, giddy-headed, hear the testimony of Solomon (Eccles. ii, 12):
> "And I turned to behold wisdom, madness and folly (40)."

Hearing the testimony of Solomon in this context means accrediting him as an authority, although, of course, if the thesis is accepted, Solomon himself must be among the misaffected, mad, melancholy, and giddy-headed. For the moment, however, Solomon is detached from his own observation simply because, in terms of the linear print experience, he stands in front of it. And he continues to occupy a privileged position in the reader's mind even when the impossibility of such a position is immediately reaffirmed. "So that, take melancholy in what sense you will, properly or improperly, in disposition or habit, for pleasure or for pain, dotage, discontent, fear, sorrow, madness for part or all, truly or metaphorically, 'tis all one (40)." (Significantly, the distinctions that are here declared invalid—" 'tis all one"—are the same distinctions that will form the basis of the divisions in the main body of the tract; and they will be no more real there than here.) It takes Solomon himself to destroy the illusion of apartness created by the authority of his name: "Surely I am more foolish than any man." The reputed wisest of men admits his folly and the category "wiseman" (non-mad), which for a time seemed to contain at least one member, collapses.

In the next paragraph, however, it is reconstituted under cover of another general indictment: "So corrupt is our judgement, we esteem wise and honest men fools (41)." Logically, the all-inclusive "our" of the first half of this statement militates against the very existence of the wise and honest men who dominate the second half; but rhetorically the weight of the sentence falls on the assertion of corruption; the esteeming of wise men fools is merely brought in to support it. In short, we are tricked into worrying about the wrong proposition and allowing the truly provocative thesis—that there *are* wise and honest men—to slip by us unexamined. It is not long, however, before the newly reconstituted distinctions are again dissolved, this time by the prose itself: " 'Tis an ordinary thing with us to account honest, devout, orthodox, divine, religious, plain dealing men idiots, asses, that cannot or will not lie and dissemble, shift, flatter . . . make good bargains, supplant, thrive . . . (42)." Since the force of the verb phrase ("to account") lessens as the sentence continues, the groups whose confusion Burton is supposedly lamenting become, in the experience of his prose, more and more confused. "Plain dealing men" "idiots, asses," " 'tis all one."

One would think that after this the hope of finding a wise and honest man would be abandoned, even by the most Diogenes-like of readers, but Burton revives it for a third time by turning to discuss a class of men who, by his own definitions, could not exist—philosophers, lovers of wisdom. At first it seems that these men will be brought in only to be added to the ever-growing list of fools. "Yea, even all these great philosophers the world hath ever had in admiration, whose works we do so much esteem . . . (42)." Obviously this sentence will end by finding in these men and their works as much folly as can be found in everyone else. But the main verb never arrives and the sentence fails to develop as anticipated. In time the "Yea, even" construction is forgotten and the reader is left listening to a round of unqualified praises for the "wise men" of antiquity, "Socrates the wisest man of his time. . . . Those seven wise men of Greece . . . Aristotle . . . wisdom itself in the abstract (42–43)." When the inevitable reversal does come—"myriads of men wiser in those days and yet all short of what they should be (43)"—it is, in a sense, too late, because we have already been lulled into accepting the credentials of these myriads at face value. The section on philosophers concludes, as every section concludes, with a new insistence on the old and familiar truth: "For we are *ad unum omnes,* all mad, *semel insanivimus omnes,* not once, but always so . . . say it of us all . . . young and old, all dote (46)." But even this relentless statement contains a Burtonian loophole in the form of an unnecessary and suspect citation of authority: "all dote, as Lactantius proves out of Seneca." If one steps back from the prose, this turning to Lactantius and Seneca is absurd, since they are both necessarily implicated in the general accusation; but the sentence moves right on past this point, disallowing a rhetorical pause, and we leave it believing both in the madness and foolishness of all and in the sanity of Lactantius and Seneca, and perhaps, in some innermost recess of our minds, believing in ourselves.

Burton is so confident of his ability to control us that at one point he openly displays the mechanism by which we have been manipulated: "It is midsummer moon still, and the dog days last all the year long, they are all mad. Whom shall I then except (117)?" The question is absurd, and the answer to it has been given many times before: no one. It is given here again, and, what is more important, it is given not by implication but openly. And yet, within a few lines this very openness, so uncharacteristic of Burton's usual procedure, becomes the means by which he once again tricks us into believing in something we know to be a fiction:

> Whom shall I then except? Ulricus Huttenus' *Nemo; nam, Nemo omnibus horis sapit, Nemo nascitur sine vitiis, Crimine Nemo caret, Nemo sorte sua vivit contentus, Nemo in amore sapit, Nemo bonus, Nemo sapiens, Nemo est ex omni parti beatus* [Nobody; for Nobody is sensible at all times; Nobody is born without fault; Nobody is free from blame; Nobody lives content with his own lot; Nobody is sane in love; Nobody is good, Nobody wise; Nobody is happy], etc., and therefore Nicholas Nemo, or Monsieur Nobody, shall go free (117).

Here the will-o'-the-wisp the reader has chased through so many pages and sections is identified as the nonperson he has always been; but, just as before he acquired a substance simply because we desired him to have one, in this passage he acquires a substance simply because he is named, and then named again. Of course, if there were an opportunity to reflect on the illusion the prose is creating, we might be able to disassociate ourselves from it; but as always, the pace of the *Anatomy* discourages reflection, and before we know it the reality of that illusion has become a presupposition of the words we are reading. "Whom shall I except in the second place?" Simply by taking this sentence in, we assent, if only for a moment, to what is assumed—that there is a "first place"—and thereby participate in the reification of a nobody into some body. If the reader is Burton's subject, he is also his plaything.

YOU SHALL FIND THEM ALL ALIKE

Burton's double game, his repeated playing of both ends (the impulse to anatomize and the impulse to assimilate) against the middle (you) has many consequences, some of which we have already noted: the speaker, in effect, disappears behind a screen of contradictory authorities and shifting scenery; the reader is deprived of a point of reference, either in the person of the author or in the material, and prevented from distancing himself from the follies of mankind; distinctions and classifications whose reality is usually assumed are called into question and finally denied. There are also future consequences in the sense that the reader's experience in these pages predetermines his response to what is to follow. It is a strange preface indeed that makes an a priori mockery of the work it introduces, but that is precisely the effect of the patterns analyzed here, and the effect is reinforced when Burton directly attacks the procedures he will employ in the body of his formal *Anatomy:*

> But make how many kinds you will, divide and subdivide,
> few men are free, or that do not impinge on some one kind

or other . . . as he that examines his own and other men's actions shall find (47).

We are of the same humours and inclinations as our predecessors were; you shall find us all alike (53).

To insist in every particular were one of Hercules' labours, there's so many ridiculous instances as motes in the sun (68).

Proceed now *a partibus ad totum,* or from the whole to the parts, and you shall find no other issue; the parts shall be sufficiently dilated in this following Preface. The whole must needs follow by a sorites or induction (78).

Begin then where you will, go backward or forward, choose out of the whole pack, wink and choose, you shall find them all alike, "never a barrel better herring (78)."

To insist in all particulars were an Herculean task (116). It would ask an expert Vesalius to anatomize every member (117).

Making kinds, dividing, subdividing, examining, insisting on particulars, proceeding *a partibus ad totum* or from the whole to the parts, beginning, choosing, anatomizing, these are the very activities to which Burton will call us for several hundreds of pages, yet here he clearly labels them exercises in futility. Not that this will prevent us from going on to the larger work, any more than the unceasing repetition of "Burton's Law"—all are mad—prevents us from seeking its exceptions. In both contexts we are pulled forward by the strongest of motives—self-interest, the hope of finding an answer to the question "whom shall I except?" and of finding in the answer a place for ourselves. So strong and deeply rooted is this motive that Burton can dangle it as bait in any number of guises and rely on us to rise to it. At one point the bait takes the form of Christianity: "Yea, but you will infer, that is true of heathens, if they be conferred with Christians (I Cor. III, 19): 'The wisdom of this world is foolishness with God' (45)." Here is a distinction one can approve and live with: a heathenish subjection to the foolishness of the world, as opposed to a Christian alliance with the wisdom of God. But the opposition barely survives its introduction, for "In some sense, *Christiani Crassiani*, Christians are Crassians, and if compared to that wisdom [God's], no better than fools." One avenue of escape closed, however, opens up the possibility of another. Christians may be fools in relation to the wisdom of God, but we need not always apply that stringent criterion. There are, after all, less rigorous standards of wisdom for the judging of secular activities. But the reader who takes this path finds that Burton has anticipated him: "But I do not so mean; even in our ordinary dealings we are no better than fools. 'All our actions . . . upbraid us of folly,' our whole course of life is but matter of laughter." In short, the "wisdom of the world" is simply a phrase, rhetorically useful if the intention is to glorify God, but certainly not something one should believe in. To the extent that we would like to believe in it, it represents still another way of avoiding the truth about ourselves ("Our whole course of life is but matter of laughter"), a way this small sequence effectively bars.

The self-defensive mechanism of the human mind is infinitely resourceful, however; any port in a storm. If these times and this place are replete with folly, perhaps we can find refuge (and an exception) in former ages and far countries:

> For where you shall see the people civil, obedient to God
> and princes, judicious, peaceable and quiet, rich, fortunate,
> and flourish, to live in peace, in unity and concord, a coun-
> try well tilled, many fair built and populous cities . . .
> that country is free from melancholy; as it was in Italy
> in the time of Augustus, now in China, now in many other
> flourishing kingdoms of Europe (79).

The reference to Italy is conveniently in the past, and the reference to China is to a country remote and mysterious. As for "many other flourishing kingdoms," that raises more questions than it answers. Even so, Italy and China *are* names, these names *are* attached to existing geographical entities, and it would seem that a place "free from melancholy" is at least a possibility, albeit a rarity. But in the extended survey of kingdoms that follows, the effects of melancholy are discovered everywhere, in ancient Italy "when Catiline rebelled (83)," in China, which is even now

"infested (96)" with wandering Tartars, and in every "flourishing" kingdom of Europe: Italy, where "luxury and riot" reign;
Spain, in bondage to "superstition and jealousy"; Germany, de-
bauched by drunkenness; the northern countries, intemperate and
gluttonous (97). So pervasive are barbarism and folly that even
America and *Terra Australis Incognita* must be purged of them,
if possible. Of course, it is not, and a section that began by contrasting England to those other places and finding in them a
hope that we, too, may be reformed, ends by declaring all such
hopes "vain and absurd":

> These are vain, absurd, and ridiculous wishes not to be
> hoped: all must be as it is, Boccalinus may cite common-
> wealths to come before Apollo, and seek to reform the
> world itself by commisioners, but there is no remedy (97).

"There is no remedy," whether one seeks it in various professions
(divinity, physic, philosophy) persons (Seneca, Democritus, Democritus Jr., the reader) or nations (England, France, China, ancient Italy). The reformation of the world is as impossible a task,
it would seem, as the anatomization of melancholy or the finding
of its cure. Burton's universe and his grand scheme break down
at precisely the same point, that is, at every point.

Thus when Burton declares, "Begin then where you will, . . .
choose out of the whole pack . . . you shall find them all alike,
'never a barrel better herring' " (78), he describes both his method
and the reader's experience. Every change of subject, every new
topic, is another barrel, a container whose contents are, for the
moment, unknown; and for that moment each barrel is the substance of a revived hope, the hope that when opened it will yield
better herrings and that we will be among them. But as Democritus
Jr. so often tells us, "you shall find them all alike"; and the finding
of them all alike is, from the reader's point of view, the action
as well as the plot of the preface. So that, despite the tendency
to digress and the absence of sustained discursive patterns, there
is a rigorous logic to the movement of the prose, a logic of elimination—"there is no remedy," "Whom shall I then except? . . .
Nobody"—and of assimilation—"all the world is melancholy . . .
every member of it." Every paragraph, every section shuts off an-

other potential route of escape for the reader who resists the personal application of the general rule. One by one the areas of an artificially segmented universe lose their distinctness, until the complete triumph of madness is not an assertion, but an experienced fact.

The last area to be inundated, the last barrel to be opened, the last refuge for the resisting mind, is its own place. Having denied us comfort and hope in the world outside, Burton invites us to turn inward to the world of the imagination. Let states persist in their excesses and persons in their crimes, "I will yet to satisfy and please myself, make an Utopia of mine own, a New Atlantis, a poetical commonwealth of mine own, in which I will freely domineer, build cities, make laws, statutes, as I list myself. And why may I not (97)?" Even at this late stage, Burton continues to involve us in his double game. On the surface this new project is an admission of defeat ("Because . . . it [purging the world of melancholy] is a thing so difficult, impossible, and far beyond Hercules' labour"); the very name, "Utopia," implies impossibility and insubstantiality. Still, the notion has a kind of conceptual reality to which the reader can attach whatever wishful thoughts have survived the disillusioning experience of the preface. In other words, it represents another potential avenue of escape, if only into illusion; for although Utopia is (literally) nowhere, it is, simply as an idea, a container or enclosure within whose confines one can hope to be free of melancholy. And, as Burton exclaims, "Why not?" The answer, unfortunately, is that while one may freely domineer in a commonwealth, one's freedom does not extend to the banishing of human nature, and if human nature enters, all that the Utopia was designed to exclude enters with it.

Burton's Utopia begins well. The setting is paradisial, *"ubi semper virens laurus . . .* where is a perpetual spring (98)."* Cities are built at the most convenient distances from each other. Rivers flow exactly where they are needed. Marketplaces, churches, recreation fields are dotted about in "opportune places (99)." The first discordant note is struck by the word "hospital": "Hospitals of all kinds, for childen, orphans, old folks, sickmen,

madmen, soldiers (99)." Madmen are exactly what we have entered Utopia to escape, and suddenly here they are at the tail end
of a list that began innocently enough with children and orphans.
A bit of the excluded world has seeped in, and more of it enters
through the agency of the "not" clause which follows:

> not built *precario,* or by gouty benefactors, who, when by
> fraud and rapine they have extorted all their lives, op-
> pressed whole provinces, societies, etc., give something to
> pious uses, build a satisfactory almshouse, school, or
> bridge, etc., at their last end, or before perhaps, which is
> no otherwise than to steal a goose and stick down a feather,
> rob a thousand to relieve ten (99).

Ostensibly this is an account of the motives that will not obtain
in Utopia, but the (verbal) act of banishing them gives them a
substance they would not otherwise have had. At some point in
this long syntactical unit the "not" ceases to be controlling, and
we watch the gouty benefactors, rapacious oppressors, and pious
robbers build their hospitals right here on Utopian territory, the
printed page. When Burton continues, "and those hospitals so
built and maintained," it is impossible to tell which hospitals he
means; those he would have in Utopia or those whose origins
have been the object of his attack. And, of course, that is exactly
the point: the distinction, not only between the two kinds of hospitals but between the supposedly different worlds they serve, is
incapable of being maintained, even as an imaginative exercise.
In the pages that follow more and more of reality intrudes. There
are still gestures in the direction of the Utopian ideal—"Few laws,
but those severely kept, plainly put down, and in the mother
tongue," "No parish to contain above a thousand auditors (102)"
—but the real force of the prose comes from the sense of imminent engulfment that attends every reference, direct and indirect,
to the excluded world.

> If it were possible, I would have such priests as should
> imitate Christ, charitable lawyers should love their neigh-
> bors as themselves, temperate and modest physicians, poli-

ticians contemn the world, philosophers should know themselves, noblemen live honestly, tradesmen leave lying and
cozening, magistrates corruption, etc.; but this is impossible (102).

"If it were possible" is a qualification that belongs in the real
world; in Utopia, possibility is bounded only by the wishes and
imagination of the framer. But the imagination of this framer cannot free itself from the very thing it would avoid. At the beginning
of this sentence the word "should" is future—hypothetical; but
by the end it is exhortative and moral—noblemen *ought to* live
honestly—and the hypothesis has been forgotten in the reality
(they don't). When Burton concludes wearily, "I must get such
as I may," he in effect admits defeat not only on the particulars—
priests, politicians, lawyers—but on the Utopia itself. That admission is formalized a little later on by these distressingly familiar words: "for men are partial and passionate, merciless,
covetous, corrupt, subject to love, hate, fear, favour, etc. (103)."
There is no hint in this statement of a particular application, no
exception of the Utopian populace or of any other group. We are
back at the same old stand, nothing has changed, and to all intents and purposes it is as if the idea of a Utopia had never been
broached.

The decision to let go of the Utopian framework is, in a curious way, made independently of either the speaker or the reader.
In the midst of a discussion of "defensive" wars (wars, too, will
have their place in the "ideal" commonwealth) [8] Burton exclaims,
*"Manum de Tabella,* I have been over tedious in this subject
(107)." What exactly is meant by "this subject" is not at all
clear. Is it this particular aspect of Utopia, its response to mili-
tary challenges? or is it the Utopia as a whole? The first words
of the following paragraph only perpetuate the ambiguity—"From
commonwealths and cities I will descend to families"—for this,

[8] Utopian wars, it seems, will differ from the wars of Europe only in the
degree or quantity of their horrors. Armies will abstain "as much as is possible
from depopulations, burnings of towns, massacring of infants, etc. (107)." This
is barely to be distinguished from the wars that were earlier called massacres,
murders, desolations, and plagues (56), and the weakness of "as much as is possible" suggests that in the end there would be no distinction at all.

too, could refer either to a further sketching in of the Utopian landscape or to a return to the interrupted "survey of the world." The availability of both frames of reference prevents us from resting with certainty in either, and there is no firm sense of closure at this point. In time, as the discussion of families proceeds without reference to Utopia, the question is forgotten. As a result, the reader has no recollection of leaving Utopia for the real world. One blends into the other without any clear line of demarcation. J. Max Patrick has complained that some readers seem not to have noticed that there was a Utopia in Burton's preface.[9] The explanation is simply that there isn't one, at least not one sustained enough to allow it to stand out. Nor should this be surprising. Nothing stands out in Burton's universe, because nothing—no person, place, object, idea—can maintain its integrity in the context of an all-embracing madness. Even syntactical and rhetorical forms—sentences, paragraphs, sections—lose their firmness in this most powerful of all solvents. The Utopia is just one more barrel, one more false promise, one more substanceless hope of sanity and order, and, like the others, it surfaces for a few brief moments before the advancing tides of melancholy rise to overwhelm and obliterate it.

I would apologize for the fanciful language of the last sentence were it not Burton's:

> We change language, habits, laws, customs, manners, but not vices, not diseases, not the symptoms of folly and madness, they are still the same. And as a river, we see, keeps the like name and place, but not water, and yet ever runs . . . our times and persons alter, vices are the same, and ever will be; look how nightengales sang of old, cocks crowed, kine lowed, sheep bleated, sparrows chirped, dogs barked, so do they still; we keep our madness still, play the fools still . . . you shall find us all alike (53).

The same metaphor is used earlier in the book to describe the speaker's style: "So that as a river runs sometimes precipitate and swift, then dull and slow; now direct, then *per ambages;* now

[9] J. Max Patrick, "'Robert Burton's Utopianism," *Philological Quarterly,* XXVII (1948), 345.

deep, then shallow; now muddy then clear; now broad, then narrow; doth my style flow (32)." And later, the river becomes a
thread, but to the same effect: "You shall find a phantastical
strain, a fustian, a bombast, a vainglorious humour, an affected
style, etc., like a prominent thread in an uneven woven cloth, run
parallel throughout (111)." The river-thread images are the perfect vehicles for the all-inclusiveness of Burton's vision; they allow for a plurality of forms within a singleness of essence, recognizing the existence of local variations, but insisting on the final
relevance of a larger perspective in the context of which those
variations are less striking than the one prominent thread: "There
is in all melancholy *similitudo dissimilis,* like men's faces, a dis-
agreeing likeness still; and as in a river we swim in the same
place, though not in the same numerical water; as the same instrument affords several lessons, so the same disease yields diversity
of symptoms (397)." This likeness of all men and of their productions operates in the present situation to dissolve the usual
distinctions between author and reader, observer and observed.
The mind of the narrator is itself an instance of what he is reporting, as are the minds of those to whom he reports. Wherever
the melancholy mind turns, it will find melancholy and relate its
findings to melancholics, in a diseased, mad, rambling irrational—
that is, melancholy—style. What we have, then, is a total unity
of unreliability, in the author, in his materials, in his readers, and
in his structure, a total unreliability and a total subjectivity.

In the face of such a depressing unity, why is the *Anatomy*
not a more uncomfortable experience than most readers report it
to be? One answer to this question has already been given: every
time a category is collapsed into the general malady, a new one
pops up to take its place and to become, for a moment, a candi-
date for the status of "exception"; as long as the prose goes on
(and it *does* go on), as long as the scene continually shifts, the
supply of unopened barrels, and therefore of hope, is assured. At
the same time (and this is the second answer to my question),
the discovery everywhere of unreliability and subjectivity finally
(and paradoxically) makes everything we come upon in the *Anatomy* perfectly reliable and objective; for in the absence of an
independent center of authority, that is of an exception, the pri-

vate and eccentric visions that fill the book become the norm and subjectivity becomes objectivity, for it is all there is; and by the same reasoning, if there is nothing but madness and melancholy, whatever mad and melancholy men say is necessarily true. When the assertion "all are mad" is proved by Lactantius out of Seneca (46), the absurdity of the pseudo-documentation is obvious: Seneca and Lactantius are no less mad than anyone else. And yet it is precisely this that validates their judgment (it takes one to know one) and makes of them reliable authorities. In these terms, the terms of the universe he both inhabits and creates, Burton's antimethod is perfectly methodical, and when he pledges to "omit all impertinent digressions, to say no more of such as are improperly melancholy (120)," he is able to keep his promise by breaking it; for in a world ordered (or disordered) by digressiveness, every digression is in order.

As for those who are "improperly melancholy," where melancholy is the standard, the concept of propriety is meaningless. Meaningless, too, are the concepts of authorship and attribution, for when all are infected with the same disease, all speak with the same, that is, one, voice. (This is reflected in the prose, in the gradual shift from full-verb phrases which specify agents, to infinitives whose subject is general, to tenseless, subjectless forms which suggest actions that are not produced but simply are.) [10] In short, *total unreliability assures total anonymity,* and makes perfect sense out of Burton's most outrageous statement: "I writ this and published this . . . it is *neminis nihil* [nothing by nobody] (122)." In this upside-down sacramental universe, where a great (but perverse) spirit rolls through all things, "I" can be equal to nobody, that is everybody, because the distinction between persons is merely a distinction between momentarily and artificially discrete manifestations of a single essence (" 'tis all mine, and none mine"). And thus Burton's disclaimers of respon-

[10] See, for example, *Anatomy of Melancholy,* p. 67: "To see a fond mother, like Aesop's ape, hug her child to death, a wittol wink at his wife's honesty, and too perspicuous in all other affairs; one stumble at a straw, and leap over a block; rob Peter, and pay Paul; scrape unjust sums with one hand, purchase great manors by corruption, fraud and cozenage, and liberally to distribute to the poor with the other, give a remnant to pious uses, etc.; penny wise, pound foolish; blind men judge of colours; wise men silent, fools talk."

sibility—not I, but Democritus, not he but "they"—carry a
weight and truth far beyond their immediate rhetorical effect. It
is not I, but the world, all, everybody, they, speaking, even when
a particular name or a limiting pronoun happens to be attached
to the utterance.[11] "Whom shall I except?" Burton asks, and the
answer is "Monsieur Nobody (117)," and because this answer is
documented so fully, the answer to another question—who wrote
this work?—is "Everybody," the world, all, they, *you*, including
the reader who is, in some sense, the author of what he is reading.
The book is finally the world speaking to a part of itself (the
reader) through the medium of a part of itself (the speaker)
about parts of itself (nations, professions, places, etc.). In this
conflation of the categories in terms of which we usually analyze
the literary experience—speaker, reader, subject, reality—all
questions of perspective and method lose their urgency. Burton
calls the preface a "confused lump," but in a way he is over-harsh,
since confusion is its unifying principle. And therefore, when he
ends by declaring "I will begin," the statement is at once ridiculous and perfectly acceptable; for, "Begin then where you will,
go backward or forward, choose out of the whole pack, wink and
choose, you shall find them all alike (78)."

THERE IS NO REMEDY

What happens in the body of the tract, not surprisingly, is
merely a larger and more schematically obvious version of what
happens in the preface. To put the matter simply, if paradoxically,
the nonmethod is more methodized. In place of the rather random
surfacing of a succession of organizing principles (professions, nations, the Utopia), the reader is confronted immediately with a
huge predigested synopsis in the form of a Ramus-like branching
diagram, complete with sections, subsections, and members of
subsections. The effect is to renew the promise—so many times
made and so many times breached—of a comprehensible and sane
universe, where the relationships between things can be grasped
and anatomized and where the regularity of cause and effect suggests at least the possibility of managing one's life. In this case

[11] On this point, see Webber, *The Eloquent "I,"* pp. 82, 99.

the promise has all the solidity a concrete visualization can confer, and its force is sustained by Burton's more or less faithful adherence to the scheme of his synopsis. But within the framework of that ever-present and ever-insistent superstructure, the same old games are being played. At one point in Partition I, Section 3, Member 1, Subsection 2, *Symptoms or signs in the Mind,* we are told this about those melancholics who fear without cause: "Yet for all this, as Jacchinus notes, 'in all other things they are wise, staid, discreet, and do nothing unbeseeming their dignity, person, or place, this foolish, ridiculous, and childish fear excepted' (388)." For a moment, this particular strain of melancholy seems no more debilitating than an occasional nervous tic, irritating perhaps and upsetting, but noticeable chiefly as an exception to a sane and normal pattern of behavior. But what Burton giveth, Burton usually taketh away, and in the second half of this same sentence, the area of sanity is narrowed to nothing: "which so much, so continuously tortures and crucifies their souls, like a barking dog that always bawls, but seldom bites, this fear ever molesteth, and, so long as melancholy lasteth, cannot be avoided (388–389)." The logic of this, as it finally unfolds, is: they are only mad when this fear possesses; this fear possesses them always ("ever molesteth"); therefore they are always mad. The sequence is obviously rhetorical, designed not to give information, but to mislead the reader into positing the existence of more order and regularity than the world actually affords.

The reader is similarly misled every time a section or subsection or member of a subsection ends and another begins, for every beginning is, at least ostensibly, a separating out (of one aspect of melancholy from all the others) and every separating out is an act of containment which implies that the subject at hand cannot only be anatomized, but controlled; but the limited focus supplied by the specifying title soon expands to the point where the silent claim of the superstructure to order and contain becomes untenable. This happens in innumerable ways, but most simply when symptoms, case histories, causes, and effects of supposedly discrete strains of melancholy are found to be interchangeable. In the discussion of "Extravagant humours," we read of these symptoms: "If he be told he hath a stinking breath, a great nose, that he is sick, or inclined to such or such a disease, he believes it eftsoons and peradventure by force of imagination will work it out (393)." In other words, an extravagantly humorous man need only hear of a disease or a defect or malady for it to become his; but this also, it seems, is a characteristic of those who "fear without cause": "some are afraid that they shall have every fearful disease they see others have, hear of or read, and dare not therefore hear or read of any such subject, no not of melancholy itself, lest by applying to themselves that which they hear or read, they should aggrevate and increase it (387)." Of course there is a certain logic to this cross-referencing. Fearing without cause *is* an extravagant humor; and one who fears without cause is very much like one who becomes melancholic upon suggestion; but then, all humors are extravagant in the sense that they are deviations from a norm (which, significantly, never appears) and all those who are humorous are irregularly (causelessly) so. And this is precisely what the reader learns as he makes his way through the hundreds of pages that comprise the three partitions. Melancholy is so pervasive that it is the cause of all effects and the effect of all causes, simultaneously symptom and disease, the prominent thread that not only runs through the divisions and subdivisions (barrels) of the superstructure, but finally undoes them. That is, as examples, case histories, signs, etc. are discovered to be the common property of every discretely partitioned unit, the reality of those partitions and the discreteness of those units becomes questionable. So powerful, finally, is the sense of continuity between sections, that within a few paragraphs of the opening sentence of any one of them, the reader forgets what particular aspect of melancholy is (supposedly) under discussion. The machinery generated and sustained by the introductory synopsis implies that a reading of the tract will sort everything out; but in the experience of that reading, everything gets mixed up, and as a result the synopsis becomes the ever-present symbol of a promise—of order, sanity, the hope of making sense of things—that is never redeemed.[12]

---

[12] Critics have long argued about the relationship of the synopsis to the material it does not quite contain. Some have tended to look for a psychological explanation, while others, like James Roy King, have emphasized the problems of

It is a promise, however that Burton repeatedly renews (as he did in the preface) even after he has himself admitted that it could not possibly be kept. The subsection from which we have been quarrying examples ends by declaring its own failure, and, by extension, the inevitable failure of all other subsections:

> The tower of Babel never yielded such confusion of tongues, as the chaos of melancholy doth variety of symptoms. There is in all melancholy *similitudo dissimilis,* like men's faces, a disagreeing likeness still; and as in a river we swim in the same place, though not in the same numerical water; as the same instrument affords several lessons, so the same disease yields diversity of symptoms (397).

The comparison to the Tower of Babel is not casual or random; the traditional image of a grandly presumptuous structure built

---

composition: "Burton's elaborate outline indicates that he intended to compose a carefully constructed, analytical book. That he did not prompts the suggestion that he compiled his outline only after he had written a number of completely independent sections. . . . One might conclude from the presence of both outline and digressions that Burton suffered from an almost comic inability to manage the fundamental problems involved in writing a book. . . . These digressions . . . represent, I think, an early layer of material, too fascinating to be discarded, too irrelevant, even after a hundred visions and revisions, to gain a place in the structural fabric of the finished book (*Studies in Six 17th Century Writers,* Athens, Ohio, 1966, pp. 80, 83–84)." Since this chapter was completed, however, two studies which present views closer to my own have appeared. In "Robert Burton and Ramist Method" (*Renaissance Quarterly,* Vol. XXIV, No. 2, Summer, 1971), David Renaker suggests that "Burton . . . took a curious revenge on Ramus. . . . Everything that Ramus had sought to banish—digressiveness, inconsistency, *copia,* the fusion of rhetoric with dialectic—ran riot over and through the meticulus pattern of the 'method' (220)." And Bridget Gellert Lyons writes (in *Voices of Melancholy,* New York, 1971): "The rigidly schematic pattern of the *Anatomy* is called into question by the extent to which it is overelaborated, by the contradictory and doubtful ideas that are brought to play on it, and by the demonstration that is made throughout of the inadequacy of theory to the complications of life (148)." But Professor Lyons and I appear to differ on an important point. Her next sentence reads: "The most strikingly artistic feature of the *Anatomy,* however, is its conscious creation of unity out of diversity." I take the "however" to mean that the *Anatomy* is unified *despite* the subversion of the schematic pattern, whereas it seems to me that its upside-down unity is the *product* of that subversion. Some of the best writing on these questions is to be found in Ruth Fox's unpublished dissertation (Ohio State, 1971), "The Tangled Chain: The Structure of Disorder in *The Anatomy of Melancholy.*"

on the shakiest of foundations is exactly right for the present work, and the reader's experience of that work accords perfectly with the experience of Burton's swimmer, for whom everything remains the same even as it changes. And yet Burton is so sure of us, so confident that no matter how many times he tells the truth, we will manage somehow to disbelieve it, that he follows this confession with still another promise of a "more sober discourse to follow": "Which howsoever they be diverse, intricate, and hard to be confined, I will adventure yet in such a vast confusion and generality to bring them into some order; and so descend to particulars (397)." Descending to particulars is something the speaker declares his intention of doing whenever the structure he has been laboring to build collapses. It is a declaration we have every reason to distrust, and yet reason has nothing to do, finally, with our susceptibility to the lure it holds out: "to bring them into some order."

There are as many instances of this pattern in the *Anatomy* as there are divisions. With every new section, the hope of "bringing them into some order" is revived, simply because the act of specifying is an act of delimiting; but the narrow and manageable focus of the introductory sentences barely survives the first page before it widens to include everything and everybody, revived hope fades, and the reader is left simply with the fact—and no cure. Joan Webber has remarked of Thomas Browne, he "always . . . pulls the sting from pain." [13] Burton always leaves it in, even to the extent of withholding the one consolation we might have expected him to offer, the consolation of Christian doctrine. This is not to say that there are not everywhere in the *Anatomy* references to Christ and to the Scriptures, but that in context these references point away from the consolation of which they are usually the vehicle. In the midst of his indictment of the contemporary world, Burton begins a sentence which would seem to attribute the deplorable state of things to the absence of specifically Christian virtues: "No charity, love, friendship, fear of God, alliance, affinity, consanguinity, Christianity . . ."; but the sentence finally asserts the inability of these virtues, whether they are present or not, to effect any material change: "No charity, love, friend-

[13] *The Eloquent "I,"* p. 181.

ship, fear of God, alliance, affinity, consanguinity, Christianity, can contain them (64)." For the moment before we read "can contain them," Christianity represents our best hope in the face of "knavery, flattery, . . . villainy," but then it is dismissed as one more ineffectual remedy against an irresistible disease. In other words, Christianity functions negatively, as a part of the documentation of the evil it would normally be expected to counter. This continues to be true even when Burton turns explicitly to Scripture; the texts he marshals build up an overwhelming case against hope and for despair:

> My second argument is grounded upon the like place of Scripture, which though before mentioned in effect, yet for some reasons is to be repeated . . . "Fools" (saith David) "by reason of their transgressions," etc. (Ps. cvii, 17) . . . So we read (Rom. ii) "Tribulation and anguish on the soul of every man that doeth evil"; but all do evil. And Isaiah lxv, 14, "My servants shall sing for joy, and ye shall cry for sorrow of heart, and vexation of mind." 'Tis ratified by the common consent of all philosophers. "Dishonesty" (saith Cardanub) . . . (73-74).

Again the movement is away from any doctrinal implications and toward a treatment of Scripture as a body of evidence that supports not a promise of relief, but a thesis of total and cosmic depravity. So that, not only is the consoling power of Christianity defused, but its sacred book loses the status of a special authority and becomes subject to the ratification of empirical observation.

This consistent refusal to release the potential that is present whenever the Scriptures are cited or even echoed has the curious effect of increasing our awareness of that potential. That is, the very fact that the scriptural references do not fulfill our normal expectations in some sense reinforces those expectations. We wait all the more self-consciously for that which has been self-consciously withheld, and at one point in the preface, it seems that our patience is about to be rewarded:

> We had need of some general visitor in our age, that should reform what is amiss; a just army of Rosy-cross men, for

they will amend all matters (they say), religion, policy, manners with arts, sciences, etc., another Attila, Tamerlane, another Hercules to strive with Acheolus, *Augae stabulum purgare,* to subdue tyrants . . . to expel thieves . . . and purge the world of monsters and Centaurs: or another Theban Crates to reform our manners, to compose quarrels and controversies, as in his time he did, and was therefore adored for a God in Athens. "As Hercules purged the world of monsters, and subdued them, so did he fight against envy, lust, anger, avarice, etc. and all those feral vices and monsters of the mind." It were to be wished we had some such visitor (96).

At first this peroration is ambiguous in precisely the manner we have come to expect. The sincerity of the speaker's "wish" is called into question when his parenthesis ("they say") calls into question the powers of the "Rosy-cross men," and one wonders whether a visit by Attila or Tamerlane would effect the kind of reformation "our age" requires. Hercules, however, is another matter. Generations of Christian allegorizers had found in his career their most fertile field, and it was not at all unusual to see Christ referred to as "our Hercules." As Hercules comes to dominate the passage, the emphasis shifts from social and political problems to the problem of the mind, that true Augean stable whose residue of original sin can be washed away only by the waters of baptism (Christ's blood): and when the "monsters" of the mind turn out to be four of the seven deadly sins, the reader feels that the identification of the desired visitor cannot be far behind.

It, of course, never arrives; even though Burton tantalizes us by making his most explicit reference to a Christ in a context which argues strongly for the necessity of his coming: "He might . . . cut off our tumultuous desires, inordinate lusts, root out atheism, impiety, heresy, schism, and superstition, which now so *crucify* the world (my emphasis)." It is after this, when the level of our expectation is perhaps higher than it has ever been before, that Burton draws back and reminds us of what we should have remembered all along:

These are vain, absurd, and ridiculous wishes not to be hoped: all must be as it is, Boccalinus may cite commonwealths to come before Apollo, and seek to reform the world itself by commisioners, but there is no remedy, it may not be redressed, *desinet homines tum demum stultescere quando esse desinent,* so long as they can wag their beards, they will play the knaves and fools . . . it is a thing so difficult, impossible, and far beyond Hercules' labours to perform (97).

There is no remedy. Except, perhaps, suicide, and Burton's treatment of that possibility is perfectly illustrative of both his method and his message, in the sense that there is one. The final movement of the last member (*Prognostics of Melancholy*) of Partition I begins with one of those self-cannibalizing sentences we encounter so often in *The Anatomy of Melancholy:* "Seldom this malady [Melancholy] procures death, except (which is the greatest most grievous calamity, and the misery of all miseries) they make away themselves, which is a frequent thing and familiar amongst them (431)." This pattern is by now so "frequent and familiar" that it constitutes a mannerism. In the brief space between "seldom" and "frequent," the exception becomes the rule, and this particular effect of melancholy, for a moment limited to a small group in special circumstances, is extended to everyone. There follows a series of quotations and examples, all of which support the resolution of those who find themselves in the grip of this disease to make away with themselves. "And in the midst of these squalid, ugly, and such irksome days, they seek at last, finding no comfort, no remedy in this wretched life, to be eased of all by death . . . 'after many tedious days, at last, either by drowning, hanging, or some fearful end, they precipitate or make away themselves; many lamentable examples are daily seen amongst us' (432)." The arguments are familiar but nonetheless persuasive, as anyone who has read the ninth canto of the first book of the *Faerie Queene* can testify ("Sleepe after toyle, port after stormie seas,/Ease after warre, death after life does greatly please"); but for the Christian reader, there is the possibility that the well-known doctrinal objections to suicide, and the accompanying consolation of the meaning for all of us of Christ's sacrifice, will be brought forward. And at least one sentence suggests that Burton is moving in just that direction:

> 'Tis a common calamity, a fatal end to this disease they are condemned to a violent death by a jury of physicians, furiously disposed, carried, headlong by their tyrannizing wills, enforced by miseries, and there remains no more to such persons, if that heavenly Physician, by His assisting grace and mercy alone, do not prevent (for no human persuasion or art can help), but to be their own butchers, and execute themselves (432).

The introduction of the Divine Physician at this point is simultaneously promising and troubling, promising because of the final consolation the reader may at least (and at last) hope to be given, troubling because it occurs in a parenthesis, and then in a parenthesis that treats the possibility rather negatively. *"If* that heavenly Physician . . . do not prevent. . . ."* Logically, in relation to the "if" clause, "do not prevent" should be read as a positive wish—may he prevent—but the force of the negative operates independently of the larger context—he will *not* prevent—especially since the sentence ends so badly. Even so, the mere suggestion (however hypothetical) of an imminent savior, in combination with occasional references to biblical figures, is enough to keep alive our anticipation of a consoling turn; that is, until the biblical perspective we have been waiting for is brought in to support the wrong position. In rapid succession, the speaker recalls the examples of Samson, Saul, Jonas, and Razis, all of whom are celebrated in the Church for killing themselves. Even Augustine and Jerome "vindicateth the same," and Ambrose "commendeth Pelagia for so doing (436)." As a result, the conviction grows that the harshness of Burton's vision will not be mitigated and the consolation of orthodox Christianity will once again be withheld. And then, suddenly, when we least expect it and have ceased to hope for it, on the last page, in the final paragraph, it comes, in the middle of a sentence:

Calenus and his Indians hated of old to die a natural death:
the Circumcellions and Donatists, loathing life, compelled
others to make them away, with many such: but these are
false and pagan positions, profane Stoical paradoxes, wicked
examples; it boots not what heathen philosophers determine in this kind, they are impious, abominable, and upon
a wrong ground. "No evil is to be done that good may come
of it"; *reclamat Christus, reclamat Scriptura* [Christ and
Scripture cry out against it], God and all good men are
against it. He that stabs another can kill his body; but he
that stabs himself kills his own soul. *Male meretur, qui dat
mendico quod edat; nam et illud quod dat, perit; et illi
producit vitam ad miseriam:* he that gives a beggar an alms
(as that comical poet said) doth ill, because he doth but
prolong his miseries. But Lactantius, *lib. 6, cap. 7, de
vero cultu,* calls it a detestable opinion, and fully confutes
it, *lib. 3 de sap. cap. 18,* and St. Austin, *Ep. 52 ad Mace-
donium, cap. 61, ad Dulcitium Tribunum;* so doth Hierome
to Marcella of Blaesilla's death, *Non recipio tales animas,*
etc., he calls such men *martyres stultae philosophiae* [the
victims of a stupid philosophy]; so doth Cyprian, *de du-
plici martyrio: Si qui sic moriantur, aut infirmitas, aut
ambitio, aut dementia cogit eos* [those who so die are
driven to it by illness or ambition or madness]; 'tis mere
madness so to do, *furor est ne moriare mori* ['tis mad for
fear of death to kill oneself] (438).

This has all the force and authority we could have wished, but
Burton will not let us rest in it; there is always one more turn to
his screw. "This only let me add," he begins mildly, and then, as
has happened so many times before, the small qualification turns
out to be so large that it becomes the entire argument:

> This only let me add, that in some cases those hard censures
> of such as offer violence to their own persons, or in some
> desperate fit to others, which sometimes they do, by stab-
> bing, slashing, etc., are to be mitigated, as in such as are
> mad, beside themselves for the time, or found to have been

> long melancholy, and that in extremity; they know not
> what they do, deprived of reason, judgement, all, as a ship
> that is void of a pilot must needs impinge upon the next
> rock of sands, and suffer shipwreck (439).

Since the category "such as are mad" includes everyone, "some
cases" becomes all cases and the Christian objections to making
away with oneself seem less conclusive than they did only a
moment ago. We end with a story which suggests that suicide is
not only justified, but necessary:

> P. Forestus hath a story of two melancholy brethren that
> made away themselves, and for so foul a fact were accord-
> ingly censured to be infamously buried, as in such cases
> they use, to terrify others, as it did the Milesian virgins of
> old; but upon farther examination of their misery and
> madness, the censure was revoked, and they were solemnly
> interred, as Saul was by David (439).

This incident is, in some ways, a small model of the volume it
concludes. A judgment is made on the basis of an abstraction,
which itself depends on a series of assumptions about the order
and purpose of life; but upon further examination, that is, when
the circumstances are laid open and anatomized, the case is seen
to be less clear than had been thought and the assumptions become
questionable.[14] When Burton rounds off this little narrative by
recalling the compassion David displayed for the suicide of Saul,
he is (audaciously) close to citing Christ, the flower of the house
of David, as one who would suspend the canon against self-slaugh-
ter; and in the next sentence he openly speculates as to whether
man's judgment may be harsher than God's: "Thus of their goods
and bodies we can dispose; but what shall become of their souls,
God alone can tell; His mercy may come . . . betwixt the bridge
and the brook, the knife and the throat."

In the synopsis, the headings that rule this section read,
"Whether it be lawful, in this case of melancholy, for a man to
offer violence to himself," and "How a melancholy or mad man,
offering violence to himself, is to be censured"; but in the end,
the criterion of lawfulness seems almost irrelevant; what really

[14] One might profitably compare this with Donne's treatment in *Biathanatos*.

matters is every man's confrontation with a world whose sickness and irrationality mirrors his own, and in that context, the only response is not the rule of law, but the fellow feeling of compassion. The whole question of suicide is finally taken away from the jurisdictions of law and religion and brought right back to where it always belonged, to you ("Thou thyself art the subject of my discourse") *"Quod cuiquam contigit, cuivis potest.* Who knows how he may be tempted? It is his case, it may be thine." Given the premises of Burton's book and the evidence marshaled in it, it *is* thine, and mine, and everyone else's, and therefore judgments are presumptuous, and hope a deception: "We ought not to be so rash and rigorous in our censures as some are; charity will judge and hope the best; God be merciful unto us all (439)!" In the context of all that has gone before, those last words—"God be merciful unto us all"—are less a prayer than a cry of desperation. One does not hear in them any conviction that God *will* be merciful; rather, one hears a note that has been sounded before in the preface, at one of those many points at which this amazing treatise "concludes":

> To conclude, this being granted, that all the world is melancholy, or mad, dotes, and every member of it, I have ended my task, and sufficiently illustrated that which I took upon me to demonstrate at first. At this present I have no more to say. *His sanam mentem Democritus,* I can but wish myself and them a good physician, and all of us a better mind (120).

In other words, I can but wish us an impossibility. The only cure for the malady Burton anatomizes is a better mind, supposedly to be given us by a "good physician," but a "good physician" who never appears in any efficacious form on this particular stage. A better mind is exactly what we do need, but that promise is one that Burton does not make, even as a rhetorical gesture. Instead, he resigns himself and us to a greater power, but a power in whom he himself has little faith, if the thrust of his own work is any evidence. Within the confines of the universe he so carefully (and yet confusedly) delineates, our universe for all intents and purposes, "there is no remedy."

BE NOT IDLE

This remains true even in the concluding subsection of the *Anatomy*, Partition III, Section 4, Member 2, Subsection 6, *Cure of Despair by Physic, Good Counsel, Comforts, etc.* (III, 408). The remedies for despair are well known; those who are afflicted with this disease of the mind should follow the "special rules" of Culmannus: "First to acknowledge all help come from God. 2. That the cause of their present misery is sin. 3. To repent and be heartily sorry for their sins. 4. To pray earnestly to God they may be eased. 5. To expect and implore the prayers of the Church, and good men's advice. 6. Physic. 7. To commend themselves to God and rely upon His mercy (III, 410)." No sooner are these rules given, however, than their efficacy, in the present context, is questioned: "But forasmuch as most men in this malady are spiritually sick, void of reason almost, overborne by their miseries and too deep an apprehension of their sins, they cannot apply themselves to good counsel pray, believe, repent." The structure of the subsection follows this pattern, alternating words of consolation or "A comfortable speech of St. Austin (414)" with the imagined response of those who are actually suffering:

> Yea, but thou urgest again, I have little comfort of this which is said, it concerns me not . . . 'tis to no purpose for me to repent, and to do worse then ever I did before (III, 412).
>     'Tis true indeed, and all-sufficient this, they do confess, if they could repent; but they are obdurate they have cauterized consciences, they are in a reprobate sense, they cannot think a good thought, they cannot hope for grace, pray, believe, repent, or be sorry for their sins (III, 414).
>     All this is true, thou repliest, but yet it concerns not thee, 'tis verified in ordinary offenders, in common sins, but thine are of an higher strain. . . . Thou art worse than a pagan, infidel, Jew, or Turk. . . . Thou hast given thy soul to the devil (III, 416).
>     Yea, that's the main matter, how shall I believe, or dis-

cern my security from carnal presumption? my faith is
weak and faint, I want those signs and fruits of sanctifica-
tion (III, 421).

Thou exceptest. These [Lazarus and Abraham] were
chief men, divine spirits, *Deo cari,* beloved of God, especially respected; but I am a contemptible and forlorn
wretch, forsaken of God, and left to the merciless fury of
evil spirits (III, 427).

In reply to these "wretched" (whose complaints are validated in
the shift from indirect—"thou repliest"—to direct discourse—
"thou art worse than a pagan") Burton can only rehearse and
rerehearse the litany of Christian consolation, but with an important, and debilitating, qualification:

'Tis a grievous case this, I do yield, and yet not to be de-
spaired . . . thou *mayst* be called at length (III, 414).

Besides, they must know this, all so molested and dis-
tempered, that although these be most execrable and grievous sins, they are pardonable yet, through God's mercy and
goodness they *may* be forgiven (III, 418).

Though these signs be languishing in thee, and not
seated in thine heart, thou must not therefore be dejected
or terrified. . . . Thou *mayst* in the Lord's good time be
converted . . . if not yet called, pray thou *mayst* be or at
least wish and desire thou *mayst* be (III, 421).

How often shall I say it? thou *mayst* perform all these
duties, Christian offices, and be restored in good time (III,
427) (Emphases all mine).

These "mays" admit the very possibility that is the source of all
despairing thoughts (that we may not, in fact, repent, confess, and
be restored) and by alternating them with the rules of general consolation, Burton weakens the personal application of the scriptural
promise, reinforcing rather than mitigating the symptoms of the
disease he is supposedly curing. Indeed, the scriptural promise is
itself the cause of these symptoms. After advising his anonymous
interlocutor (and the reader) to follow David's advice in Psalm 1,
"Meditate on his law day and night," Burton turns on his au-

thority (as he has so many times before) and exclaims: "Yea, but this meditation is that mars all, and mistaken makes many men far worse, misconceiving all they read or hear, to their own overthrow; the more they search and read Scriptures, or divine treatises, the more they puzzle themselves, as a bird in a net, the more they are entangled, and precipitated into this preposterous gulf (419)." "Think on God's word," say Donne, Herbert, Bunyan, Milton, "and be saved"; "think on God's word," says Burton, "and be *mad*."

What is to be done, then, if the Word that was to be our cure is instead our affliction? Burton offers a succession of answers to this question. First he considers (and holds out as a bait) "that plausible doctrine of universal grace, which many Fathers, our late Lutherans and modern papists do still maintain that we have free will of ourselves, and that grace is common to all that will believe (421)"; but for all its plausibility and attractions (attractions that we are made to feel) this doctrine must at last be dismissed, because "we teach otherwise (423)." Next he turns to a number of popular remedies—"certain amulets, herbs, and precious stones (429)," "Fires to be made in rooms where spirits haunt (430)," "have the party affected wink (430)," "shoot a pistol at them (430)"—but these are obviously what Burton in the end calls them, "counterfeit . . . , to no purpose, . . . fopperies and fictions (431)." "Last of all" we hear the only advice that makes Burtonian sense:

> Last of all: If the party affected shall certainly know this malady to have proceeded from too much fasting, meditation, precise life, contemplation of God's judgements. . . . Let him read no more such tracts or subjects, hear no more such fearful tones, avoid such companies. . . . Only take this for a corollary and conclusion, as thou tenderest thine own welfare in this and all other melancholy, thy good health of body and mind, observe this short precept, give not way to solitariness and idleness. "Be not solitary, be not idle (III, 431–432)."

"Be not solitary, be not idle," or, in other words, don't think about it, keep your mind off it, keep your mind moving, *be ye distracted*. This is finally the "word" that replaces God's word as the cure (if it be cure) of melancholy, and it returns us to the beginning of this section where God and his word are specified as the very causes of melancholy:

> Before I can come to treat of these several errors and ob-
> liquities, their cause, symptoms, affections, etc., I must say
> something necessarily of the object of this love, God Him-
> self, what this love is, how it allureth, whence it proceeds,
> and (which is the cause of all our miseries) how we mis-
> take, wander and swerve from it (III, 313).

Religious melancholy is a species of love melancholy (311), and in this sentence it is treated as a perversion of a laudable impulse. It is only the "mistakes" in this kind that cause all our misery. What follows will be something less than a surprise to anyone who has come this far in the *Anatomy*. The healthy norm from which the disease is a deviation never appears, while the examples of those who "wander and swerve from it" increase and multiply. For every reference to the practitioners of a "true religion" where "the true God is truly worshipped (III, 320)," there are ten pages documenting the ubiquity of idolatry and super-stition:

> Now for the extent, as I say, the world itself is the subject
> of it . . . all times have been misaffected, past, present,
> "There is not one that doth good, no not one, from the
> prophet to the priest," etc. (III, 321).
>
> In all ages what a small portion hath the true Church
> ever been! . . . The patriarchs and their families, the Is-
> raelites, a handful in respect, Christ and his apostles, and
> not all of them, neither. Into what straits hath it been com-
> pinged, a little flock! how hath superstition on the other
> side dilated herself, error, ignorance, barbarism, folly, mad-
> ness. . . . Philosophers, dynasts, monarchs, all were in-
> volved and overshadowed in this mist, in more than Cim-
> merian darkness (III, 322).
>
> A fifth part of the world, and hardly that, now profess-
> eth Christ, but so inlarded and interlaced with several su-

perstitions, that there is scarce a sound part to be found
(III, 323).

What religion is, and of what parts it doth consist,
every catechism will tell you, what symptoms it hath, and
what effects it produceth: but for their superstitions, no
tongue can tell them, no pen express, they are so many
(III, 347).

We have myriads of examples in this kind . . . and
therefore not without good cause, *intolerabilem perturba-
tionem,* Seneca calls it, as well he might, an intolerable
perturbation, that causeth such dire events, folly, madness,
sickness, despair, death of body and soul, and hell itself
(III, 375).

In the course of this long section with its "myriads of examples,"
the "properly" religious man becomes a will-o'-the-wisp; like the
"sane" and "wise" man who never appears in the preface (or
like the "true friend" in Bacon's essay), he is a chimerical member of an empty category. The catechism may imply his reality,
but in the reality of Burton's pages, taken from life, he is nowhere to be found.

In time, the familiar question obtrudes itself—what is the
remedy?—and the answer is given and dismissed in the same
sentence: "To purge the world of idolatry and superstition will
require some monster-taming Hercules, a divine Aesculapius, or
Christ Himself to come in his own person, to reign a thousand
years on earth before the end as the millenaries will have Him
(III, 375)." The unfolding clauses carry us in successive and
graduated stages from promise to promise; from the suggestiveness of Hercules, to the charged metaphor of the Divine Physician, to the apparent imminence of Christ's second coming; but
scarcely is this ultimate promise proffered before it is taken away,
and returned, discredited, to the "millenaries" who are foolish
(mad) enough to believe in it. This is the opening sentence of a
subsection entitled *Cure of Religious Melancholy,* and the blast-
ing of its facile hopes (and therefore of the hopes of the section
it introduces) hearkens back to the preface and an earlier call
for a Hercules who "should reform what is amiss (I, 96)." De-

mocritus's conclusion there is the conclusion urged on us here: "These are vain, absurd, ridiculous wishes not to be hoped . . . there is no remedy, it may not be redressed . . . it is a thing so difficult, and far beyond Hercules' labours to perform (I, 97)." Hercules will not appear to clean our Augean stables. Christ will not come to reign a thousand years. We are alone, with only ourselves to rely on, and those selves mad and melancholy. If there were a remedy, a cure, it would have to be nothing less than the fulfillment of the wish the speaker expresses when we first meet him, and again when he prepares to exit from our stage:

> I have no more to say. *His sanam mentem Democritus,* I can only wish myself and them a good physician, and all of us a better mind (I, 120).
> What shall we wish them, but *sanam mentem* and a good physician (III, 324).

The good physician has been invoked and implored, but there is little evidence that he has heard. And a better mind is a gift beyond Burton's power to confer. In its place he can only offer an experience that enables us, for a time, to follow the advice he tenders in the closing paragraph—"Be not solitary, be not idle." As Miss Webber has observed, Burton "never leaves the reader alone (100)." Nor does he leave us idle. He pushes us, prods us, leads us on, trips us up, laughs at us, laughs with us, makes us laugh at him. *He keeps us busy.* "I write of melancholy, by being busy to avoid melancholy (I, 20)." By busily reading of melancholy we may avoid it too. If Burton cannot give us a better mind, he can perhaps give us a mind not too much involved with its own pain. *The Anatomy of Melancholy,* in all of its distracting confusion, is finally something of a mercy, and it is the only mercy to be found within its confines.

A better mind is exactly what Herbert, Milton, Donne, Bacon, Bunyan, Plato, and Augustine labor to give us through the experience of their prose and poetry, for they are good physicians. I have included Burton in this volume partly because he has so much in common with these men and is, at the same time, so markedly different. Like Bacon, Burton is concerned with the disparity between a prescriptive moralism and the intractable reality of everyday life, and to some extent his *Anatomy,* as much as Bacon's *Essays,* impresses upon us the unavailability of easy answers. Like Herbert, he simultaneously weaves himself into the sense and disappears finally into the fabric he has woven; when he declares that this is a book written by nobody, we believe him, for very much the same reasons we believe Herbert when he signs someone else's name to his poems. Like Donne, he promises to explain and clarify, but his explanations are circular and his clarifications confusing; and his categories are no firmer than the distinctions Donne fails to maintain between joy and fear, up and down, I and God. Like both Bunyan and Milton, he unbuilds the superstructure of his great work until finally it stands for a failure to effect a declared intention; the apparatus of the *Anatomy* is finally no more controlling and determining than the book and chapter divisions of *The Reason of Church Government* or the spatial continuum of *The Pilgrim's Progress.* Like all of these, Burton is continually calling attention to what his art is *not* doing; and what his art is not doing is making sense of things. That is, like Herbert, Milton, Bunyan, Bacon, and Donne, Burton does not divide the universe into discrete and manageable entities whose configurations and values correspond to our human idea of the way things should be, although he often promises, as do the others, to do just that.

In addition to these shared concerns and motives, Burton and his seventeenth-century brethren have recourse to a common pool of stylistic and rhetorical devices, the disappointment of deliberately primed expectations, the conspicuous breakdown of discursive forms—sentences, paragraphs, chapters, whole structures— syntactical ambiguities that subvert an assertion even as it is made, the pursuing of lines of argument to tautological conclusions, and so on. And yet for all of these similarities, the experience of Burton's prose is not at all like the experiences we have described in the earlier chapters of this study. The difference is to be located in something that is missing in Burton, something so crucial that its absence transforms the meaning and even the value of all that he shares with the others. In the prose of Bunyan, Donne, Bacon, and Milton, and in the poetry of Herbert, the undermining of discursive forms and the related devaluation of rational thought is but one half of a movement which is completed only when the availability of something better is affirmed. That affirmation is withheld in the *Anatomy,* and as a result the negativity of the work's rhetorical thrust is never redeemed. It is as if the movement of Donne's *Devotions* did not include the reconciling prayer, and reader and protagonist alike were trapped in the cycle of meditation and expostulation; or as if the cyclic pattern traced out by Christian's errors in *The Pilgrim's Progress* did not continually intersect with a pattern of heavenly intervention; or as if the emptiness of ratiocinative content in *The Reason of Church Government* were not more than balanced by the force of Milton's declared faith; or as if the conviction of personal weakness in Herbert's poetry were not transformed into strength by his realization that "all things are more ours for their being his"; or as if Bacon did not conduct his debunking experiments within a framework that suggested at least the possibility of finding replacements for the moral abstractions his method rejected. In short, while the *Anatomy* more overtly than the other works we have examined undermines the reader's ability to make judgments and determine value, the only consolation it offers is the unhelpful assertion that we are all in the same boat.[15] The experience of Burton's prose may involve the absorption of our personal weaknesses into some-

---

[15] This is precisely the point of the *Consolatory Digression* in Partition II, where the reader is advised to "comfort thyself with other men's misfortunes (II, 131)." To the wretch who complains of his situation, Burton replies that the case of others is just as bad or even worse. Are you poor? And do you believe that wealth would make you happy? "Many rich men . . . that lie on down beds, with delicacies pampered every day, in their well furnished houses, live at less heart's ease, with more anguish, more bodily pain, and through their intemperance more bitter hours, than many a poor prisoner or galley slave (II, 171)." Note that the prisoner or galley slave is not told that he suffers no pain or experiences no anguish, but that those who seem better off than he is are not. As always, Burton's arguments level *downward,* putting everyone on an equally miserable footing, and as a result, happiness becomes, like non-melancholic, an empty category, an illusion. Indeed, adversity is finally preferred to prosperity, because it offers less scope to immoderate folly and precludes disappointment. The preference, however, is for the lesser of two evils—"both bad . . . the one miserably happy, the other happily miserable (II, 172)"—and Burton's conclusion is the same here as elsewhere: "There is no remedy . . . kings and princes, wise, grave, prudent, holy good men, divine, all are . . . served alike (II, 201)."

thing larger, but that something larger is merely a cosmic version of what has supposedly been transcended.

I have emphasized this difference within similarity because I wish to counter an impression the methodology of this study may have unavoidably conveyed, the impression that there is a fixed relationship between the presence of certain rhetorical and stylistic devices and either intention or meaning. What the *Anatomy* shows is that the same descriptively observable techniques, in the service of different visions, may mean differently, and that only the analysis in time of the total reading experience will prevent the drawing of premature and facile conclusions.

Sir Thomas Browne's *Religio Medici* is a case in point, one even more interesting than the *Anatomy* because it shares nearly everything with the works from which it must finally be differentiated.

 VII

# The Bad Physician: The Case of
# Sir Thomas Browne

### I AM AVERSE FROM NOTHING

The *Religio Medici* is the most consistent and overt celebration of the vision whose literary effects we have been examining. Browne's commitment to the devaluing of rational thought and the subsequent exaltation of knowledge through faith is evident on every page, and nowhere so felicitously as in this most famous of passages:

> I love to lose myself in a mystery, to pursue my reason to
> an *O altitudo!* 'Tis my solitary recreation to pose my ap-
> prehension with those involved aenigmas and riddles of the
> Trinity, with Incarnation and Resurrection. I can answer
> all the objections of Satan and my rebellious reason with
> that odde resolution I learned of *Tertullian, Certum est,*
> *quia impossibile est* (I, 9).[1]

This will almost serve as a program for what happens to the reader in the *Religio;* his reason is exercised (and teased) to the point where its insufficiency becomes self-evident, and ratiocination gives way to faith professing assertion; and in the process, of course, the machinery of reason—linguistic, logical, rhetorical —becomes the vehicle of its own abandonment:

[1] The text is that prepared by Vittoria Sanna as printed in Vol. I of *The Works of Sir Thomas Browne,* ed. Geoffrey Keynes (Chicago, 1964).

That there is but one world, is a conclusion of faith. *Aristotle* with all his Philosophy hath not beene able to prove it, and as weakely that the world was eternall; that dispute much troubled the pennes of the antient Philosophers [who saw no further than the first matter]; but *Moses* [hath] decided that question, and all is salved with the new terme of a creation, that is, a production of something out of nothing; and what is that? Whatsoever is opposite to something or more exactly, that which is truely contrary unto God: for he onely is, all others have an existence with dependency and are something but by a distinction; and herein is Divinity conformant unto Philosophy, and generation not onely founded on contrarieties, but also creation; God being all things is contrary unto nothing out of which were made all things, and so nothing became something, and *Omneity* informed *Nullity* into an essence (I, 35).

This passage (which might have been taken from one of Donne's sermons) turns on the exploitation of the slight dissonance created by the juxtaposition of "conclusion" and "faith." We are told at once that the proposition "there is but one world" is incapable of rational verification, but the point is really made only when our tendency to rationalize everything is given full and self-defeating play.

Browne's strategy is simple, even obvious, but nonetheless effective. The form of his sentences, in conjunction with a series of prominently displayed logical connectives—"that is," "whatsoever," "more exactly," "for," "and herein," "and so"—suggests that the reader is experiencing a progressive clarification of the word and concept "creation" ("and what is that?"). But each attempt at redefinition and refining serves largely to introduce new problems, both linguistic and logical, and there is a growing disparity between the triumphant march of the surface rhetoric (toward a point of QED) and the reader's deepening confusion. "And what is that?" asks Browne obligingly, as if to acknowledge the difficulty of comprehending "a production of something out of nothing"; but his answer—"Whatsoever is opposite to something"—is unhelpfully tautologous, and its elaboration—"that which is truely contrary unto God"—returns us in a circle to the original question, "and what is *that?*"

At this point, the simple declarative "for he onely is" will be welcomed with relief, if only because it is at least intelligible; but it also implies the futility of the process it interrupts: for if the existence of anything other than God can be affirmed only by a linguistic and perceptual distortion, "are something but by a distinction," the attempt to locate or specify "that which is truely contrary unto God" is prima facie absurd. Nevertheless, we go on, carried forward by the current of the prose into a flood of closely packed quasi-philosophical terms—"Divinity," "conformant," "Philosophy," "generation," "contrarieties," "creation"—which only increases the confusion of the preceding sentences. The reader is exactly where he was at the beginning of the sequence, still waiting for the clarification he has so often been promised.

And it seems for a moment that his patience is to be rewarded: "God, being all things, is contrary unto nothing." One can make sense of this by decompounding "nothing" into "no thing": since God is the essence of all things, there exists no thing which is contrary unto him. If the reasoning is circular, it is at least comprehensible. But even this small comfort is taken away, when the succeeding clause requires that we recombine "no" and "thing" and confer on the compound abstraction the status of a substance "out of which were made all things." The mind, literally, boggles. And before there is time to adjust, Browne proceeds triumphantly to his grandly obfuscating conclusion: "and so nothing became something, and *Omneity* informed *Nullity* into an essence."

The only possible response to this bastard scholasticism is laughter, even though the joke is on the reader who has been led to expect something more portable. (There may even be a secret joke in the anagram formed by the first letters of *Omneity, Nullity,* and essence.) The point, however, is a serious one, and in the next sentence it is made unambiguously, and with a force that is directly attributable to our experience of the preceding section: "The whole creation is a mystery (I, 36)." The effect is not unlike that achieved in Herbert's "Even-Song" when the drawing together of "day" and "night" is followed immediately by the declaration "My God, thou art all love."

This passage is typical of what one finds on every page of the *Religio Medici*. In section 12 of Part I, the rational understanding is broken on the question of whether or not miracles have ceased:

> THAT Miracles are ceased, I can neither prove, nor absolutely deny, much lesse define the time and period of their cessation; that they survived Christ, is manifest upon record of Scripture; that they outlived the Apostles also, and were revived at the conversion of Nations, many yeares after, we cannot deny, if wee shall not question those Writers whose testimonies wee doe not controvert, in points that make for our owne opinions; therefore that may have some truth in it that is reported of the Jesuites and their Miracles in the Indies, I could wish it were true, or had any other testimony then their owne Pennes (I, 27):

While in section 35 the prose pulls the reader forward in the direction of a point of clarity that is never reached, here the reader is always looking backward, in the direction of a point of clarity from which the movement of the prose is taking him away. The basic pattern is established in the opening sentence and then simply repeated. For the moment it takes to read the first clause, the cessation of miracles is assumed to be a fact (in constructions of this type "That" is usually taken to mean "the fact that"); but its status becomes less clear and the reader less sure of his ground as the sentence continues. Were the cessation of miracles simply denied, that denial itself would serve as a new point of reference; but Browne forestalls certainty in any direction. A word like "absolutely" ("nor absolutely deny") has no other function but to suggest, misleadingly, that it is only a question of a conclusive piece of information; if we were only in possession of that, a documented denial would readily follow. But at the end of the sentence, the phrase "of their cessation" indirectly revives the possibility that miracles have indeed ceased. The reader moves first toward one and then the other of the opposing alternatives, and, as he does, the beacon of that first clause brightens and dims.

(One recalls our similar experience of "yonder shining light" in *The Pilgrim's Progress*.)

Once bitten, twice shy. When the next member begins, "that they survived Christ, is," the reader expects that Browne will pull the rug out from under him again, but instead he finds "is manifest upon record of Scripture." And when the same construction is put to an innocent use a second and a third time—"that they out-lived the Apostles also and [that they] were revived at the conversion of Nations . . . we cannot deny"—the case for the survival of miracles is apparently confirmed. It is then, when the reader is newly vulnerable, that Browne adds the qualifying "if wee shall not question those Writers," and retroactively discredits the evidence he has been marshaling. In a short space "testimonies" become "opinions" and then "reports," as the avenues of uncertainty multiply. There may be some truth to what the Jesuits say of their miracles in the Indies, but then again there may not be. The more information the reader is given, the less inclined he is to draw any conclusions from it. Browne builds his argument with one hand, while with the other he impugns the credibility of his sources, leaving the reader where Burton so often leaves him, poised uneasily between two equally unauthorized authorities.

The question of record is finally settled by leaving it behind. Why wonder about the cessation of miracles, in the narrow sense of extraordinary physical occurrences, when the ordinary course of nature is a daily miracle? "For this is also a miracle, not only to produce effects against or above Nature, but before Nature; and to create Nature, as great a miracle, as to contradict or transcend her." One need only affirm the ability of God to "do all things," even the working of contradictions, "for, strictly, his power is [but] the same with his will, and they both, with all the rest, doe make but one God." In its funnel-like rush toward the phrase "one God," this concluding sentence recapitulates the movement of the entire section, from the posing of a problem in temporal and spatial terms to its (literal) resolution by rising above those terms ("they," "both," "rest") and the divided vision which informs them. ("We say amisse/This or that is/Thy word

is all, if we could spell.") In short, an "O altitudo," in the course
of which the rational intellect is allowed to play itself out before
rushing to embrace what Browne holds to be the "fundamental
point of Religion, the Unity of God (I, 26)."

This is the pattern, not only of section 27, but of every section in the *Religio*. Browne's "O altitudos" always leave us in
rapt contemplation of a world unified by God's informing presence, a world in which other things are "but by a distinction."
And always we are brought to this insight by the vocabulary of
distinguishing (that is, the vocabulary of reasoning), which is
made to subvert its customary ends and affirm against itself. It
is a process, to use Browne's felicitous phrase, of "distinguishing
*into* (I, 53)," although for a time it wears the livery of the more
usual "distinguishing *from*."

In the early sections, for example, Browne makes a great show
of distinguishing himself from other men by recalling his peculiar
habits, opinions, and beliefs; but so generous and assimilative is
his nature, that he is finally distinguishable only by a distinction-
effacing tolerance. I style myself, he declares in section 1, "a Christian." This is, he admits, a "Name . . . too general . . . there
being a Geography of Religions as well as [of] Lands, and every
Clime distinguished not onely by their Laws and limits, but circumscribed by their Doctrines and Rules of Faith (I, 2)." The
verbs of this long dependent clause ("distinguished," "circumscribed") encourage us to anticipate the further division of the
class "Christian"; while the nouns ("Lands," "Clime," "Laws,"
"Doctrines," "Rules") project categories which will presumably
form the basis of a precisely differentiating analysis of Browne's
faith. In other words, the prose moves steadily away from the general name, and toward the more specific name that we expect to
hear when Browne declares, "To be particular, I am. . . ." But
the name is withheld, and in its place we are given a pointedly
nonexclusive list of those to whom it would have applied:

> To be particular, I am of that reformed new-cast Religion,
> wherein I dislike nothing but the name; of the same be-
> liefe [which] our Saviour taught, the Apostles dissemi-
> nated, the Fathers authorised, and the Martyrs confirmed;

but by the sinister ends of Princes, the ambition & avarice of Prelates, and the fatall corruption of times, so decaied, impaired, and fallen from its native beauty, that it required the carefull and charitable hand of these times to restore it to its primitive integrity.

The designation "Reformed new-cast" is immediately contradicted by the pedigree that follows. Browne's faith is neither "new-cast" nor "particular," since it includes everyone, past and present, who subscribes to "the same belief [which] our Saviour taught." In a word, or a name, it is the faith of a Christian. From the general name, the ever-narrowing focus of Browne's prose has brought us to—the general name. Only the Papists, it would seem, will be denied its sanction, but they, too, are brought under the protection of Browne's beneficent umbrella. "There is," after all, "between us one common name . . . we being all Christians." The end of section 3 finds Browne admitting his attendance at Roman rites and approving the ceremonies of Greek and African churches, "whereof the wiser zeales doe make a Christian use."

So much, then, for the promise of distinguishing and particularizing with which this sequence began. Its renewal in the opening sentence of section 5 is precisely and self-consciously ambiguous: "But to difference myself neerer . . ." The plain sense of this requires that for "neerer" we read "more precisely"; but the more usual reading of "closer" or "less far away" is equally available, and in conjunction with the infinitive "to difference," it points to the paradoxical movement of the preceding pages: a differencing which brings together, a distinguishing *into*. Rather than identifying (that is, distinguishing) himself, Browne finally surrenders his identity in an excess of fellowship: "I could never divide my selfe from any man (I, 6)." In subsequent sections, he differences himself nearer to "Hereticks" ("they hold, as we do, there is but one God"), Jews ("It is the promise of Christ to make us all one Flock"), and the practitioners of vice ("for contraries . . . are yet the life of one another"). The tenor of Browne's belief, "This general and indifferent temper of mine (II, 2)" is a tolerance so large that it ends in the happy loss of his individuality. "In brief, I am averse from nothing (II, 1)."

In this, of course, Browne imitates his God, who is averse from nothing because out of him were made all things, "which are something but by a distinction." It is this distinction, in all of its individuations, that is transcended on every page of the *Religio Medici*. The "O altitudos" to which the prose repeatedly rises are achieved at the expense of the discretely segmented world in terms of which we validate our separate existences. This involves the denial not only of the differences between persons and nations and sects, but of the more abstract distinctions that mislead us into differentiating qualitatively between aspects of God's perfect whole. One should not, for example, call some things beautiful and others ugly:

> I hold there is a general beauty in [all] the works of God, and therefore no deformity in any kind or species of creature whatsoever: I cannot tell by what Logick we call a Toad, a Beare, or an Elephant, ugly; they being created in those outward shapes and figures which best expresse the actions of their inward formes; and having past [with approbation] that generall visitation of God, who saw that all that he had made was good, that is, conformable to his will, which abhors deformity, and is the rule of order and beauty. There is [therefore] no deformity but in monstrosity, wherein notwithstanding there is a kind of beauty, Nature so ingeniously contriving those irregular parts, as they become sometimes more remarkable than the principall Fabrick. To speake yet more narrowly, there was never anything ugly, or mis-shapen, but the Chaos; wherein not withstanding, to speake strictly, there was no deformity, because no forme; nor was it yet impregnate by the voyce of God: Now nature is not at variance with art, nor art with nature; they being both the servants of his providence: Art is the perfection of Nature: Were the world now as it was the sixt day, there were yet a Chaos: Nature hath made one world, and Art another. In briefe, all things are artificiall, for Nature is the Art of God (I, 16).

In this passage, the vocabulary of aesthetic discrimination is systematically abused, until it becomes impossible to take it or its assumptions seriously. Repeatedly, the reader is invited to assume a posture of judgment—against monstrosity, deformity, chaos—only to be met with a qualification ("wherein not withstanding") that delimits the area within which the standards of judgment apply; finally, that area is narrowed to nothing because it has been widened to include everything. That is, by discrediting the "logick" of ugliness, Browne takes away the *distinguishing* force of "beauty," which becomes an indiscriminate term for anything "impregnate by the voyce of God," that is, for everything. In this context, the phrases "to speake yet more narrowly" and "to speake strictly" are pointedly self-derisive; for their usual reference is to the action of dividing and specifying, while here they find themselves in the service of a cosmic reconciliation.

This is the basis of James Winney's criticism of Browne's prose:

> In fact he is incapable of speaking strictly because . . . he has neglected to define his terms. If there was no deformity in Chaos "because no form," then Chaos was neither ugly nor misshapen, and Browne's demonstration falls to the ground. . . . Browne has deliberately confused the sense of words, making the concept "monstrous" include "beautiful" as an implicit idea: a piece of verbal juggling which has no reference to the reality denoted by these terms. . . . Browne's thought is at the mercy of his vocabulary.[2]

I would argue, rather, that Browne does in fact define his terms, but that he defines them out of existence, and that, as a result, his "thought," by which I take Winney to mean his systematic thinking, disqualifies itself as a vehicle for the questions it pretends to consider. The sense of his words *is* confused, not however because he is confused, but because the reality to which they normally have reference and by virtue of which they have meaning is being left behind for the more inclusive reality that is revealed (in two senses) in the phrase "impregnate by the voyce of God." This demonstration is *meant* to fall to the ground and to carry with it the divisive vision it assumes and perpetuates.

Indeed, whenever Browne speaks "more narrowly" or "like a

[2] *Religio Medici,* ed. James Winney (Cambridge, 1963), pp. xxvii–xxviii.

philosopher," it is to preside over the self-destruction of the terms and concepts that comprise rational philosophic discourse. At one point he speaks like an astronomer and it is the vocabulary of distance and place that is deprived of meaning:

> The earth is a point not onely in respect of the heavens above us, but of that heavenly and celestiall part within us: that masse of flesh that circumscribes me, limits not my mind: that surface that tells the heavens it hath an end, cannot perswade me I have any; I take my circle to be above three hundred and sixty; though the number of the Arke do measure my body, it comprehendeth not my minde: whilst I study to finde how I am a Microcosme or little world, I finde my selfe something more than the great (II, 11).

As the first part of this sentence unfolds, it seems to confirm our everyday sense of a world where objects occupy discrete places at measurable distances from one another. In fact, the simple act of reading the sentence involves us inescapably in arranging its noun-objects in a pattern of spatial relationships: the earth is seen (literally) as a large mass above which hangs the even larger mass of the heavens and upon which stand the dwarfed figures of Browne and his audience ("us"). Our natural tendency to stabilize these relationships will be strengthened by the "not onely . . . but" construction which exerts a confining and organizing pressure both on the words within it and the mind that is negotiating it. It is, in short, a directing construction and it directs us to continue in a way of thinking that is natural and self-satisfying.

All this is changed by a single word, "within." Ostensibly "within" completes the argument of the first clause, but it is a spatial indicator of a very different kind from "above," with which it is directly linked by the cadences of the sentence. Suddenly, the objects that had been fixed in their respective positions become interpenetrable, and the largest of them is discovered to reside "within" the smallest. The language of spatial configuration has been retained, but in a context—of inner space—that makes nonsense of it, and of the proportional statement we have half formulated: as we are to the earth, so is the earth to the heavens. Once again the demonstration (the syntax is itself a form of demonstrative argument) falls to the ground along with the superstructure of assumptions it implies.

In the members that follow, this sequence is repeated. Again and again, the vocabulary of measurement and limit presses in on us, and again and again we are released as that same vocabulary consumes itself in paradox and contradiction. The constricting force of "masse," "flesh," "circumscribes," and "limits" is countered and dispersed by a simple "not." The image of a circle is invoked, only to be blurred when we are told that it is "above three hundred and sixty." The precise measurements of the ark are declared irrelevant to the comprehension (measurement) of the mind. And the basis of a traditional proportional analogy is overturned when the little world declares itself to be more than the great. (In this context, what, if anything do "little," "more," and "great" mean?) As the frames of reference that comprise our understanding are discredited and jettisoned, a need is created for something to take their place; and that need is met by a simple forceful declaration: "There is surely a peece of Divinity in us."

This is, of course, the insight that awaits us at the end of each of the passages we have examined. The "O altitudo" that is characteristic of Browne's thought is faithfully reflected in the movement of his prose, which is everywhere the same. The separate sections of *Religio Medici* pretend to consider a variety of subjects, but each of them winds obliquely, but predictably, toward a reaffirmation of the imminence of God's presence, ending in many instances with words and phrases that directly proclaim the supreme reality of his indwelling spirit—"one point without division," "invisible Fabrick," "hand of God," "life to come," "resurrection," "immortality," "Saviour," "Christ." [3] As a result, the reader is continually experiencing the truth of Browne's assertions about the world we live in:

> There is a neerer way to heaven than *Homers* chaine; an easie Logick may conjoyne heaven and earth in one argument, and with lesse than a Sorites resolve all things into God. For though wee Christen effects by their most sensible

[3] No less than 32 of the sections end this way.

and nearest causes, yet is God the true and infallible cause
of all, whose concourse, though it be generall, yet doth it
subdivide it selfe into the particular actions of everything,
and is that spirit, by which each singular essence not onely
subsists, but performes its operations (I, 18).

The "easie Logick" that conjoins Heaven and earth is the logic
of the reading experience; for, although we are repeatedly asked
to consider "particular" things and actions, our attention is invariably directed *away* from what is "nearest" them to "that
spirit" by which they subsist and perform their operations. In a
word, the prose *resolves,* and what it resolves is "all things into
God." All that is "truly amiable," Browne tell us, "is God, or as
it were a divided piece of him," a statement that might well apply
to the *Religio Medici* whose structure imitates the *univ*erse it
celebrates, a conglomeration of "singular essences" (divided
pieces), each of which bears a uniform significance.

"Structure" is perhaps the wrong word, for Browne refuses to
structure, to subordinate, to divide, to distinguish, insisting everywhere on the essential homogeneity of whatever is discretely perceived. The numbered sections of the *Religio Medici* are no more
indicative of an argument or a progress than the books and chapters of *The Reason of Church Government* or the road map of
*The Pilgrim's Progress.* Within the artificial enclosures they create, the reader is forever rising to (or being deposited on) the
same truth, and his experience is finally answerable to the "alle-
gorical description (I, 10)" of which Browne was so fond: "a
circle whose circumference is nowhere and center everywhere."

#### IF THERE RISE DOUBTS, I DO FORGET THEM

Like one of Milton's reasons, the conclusion to the preceding
pages implies itself: there are many points of contact between
Browne and the authors with whom the earlier chapters of this
study have been concerned. Indeed, one might say that the *Religio Medici* is a storehouse (or is it a museum?) of the wares
they commonly display. All of this, however, is preliminary to a
quite different argument: in spite of everything that he shares

with Donne, Milton, Herbert, Bacon, and Bunyan, Browne is not really like them at all. What distinguishes him is (1) an attitude toward his materials, which is, in turn, reflected in (2) the rhetorical thrust of his prose, and finally realized in (3) the demands made or not made on the reader.

To take the last point first: what is required of the reader of *Religio Medici* is, as Gilbert Phelps has observed, admiration.[4] In the prose of Donne and Milton, and the poetry of Herbert, the stylistic effects—the dislocations, ambiguities, confusions of tenses —are in the service of the commonplaces of Christian belief. In the *Religio Medici*, the commonplaces of Christian belief are in the service of a succession of stylistic effects, and our attention is continually being diverted from the implications (personal and cosmic) of Browne's statements to the skill he displays in making them. In the penultimate section of Part II, for example, the love of God is contrasted with the love we may expect from our nearest relations. It is a familiar theme—the transience of human loyalties—and at first we are invited to apply it personally: "Let us call to assize the loves of our parents, the affection of our wives and children, and they are all dumbe showes, and dreames, without reality truth, or constancy." But as the assize is called, the intricacies of the exercise replace the sentiment as the focus of our attention:

> for first there is a strong bond of affection betweene us and our parents; yet how easily dissolved? We betake our selves to a woman, forgetting our mother in a wife, the wombe that bare us in that that shall [but] beare our image. This woman blessing us with children, our affection leaves the levell it held before and sinkes from our bed unto our issue and picture of [our] posterity, where affection holds no steady mansion. They growing up in yeares [either] desire our ends, or applying themselves to a woman, take a lawfull way to love another better than our selves. Thus I perceive a man may bee buried alive and behold his grave in his owne issue (II, 14).

4 "The Prose of Donne and Browne," in *From Donne to Marvell*, ed. Boris Ford (Baltimore, 1956), p. 120.

With each turn of the rhetorical screw, our anticipation of what will follow is heightened, but it is an anticipation of manner, not matter. We attend to the transmigration of the affections, not because of any real interest or concern, but because we wonder where Browne will go next and how he will get there. What Phelps observes of an excerpt from *The Garden of Cyrus* is to the point here: "The effect is to make the reader curious . . . but not excited. There is no pressure or urgency." Actually, there is pressure, but it is pressure on Browne (who has also generated it) to complete the logic of his conceit. The note sounded in "Thus I perceive" is one of triumph—"I've done it"—and it introduces a paradox, not of faith but of wit. In this purely verbal context, the phrases "buried alive" and "behold his grave" are emptied of their conventional (and personal) force; they are, in fact, meaningless, referring to nothing in our extraliterary experience, but only to the successful conclusion of a virtuoso performance. One might profitably compare this passage with the rehearsal in *Death's Duell* of our progress from death to death. The reader or hearer of Donne's sermon believes several times that he is at the worst, only to find that the worst is yet to come. Here the worst is over when the sequence begins and the reader is free to lose himself, and his sense of responsibility to the content, in the elaboration of the figure.

In one of the more celebrated sections of the *Religio Medici*, the pattern is exactly the same:

> *Worke out your salvation with feare and trembling.* That which is the cause of my election, I hold to be the cause of my salvation, which was the mercy, and beneplacit of God, before I was, or the foundation of the world. *Before Abraham was, I am,* is the saying of Christ; yet is it true in some sense if I say it of my selfe, for I was not onely before my selfe, but *Adam,* that is, in the Idea of God, and the decree of that Synod held from all Eternity. And in this sense, I say, the world was before the Creation, and at an end before it had a beginning; and thus was I dead before I was alive; though my grave be *England,* my dying place

was Paradise, and *Eve* miscarried of mee before she conceiv'd of *Cain* (I, 59).

Once again we are invited to consider a serious, if commonplace,
argument: while man thinks of salvation in terms of the future,
in God's eternal present, the determining decree has already been
published and promulgated. In "some sense" then (though surely
not in common sense) one can say with Christ "Before Abraham
was, I am" and claim a place in both time and eternity. There is
wit here, to be sure, but it points away from itself to the inability of a time-bound consciousness to comprehend the workings of God's mercy. If Browne were to leave the point here, it
would be seriously made; but he continues—one can almost hear
him muse, "I wonder how long I can keep this up"—and the wit
becomes self-generating and self-referring, a rapid-fire series of
"one-liners," culminating in a perfectly turned and self-consciously
outrageous statement of paradox: "and *Eve* miscarried of mee before she conceiv'd of *Cain*." Of course, the more the reader responds to the performance *qua* performance, the less he is committed to its "message"; and in the end "miscarried" and *"Cain"*
are divested of their pejorative connotations (indeed, of any connotations) and are valued only for their function in a structure of
verbal art. Questions of salvation and eternity have literally been
forgotten.

I have said many times that it is characteristic of self-consuming artifacts to call attention to what they are *not* doing, and
therefore to their ultimate insufficiency before the great problems
of the spiritual life. Browne's prose betrays no such modesty. It
repeatedly calls attention to what it *is* doing, and what it is doing
is displaying Browne to advantage, even when the content is, on
its face, prejudicial to him:

> The heart of man is the place the devill dwels in; I feele
> somtimes a hell within my selfe, *Lucifer* keeps his court
> in my brest, Legion is revived in me. There are as many
> hels as *Anaxagoras* conceited worlds; there was more than
> one hell in *Magdalen,* when there were seven devils; for
> every devill is an hell unto himselfe: hee holds enough of

torture in his owne *ubi,* and needs not the misery of circumference to afflict him, and thus a distracted conscience here is a shadow or introduction unto hell hereafter (I, 51).

Nothing is more firmly rooted in the seventeenth-century sensibility than a tendency to introspection and self-criticism; and in the tradition of spiritual autobiography, nothing is more commonplace than the assertion by the first-person voice that "I feele sometimes a hell within my selfe"; but in the present context it becomes obvious that Browne doesn't feel anything, except the impulse to *amplificatio.* His interest in the idea of hell and its location within him is purely formal; it can be turned over (*"Lucifer* keeps his court in my brest"), caressed ("Legion is revived in me"), played with ("There are as many hels as *Anaxagoras* conceited worlds"). It can even form the basis of a new mathematics ("there was more than one hell in *Magdalen,* when there were seven devils . . ."). What it cannot do, at least on this occasion, is sustain itself as a serious proposition. The reality of hell, as the place and condition of our eternal damnation, gives way to the literary reality of an extended "recreation." Any "idea," no matter how potentially threatening, can be domesticated, if one toys with it long enough; [5] and when Browne declares at the beginning of the next section, "I have almost forgot the Idea of Hell," he speaks for the reader as well as for himself.

Forgetting is what the *Religio Medici* encourages its readers to do. "If . . . there rise any doubts in my way," Browne tells us in I.6, "I doe forget them." More than any other statement, this distinguishes Browne from his seventeenth-century brethren who in various ways make of their doubts (and of ours) the occasion for an exhaustive and painful process of self-exploration. Browne, however, as Joan Webber has so finely said, "pulls the sting from pain" [6] and so releases his reader from any real obligation to the issues his prose pretends to raise. His vaunted tolerance is really indifference: he doesn't want to be bothered and he doesn't want to bother us either. The reader of Donne's *Devotions* or Milton's *Paradise Lost* or Bunyan's *The Pilgrim's Prog-*

[5] On this point, see Joan Webber, *The Eloquent "I"* (Madison, 1968), pp. 173, 181.

[6] *Ibid.,* p. 181.

*ress* or Herbert's *The Temple* is often brought face to face with truths (about himself and his abilities) he would prefer to ignore or avoid. Browne will gesture in the direction of these truths and even allow us for a time to feel the pressure of their implications, but in the end he will always leave us some easy avenue of escape. In section 54 of Part I for example, he confronts, and for a time makes us confront, one of the hardest points of Christian belief:

THERE is no salvation to those that beleeve not in Christ, that is, say some, since his Nativity, and as Divinity affirmeth, before also; which makes me much apprehend the end of those honest Worthies and Philosophers which died before his Incarnation. It is hard to place those soules in Hell whose worthy lives doe teach us vertue on earth; methinks amongst those many subdivisions of hell, there might have bin one Limbo left for these: What a strange vision will it be to see their poeticall fictions converted into verities, & their imaginary & fancied Furies, into reall Devils? how strange to them will sound the History of *Adam,* when they shall suffer for him they never heard of? [7]

The first sentence is Baconian in strategy, the uncompromising assertion, followed by a qualification ("that is, say some") which suggests the possibility of exceptions. It is a possibility the speaker finds attractive, for "it is hard to place those soules in Hell whose worthy lives doe teach us vertue on earth." If it is hard for Browne, it is equally hard for the reader, whose reluctance to credit the damnation of "those honest Worthies" reflects an anxiety about the eventual disposition of his own case. (There but for the Grace of God, indeed!) When Browne wonders aloud, "How strange . . . when they shall suffer for him they never

[7] This question and others like it were very seriously asked in the Renaissance. See D. C. Allen, *Mysteriously Meant* (Baltimore, 1970), pp. 40–51 for a concise history of the debate over the salvation of pagan souls. During the seventeenth century, Allen observes, "the question of the redemption of the pious pagan twisted back and forth between optimistic and pessimistic convictions so that a dead philosopher saved by one redeemer might be sent to the pit by another (46)." Thus Browne could assume that the issues he raised in this section were still alive in the minds of his readers.

heard of," he is deliberately encouraging the doubts and murmurings that he elsewhere labels "arrogant" and "presumptuous." But in the manner of Milton and Herbert, or so it would seem, the rationalizing tendencies of the carnal understanding are given reign only so that their dangers can be more forcefully exposed. Once the reader has fallen in with the speaker's questionings, he is met with this rebuke: "It is an insolent part of reason, to controvert the works of God or question the justice of his proceedings." In what follows, this harsh and unrelenting judgment is reaffirmed, although the gentler perspective continues to be acknowledged in the speaker's regretful tones: "It will therefore, and must at last appeare, that all salvation is through Christ; which verity I feare these great examples of vertue must confirme, and make it good, how the perfectest actions of earth have no title or claime unto Heaven." In its recognition of the difficulties it poses, this concluding sentence is faithful to the controlled ambivalence of the entire sequence. The sweeping dismissal of human values is, to some extent, humanized by the admission of fellowship in the words "I feare"; but, at the same time, that dismissal is left standing, and we are given no choice but to accept.

Or so it seems, for a second or two. The first sentence of the following section reads: "Nor truely doe I think the lives of these or any other were ever correspondent, or in all points conformable unto their doctrines." Or, in other words, I take it all back, April Fool's, I didn't mean it, I was merely pretending, don't worry about it, *forget it*. At exactly the point where a reader of Herbert or Milton or Bunyan would have been drawn even further into the text, Browne's reader is allowed to disassociate himself from its concerns. Only a moment ago, his personal sense of well-being was threatened because men of exemplary virtue had been declared ineligible for heaven; but when the perfection of that virtue is denied, there is no longer any (necessary) inference to be made from their situation to his, and the preceding paragraph is suddenly no more threatening than any other literary exercise. It is a brilliant tour de force, a demonstration of the techniques of devotional writing which stops conspicuously short of the moral pressure that genre usually exerts.

And this is always where Browne stops and pulls the sting.

Even when he brings us, as he so often does, from the segmented world of distinguishable entities to an intuition of God's unifying presence, the ascent is easy, with none of the discarding of veils and values that makes the prose of other stylists so strenuous; and the moment of insight reflects backward to his skill ("he's done it again") rather than inward to our edification. In brief, what sets Browne apart from those with whom he shares so much is the absence in his work of their intentions, which are rhetorical in a very special sense. They seek to *change* the minds of their readers; they have designs on us; they are out to do us good; and they require our participation in what is, more often than not, the painful and exhausting process of self-examination and self-criticism. Bacon's style of presentation provokes the reader to question the adequacy of his received opinions and the completeness of his received systems of knowledge; the "present satisfaction" of a coherent literary experience is deliberately sacrificed for an uneasiness that is a stimulus to "further inquiry"; in Herbert's poetry the reader is required to give up, one by one, his claims to an independent existence, even to the extent (in some poems) of surrendering his powers of interpretation; when Bunyan promises "This book will make a traveller of thee," he keeps his promise by forcing the reader to claim a share in the errors and sins of Christian and his companions; at least half of Milton's readers are alienated and discomforted when he insists that each of us measure himself against an unyielding standard of righteousness and illumination; in *Death's Duell*, the reader is teased into asking questions that only point up his inability to answer them, and in the end he is brought literally to his knees; and if the reader is the *subject* of the *Anatomy of Melancholy*, he is in his preeminence the *object* of taunts, laughter, rebukes, and scorn. In all of these works, an uncomfortable and unsettling experience is offered as the way to self-knowledge, in the hope that self-knowledge will be preliminary to the emergence of a better self, with a better (or at least more self-aware) mind. And by offering that experience rather than another, these works shift the focus of attention from themselves and from what is happening in their formal confines to the reader and what is happening in the confines of his mind and heart.

These, then, are the characteristics of what I have called the aesthetic of the good physician (actually an anti-aesthetic), and on every point Browne stands on the opposite side. He draws attention not *away* from, but *to,* himself; his words are not seeds, spending their lives in salutary and self-consuming effects, but objects, frozen into rhetorical patterns which reflect on the virtuosity of their author; the experience of his prose has its climaxes not in moments of insight and self-knowledge, but in moments of wonder and admiration for the art that has produced it; rather than provoking us to a distrust of its procedures and conclusions, the *Religio Medici,* solicits and wins our confidence. It is therefore not self-consuming, but self-indulgent, and in two directions: for the confidence it wins is reflected in the confidence it leaves us, a *self*-confidence, which is the result of never having been really pained or challenged; Browne does not say to us, "awake, remember, change," but "take it easy, don't let it bother you, let it be."

To all this, it could be replied that Browne would claim no more and that he should not be judged by standards he would not have acknowledged. What Browne does, he does beautifully, and there is no reason to fault him simply because he is not Herbert. And, after all, it is a strange criticism that complains because a man's work is fun to read.

These are precisely the terms in which his admirers praise him:

> Anglican Browne liberates himself from Baxter's pain by emphasizing style more than meaning . . . thus floating above the century's ills, as it were, rather than being submerged by them, and creating an art as fragile and spectacular as a prism. The ambiguities and mysteries of it are there to be enjoyed in themselves.[8]
>
> He makes a game of doubt and allows himself much play of fancy in his style. . . . He has seen that the world is not an inn but a hospital, and *therefore* he will make his affirmation. Such a claim can be made more confidently of Milton and Shakespeare, because with them the late art is clearly born of a lifetime of tragic insight and artistic

[8] Webber, *The Eloquent "I,"* p. 152.

discipline. With Browne, one often has the sense that the tragic insight is at best willed and at worst a cliche. Yet his point is, I think, the same as theirs.[9]

His religious experience has a profoundly different substance and color from that represented by the divine poetry of Donne or Herbert . . . these men derived much of their best poetry from the experience of spiritual combat, from their personal struggle over rebellion and obedience, exile or union. . . . Such struggle was evidently not an aspect of Brown's religious life.[10]

It [*RM*] definitely lacks the drama of Augustine's *Confessions,* the drama that issues from religious conversion. . . . But nowhere else can we find a presentation of a mind so securely anchored in the Anglican *via media* that is equally compelling. Never has complacency been so dazzling and the transport that accompanies the contemplation of mysteries so serene.[11]

Miss Webber and Mr. Nathanson are eloquent and persuasive, but also not a little defensive. Their praises gesture nervously in the direction of the other authors who share Browne's century and (superficially) his concerns, and the category they construct for him is both special and diminishing. Moreover, the judgment these pages make on Browne is one he invites when he enrolls himself, both by posture and choice of subject, in a tradition less concerned with the winning of applause and the making of better artifacts, than with the sounding of souls and the making of better persons. In terms of that tradition, which has been the subject and the author of this book, he is the bad physician.

[9] *Ibid.,* p. 182.
[10] Leonard Nathanson, *The Strategy of Truth* (Chicago, 1968), p. 98.
[11] *Ibid.,* p. 175.

 VIII

# Epilogue: The Plain Style Question

In general, this study has not addressed itself to the solving of problems in intellectual history, yet it seems to me that the conclusions it reaches suggest the possibility of formulating a new answer to a very old question: what is it that polarizes seventeenth-century style, and why is it that by the end of the century the opposition of styles has become so much less pronounced? There have been many attempts to answer this question, and their history forms a sequence that corresponds in many ways to my characterization of a self-consuming artifact. Thus, Morris Croll constructs a theory of seventeenth-century style that depends on the opposition of Ciceronian to Senecan or Attic, the one in the service of prevailing orthodoxies, the other reflecting "exactly those athletic movements of the mind by which it arrives at a sense of reality and the true knowledge of itself and the world." [1] It is the latter, Croll declares, that comes to predominate in the seventeenth century, finding one expression in the language of Baconian inquiry, another in the plain style of the Puritan sermonists, and still another in the rationalism of the Restoration. To this, R. F. Jones replies that the roster of anti-Ciceronians includes several stylists against whom the Restoration reformers "were in open revolt," [2] and, at any rate, a "theory which places Sir Thomas Browne and John Dryden, Jeremy Taylor and John

[1] *Style, Rhetoric and Rhythm: Essays by Morris W. Croll,* ed. J. Max Patrick et al. (Princeton, 1966), p. 67.
[2] R. F. Jones, *The Seventeenth Century* (Stanford, 1951), p. 106.

Tillotson in the same stylistic category is puzzling (158)." Jones solves the puzzle by hanging everything on an alternative opposition, on the one hand the style of the new science, fostered and promulgated by the members of the Royal Society, and on the other hand, the style of everyone else, that is of everyone whose writings display the rhetorical ornament, convoluted syntax, and interlarding of Greek and Latin quotations that were to be banished in favor of the ideal of so many words to so many things. In this scheme, Croll's anti-Ciceronians become conservative rather than revolutionary figures, and we have a new alignment based on the assumption that a commitment to the "linguistic platform (76)" of the new science is decisive. It is an assumption that Robert Adolph, who is on balance more a Jonesian than a Crollian, challenges; for, as he points out, while some Restoration plain stylists are either members of the Royal Society or influenced by it, others are "untouched by or hostile to the New Philosophy" and yet we find them "advocating identical stylistic programs using identical arguments." [3] "Thus," Adolph concludes, "from sources remote from, opposed to, or antedating the Royal Society came similar stylistic ideals (210)," and one must therefore give up the notion that the decisive or explanatory influence in the fashioning of late seventeenth-century style was the rise of science. Indeed, "there is as much evidence that the reform of the sermon influenced the Society's view of style as that 'science' affected the preachers."

It will not do, however, to look to the controversy between Puritan and Anglican for a solution to the puzzle, if only because the two parties refuse to stay on their respective sides of the fence. In Perry Miller's classic study of *The New England Mind,* the Puritans, under the influence of Ramist logic and method, oppose the orderly disposition of axiomatic sentences to the jingling schemes and scholastic "crumblings" of the Anglican rhetoricians; but in Jones's version of the story, the Anglican reformers, under the influence of Glanville and Sprat, do battle against the rhetorical excesses of the Puritan dissenters. Have the Puritans and

---

[3] Robert M. Adolph, *The Rise of Modern Prose Style* (Cambridge, Mass., 1968), pp. 190–191.

Anglicans changed places? Not at all, according to Harold Fisch
who insists that the Puritans are consistent in their promotion of a
plain style. Jones's presentation of evidence "is positively misleading," [4] and indeed, Fisch contends, each side accused the other of
identical vices and drew their arguments from common *Puritan*
sources. This raises the intriguing possibility that there was no
Restoration reform of prose style and that the so-called "rhetorical" preacher was a phantom opponent who could be invoked by
anyone who found it convenient to do so, but who could not himself be found. Irène Simon, for one, has some difficulty finding
him; she is struck by the "reasonableness" and "moderate tone" [5]
of the vilified Puritans; she speculates that perhaps "the Puritans'
temper had changed; perhaps the repeated attacks on their jargon
had put a curb on their fancy (72)," for surely (and this seems
almost plaintive), "the witty or the florid style of preaching must
have lingered in some places, or the reformers would hardly have
felt it necessary to refer so often to this false kind of eloquence (59)."

To borrow a line from Milton's Lady, "Shall I go on / Or have
I said enough?" Ciceronian-Attic, Scientific-Rhetorical, Puritan-
Anglican, Commonwealth-Restoration, none of them seems to
work. What we need, as Adolph observes, is "some other explanation (25)," some influence that "can be found to impel consciously
or unconsciously all or most of our theorists, who are all advocating and writing more or less the same style (191)." For this honor
Adolph nominates the ethic of "utility": "Utility, much more than
anything else hovers in the background as the ultimate basis of
the new ideals (193)." "Not only the religious writers but philosophers and literary critics . . . developed a theory of style
which was indistinguishable from that of the Royal Society. . . .
Again the influences on these theorists are to be found not so
much in 'science' but in the general feeling that prose should exist
primarily for purposes of useful communication (210)." The
trouble with this is not that it doesn't work, but that it works at

[4] Harold Fisch, "The Puritans and the Reform of Prose Style," *ELH*, XIX
(1952), 242.

[5] Irène Simon, *Three Restoration Divines: Barrow, South, Tillotson* (Paris,
1967), p. 29.

the expense of the distinctions it is supposed to explain. Adolph solves the problem of seventeenth-century style by generalizing it out of existence and in the process the dimensions of any number of writers are flattened out. I have already noted (pp. 88–89) how in his rush to put Bacon in the utilitarian camp, Adolph ignores or misinterprets the many statements, in the *Novum Organum* and elsewhere, *against* the straightforward conveying of sense that is supposedly the hallmark of utilitarian prose. Of course, Bacon's prose is, in fact, utilitarian in the context of his wish to "invite men to enquire farther" by denying them satisfaction in the present; but in Adolph's view, the ethic of utility finds expression only in a plain and easy style, and he is unable to deal with a style that is useful *because* it is difficult. Not only is his key term too broad and vague to do the job, but his understanding of it is too inflexibly tied to one kind of experience and one set of formal features.

The rhetoric of the preceding paragraphs suggests that I alone have the answer to the question that has confounded two generations of scholars. It is probably more accurate to say that I have *an* answer, for no doubt in time someone else will point out that it is at best partial and at worst distorting. Nevertheless, I propose, like Bacon, to offer my present understanding of the matter, so that men "may see whether there be any error connected with it and may arouse themselves to devise proofs more trust-worthy." In brief, it seems to me that seventeenth-century style is not polarized by a distinction between Ciceronians and anti-Ciceronians, or by a controversy between Puritans and Anglicans, or by the incompatibility of the rhetorical and scientific ideals, or by the difference between a prose that is useful and a prose in the service of "self-revelation (Adolph, 193)," but by two views of the human mind and its capabilities. On the one hand there is the assumption that the mind, either in its present state or in some future state of repair, is adequate to the task of comprehending and communicating the nature and shape of reality; and on the other, the assumption that the mind is a prisoner of its inherent limitations, and that the apprehension, in rational or discursive terms, of ultimate truth, is beyond it.

In short, for a political, social, or religious opposition, I substitute an opposition of epistemologies, one that finds its expression in two kinds of reading experiences: on one side the experience of a prose that leads the auditor or reader step-by-step, in a logical and orderly manner, to a point of certainty and clarity; and on the other, the experience of a prose that undermines certainty and moves away from clarity, complicating what had at first seemed perfectly simple, raising more problems than it solves. Within this large opposition there are, of course, distinctions to be made, and in the preceding pages I have tried to make them; but in general the contrast holds, between a language that builds its readers' confidence by building an argument they can follow, and a language that, by calling attention to the insufficiency of its own procedures, calls into question the sufficiency of the minds it unsettles. To the paired terms of my predecessors—Anglican-Puritan, Painted-Plain, Ciceronian-Senecan, Scientific-Rhetorical, Utilitarian-Frivolous—I add a new pair, Self-Satisfying and Self-Consuming.

The great advantage of this new polarization is its combination of precision and flexibility, for it escapes the rigidity of other classifications without blurring the differences they affirm. Thus Donne and Bunyan can quite properly be cited (by Joan Webber) as paradigm instances of contrasting world views and styles, and yet be one in their tendency to subvert rational and discursive structures. And conversely, Donne and Browne may share nearly everything, including patterns of style and devices of rhetoric, and yet differ on this one crucial point. Epistemological distinctions operate independently of party label and can even at times divide the corpus of a single author. Bacon is on one side in *The Advancement of Learning,* when he is concerned "to win consent or belief (*Sp.* III, 405)," but he is on the other in the *Essays,* where he is concerned to disabuse his readers of beliefs they already hold; now he gives present satisfaction, now he deliberately withholds it. Epistemological distinctions also operate independently of formal categories. In formal terms, the *Essays* are properly characterized as plain, and it is the availability of such a characterization that has led so many to mistake their essence. Adolph is only the last in a long line when he speaks of a Bacon essay as a "dispassionate survey of the available literature (73)," a progression of "distilled certainties" delivered in a language which, because it tends to "clarify, illustrate, restrict," reflects the philosopher's "faith in the instructed intellect (31–32)." This, I think, is precisely wrong, and it is wrong because Adolph reads directly from the formally describable features of a style to the experience it gives: if the prose is distinguished by short and pithy members, by a "commonsensical" Anglo-Saxon vocabulary, and by the absence of full periods and rhetorical flourishes, then it must be easy to understand and easy understanding must be what it seeks to promote. The prose of Bacon's *Essays* answers to this description, but the experience of reading them is strenuous and easy understanding is what they warn against. In *The Advancement of Learning,* the relationship is reversed: the prose is Ciceronian and full, the manner formal, the parade of learning formidable, and yet the experience is by and large comfortable, not without effort, but also not without the reward and satisfaction of following and comprehending an unfolding argument. A florid style that makes plain and a plain style that confuses and unsettles: it would be difficult to accommodate this reverse fit within a scheme that requires an isomorphic relationship between the formal features of a style and what it is or does, and it is the freedom from such requirements that makes a classification by epistemologies so flexible. Of course, the occasional isomorphism which critics have made the basis of their typologies does exist (as in the example of Cotton on one side and Andrewes on the other), but it is the exception, not the rule, and one cannot hope for descriptive adequacy from a theory that actively seeks it. My theory compels me neither to seek it nor to deny it when it occurs, and I am therefore free to acknowledge the distinctions of my predecessors without being straitened by them. Anglicans, Puritans, Roundheads, Cavaliers, Senecans, Ciceronians, Libertines, Aphorists, they all remain; and, retaining their separate identities, these and other parties can be sometimes on one side, sometimes on the other, of the epistemological divide. In short, this is an explanation that does not explain away.

One of the things it explains is what happens at the end of the century, when, as so many have remarked, the plain style wins the day. The fact itself is not in dispute, and it is a puzzle only if the plain style is identified with a particular party or point of view, for then the question of influence and counterinfluence becomes paramount. If, however, the plain style has always been available for appropriation by any party, then its appropriation by *all* parties in the Restoration is a phenomenon independent of the ascendancy or decline of any one of them. And this is indeed the case: the oppositions that make the intellectual structures of the century so pervasively binary survive into its final quarter; what does not survive is one of the distinctions by which particular positions were at times (and then inconsistently) set off from each other. I refer, of course, to the distinction between a self-satisfying and a self-consuming style; the latter is simply not available, because the assumption that underlies it—the assumption that the apprehension of ultimate truth is beyond the capacity of the rational understanding—is no longer respectable. No one is now willing to say, with Donne, that he intends "to trouble the understanding, to displace, and to discompose, and disorder the judgement"; [6] and indeed everyone is loudly professing exactly the opposite intention, not to trouble the judgment, but to conform in every way possible to its procedures, to dispose arguments in a methodical and orderly progression and so affirm, in Adolph's phrase, "a faith in the instructed intellect."

In short, there has been an epistemological shift that cuts across party lines—everyone now believes (or declares himself to believe) in the ability of the mind to be instructed in the truth, although different versions of what the truth is continue to be put forward—and it is this shift, rather than any of its several manifestations, that is responsible for the stylistic homogeneity of the period. Adolph is correct to seek some "decisive influence" that will explain why "all or most of our theorists . . . are all advocating and writing more or less the same style (191)"; but when he finds it in utility, he mistakes a tributary for the main stream; for the utilitarian "aim" (as he describes it) of persuasively making things easier for the reader to understand (176), is possible only if understanding is assumed to be easy; that is, if at some level the purview of human knowledge and the dimensions of reality are co-extensive. Now we see through a glass darkly, as-

[6] *Sermons,* ed. Potter and Simpson, Vol. II, 282.

serts the Apostle, and with him Augustine, Donne, Herbert, Milton, Bunyan, and, in a limited sense, Bacon; but for many in the Restoration the glass has been made clear by the power of reason, whose workings are believed to yield a direct and undistorted access to the order of things as they have been disposed by God. This is certainly the case with the propagandists of the Royal Society, and it is also true, as Irène Simon has so conclusively demonstrated, of the Anglican reformers, who are convinced "that reason if rightly directed" is able to "arrive at the truths of Christianity (115)." This same belief is also responsible for the hostility to metaphor, which is, in essence, a bias in favor of clear and logical thinking. On every front, as Miss Simon remarks, we find theorists expounding "an epistemology that warranted the objectivity of knowledge (92)," and it is in the name of that objectivity, and therefore of a faith in the sufficiency of the rational intelligence, that the plain style triumphs.[7]

The triumph of the plain style, then, is a triumph of epistemology. In the first half of the century, the plain style could still be regarded as one of a number of rhetorical options, and the decision to use it did not necessarily reflect a consistent religious and philosophical position; but in the Restoration, a pressure for consistency, that is for isomorphism, is exerted by a naive and optimistic epistemology, and the plain style is no longer optional, but mandatory, and mandatory not as a literary choice, but as a manifestation of a faith in rational discourse. It is only in the context of such a faith that the plain style as a program, as a philosophic and quasi-religious ideal, is tenable; for in its absence, the orderly disposition of logical arguments can claim nothing more than a measure of formal elegance. And, indeed, if sensible perception and the laws of reason operate in a closed and self-confirming circle, a style that is faithful to them is ultimately solipsistic, a style not for telling, but for evading, the truth.

Of course, it depends finally on what the truth is taken to be. In the end the question of the plain style must remain open, for

---

[7] Of course, as Miss Simon points out, the Anglican preachers continue to assert the subservience of reason to faith and revelation; but the watchwords are "cooperation" and "harmony," and in practice the limitations on reason are more honored in the breach than in the observance.

one man's plain is another man's distortion. Making plain, after all, can have two senses, clarifying or simplifying (*making* plain), and in the latter sense the plain style of the Restoration is a self-validating (because it is self-satisfying) cheat, while the true plain style would be one that makes plain the impossibility and presumption of making plain. (The literature is shot through with an equivocation between the plain style as a formal criterion and making plain as a criterion of experience.) In other words, it may very well be that the true plain style is self-consuming.

 APPENDIX

# Literature in the Reader: Affective Stylistics[1]

[1] This essay first appeared in *New Literary History*, Vol. II (Autumn, 1970), 123–162. Although I would no longer stand behind its every statement, it is here reprinted in full, except for a small section on the *Phaedrus*.

## MEANING AS EVENT

If at this moment someone were to ask, "what are you doing?" you might reply, "I am reading," and thereby acknowledge the fact that reading is an activity, something *you do*. No one would argue that the act of reading can take place in the absence of someone who reads—how can you tell the dance from the dancer? —but curiously enough when it comes time to make analytical statements about the end product of reading (meaning or understanding), the reader is usually forgotten or ignored. Indeed in recent literary history he has been excluded by legislation. I refer, of course, to the *ex cathedra* pronouncements of Wimsatt and Beardsley in their enormously influential article "The Affective Fallacy":

> The Affective Fallacy is a confusion between the poem and its *results* (what it *is* and what it *does*). . . . It begins by trying to derive the standards of criticism from the psychological effects of the poem and ends in impressionism and relativism. The outcome . . . is that the poem itself,

as an object of specifically critical judgment, tends to disappear.[2]

In time, I shall return to these arguments, not so much to refute them as to affirm and embrace them; but I would first like to demonstrate the explanatory power of a method of analysis which takes the reader, as an actively mediating presence, fully into account, and which, therefore, has as its focus the "psychological effects" of the utterance. And I would like to begin with a sentence that does not open itself up to the questions we usually ask.

> That Judas perished by hanging himself, there is no certainty in Scripture: though in one place it seems to affirm it, and by a doubtful word hath given occasion to translate it; yet in another place, in a more punctual description, it maketh it improbable, and seems to overthrow it.

Ordinarily, one would begin by asking "what does this sentence mean?" or "what is it about?" or "what is it saying?" all of which preserve the objectivity of the utterance. For my purposes, however, this particular sentence has the advantage of not saying anything. That is, you can't get a fact out of it which could serve as an answer to any one of these questions. Of course, this difficulty is itself a fact—of response; and it suggests, to me at least, that what makes problematical sense as a statement makes perfect sense as a strategy, as an action made upon a reader rather than as a container from which a reader extracts a message. The strategy or action here is one of progressive decertainizing. Simply by taking in the first clause of the sentence, the reader commits himself to its assertion, "that Judas perished by hanging himself" (in constructions of this type "that" is understood to be shorthand for "the *fact* that"). This is not so much a conscious decision as it is an anticipatory adjustment to his projection of the sentence's future contours. He knows (without giving cognitive form to his knowledge) that this first clause is preliminary to some larger assertion (it is a "ground") and he must be in control of it if he is to move easily and confidently through what follows; and in the

---

[2] *The Verbal Icon* (Lexington, Ky., 1954), p. 21.

context of this "knowledge," he is prepared, again less than consciously, for any one of several constructions:

That Judas perished by hanging himself, *is* (an example for us all).

That Judas perished by hanging himself, *shows* (how conscious he was of the enormity of his sin).

That Judas perished by hanging himself, *should* (give us pause).

The range of these possibilities (and there are, of course, more than I have listed) narrows considerably as the next three words are read, "there is no." At this point, the reader is expecting, and even predicting, a single word—"doubt"; but instead he finds "certainty"; and at that moment the status of the fact that had served as his point of reference becomes *un*certain. (It is nicely ironic that the appearance of "certainty" should be the occasion for doubt, whereas the word "doubt" would have contributed to the reader's certainty.) As a result, the terms of the reader's relationship to the sentence undergo a profound change. He is suddenly involved in a different kind of activity. Rather than following an argument along a well-lighted path (a light, after all, has gone *out*), he is now looking for one. The natural impulse in a situation like this, either in life or in literature, is to go forward in the hope that what has been obscured will again become clear; but in this case going forward only intensifies the reader's sense of disorientation. The prose is continually opening, but then closing, on the possibility of verification in one direction or another. There are two vocabularies in the sentence; one holds out the promise of a clarification—"place," "affirm," "place," "punctual," "overthrow"—while the other continually defaults on that promise— "Though," "doubtful," "yet," "improbable," "seems"; and the reader is passed back and forth between them and between the alternatives—that Judas did or did not perish by hanging himself—which are still suspended (actually it is the reader who is suspended) when the sentence ends (trails off? gives up?). The indeterminateness of this experience is compounded by a superfluity of pronouns. It becomes increasingly difficult to tell what "it" refers to, and if the reader takes the trouble to retrace his steps, he is simply led back to "that Judas perished by hanging himself"; in short, he exchanges an indefinite pronoun for an even less definite (that is, certain) assertion.

Whatever is persuasive and illuminating about this analysis (and it is by no means exhaustive) is the result of my substituting for one question—what does this sentence mean?—another, more operational question—what does this sentence do? And what the sentence does is give the reader something and then take it away, drawing him on with the unredeemed promise of its return. An observation about the sentence as an utterance—its refusal to yield a declarative statement—has been transformed into an account of its experience (not being able to get a fact out of it). It is no longer an object, a thing-in-itself, but an *event,* something that *happens* to, and with the participation of, the reader. And it is this event, this happening—all of it and not anything that could be said about it or any information one might take away from it—that is, I would argue, the *meaning* of the sentence. (Of course, in this case there is no information to take away.)

This is a provocative thesis whose elaboration and defense will be the concern of the following pages, but before proceeding to it, I would like to examine another utterance which also (conveniently) says nothing:

Nor did they not perceive the evil plight.

The first word of this line from *Paradise Lost* (I, 335) generates a rather precise (if abstract) expectation of what will follow: a negative assertion which will require for its completion a subject and a verb. There are then two "dummy" slots in the reader's mind waiting to be filled. This expectation is strengthened (if only because it is not challenged) by the auxiliary "did" and the pronoun "they." Presumably, the verb is not far behind. But in its place the reader is presented with a second negative, one that cannot be accommodated within his projection of the utterance's form. His progress through the line is halted and he is forced to come to terms with the intrusive (because unexpected) "not." In effect what the reader *does,* or is forced to do, at this point, is ask a question—did they or didn't they?—and in search of an answer he either rereads, in which case he simply repeats the sequence of mental operations, or goes forward, in which case he finds the anticipated verb, but in either case the syntactical uncertainty remains unresolved.

It could be objected that the solution to the difficulty is simply to invoke the rule of the double negative; one cancels the other and the "correct" reading is therefore "they did perceive the evil plight." But however satisfactory this may be in terms of the internal logic of grammatical utterances (and even in those terms there are problems),[3] it has nothing to do with the logic of the reading experience or, I would insist, with its meaning. That experience is a temporal one, and in the course of it the two negatives combine, not to produce an affirmative, but to prevent the reader from making the simple (declarative) sense which would be the goal of a logical analysis. To clean the line up is to take from it its most prominent and important effect—the suspension of the reader between the alternatives its syntax momentarily offers. What is a problem if the line is considered as an object, a thing-in-itself, becomes a *fact* when it is regarded as an occurrence. The reader's inability to tell whether or not "they" do perceive and his involuntary question (or its psychological equivalent) are events in his encounter with the line, and as events they are part of the line's *meaning,* even though they take place in the mind, not on the page. Subsequently, we discover that the answer to the question "did they or didn't they," is, "they did and they didn't." Milton is exploiting (and calling our attention to) the two senses of "perceive": they (the fallen angels) do perceive the fire, the pain, the gloom; physically they see it; however they are blind to the moral significance of their situation; and in that sense they do not perceive the evil plight in which they are. But that is another story.

Underlying these two analyses is a method, rather simple in concept, but complex (or at least complicated) in execution. The concept is simply the rigorous and disinterested asking of the question, what does this word, phrase, sentence, paragraph, chapter, novel, play, poem, *do?*; and the execution involves *an analysis of the developing responses of the reader in relation to the words as*

---

[3] Thus the line could read: "They did not not perceive," which is not the same as saying they did perceive. (The question is still open.) One could also argue that "nor" is not really a negative.

*they succeed one another in time*. Every word in this statement bears a special emphasis. The analysis must be of the developing responses to distinguish it from the atomism of much stylistic criticism. A reader's response to the fifth word in a line or sentence is to a large extent the product of his responses to words one, two, three, and four. And by response, I intend more than the range of feelings (what Wimsatt and Beardsley call "the purely affective reports"). The category of response includes any and all of the activities provoked by a string of words: the projection of syntactical and/or lexical probabilities; their subsequent occurrence or non-occurrence; attitudes toward persons, or things, or ideas referred to; the reversal or questioning of those attitudes; and much more. Obviously, this imposes a great burden on the analyst who in his observations on any one moment in the reading experience must take into account all that has happened (in the reader's mind) at previous moments, each of which was in its turn subject to the accumulating pressures of its predecessors. (He must also take into account influences and pressures predating the actual reading experience—questions of genre, history, etc.—questions we shall consider later.) All of this is included in the phrase "in time." The basis of the method is a consideration of the *temporal* flow of the reading experience, and it is assumed that the reader responds in terms of that flow and not to the whole utterance. That is, in an utterance of any length, there is a point at which the reader has taken in only the first word, and then the second, and then the third, and so on, and the report of what happens to the reader is always a report of what has happened *to that point*. (The report includes the reader's set toward future experiences, but not those experiences.)

The importance of this principle is illustrated when we reverse the first two clauses of the Judas sentence: "There is no certainty that Judas perished by hanging himself." Here the status of the assertion is never in doubt because the reader knows from the beginning that it is doubtful; he is given a perspective from which to view the statement and that perspective is confirmed rather than challenged by what follows; even the confusion of pronouns in the second part of the sentence will not be disturbing to him, because it can easily be placed in the context of his initial response. There is no difference in these two sentences in the information conveyed (or not conveyed), or in the lexical and syntactical components,[4] only in the way these are received. But that one difference makes *all* the difference—between an uncomfortable, unsettling experience in which the gradual dimming of a fact is attended by a failure in perception, and a wholly self-satisfying one in which an uncertainty is comfortably certain, and the reader's confidence in his own powers remains unshaken, because he is always in control. It is, I insist, a difference in meaning.

The results (I will later call them advantages) of this method are fairly, though not exhaustively, represented in my two examples. Essentially what the method does is *slow down* the reading experience so that "events" one does not notice in normal time, but which do occur, are brought before our analytical attentions. It is as if a slow-motion camera with an automatic stop action effect were recording our linguistic experiences and presenting them to us for viewing. Of course the value of such a procedure is predicated on the idea of *meaning as an event,* something that is happening between the words and in the reader's mind, something not visible to the naked eye, but which can be made visible (or at least palpable) by the regular introduction of a "searching" question (what does this do?). It is more usual to assume that meaning is a function of the utterance, and to equate it with the information given (the message) or the attitude expressed. That is, the components of an utterance are considered either in relation to each other or to a state of affairs in the outside world, or to the state of mind of the speaker-author. In any and all of these variations, meaning is located (presumed to be imbedded) *in* the utterance, and the apprehension of meaning is an act of extraction.[5] In short, there is little sense of process and even less of the reader's actualizing participation in that process.

This concentration on the verbal object as a thing in itself and as a repository of meaning has many consequences, theoretical

---

[4] Of course, "That" is no longer read as "the fact that," but this is because the order of the clauses has resulted in the ruling out of that possibility.

[5] This is not true of the Oxford school of ordinary language philosophers (Austin, Grice, Searle) who discuss meaning in terms of hearer-speaker relationships and intention-response conventions, i.e., "situational meaning."

and practical. First of all, it creates a whole class of utterances, which, because of their alleged transparency, are declared to be uninteresting as objects of analysis. Sentences or fragments of sentences that immediately "make sense" (a deeply revealing phrase if one thinks about it) are examples of ordinary language; they are neutral and styleless statements, "simply" referring, or "simply" reporting. But the application to such utterances of the question "what does it do?" (which assumes that something is *always* happening) reveals that a great deal is going on in their production and comprehension (*every linguistic experience is affecting and pressuring*), although most of it is going on so close up, at such a basic, "preconscious" level of experience, that we tend to overlook it. Thus the utterance (written or spoken) "there is a chair" is at once understood as the report either of an existing state of affairs or of an act of perception (I see a chair). In either frame of reference, it makes immediate sense. To my mind, however, what is interesting about the utterance is the *sub rosa* message it puts out *by virtue of* its easy comprehensibility. Because it gives information directly and simply, it asserts (silently, but effectively) the "givability," directly and simply, of information; and it is thus an extension of the ordering operation we perform on experience whenever it is filtered through our temporal-spatial consciousness. In short, it *makes* sense, in exactly the way we make (i.e., manufacture) sense of whatever, if anything, exists outside us; and by making easy sense it tells us that sense can be easily made and that we are capable of easily making it. A whole document consisting of such utterances—a chemistry text or a telephone book—will be telling us that all the time; and *that*, rather than any reportable "content," will be its *meaning*. Such language can be called "ordinary" only because it confirms and reflects our ordinary understanding of the world and our position in it; but for precisely that reason it is *extra*ordinary (unless we accept a naive epistemology which grants us unmediated access to reality) and to leave it unanalyzed is to risk missing much of what happens—to us and through us—when we read and (or so we think) understand.

In short, the problem is simply that most methods of analysis operate at so high a level of abstraction that the basic data of the *meaning experience* is slighted and/or obscured. In the area of specifically literary studies, the effects of a naive theory of utterance meaning and of its attendant assumption of ordinary language can be seen in what is acknowledged to be the sorry state of the criticism of the novel and of prose in general. This is usually explained with reference to a distinction between prose and poetry, which is actually a distinction between ordinary language and poetic language. Poetry, it is asserted, is characterized by a high incidence of deviance from normal syntactical and lexical habits. It therefore offers the analyst-critic a great many points of departure. Prose, on the other hand (except for Baroque eccentrics like Thomas Browne and James Joyce) is, well, just prose, and just there. It is this helplessness before all but the most spectacular effects that I would remedy; although in one way the two examples with which this essay began were badly chosen, since they were analyses of utterances that are obviously and problematically deviant. This, of course, was a ploy to gain your attention. Assuming that I now have it, let me insist that the method shows to best advantage when it is applied to unpromising material. Consider for example this sentence (actually part of a sentence) from Pater's "Conclusion" to *The Renaissance,* which, while it is hardly the stuff of everyday conversation, does not, at first sight, afford much scope for the critic's analytical skill:

> That clear perpetual outline of face and limb is but an image of ours.

What can one say about a sentence like this? The analyst of style would, I fear, find it distressingly straightforward and nondeviant, a simple declarative of the form X is Y. And if he were by chance drawn to it, he would not be likely to pay very much attention to the first word—"That." It is simply there. But of course it is not simply there; it is *actively* there, doing something, and what that something is can be discovered by asking the question "what does it do?" The answer is obvious, right there in front of our noses, although we may not see it until we ask the question. "That" is a demonstrative, a word that points *out,* and as one takes it *in,* a sense of its referent (yet unidentified) is established. Whatever "that" is, it is outside, at a distance from the observer-reader; it is "pointable to" (pointing is what the word "that" does), something of substance and solidity. In terms of the reader's response, "that" generates an expectation that impels him forward, the expectation of finding out *what* "that" is. The word and its effect are the basic data of the meaning experience and they will direct our description of that experience because they direct the reader.

The adjective "clear" works in two ways; it promises the reader that when "that" appears, he will be able to see it easily, and, conversely, that it can be easily seen. "Perpetual" stabilizes the visibility of "that" even *before* it is seen and "outline" gives it potential form, while at the same time raising a question. That question—outline of what?—is obligingly answered by the phrase "of face and limb," which, in effect, fills the outline in. By the time the reader reaches the declarative verb "is"—which sets the seal on the objective reality of what has preceded it—he is fully and securely oriented in a world of perfectly discerned objects and perfectly discerning observers, of whom he is one. But then the sentence turns on the reader, and takes away the world it has itself created. With "but" the easy progress through the sentence is impeded (it is a split second before one realizes that "but" has the force of "only"); the declarative force of "is" is weakened and the status of the firmly drawn outline the reader has been pressured to accept is suddenly uncertain; "image" resolves that uncertainty, but in the direction of insubstantiality; and the now blurred form disappears altogether when the phrase "of ours" collapses the distinction between the reader and that which is (or was) "without" (Pater's own word). Now you see it (that), now you don't. Pater giveth and Pater taketh away. (Again this description of the reader's experience is an analysis of the sentence's meaning and if you were to ask, "but, what does it mean?" I would simply repeat the description.)

What is true of this sentence is true, I believe, of much of what we hold ourselves responsible for as critics and teachers of literature. There is more to it, that is, to its experience, than meets the casual eye. What is required, then, is a method, a machine if you will, which in its operation makes observable, or at least accessible, what goes on below the level of self-conscious response. Everyone would admit that something "funny" happens in the "Judas" sentence from Browne's *Religio Medici* and that there is a difficulty built into the reading and understanding of the line from *Paradise Lost;* but there is a tendency to assume that the Pater sentence is a simple assertion (whatever that is). It is, of course, nothing of the kind. In fact it is not an assertion at all, although (the promise of) an assertion is one of its components. It is an experience; it occurs; it does something; it makes us do something. Indeed, I would go so far as to say, in direct contradiction of Wimsatt-Beardsley, that what it does is what it means.

THE LOGIC AND STRUCTURE OF RESPONSE

What I am suggesting is that there is no direct relationship between the meaning of a sentence (paragraph, novel, poem) and what its words mean. Or, to put the matter less provocatively, the information an utterance gives, its message, is a constituent of, but certainly not to be identified with, its meaning. It is the experience of an utterance—*all* of it and not anything that could be said about it, including anything I could say—that *is* its meaning.

It follows, then, that it is impossible to mean the same thing in two (or more) different ways, although we tend to think that it happens all the time. We do this by substituting for our immediate linguistic experience an interpretation or abstraction of it, in which "it" is inevitably compromised. We contrive to forget what has happened to us in our life with language, removing ourselves as far as possible from the linguistic event before making a statement about it. Thus we say, for example, that "the book of the father" and "the father's book" mean the same thing, forgetting that "father" and "book" occupy different positions of emphasis in our different experiences; and as we progress in this forgetting, we become capable of believing that sentences as different as these are equivalent in meaning:

This fact is concealed by the influence of language, moulded by science, which foists on us exact concepts as though they represented the immediate deliverances of experience.                                    A. N. WHITEHEAD

And if we continue to dwell in thought on this world,
not of objects in the solidity with which language invests
them, but of impressions, unstable, flickering, inconsistent,
which burn and are extinguished with our consciousness
of them, it contracts still further.

WALTER PATER

It is (literally) tempting to say that these sentences make
the same point: that language which pretends to precision operates to obscure the flux and disorder of actual experience. And
of course they do, if one considers them at a high enough level
of generality. But as individual experiences through which a
reader lives, they are not alike at all, and neither, therefore,
are their meanings.

To take the Whitehead sentence first, it simply doesn't mean
what it says; for as the reader moves through it, he experiences
the stability of the world whose existence it supposedly denies.
The word "fact" itself makes an exact concept out of the idea
of inexactness; and by referring backward to find its referent—
"the radically untidy ill-adjusted character of . . . experience"
—the reader performs the characteristic action required of him
by this sentence, the fixing of things in their places.

There is nothing untidy either in the sentence or in our experience of it. Each clause is logically related to its predecessors
and prepares the way for what follows; and since our active attention is required only at the points of relation, the sentence is
divided *by us* into a succession of discrete areas, each of which
is dominated by the language of certainty. Even the phrase "as
though they represented" falls into this category, since its stress
falls on "they represented" which then thrusts us forward to
the waiting "deliverances of experience." In short, the sentence,
in its action upon us, declares the tidy well-ordered character of
actual experience, and that is its meaning.

At first the Pater sentence is self-subverting in the same way.
The least forceful word in its first two clauses is "not," which is
literally overwhelmed by the words that surround it—"world,"
"objects," "solidity," "language"; and by the time the reader
reaches the "but" in "but of impressions," he finds himself in-

habiting (dwelling in) a "world" of fixed and "solid" objects.
It is of course a world made up of words, constructed in large
part by the reader himself as he performs grammatical actions
which reinforce the stability of its phenomena. By referring
backwards from "them" to "objects," the reader accords "objects" a place in the sentence (whatever can be referred back to
must be somewhere) and in his mind. In the second half of
the sentence, however, this same world is unbuilt. There is still
a backward dependence to the reading experience, but the point
of reference is the word "impressions"; and the series which follows it—"unstable," "flickering," "inconsistent"—serves only to
accentuate its *in*stability. Like Whitehead, Pater perpetrates the
very deception he is warning against; but this is only one part
of his strategy. The other is to break down (extinguish) the coherence of the illusion he has created. Each successive stage of
the sentence is less exact (in Whitehead's terms) than its predecessors, because at each successive stage the reader is given less
and less to hold on to; and when the corporeality of "this world"
has wasted away to an "it" ("it contracts still further"), he is
left with nothing at all.

One could say, I suppose, that at the least these two sentences
gesture toward the same insight; but even this minimal statement makes me uneasy, because "insight" is another word that
implies "there it is, I've got it." And this is exactly the difference
between the two sentences: Whitehead lets you get "it" ("the
neat, trim, tidy, exact world"), while Pater gives you the experience of having "it" melt under your feet. It is only when
one steps back from the sentences that they are in any way
equivalent; and stepping back is what an analysis in terms of
doing and happenings does not allow.

The analysis of the Pater sentence illustrates another feature of the method, its independence of linguistic logic. If a
casual reader were asked to point out the most important word
in the second clause—"not of objects in the solidity with which
language invests them"—he would probably answer "not," because as a logical marker "not" controls everything that follows
it. But as one component in an experience, it is hardly controlling
at all; for as the clause unfolds, "not" has less and less a claim

on our attention and memories; working against it, and finally overwhelming it, as we saw, is an unbroken succession of more forceful words. My point, of course, is that in an analysis of the sentence as a thing in itself, consisting of words arranged in syntactological relationships, "not" would figure prominently, while in an experiential analysis it is noted chiefly for its weakness.

The case is even clearer and perhaps more interesting in this sentence from one of Donne's sermons:

> And therefore as the mysteries of our religion, are not the objects of our reason, but by faith we rest on God's decree and purpose, (it is so, O God, because it is thy will it should be so) so God's decrees are ever to be considered in the manifestation thereof.

Here the "not"—again logically controlling—is subverted by the very construction in which it is imbedded; for that construction, unobtrusively, but nonetheless effectively, pressures the reader to perform exactly those mental operations whose propriety the statement of the sentence—what it is saying—is challenging. That is, a paraphrase of the material before the parenthesis might read—"Matters of faith and religion are not the objects of our reason"; but the simple act of taking in the words "And therefore" involves us unavoidably in reasoning about matters of faith and religion; in fact so strong is the pull of these words that our primary response to this part of the sentence is one of anticipation; we are waiting for a "so" clause to complete the logically based sequence begun by "And therefore as." But when that "so" appears, it is not at all what we had expected, for it is the "so" of divine fiat—it is so O God because it is thy will it should be so—of a causality more real than any that can be observed in nature or described in a natural (human) language. The speaker, however, completes his "explaining" and "organizing" statement as if its silent claim to be a window on reality were still unquestioned. As a result the reader is alerted to the inadequacy of the very process in which he is (through the syntax) involved, and at the same time he accepts the necessity, for limited human beings, of proceeding within the now discredited assumptions of that process.

Of course, a formalist analysis of this sentence would certainly have discovered the tension between the two "so's," one a synonym for therefore, the other shorthand for "so be it," and might even have gone on to suggest that the relationship between them is a mirror of the relationship between the mysteries of faith and the operations of reason. I doubt, however, that a formalist analysis would have brought us to the point where we could see the sentence, and the mode of discourse it represents, as a self-deflating joke ("thereof" mocks "therefore"), to which the reader responds and of which he is a victim. In short, and to repeat myself, to consider the utterances apart from the consciousness receiving it is to risk missing a great deal of what is going on. It is a risk which analysis in terms of "doings and happenings" [6] works to minimize.

Another advantage of the method is its ability to deal with sentences (and works) that don't mean anything, in the sense of not making sense. Literature, it is often remarked (either in praise or with contempt), is largely made up of such utterances. (It is an interesting comment, both on Dylan Thomas and the proponents of a deviation theory of poetic language, that their examples so often are taken from his work.) In an experiential analysis, the sharp distinction between sense and nonsense, with the attendant value judgments and the talk about truth content, is blurred, because the place where sense is made or not made is the reader's mind rather than the printed page or the space between the covers of a book. For an example, I turn once again, and for the last time, to Pater: "This at least of flame-like, our life has, that it is but the concurrence, renewed from moment to moment, of forces parting sooner or later on their ways."

This sentence deliberately frustrates the reader's natural desire to organize the particulars it offers. One can see, for instance, how different its experience would be if "concurrence of forces" were substituted for "concurrence, renewed from moment to moment, of forces." The one allows and encourages the formation of a physical image which has a spatial reality; the mind imagines

[6] I borrow this phrase from P. W. Bridgman, *The Way Things Are.*

(pictures) separate and distinct forces converging, in an orderly fashion, on a center where they form a new, but still recognizable and manageable (in a mental sense) force; the other determinedly prevents that image from forming. Before the reader can respond fully to "concurrence," "renewed" stops him by making the temporal status of the motion unclear. Has the concurrence already taken place? Is it taking place now? Although "from moment to moment" answers these questions, it does so at the expense of the assumptions behind them; the phrase leaves no time for anything so formal and chartable as a "process." For "a moment," at "of forces," there is a coming together; but in the next moment, the moment when the reader takes in "parting," they separate. Or do they? "Sooner or later" upsets this new attempt to find pattern and direction in "our life" and the reader is once more disoriented, spatially and temporally. The final deterrent to order is the plural "ways," which prevents the mind's eye from traveling down a single path and insists on the haphazardness and randomness of whatever it is that happens sooner or later.

Of course this reading of the sentence (that is, of its effects) ignores its status as a logical utterance. "Concurrence, renewed from moment to moment, of forces" is meaningless as a statement corresponding to a state of affairs in the "real" world; but its refusal to mean in that discursive way creates the experience that is its meaning; and an analysis of that experience rather than of logical content is able to make sense of one kind—experiential sense—out of nonsense.

A similar (and saving) operation can be performed on units larger than the sentence. . . . Whatever the size of the unit, the focus of the method remains the reader's experience of it, and the mechanism of the method is the magic question, "what does this ——— do?" Answering it, of course, is more difficult than it would be for a single sentence. More variables creep in, more responses and more different kinds of responses have to be kept track of; there are more contexts which regulate and modulate the temporal flow of the reading experience. Some of these problems will be considered below. For the present, let me say that I have usually found that what might be called the basic experience of a work (do *not* read basic meaning) occurs at every level. As an example, we might consider, briefly, *The Pilgrim's Progress*.

At one point in Bunyan's prose epic, Christian asks a question and receives an answer:

*Chr.*  Is this the way to the Celestial City?
*Shep.*  You are just in your way.

The question is asked in the context of certain assumptions about the world, the stability of objects in it, the possibility of knowing, in terms of measurable distances and locatable places, where you are; but the answer, while it is perfectly satisfactory within that assumed context, also challenges it, or, to be more precise, forces the reader to challenge it by forcing him to respond to the pun on the word "just." The inescapability of the pun reflects backward on the question and the world view it supports; and it gestures toward another world view in which spatial configurations have moral and *inner* meanings, and being in the way is independent of the way you happen to be in. That is, if Christian is to be truly in the way, the way must first be in him, and then he will be in it, no matter where—in what merely *physical* way—he is.

All of this is *meant,* that is experienced, in the reader's encounter with "just" which is a comment not only on Christian for asking the question, but on the reader for taking it seriously, that is, simply. What has happened to the reader in this brief space is the basic experience of *The Pilgrim's Progress*. Again and again he settles into temporal-spatial forms of thought only to be brought up short when they prove unable to contain the insights of Christian faith. The many levels on which this basic experience occurs would be the substance of a full reading of *The Pilgrim's Progress*, something the world will soon have, whether it wants it or not.

The method, then, is applicable to larger units and its chief characteristics remain the same: (1) it refuses to answer or even ask the question, what is this work about; (2) it yields an analysis not of formal features, but of the developing responses of the reader in relation to the words as they succeed one another in time; (3) the result will be a description of the structure of response which may have an oblique or even (as in the case of *The Pilgrim's Progress*), a contrasting relationship to the structure of the work as a thing in itself.

THE AFFECTIVE FALLACY FALLACY

In the preceding pages I have argued the case for a method of analysis which focuses on the reader rather than on the artifact, and in what remains of this essay I would like to consider some of the more obvious objections to that method. The chief objection, of course, is that affective criticism leads one away from the "thing itself" in all its solidity to the inchoate impressions of a variable and various reader. This argument has several dimensions to it, and will require a multidirectional answer.

First, the charge of impressionism has been answered, I hope, by some of my sample analyses. If anything, the discriminations required and yielded by the method are too fine for even the most analytical of tastes. This is in large part because in the category of response I include not only "tears, prickles," and "other psychological symptoms," [7] but all the precise mental operations involved in reading, including the formulation of complete thoughts, the performing (and regretting) of acts of judgment, the following and making of logical sequences; and also because my insistence on the cumulative pressures of the reading experience puts restrictions on the possible responses to a word or a phrase.

The larger objection remains. Even if the reader's responses can be described with some precision, why bother with them, since the more palpable objectivity of the text is immediately available ("the poem itself, as an object of specifically critical judgment, tends to disappear"). My reply to this is simple. The objectivity of the text is an illusion, and moreover, a dangerous illusion, because it is so physically convincing. The illusion is one of self-sufficiency and completeness. A line of print or a page or a book is so obviously *there*—it can be handled, photographed, or put away—that it seems to be the sole repository of whatever value and meaning we associate with it. (I wish the pronoun could be avoided, but in a way *it* makes my point.) This is, of course, the unspoken assumption behind the word "content." The line or page or book *contains*—everything.

The great merit (from this point of view) of kinetic art is that

[7] Wimsatt and Beardsley, *The Verbal Icon*, p. 34.

it forces you to be aware of "it" as a changing object—and therefore no "object" at all—and also to be aware of yourself as cor-
respondingly changing. Kinetic art does not lend itself to a static
interpretation because it refuses to stay still and doesn't let you
stay still either. In its operation it makes inescapable the actualizing role of the observer. Literature is a kinetic art, but the physical
form it assumes prevents us from seeing its essential nature, even
though we so experience it. The availability of a book to the hand,
its presence on a shelf, its listing in a library catalogue—all of
these encourage us to think of it as a stationary object. Somehow
when we put a book down, we forget that while we were reading,
*it* was moving (pages turning, lines receding into the past) and
forget too that *we* were moving with it.

A criticism that regards "the poem itself as an object of specifically critical judgment" extends this forgetting into a principle; it transforms a temporal experience into a spatial one; it
steps back and in a single glance takes in a whole (sentence, page,
work) which the reader knows (if at all) only bit by bit, moment
by moment. It is a criticism that takes as its (self-restricted) area
the physical dimensions of the artifact and within these dimensions it marks out beginnings, middles, and ends, discovers frequency distributions, traces out patterns of imagery, diagrams
strata of complexity (vertical of course), all without ever taking
into account the relationship (if any) between its data and their
affective force. Its question is what goes into the work rather than
what does the work go into. It is "objective" in exactly the wrong
way, because it determinedly ignores what is objectively true
about the *activity* of reading. Analysis in terms of doings and
happenings is on the other hand truly objective because it recognizes the fluidity, "the movingness," of the meaning experience
and because it directs us to where the action is—the active and
activating consciousness of the reader.

But what reader? When I talk about the responses of "the
reader," am I not really talking about myself, and making myself
into a surrogate for all the millions of readers who are not me at
all? Yes and no. Yes in the sense that in no two of us are the responding mechanisms exactly alike. No, if one argues that because
of the uniqueness of the individual, generalization about response

is impossible. It is here that the method can accommodate the insights of modern linguistics, especially the idea of "linguistic competence," "the idea that it is possible to characterize a linguistic system that every speaker shares." [8] This characterization, if it were realized, would be a "competence model," corresponding more or less to the internal mechanisms which allow us to process (understand) and produce sentences that we have never before encountered. It would be a spatial model in the sense that it would reflect a system of rules preexisting, and indeed making possible, any actual linguistic experience.

The interest of this for me is its bearing on the problem of specifying response. If the speakers of a language share a system of rules that each of them has somehow internalized, understanding will, in some sense, be uniform; that is, it will proceed in terms of the system of rules all speakers share. And insofar as these rules are constraints on production—establishing boundaries within which utterances are labeled "normal," "deviant," "impossible," and so on—they will also be constraints on the range, and even the direction, of response; that is, they will make response, to some extent, predictable and normative. Thus the formula, so familiar in the literature of linguistics, "Every native speaker will recognize. . . ."

A further "regularizing" constraint on response is suggested by what Ronald Wardhaugh, following Katz and Fodor, calls "semantic competence," a matter less of an abstract set of rules than of a backlog of language experience which determines probability of choice and therefore of response. "A speaker's semantic knowledge," Wardhaugh contends,

> . . . is no more random than his syntactic knowledge . . . ; therefore, it seems useful to consider the possibility of devising, for semantic knowledge, a set of rules similar in form to the set used to characterize syntactic knowledge. Exactly how such a set of rules should be formulated and exactly what it must explain are to a consid-

[8] Ronald Wardhaugh, *Reading: A Linguistic Perspective* (New York, 1969), p. 60.

erable extent uncertain. At the very least the rules must characterize some sort of norm, the kind of semantic knowledge that an ideal speaker of the language might be said to exhibit in an ideal set of circumstances—in short, his semantic competence. In this way the rules would characterize just that set of facts about English semantics that all speakers of English have internalized and can draw upon in interpreting words in novel combinations. When one hears or reads a new sentence, he makes sense out of that sentence by drawing on both his syntactic and his semantic knowledge. The semantic knowledge enables him to know what the individual words mean and how to put these meanings together so that they are compatible (p. 90).

The resulting description could then be said to be a representation of the kind of system that speakers of a language have somehow internalized and that they draw upon in interpreting sentences (p. 92).

Wardhaugh concedes that the "resulting description" would resemble rather than be equivalent to the system actually internalized, but he insists that "What is really important is the basic principle involved in the total endeavor, the principle of trying to formalize in as explicit a way as possible the semantic knowledge that a mature listener or reader brings to his task of comprehension and that underlies his actual behavior in comprehension (p. 92)." (Interestingly enough, this is a good description of what Empson tries to do, less systematically of course, in *The Structure of Complex Words*.) Obviously the intersection of the two systems of knowledge would make it possible to further restrict (make predictable and normative) the range of response; so that one could presume (as I have) to describe a reading experience in terms that would hold for all speakers who were in possession of both competences. The difficulty is that at present we do not have these systems. The syntactic model is still under construction and the semantic model has hardly been proposed. (Indeed, we will need not a model, but models, since "the semantic knowledge that a mature . . . reader brings to his task of comprehension" will vary with each century or period.[9]) Nevertheless, the incompleteness of our knowledge should not prevent us from hazarding analyses on the basis of what we presently know about what we know.

Earlier, I offered this description of my method: "an analysis of the developing responses of the reader to the words as they succeed one another on the page." It should now be clear that the developing of those responses takes place within the regulating and organizing mechanism, preexisting the actual verbal experience, of these (and other) competences. Following Chomsky, most psychologists and psycholinguists insist that understanding is more than a linear processing of information.[10] This means, as Wardhaugh points out that "sentences are not just simple left to right sequences of elements" and that "sentences are not understood as a result of adding the meaning of the second to that of the first, the third to the first two, and so on (p. 54)." In short, something other than itself, something existing outside its frame of reference, must be modulating the reader's experience of the sequence.[11] In my method of analysis, the temporal flow is monitored and structured by everything the reader brings with him, by his competences; and it is by taking these into account as they interact with the temporal left to right reception of the verbal string, that I am able to chart and project *the* developing response.

It should be noted however that my category of response, and especially of meaningful response, includes more than the transformational grammarians, who believe that comprehension is a function of deep structure perception, would allow. There is a tendency, at least in the writings of some linguists, to downgrade

[9] That is to say, there is a large difference between the two competences. One is uniform through human history, the other different at different points in it.

[10] *Syntactic Structures* (The Hague, 1957), pp. 21–24.

[11] See Wardhaugh, p. 55: "Sentences have a 'depth' to them, a depth which grammatical models such as phrase structure models and generative-transformational models attempt to represent. These models suggest that if a left-to-rightness principle is relevant to sentence processing, it must be a left-to-rightness of an extremely sophisticated kind that requires processing to take place concurrently at several levels, many of which are highly abstract: phonological or graphological, structural, and semantic."

surface structure—the form of actual sentences—to the status of a husk, or covering, or veil; a layer of excrescences that is to be peeled away or penetrated or discarded in favor of the kernel underlying it. This is an understandable consequence of Chomsky's characterization of surface structure as "misleading" and "uninformative" [12] and his insistence (somewhat modified recently) that deep structure alone determines meaning. Thus, for example, Wardhaugh writes that "Every surface structure is interpretable only by reference to its deep structure (p. 49)" and that while "the surface structure of the sentence provides clues to its interpretation, the interpretation itself depends on a correct processing of these clues to reconstruct all the elements and relationships of the deep structure." Presumably the "correct processing," that is, the uncovering of the deep structure and the extraction of deep meaning, is the only goal, and whatever stands in the way of that uncovering is to be tolerated, but assigned no final value. Clues, after all, are sometimes misleading and give rise to "mistakes."

> For example, we sometimes anticipate words in a conversation or text only to discover ourselves to be wrong, or we do not wait for sentences to be completed because we assume we know what their endings will be. . . . Many of the mistakes students make in reading are made because the students have adopted inappropriate strategies in their processing (pp. 137–138).

In my account of reading, however, the temporary adoption of these inappropriate strategies is itself a response to the strategy of an author; and the resulting mistakes are part of the experience provided by that author's language, and therefore part of its meaning. Deep structure theorists, of course, deny that differences in meaning can be located in surface forms. And this for me vitiates the work of Richard Ohmann, who does pay attention to the temporal flow, but only so that he can uncover beneath it the deep structure, which, he assumes, is really doing the work.

The key word is, of course, experience. For Wardhaugh, reading (and comprehension in general) is a process of extraction.

12 *Language and Mind* (New York, 1968), p. 32.

"The reader is required to get the meaning from the print in front of him (p. 139)." For me, reading (and comprehension in general) is an event, no part of which is to be discarded. In that event, which is the actualization of meaning, the deep structure plays an important role, but it is not everything; for we comprehend not in terms of the deep structure alone, but in terms of a *relationship* between the unfolding, in time, of the surface structure and a continual checking of it against our projection (always in terms of surface structure) of what the deep structure will reveal itself to be; and when the final discovery has been made and *the* deep structure is perceived, all the "mistakes," the positing, on the basis of incomplete evidence, of deep structures that failed to materialize, will not be canceled out. They have been experienced; they have existed in the mental life of the reader; they *mean*. (This is obviously the case in our experience of the line "Nor did they not perceive the evil plight.")

All of which returns us to the original question. Who is *the* reader? Obviously, my reader is a construct, an ideal or idealized reader; somewhat like Wardhaugh's "mature reader" or Milton's "fit" reader, or to use a term of my own, *the* reader is the *informed* reader. The informed reader is someone who

> 1. is a competent speaker of the language out of which the text is built up.
> 2. is in full possession of "the semantic knowledge that a mature . . . listener brings to his task of comprehension." This includes the knowledge (that is, the experience, both as a producer and comprehender) of lexical sets, collocation probabilities, idioms, professional and other dialects, etc.
> 3. has *literary* competence.

That is, he is sufficiently experienced as a reader to have internalized the properties of literary discourses, including everything from the most local of devices (figures of speech, etc.) to whole genres. In this theory, then, the concerns of other schools of criticism—questions of genre, conventions, intellectual background, etc.—*become redefined in terms of potential and probable re-*

*sponse,* the significance and value a reader can be expected to attach to the idea "epic," or to the use of archaic language, or to anything.

The reader, of whose responses I speak, then, is this informed reader, neither an abstraction, nor an actual living reader, but a hybrid—a real reader (me) who does everything within his power to make himself informed. That is, I can with some justification project my responses into those of "the" reader because they have been modified by the constraints placed on me by the assumptions and operations of the method: (1) the conscious attempt to become the informed reader by making my mind the repository of the (potential) responses a given text might call out and (2) the attendant suppressing, insofar as that is possible, of what is personal and idiosyncratic and 1970ish in my response. In short, the informed reader is to some extent processed by the method that uses him as a control. Each of us, if we are sufficiently responsible and self-conscious, can, in the course of employing the method become the informed reader and therefore be a more reliable reporter of his experience.

(Of course, it would be easy for someone to point out that I have not answered the charge of solipsism, but merely presented a rationale for a solipsistic procedure; but such an objection would have force only if a better mode of procedure were available. The one usually offered is to regard the work as a thing in itself, as an object; but as I have argued above, this is a false and dangerously self-validating objectivity. I suppose that what I am saying is that I would rather have an acknowledged and controlled subjectivity than an objectivity which is finally an illusion.)

In its operation, my method will obviously be radically historical. The critic has the responsibility of becoming not one but a number of informed readers, each of whom will be identified by a matrix of political, cultural, and literary determinants. The informed reader of Milton will not be the informed reader of Whitman, although the latter will necessarily comprehend the former. This plurality of informed readers implies a plurality of informed reader aesthetics, or no aesthetic at all. A method of analysis that yields a (structured) description of response has built into it an *operational* criteria. The question is not how good it is, but how does it work; and both question and answer are framed in terms of local conditions, which include local notions of literary value.

This raises the problem of the consideration of local beliefs as a possible basis of response. If a reader does not share the central concerns of a work, will he be capable of fully responding to it? Wayne Booth has asked that question: "But is it really true that the serious Catholic or atheist, however sensitive, tolerant, diligent, and well-informed about Milton's beliefs he may be, enjoys *Paradise Lost* to the degree possible to one of Milton's contemporaries and co-believers, of equal intelligence and sensitivity?" [13] The answer, it seems to me, is no. There are some beliefs that cannot be momentarily suspended or assumed. Does this mean, then, that *Paradise Lost* is a lesser work because it requires a narrowly defined ("fit") reader? Only if we hold to a universal aesthetic in the context of which value is somehow correlated with the number of readers who can experience it fully, irrespective of local affiliations. My method allows for no such aesthetic and no such fixings of value. In fact it is oriented *away* from evaluation and toward description. It is difficult to say on the basis of its results that one work is better than another or even that a single work is good or bad. And more basically, it doesn't permit the evaluation of literature as literature, as apart from advertising or preaching or propaganda or "entertainment." As a report of a (very complex) stimulus—response relationship, it provides no way to distinguish between literary and other effects, except, perhaps, for the components which go into one or the other; and no one, I assume, will assent to a "recipe" theory of literary difference. For some this will seem a fatal limitation of the method. I welcome it, since it seems to me that we have for too long, and without notable results, been trying to determine what distinguishes literature from ordinary language. If we understood "language," its constituents and its operations, we would be better able to understand its subcategories. The fact that this method does not begin with the assumption of literary superiority or end with its affirmation, is, I think, one of its strongest recommendations.

[13] *The Rhetoric of Fiction* (Chicago, 1961), p. 139.

This is not to say that I do not evaluate. The selection of texts for analysis is itself an indication of a hierarchy in my own tastes. In general I am drawn to works which do not allow a reader the security of his normal patterns of thought and belief. It would be possible, I suppose, to erect a standard of value on the basis of this preference—a scale on which the most unsettling of literary experiences would be the best (perhaps literature is what disturbs our sense of self-sufficiency, personal and linguistic)—but the result would probably be more a reflection of a personal psychological need than of a universally true aesthetic.

Three further objections to the method should be considered if only because they are so often made in my classes. If one treats utterances, literary or otherwise, as strategies, does this not claim too much for the conscious control of their producer-authors? I tend to answer this question by begging it, by deliberately choosing texts in which the evidence of control is overwhelming. (I am aware that to a psychoanalytic critic, this principle of selection would be meaningless, and indeed, impossible.) If pressed I would say that the method of analysis, apart from my own handling of it, does not require the assumption either of control or of intention. One can analyze an effect without worrying about whether it was produced accidentally or on purpose. (However I always find myself worrying in just this way, especially when reading Defoe.) The exception would be cases where the work includes a statement of intention ("to justify the ways of God to man"), which, because it establishes an expectation on the part of a reader, becomes a part of his experience. This, of course, does not mean that the stated intention is to be believed or used as the basis of an interpretation, simply that it, like everything else in the text, draws a response, and, like everything else, it must be taken into account.

The second objection also takes the form of a question. If there is a measure of uniformity to the reading experience, why have so many readers, and some equally informed, argued so well and passionately for differing interpretations? This, it seems to me, is a pseudo-problem. Most literary quarrels are not disagreements about response, but about a response to a response. What happens to one informed reader of a work will happen, within a range of nonessential variation, to another. It is only when readers become literary critics and the passing of judgment takes precedence over the reading experience, that opinions begin to diverge. The act of interpretation is often so removed from the act of reading that the latter (in time the former) is hardly remembered. The exception that proves the rule, and my point, is C. S. Lewis, who explained his differences with Dr. Leavis in this way: "It is not that he and I see different things when we look at *Paradise Lost.* He sees and hates the very same things that I see and love."

The third objection is a more practical one. In the analysis of a reading experience, when does one come to the point? The answer is, "never," or, no sooner than the pressure to do so becomes unbearable (psychologically). Coming to the point is the goal of a criticism that believes in content, in extractable meaning, in the utterance as a repository. Coming to the point fulfills a need that most literature deliberately frustrates (if we open ourselves to it), the need to simplify and close. Coming to the point should be resisted, and in its small way, this method will help you to resist.

### OTHER VERSIONS, OTHER READERS

Some of what I have said in the preceding pages will be familiar to students of literary criticism. There has been talk of readers and responses before and I feel some obligation at this point both to acknowledge my debts and to distinguish my method from others more or less like it.[14]

---

[14] What follows is by no means exhaustive; it is selective in three directions. First I arbitrarily exclude, and therefore lump together in one undifferentiated mass, all those whose models of production and comprehension are primarily spatial; all those who are more interested in what goes into a work than what goes into and out of the reader; all those who offer top to bottom rather than left to right analyses: statisticians of style (Curtis Hayes, Josephine Miles, John Carroll), descriptive linguists (Halliday and Company), formalist-structuralists (Roman Jakobson, Roland Barthes), and many more. (In the longer study to which this essay is preliminary, these men and women will be considered and discriminated.) I am also selective in my discussion of psychologically oriented critics; and within that selection I must make further apologies for considering their work only in relation to my own methodological concerns which are on the whole narrower and less ambitious than theirs. In short, with the possible exception of Michael Riffaterre, I shall do less than justice to my predecessors.

One begins of course with I. A. Richards, whose principal article of faith sounds very much like mine:

> . . . the belief that there is such a quality or attribute,
> namely Beauty, which attaches to the things which we
> rightly call beautiful, is probably inevitable for all reflec-
> tive persons at a certain stage of their mental develop-
> ment.
>
> Even among those who have escaped from this delu-
> sion and are well aware that we continually talk as though
> things possess qualities, when what we ought to say is that
> they cause effects in us of one kind or another, the fallacy
> of "projecting" the effect and making it a quality of its
> cause tends to recur. . . .
>
> Whether we are discussing music, poetry, painting,
> sculpture or architecture, we are forced to speak as though
> certain physical objects . . . are what we are talking
> about. And yet the remarks we make as critics do not ap-
> ply to such objects but to states of mind, to experiences.[15]

This is obviously a brief for a shift of analytical attention away
from the work as an object to the response it draws, the experience it generates; but the shift is, in Richards's theory, preliminary
to *severing* one from the other, whereas I would insist on their
precise interaction. He does this by distinguishing sharply between
scientific and emotive language:

> A statement may be used for the sake of the *reference*
> true or false, which it causes. This is the *scientific* use of
> language. But it may also be used for the sake of the ef-
> fects in emotion and attitude produced by the reference it
> occasions. This is the *emotive* use of language. The dis-
> tinction once clearly grasped is simple. We may either use
> words for the sake of the references they promote, or we
> may use them for the sake of the attitudes and emotions
> which ensue (p. 267).

But may we? Isn't it the case, rather, that in any linguistic
experience we are internalizing attitudes and emotions, even if the

15 *Principles of Literary Criticism* (New York, 1959 [1924]), pp. 20–22.

attitude is the pretension of no attitude and the emotion is a passionate coldness? Richards's distinction is too absolute and in his literary theorizing it becomes more absolute still. Referential language, when it appears in poetry, is not to be attended to as referential in any sense. Indeed, it is hardly to be attended to at all. This is in general the thesis of *Science and Poetry:* [16]

> The intellectual stream is fairly easy to follow; it follows itself, so to speak; but it is the less important of the two. In poetry it matters only as a *means* (p. 13).

> A good deal of poetry and even some great poetry exists (e.g., some of Shakespeare's Songs and, in a different way, much of the best of Swinburne) in which the sense of the words can be *almost* entirely missed or neglected without loss (pp. 22–23).

> Most words are ambiguous as regards their plain sense, especially in poetry. We can take them as we please in a variety of senses. The sense we are pleased to choose is the one which most suits the impulses already stirred through the form of the verse. . . . Not the strictly logical sense of what is said, but the tone of voice and the occasion are the primary factors by which we interpret (p. 23).

> It is never what a poem *says* which matters, but what it *is* (p. 25).

Well what is it? And what exactly is the "form of the verse" which is supposed to displace our interest in and responsibility to the sense? The answers to these questions, when they come, are disturbing: the cognitive structure of poetic (read literary) language is a conduit through which a reader is to pass untouched and untouching on his way to the *impulse* which was the occasion of the poem in the first place:

> The experience itself, the tide of impulses sweeping through the mind, is the source and the sanction of the words . . . to a suitable reader . . . the words will reproduce in his mind a similar play of interests putting him for the while into a similar situation and leading to the same response.

[16] London, 1926.

> Why this should happen is still somewhat of a mystery. An extraordinarily intricate concourse of impulses brings the words together. Then in another mind the affair in part reverses itself, the words bring a similar concourse to impulses (pp. 26–27).

Declining to identify message with meaning, Richards goes too far and gives the experience of decoding (or attempting to decode) the message no place in the actualization of meaning. From feeling to words to feeling, the passage should be made with as little attention as possible to the sense, which is usually "fairly easy to follow" (disposable, like a straw). In fact, attention to the sense can be harmful, if one takes it too seriously. Assertions in poetry are "pseudo-statements": "A pseudo-statement is a form of words which is justified entirely by its effect in releasing or organizing our impulses and attitudes (due regard being had for the better or worse organizations of these *inter se*); a statement, on the other hand, is justified by its truth, i.e., its correspondence . . . with the fact to which it points (p. 59)." This would be unexceptionable, were Richards simply warning against applying the criterion of truth-value to statements in poetry; but he seems to mean that we should not experience them as statements at all, even in the limited universe of a literary discourse. That is, very little corresponding to cognitive processes should be going on in our minds when we read poetry, lest the all-important release of impulses be impaired or blocked. Contradictions are not to be noted or worried about. Logical arguments need not be followed too closely ("the relevant consequences are . . . to be arrived at by a partial relaxation of logic"). But while this may be the response called forth by some poetry (and prose), it is by no means universally true that in reading literature we are always relieved of our responsibility to logic and argument. Very often, and even when the sense is "fairly easy to follow," cognitive processes— calculating, comparing, deducting, etc.—form the largest part of our response to a work, and any description of its effects must take this into account. Richards arbitrarily limits the range of meaningful response to feelings (impulses and attitudes) and of course here I cannot follow him. (In seventeenth-century literature, for example, the impact of a work often depends on the encouragement and manipulation of ratiocinative patterns of response.)

The range of response is further narrowed when Richards argues for a hierarchy of experiences. What is the best life one can live, he asks? "The best life . . . which we can wish for our friend will be one in which as much as possible of himself is engaged (as many of his impulses as possible). The more he lives and the less he thwarts himself the better. . . . And if it is asked, what does such life feel like . . . the answer is that it feels like and is the experience of poetry (p. 33)." The best poetry then is the poetry that gives the most impulses, with the greatest intensity, and, presumably, with the least ratiocinative interference. It is hardly surprising, given this theory of poetic value, that Richards is not really interested in the sequence of the reading experience. His analysis of reading a poem (*Principles,* chapter XVI) is spatial, in terms of isolated word-impulse relationships, exactly what we might expect from an aesthetic which regards the ligatures of thought as a kind of skeletal container, holding the experience in, but not forming any considerable part of it.

Richards's theories and his prejudices weigh heavily on his protocols and account, in part, for their miserable performance in *Practical Criticism.*[17] They begin, not with a sense of responsibility to language in all of its aspects, but with a license and, indeed, an obligation to ignore some of them. They are simply reporting on the impulses and attitudes they experience while reading, presumably under the influence of Richards's anticognitive bias. It is ironic and unfortunate that the case against analysis in terms of reader response is often made by referring to the example of a group of readers whose idea of response was disastrously narrow, and whose sensitivity to language was restricted to only one of its registers. If *Practical Criticism* makes any case, it is a case for the desirability of my informed reader; for it shows what happens when people who have never thought about the language they use every day are suddenly asked to report precisely on their experience of poetry, and even worse, are asked to do so in the context of an assumption of poetic "difference."

[17] London, 1929.

In all of this, of course, I have been anticipated by William Empson:

> . . . when you come down to detail, and find a case where there are alternative ways of interpreting a word's action, of which one can plausibly be called Cognitive and the other Emotive, it is the Cognitive one which is likely to have important effects on sentiment or character, and in general it does not depend on accepting false beliefs. But in general it does involve a belief of some kind, if only the belief that one kind of life is better than another, so that it is no use trying to chase belief-feelings out of the poetry altogether.
>
> The trouble I think is that Professor Richards conceives the Sense of a word in a given use as something single, however "elaborate," and therefore thinks that anything beyond that Sense has got to be explained in terms of feelings, and feelings of course are Emotions, or Tones. But much of what appears to us as a "feeling" (as is obvious in the case of a complex metaphor) will in fact be quite an elaborate structure of related meanings. The mere fact that we can talk straight ahead and get the grammar in order shows that we must be doing a lot more rational planning about the process of talk than we have to notice in detail.[18]

Empson agrees with Richards that there are "two streams of experience in reading a poem, the intellectual and the active and emotional" but he objects to the suggestion that the interconnection between them "had better be suppressed (p. 11)." In short, his position, at least on this point, is very close to (and is probably one of the causes of) my own. And his insistence that words carry with them discriminations of sense and feeling of which we are not always consciously aware goes a long way to making my case for the complexity, again largely unconscious, of the response these same words evoke.

We differ, however, in the scope and direction of our analyses. Empson does not follow the form of the reader's experience, but some form, usually arbitrary, which allows him to explore in depth

[18] *The Structure of Complex Words* (London, 1951), pp. 10, 56–57.

isolated moments or potential moments in that experience. (I say potential because his emphasis is often on what has gone into a word rather than an account of its effect.) Why *seven* types of ambiguity? I like the explanation offered recently by Roger Fowler and Peter Mercer: "Empson's categories are thrown off with a marvellous disbelieving *panache*—if there had been eight and not the magical seven we might have had to worry—but there are only as few or as many types as you want." [19] As you *need* to write a book, that is to generate a sufficient number of categories to contain and at least keep physically separate the points you would like to make. The categories of *The Structure of Complex Words* are to be taken no more seriously, that is, absolutely, than the seven types, and of course Empson never asks that you do. They are simply (or not so simply) containers, and boundaries, artificial, but necessary, if he is to manage the discussion (which is often a matter of keeping a great many balls in the air at once) and if we are to have the aid and comfort of some sort of ordering principle as we follow him.

The results, as Fowler and Mercer point out, are "scores of analyses probably unequalled in brilliance, if also at times, unequalled in ingenuity, which proceed for the most part as fragmented . . . imitations of the many-dimensional poetic object (p. 58)." The method tends to be atomistic, for it generates in-depth analyses of lexical and semantic complexity without the restraint imposed by the consideration of the mind's involvement with the ligatures of thought. And if it is true, as some have argued, that Empson equates value with this kind of complexity (a standard not unlike Richards's intensity and frequency of impulse), one can see why he would avoid any methodological strategy which would prevent him from fully attending to it. (In my analyses, the range of associations, and therefore of response, is always being narrowed and directed by decisions made or actions taken as a result of earlier events in the meaning experience.) Even when Empson considers whole poems—he is more likely to subsume parts of poems under his various categories—the atomism and fragmentation is obvious. What he always looks for, or constructs,

[19] "Criticism and the Language of Literature: Some Traditions and Trends in Great Britain," *Style*, III (1969), 59.

is some classificatory mechanism which relieves him of the responsibility for a sequential reading of the poem. The most obvious device is the emphasis on a single word, for instance, "all" in *Paradise Lost;* but even here he does not follow the word through the poem, but sets up "classes" of occurrence ordered on the basis of certain emotions (p. 102). In *Some Versions of Pastoral,* the categories of Bentleyan error serve the same purpose; and the thesis which later becomes *Milton's God*—a book on the argument of *Paradise Lost,* notable for the *absence* of semantic analysis—is developed in the spaces *between* the explorations of verbal texture rather than as a consequence of them.

The reading of Marvell's "Garden" displays the same characteristics. Here there is a gesture in the direction of considering the poem in the order of its stanzas, but at a certain point Empson surrenders to his genius: *"Green* takes on great weight here . . . because it has been a pet word of Marvell's before. To list the uses before the satires may seem an affectation of pedantry, but shows how often the word was used; and they are pleasant things to look up." [20] Empson is off and running, from Lawrence to Whitman to Wordsworth to Donne to Shakespeare to Homer to Milton and even (or inevitably) Buddha, returning to "The Garden" only in a closing sentence whose impact is derived from our awareness of its arbitrariness. It doesn't conclude the essay or the reading of the poem; it merely *closes off* this particular section of the lifelong dialogue Empson is having with his language, its creations and their creators. And who would want it otherwise? What Empson does, he does better than anyone else; but he does not analyze the developing responses of the reader to the words as they succeed one another in time.

Finally, I come to Michael Riffaterre whose work has only recently been called to my attention. Mr. Riffaterre *is* concerned with the reader's developing responses, and insists on the constraints imposed on response by the left to right sequence of a temporal flow, and he objects, as I do, to methods of analysis that yield descriptions of the observable features of an utterance without reference to their reception by the reader. In a reply to a reading by Jakobson and Levi-Strauss of Baudelaire's "Les Chats,"

[20] *Some Versions of Pastoral* (Norwalk, Conn., n.d.), p. 121.

Riffaterre makes his position on these points very clear.[21] The systems of correspondences yielded by a structuralist analysis are not necessarily perceived or attended to by the reader; and the resulting data, encased as it often is in formidable spatial schematizations, often prevents us from looking at what is going on in the act of comprehension. The question, Riffaterre insists, is "whether unmodified structural linguistics is relevant at all to the analysis of poetry (p. 202)." The answer, it seems to me, is yes and no. Clearly we must reject any claims made for a direct relationship between structurally derived descriptions and meaning; but it does not follow for me, as it does for Riffaterre, that the data of which such descriptions consist is therefore irrelevant:

> The authors' method is based on the assumption that any structural system they are able to define in the poem is necessarily a poetic structure. Can we not suppose, on the contrary, that the poem may contain certain structures that play no part in its function and effect as a literary work of art, and that there may be no way for structural linguists to distinguish between these unmarked structures and those that are literarily active? Conversely, there may well be strictly poetic structures that cannot be recognized as such by an analysis not geared to the specificity of poetic language (p. 202).

Here the basis for both my agreement and disagreement with Riffaterre is clear. He is a believer in two languages, ordinary and poetic, and therefore in two structures of discourse and two kinds of response; and he believes consequently, that analysis should concern itself with "turning up" features, of language, structure and response, that are specifically poetic and literary.

> Poetry is language, but it produces effects that language in everyday speech does not consistently produce; a reasonable assumption is that the linguistic analysis of a poem should turn up specific features, and that there is a casual relationship between the presence of these features in the

---

[21] "Describing Poetic Structures," *Yale French Studies,* XXXVI–XXXVII (1966).

text and our empirical feeling that we have before us a poem. . . . In everyday language, used for practical purposes, the focus is usually upon the situational context, the mental or physical reality referred to. . . . In the case of verbal art, the focus is upon the message as an end in itself, not just as a means . . . (p. 200).

This is distressingly familiar deviationist talk, with obvious roots in Mukarovsky's distinction between standard language and poetic language and in Richards's distinction between scientific and emotive language. Riffaterre's conception of the relation between standard and poetic language is more flexible and sophisticated than most, but nevertheless his method shares the weakness of its theoretical origins, the a priori assumption that a great deal doesn't count. Deviation theories always narrow the range of meaningful response by excluding from consideration features or effects that are not poetic; and in Riffaterre's version, as we shall see, the range of poetic effects is disastrously narrow, because he restricts himself only to that which is called to a reader's attention in the most spectacular way.

For Riffaterre, stylistic study is the study of SDs or stylistic devices which are defined as those mechanisms in the text which "prevent the reader from inferring or predicting any important feature. For predictability may result in superficial reading; unpredictability will compel attention: the intensity of reception will correspond to the intensity of the message." [22] Talking about style then is talking about moments in the reading experience when attention is compelled because an expectation has been disappointed by the appearance of an unpredictable element. The relationship between such moments and other moments in the sequence which serve to highlight them is what Riffaterre means by the "stylistic context":

> The stylistic context is a linguistic *pattern suddenly broken by an element which was unpredictable,* and the contrast resulting from this interference is the stylistic stimulus. The rupture must not be interpreted as a dissociating principle. The stylistic value of the contrast lies in

[22] "Criteria for Style Analysis," *Word,* XV (1959), 158.

the relationship it establishes between the two clashing elements; no effect would occur without their association in a sequence. In other words, the stylistic contrasts, like other useful oppositions in language, create a structure (p. 171).

Riffaterre is more interesting than other practitioners of "contrast" stylistics because he locates the disrupted pattern in the context rather than in any preexisting and exterior norm. For if "in the style norm relationship we understood the norm pole to be universal (as it would be in the case of the linguistic norm), we could not understand how a deviation might be an SD on some occasions and on others, not ('Criteria,' p. 169)." This means, as he points out in "Stylistic Context," [23] that one can have the pattern *Context-SD starting new context—SD:* "The SD generates a series of SDs of the same type (e.g., after an SD by archaism, proliferation of archaisms); the resulting saturation causes these SDs to lose their contrast value, destroys their ability to stress a particular point of the utterance and reduces them to components of a new context; this context in turn will permit new contrasts." In the same article (pp. 208–209) this flexible and changing relationship is redefined in terms of microcontext ("the context which creates the opposition constituting the SD") and macrocontext ("the context which modifies this opposition by reinforcing or weakening it"). This enables Riffaterre to talk about the relationship between local effects and a series of local effects which in its entirety or duration determines to some extent the impact of its members; but the principle of contextual norm, and its advantages, remains the same.

Those advantages are very real; attention is shifted away from the message to its reception, and therefore from the object to the reader. (Indeed in a later article Riffaterre calls for a "separate linguistics of the decoder" and argues that SF, the impact made on the reader, "prevails consistently over referential function," especially in fiction.[24]) No fixed and artificial inventory of stylistic devices is possible, since in terms of contextual norms anything can be a stylistic device. The temporal flow of the reading experi-

[23] *Word,* XVI (1960).

[24] "The Stylistic Function," *Proceedings of the 9th International Congress of Linguistics* (Cambridge, 1962), pp. 320, 321.

ence is central and even controlling; it literally locates, with the help of the reader, the objects of analysis. The view of language and of comprehension is nonstatic; the context and SDs are moving and shifting; the reader is moving with them and through his responses, creating them, and the critic is moving too, placing his analytic apparatus now here, now there.

All of this, however, is vitiated for me by the theory of language and style in the context (that word again) of which the methodology operates. I refer of course to the positing of two kinds of language and the resulting restriction of meaningful or interesting response to effects of surprise and disruption. Riffaterre is very forthright about this:

> *Stylistic facts can be apprehended only in language,*
> *since that is their vehicle;* on the other hand, *they must*
> *have a specific character,* since other*wise they could not be*
> *distinguished from linguistic facts.* . . .
>
> It is necessary to gather first all those elements which present stylistic features, and secondly, to subject to linguistic analysis only these, to the exclusion of all others (which are stylistically irrelevant). Then and only then will the confusion between style and language be avoided. For this sifting, preliminary to analysis, we must find specific criteria to delineate the distinctive features of style. . . .
>
> *Style* is understood as an emphasis (expressive, affective, or aesthetic) added to the information conveyed by the linguistic structure, without alteration of meaning. Which is to say that language expresses and that style stresses.[25]

"Stylistic facts"—"Linguistic facts," "stylistically irrelevant," "distinctive features of style," "emphasis . . . added to the information . . . without alteration of meaning." This is obviously more than a distinction, it is a hierarchy in which the lower of the two classes is declared uninteresting and, what is more important, *inactive*. That is, the stress of style is doing something and is therefore the proper object of attention, while the expression, the

[25] "Criteria for Style Analysis," pp. 154–155.

encoding and decoding of information, the meaning, is just there, and need not be looked into very closely. (Language expresses, style stresses.) One could quarrel with this simply on the basis of its radical separation of style and meaning, and with its naive equation of meaning with information; but for my purposes it is enough to point out the implications for the specifying and analyzing of response. Underlying Riffaterre's theorizing is the assumption that for long stretches of language, in both ordinary and literary discourse, there is no response worth talking about because nothing much is happening. (Minimal decoding, minimal response.)

This assumption is reflected at every level of his operation. It is the basis of his distinction between what is and what is not a literary structure. It is the basis too, of the context-SD relationship that obtains once a literary structure has been identified. That relationship is, as Riffaterre says, one of "binary opposition" in which "the poles cannot be separated." [26] Of course these are variable, not fixed, poles; but within their individual relationships one is always doing nothing but preparing the way (passively) for the other, for the "big moment" when the contextual pattern is disrupted and attention is compelled (that is, response occurs). And finally, it is the basis of Riffaterre's use of the reader as a locating device. Since all the features yielded by a linguistic analysis are not poetically active, there must be a way of isolating those features that are; and since these are the features that disrupt pattern and compel attention, we shall locate them by attending to the responses of actual readers, whether they are readers in our classroom-laboratory or readers who have left us a record of their experience in footnotes or articles. Riffaterre's reader is a composite reader (either the "average reader" or "super-reader"), not unlike my informed reader. The difference, of course, is that his experience is considered relevant only at those points where it becomes unusual or "effortful." "Each point of the text that holds up the superreader is tentatively considered a component of the poetic structure. Experience indicates that such units are always pointed out by a number of informants." [27]

I am less bothered by the idea of a super-reader than by what

[26] "Stylistic Context," p. 207.    [27] "Describing Poetic Structures," pp. 215–216.

happens to his experience in the course of a Riffaterrian analysis. It, too, will become binary in structure, a succession of highlighted moments alternating with and created by intervals of contextual norm, more cyclical than linear, and of course, in a large part of it, nothing will be happening. At one point in his reading of "Les Chats," Riffaterre comes upon the line *"Ils cherchent le silence"* and here is what he has to say:

> Informants unanimously ignore *Ils cherchent le silence.* Undoubtedly *cherchent* is the poetic or high-tone substitute for *rechercher* or *aimer,* but this is no more than the normal transformation of prose into verse: the device marks genre, as do verse and stanza, setting the context apart from everyday contexts. It is expected and not surprising.[28]

In other words, nobody noticed it or had any trouble with it; it's perfectly ordinary; therefore it's not doing anything and there's nothing to say about it.

Even when Mr. Riffaterre finds something to talk about, his method does not allow him to do much with it. This analysis of a sentence from *Moby Dick* is a case in point:

> "And heaved and heaved, still unrestingly heaved the black sea, as if its vast tides were a conscience. . . ." We have here a good example of the extent to which decoding can be controlled by the author. In the above instance it is difficult for the reader not to give his attention to each meaningful word. The decoding cannot take place on a minimal basis because the initial position of the verb is unpredictable in the normal English sentence, and so is its repetition. The repetition has a double role of its own, independent of its unpredictability: it creates the rhythm, and its total effect is similar to that of explicit speech. The postponement of the subject brings unpredictability to its maximum point; the reader must keep in mind the predicate before he is able to identify the subject. The "reversal" of the metaphor is still another example of contrast with the context. The reading speed is reduced by these hurdles, at-

28 *Ibid.,* p. 223.

tention lingers on the representation, the stylistic effect is created.[29]

"Stylistic effect is created." But to what end? What does one do with the SDs or with their convergence once they have been located by the informer-reader? One cannot go from them to meaning, because meaning is independent of them; they are stress. ("Stress" occupies the same place in Riffaterre's affections as does "impulse" in Richards's and they represent the same narrowing of response.) We are left with a collection of stylistic effects (of a limited type), and while Mr. Riffaterre does not claim transferability for them, he does not claim anything else either, and their interest is to me at least an open question. (I should add that Riffaterre's analysis of "Les Chats" is brilliant and persuasive, as is his refutation of the Jakobson–Levi-Strauss position. It is an analysis, however, which depends on insights his own method could not have generated. He will not thank me for saying so, but Mr. Riffaterre is a better critic than his theory would allow.)

The difference between Riffaterre and myself can be most conveniently located in the concept of "style." The reader may have wondered why in an essay subtitled, "Affective Stylistics," the word has been so little used. The reason is that my insistence that everything counts and that something (analyzable and significant) is always happening, makes it impossible to distinguish, as Riffaterre does, between "linguistic facts" and "stylistic facts." For me, a stylistic fact is a fact of response, and since my category of response includes everything, from the smallest and least spectacular to the largest and most disrupting of linguistic experiences, everything is a stylistic fact, and we might as well abandon the word since it carries with it so many binary hostages (style *and*—).

This, of course, commits me to a monistic theory of meaning; and it is usually objected to such theories that they give no scope to analysis. But my monism permits analysis, because it is a monism of effects, in which meaning is a (partial) product of the utterance-object, but not to be identified with it. In this theory, the message the utterance carries—usually one pole of a binary relationship in which the other pole is style—is in its operation (which someone like Richards would deny) one more effect, one more

[29] "Criteria for Style Analysis," pp. 172–173.

drawer of response, one more constituent in the meaning experience. It is simply not *the* meaning. Nothing is.

Perhaps, then, the word "meaning" should also be discarded, since it carries with it the notion of message or point. The meaning of an utterance, I repeat, is its experience—all of it—and that experience is immediately compromised the moment you say anything about it. It follows, then, that we shouldn't try to analyze language at all. The human mind, however, seems unable to resist the impulse to investigate its own processes; but the least (and probably the most) we can do is proceed in such a way as to permit as little distortion as possible.

CONCLUSION

From controversy, I descend once more to the method itself and to a few final observations.

First, strictly speaking, it is not a method at all, because neither its results nor its skills are transferable. Its results are not transferable because there is no fixed relationship between formal features and response (reading has to be done every time); and its skills are not transferable because you can't hand it over to someone and expect him at once to be able to use it. (It is not portable.) It is, in essence, a language-sensitizing device, and as the "ing" in sensitizing implies, its operation is long term and never ending (never coming to the point). Moreover, its operations are interior. It has no mechanism, except for the pressuring mechanism of the assumption that more is going on in language than we consciously know; and, of course, the pressure of this assumption must come from the individual whose untrained sensitivity it is challenging. Becoming good at the method means asking the question "what does that . . . . . . . do?" with more and more awareness of the probable (and hidden) complexity of the answer; that is with a mind more and more sensitized to the workings of language. In a peculiar and unsettling (to theorists) way, it is a method which processes its own user, who is also its only instrument. It is self-sharpening and what it sharpens is *you*. In short, it does not organize materials, but transforms minds.

For this reason, I have found it useful as a teaching method, at every level of the curriculum. Characteristically I begin a course by putting some simple sentences on the board (usually "He is sincere" and "Doubtless, he is sincere") and asking my students to answer the question, "what does that . . . . . . . do?" The question is for them a new one and they always reply by answering the more familiar question, "what does . . . . . . . mean?" But the examples are chosen to illustrate the insufficiency of this question, an insufficiency they soon prove from their own classroom experience; and after a while they begin to see the value of considering effects and begin to be able to think of language as an experience rather than as a repository of extractable meaning. After that, it is a matter of exercising their sensitivities on a series of graduated texts—sentences of various kinds, paragraphs, an essay, a poem, a novel—somewhat in the order represented by the first section of this paper. And as they experience more and more varieties of effect and subject them to analysis, they also learn how to recognize and discount what is idiosyncratic in their own responses. Not incidentally, they also become incapable of writing uncontrolled prose, since so much of their time is spent discovering how much the prose of other writers controls them, and in how many ways. There are, of course, devices—the piecemeal left to right presentation of texts via a ticker-tape method, the varying of the magic question (what would have happened were a word not there or somewhere else?)—but again the area of the method's operation is interior and its greatest success is not the organizing of materials (although that often occurs), but the transforming of minds.

In short, the theory, both as an account of meaning and as a way of teaching, is full of holes; and there is one great big hole right in the middle of it, which is filled, if it is filled at all, by what happens inside the user-student. The method, then, remains faithful to its principles; it has no point of termination; it is a process; it talks about experience and is an experience; its focus is effects and its result is an effect. In the end the only unqualified recommendation I can give it is that it works.[30]

---

[30] Since this essay was written I have had the opportunity to read Walter J. Slatoff's *With Respect to Readers: Dimensions of Literary Response* (Ithaca, N.Y., 1970), a new book which addresses itself, at least rhetorically, to many of the issues raised here. The direction Slatoff takes, however, is quite different from mine.

The chief difference (and difficulty) is Slatoff's notion of what constitutes "response." In his analyses, response is something that occurs either before or after the activity of reading. What concerns him is really not response, in the sense of the interaction between the flow of words on the page and an active mediating consciousness, but a response to that response. Recalling Conrad Aiken's description of Faulkner's novels as "a calculated system of screens and obtrusions, of confusions and ambiguous interpolations and delays," Slatoff makes the following distinction on the basis, or so he would claim, of a "divergence in responses":

> Some actively enjoy the delays and suspensions of a writer like Faulkner; others can barely abide them; still others are deeply ambivalent. Similarly we must vary greatly in our instinctive responses . . . (p. 62).

Now response here clearly means what a reader is, by nature, disposed to like or dislike; and in that context there is surely a divergence. But there is no divergence at the level of response which is preliminary to this disposition. Whether the reader likes or dislikes or both likes and dislikes the experience of Faulkner's delays he will, in common with every other reader, experience them. That is, he will negotiate the confusions, struggle through the screens, endure the suspensions; and of course this uniformity of experience (and of response) is acknowledged by Slatoff himself when he makes it the basis of his observation of difference.

It could be said, I suppose, that Slatoff and I are simply interested in different stages of response: I am concerned with the response that *is* the act of perception, the moment to moment experience of adjusting to the sequential demands of prose and poetry; while he speculates on the "divergent" attitudes (what he really means by "response") a reader might take toward that experience after he has had it. But the case is more serious than that because Slatoff confuses the two (I wonder if they can really be separated) and makes the variability of one the basis of denying the uniformity of the other, even though it is that uniformity which makes talk about divergence possible.

The two thesis chapters of the book are entitled "Varieties of Involvement" and "The Divergence of Responses," and it becomes increasingly clear that the variations and divergences occur when a finished reader encounters a finished work. That is, in his theory the work is a repository of properties and meanings (corresponding to the intention of the author) which then come into contact with a reader more or less comfortable to them. In other words, his is an "adversary" model—work *vs.* reader—in which readers, rather than actualizing meanings, react to it on the basis of attitudes they hold prior to the encounter.

In the end, Slatoff's program for putting the reader back into reading amounts to no more than this: acknowledging the fact that a reader has likes and dislikes which are not always compatible with the likes and dislikes informing a particular work. Despite his pronouncements to the contrary, Slatoff finally effects a radical divorce between work and reader and, what is more important, between reader and meaning. They are fixed in their respective positions before they meet, and their interaction does nothing but define the degree of their incompatibility. This is all that Slatoff intends by the phrase "divergence of response," and since the divergence is from a received (handed over) meaning—a response *after* the fact whereas in my model the response *is* the fact—it can be tolerated without compromising the integrity of the work. Indeed it can be celebrated, and this is exactly what Slatoff proceeds to do in the name, of course, of relevance.

# Index

Adolph, Robert, *The Rise of Modern Prose Style*, 88n, 375, 377, 378, 380
Allen, D. C., "Donne's Knowledge of Renaissance Medicine," 2n; *Mysteriously Meant*, 369n
Ames, William, 71
Arber, Edward, *A Harmony of Bacon's Essays*, 78, 122
Arbesmann, Rudolf, "The Concept of *Christus Medicus* in St. Augustine," 2n
Augustine, Saint, 153; *City of God*, 55; *Confessions*, 47–48; *De Beata Vita* 47; *On Christian Doctrine*, 2, 21–43, 69, 160, 194, 349, 381

Bacon, Sir Francis, 13n, 46, 77, 78–155, 220, 349, 350, 351, 378–379, 381; *The Advancement of Learning*, 78, 86, 89, 90, 150, 378, 379; "The Case De Rego Inconsulto," 129; *Colours of Good and Evil*, 91n; *The Great Instauration*, 83, 84; *Novum Organum*, 79, 83, 84, 90, 94, 99, 110, 124, 149, 151, 377; "Of Adversity," 95–99; 101; "Of Ambition," 118–120; "Of Cunning," 99, 127–134, 149; "Of Fortune," 116; "Of Friendship," 116, 134–149, 150–151; "Of Goodness and Goodness of Nature," 113–118; "Of Love," 81–83, 90–92, 108–113; "Of Marriage and Single Life," 122–125; "Of Riches," 94; "Of Simulation and Dissimulation," 101–108; "Of Suitors," 120–122; "Of Suspicion," 94; "Of Truth," 95, 99, 116; "Of Usury," 93–94, 95, 99

Baudelaire, Charles Pierre, "Les Chats," 417, 423, 424
Beardsley, Monroe. *See* Wimsatt, William K.
Beaty, Nancy Lee. *The Craft of Dying*, 64n
Bloomfield, Morton W., *The Seven Deadly Sins*, 56n
Boll, Franz, *Die Lebensalter*, 56n
Booth, Wayne, *The Rhetoric of Fiction*, 408
Bowers, Fredson, "Herbert's Sequential Imagery," 162n
Bridgman, P. W., *The Way Things Are*, 397n
Browne, Sir Thomas, 66, 352, 378; *The Garden of Cyrus*, 366; *Religio Medici*, 50, 158, 353–373, 384–386, 388–389, 393
Bunyan, John, 4, 349, 350, 371, 378, 381; *The Pilgrim's Progress*, 6–7, 13n, 23, 25, 49, 224–264, 351, 368–369, 399
Burton, Robert, 4; *Anatomy of Melancholy*, 13n, 108, 302, 303–352, 371
Bush, Douglas, *Oxford History of English Literature*, 79, 80, 92

Chomsky, Noam, *Language and Mind*, 405; *Syntactic Structures*, 404
Colish, Marcia, L., *The Mirror of Language*, 42n
Cotton, John, *The Way of Life or Gods Way*, 71–72
Crane, R. S., "The Relation of Bacon's *Essays* to his Programme for the Advancement of Learning," 78–79, 125, 149, 150